Bloom's Modern Critical Interpretations

Bloom's Modern Critical Interpretations

Fyodor Dostoevsky's
CRIME AND PUNISHMENT

Edited and with an introduction by
Harold Bloom
Sterling Professor of the Humanities
Yale University

CHELSEA HOUSE
PUBLISHERS
A Haights Cross Communications ✔ Company
Philadelphia

©2004 by Chelsea House Publishers, a subsidiary of
Haights Cross Communications.

A Haights Cross Communications Company

Introduction © 2004 by Harold Bloom.

Printed and bound in the United States of America.

10 9 8 7 6 5 4 3 2 1

Library of Congress Cataloging-in-Publication Data

Crime and Punishment / edited and with an introduction by Harold Bloom.
     p. cm. — (Bloom's modern critical interpretations)
Includes bibliographical references and index.
  ISBN 0-7910-7579-6
  1. Dostoyevsky, Fyodor, 1821–1881. Prestuplenie inakazanie. I.
Bloom, Harold. II. Series.
  PG3325.P73C75 2003
  891.73'3dc21

                                                        2003006758

Contributing editor: Pamela Loos

Cover design by Terry Mallon

Cover: © The State Russian Musuem / CORBIS

Layout by EJB Publishing Services

Chelsea House Publishers
1974 Sproul Road, Suite 400
Broomall, PA 19008-0914

www.chelseahouse.com

Contents

Editor's Note

My introduction centers upon Raskolnikov's quest for metaphysical freedom and power, a quest he does not so much repudiate as simply abandon.

Raskolnikov's failure to repent, together with the extraordinary consciousness of Svidrigailov, is rightly seen by A.D. Nuttall as calling the Christian design of the novel into question.

Carnivalization, the great subject of the Russian critic Mikhail Bakhtin, is seen by him as creating Dostoevsky's characteristic genre.

Harriet Murav follows Bakhtin but adds the idea that *Crime and Punishment* is a critique of any psychology of motives.

The novel's Epilogue, which seems a weakness to many critics (myself included), is defended by David Matual as an inevitable component in Raskolnikov's supposed transformation.

Liza Knapp, analyzing Dostoevsky's implicit metaphysics, finds an identity between inertia and death in the novelist's vision.

In Naomi Rood's reading, *Crime and Punishment* is akin to prophetic element in the tragedies of Sophocles.

Olga Meerson explicates the nature of taboo in relation to Raskolnikov, while Victor Terras sets forth Dostoevsky's mastery of montage.

The spiritual emblem of clothing in the novel is mapped out by Janet Tucker, after which Henry M.W. Russell studies the Christian need for humiliation, in Dostoevsky's view.

Antony Johae uncovers the iconography of dreams in *Crime and Punishment*, while Linda Ivanits concludes this volume by discussing its use of the two Lazaruses in the New Testament, the one resurrected by Jesus and the other who is scorned by the rich glutton but who goes to Abraham's bosom in the afterlife.

HAROLD BLOOM

Introduction

Rereading *Crime and Punishment*, I am haunted suddenly by a recollection of my worst experience as a teacher. Back in 1955, an outcast instructor in the then New Critical, Neo-Christian Yale English department dominated by acolytes of the churchwardenly T.S. Eliot, I was compelled to teach *Crime and Punishment* in a freshman course to a motley collection of Yale legacies masquerading as students. Wearied of their response to Dostoevsky as so much more Eliotic Original Sin, I endeavored to cheer myself up (if not them) by reading aloud in class S. J. Perelman's sublime parody "A Farewell to Omsk," fragments of which are always with me, such as the highly Dostoevskian portrayal of the tobacconist Pyotr Pyotrovitch:

> "Good afternoon, Afya Afyakievitch!" replied the shopkeeper warmly. He was the son of a former notary public attached to the household of Prince Grashkin and gave himself no few airs in consequence. Whilst speaking it was his habit to extract a greasy barometer from his waistcoat and consult it importantly, a trick he had learned from the Prince's barber. On seeing Afya Afyakievitch he skipped about nimbly, dusted off the counter, gave one of his numerous offspring a box on the ear, drank a cup of tea, and on the whole behaved like a man of the world who has affairs of moment occupying him.

Unfortunately, my class did not think this funny and did not even enjoy the marvelous close of Perelman's sketch:

"Don't take any flannel kopecks," said Afya gloomily. He dislodged a piece of horse-radish from his tie, shied it at a passing Nihilist, and slid forward into the fresh loam.

Dostoevsky had his own mode of humor, but he might not have appreciated Perelman either. *Crime and Punishment* is less apocalyptic than *The Brothers Karamazov*, but it is apocalyptic enough. It is also tendentious in the extreme, which is the point of Perelman's parody, but Dostoevsky is so great a tragedian that this does not matter. Raskolnikov is a powerful representation of the will demonized by its own strength, while Svidrigailov is beyond that, and stands on the border of a convincing phantasmagoria. Until the unfortunate epilogue, no other narrative fiction drives itself onwards with the remorseless strength of *Crime and Punishment*, truly a shot out of hell and into hell again. To have written a naturalistic novel that reads like a continuous nightmare is Dostoevsky's unique achievement.

Raskolnikov never does repent and change, unless we believe the epilogue, in which Dostoevsky himself scarcely believed. Despair causes his surrender to Porfiry, but even his despair never matches the fierce ecstasy he has achieved in violating all limits. He breaks what can be broken and yet does not break himself. He cannot be broken, not because he has found any truth, objective or psychological, but because he has known, however momentarily, the nihilistic abyss, a Gnostic freedom of what is beyond our sense of being creatures in God's creation. Konstantin Mochulsky is surely right to emphasize that Raskolnikov never comes to believe in redemption, never rejects his theory of strength and power. His surrender, as Mochulsky says, "is not a sign of penitence but of pusillanimity." We end up with a pre-Christian tragic hero ruined by blind fate, at least in his own vision. But this is about as unattractive as a tragic hero can be, because Raskolnikov comes too late in cultural history to seem a Prometheus rather than a bookish intellectual. In a Christian context, Prometheus assimilates to Satan, and Raskolnikov's pride begins to seem too satanic for tragedy.

Raskolnikov hardly persuades us on the level of Dostoevsky's Christian polemic, but psychologically he is fearsomely persuasive. Power for Raskolnikov can be defined as the ability to kill someone else, anyone at all, rather than oneself. I meet Raskolnikov daily, though generally not in so extreme a form, in many young contemporaries who constitute what I would call the School of Resentment. Their wounded narcissism, turned against the self, might make them poets or critics; turned outward, against others, it makes them eminent unrest-inducers. Raskolnikov does not move our sympathy *for him*, but he impresses us with his uncompromising intensity.

Svidrigailov may have been intended as Raskolnikov's foil, but he got away from Dostoevsky, and runs off with the book, even as old Karamazov nearly steals the greater work away from the extraordinary Dmitri. Raskolnikov is too pure a Promethean or devil to be interested in desire, unless the object of desire be metaphysical freedom and power. He is a kind of ascetic Gnostic, while Svidrigailov is a libertine Gnostic, attempting to liberate the sparks upward. If Raskolnikov portrays the madness of the Promethean will, then Svidrigailov is beyond the will, as he is beyond the still-religious affirmations of atheism. He lives (if that can be the right word) a negativity that Raskolnikov is too much himself to attain. Raskolnikov killed for his own sake, he tells Sonia, to test his own strength. Svidrigailov is light years beyond that, on the way downwards and outwards into the abyss, his foremother and forefather.

The best of all murder stories, *Crime and Punishment* seems to me beyond praise and beyond affection. Dostoevsky doubtless would impress me even more than he does already if I could read Russian, but I would not like him any better. A vicious obscurantism inheres in the four great narratives, including *The Idiot* and *The Possessed*, and it darkens *Crime and Punishment*. Only *The Brothers Karamazov* transcends Dostoevsky's hateful ideology because the Karamazovs sweep past the truths that the novelist continues to shout at us. Tolstoy did not think that Dostoevsky's final and apocalyptic novel was one of the summits of the genre, but then he liked to think of Dostoevsky as the Russian Harriet Beecher Stowe and would have wanted old Karamazov to have resembled Simon Legree.

What seems to me strongest in Dostoevsky is the control of visionary horror he shares with Blake, an imaginative prophet with whom he has absolutely nothing else in common. No one who has read *Crime and Punishment* ever can forget Raskolnikov's murder of poor Lizaveta:

> There in the middle of the floor, with a big bundle in her arms, stood Lizaveta, as white as a sheet, gazing in frozen horror at her murdered sister and apparently without the strength to cry out. When she saw him run in, she trembled like a leaf and her face twitched spasmodically; she raised her hand as if to cover her mouth, but no scream came and she backed slowly away from him towards the corner, with her eyes on him in a fixed stare, but still without a sound, as though she had no breath left to cry out. He flung himself forward with the axe; her lips writhed pitifully, like those of a young child when it is just beginning to be frightened and stands ready to scream, with its eyes fixed on the object of its fear. The wretched Lizaveta was so simple, brow-beaten, and utterly terrified that she did not even put up her arms

to protect her face, natural and almost inevitable as the gesture would have been at this moment when the axe was brandished immediately above it. She only raised her free left hand a little and slowly stretched it out towards him as though she were trying to push him away. The blow fell on her skull, splitting it open from the top of the forehead almost to the crown of the head, and felling her instantly. Raskolnikov, completely beside himself, snatched up her bundle, threw it down again, and ran to the entrance.

Nothing could be more painfully effective than: "She only raised her free left hand a little and slowly stretched it out towards him as though she were trying to push him away." We think of the horrible dream in which Raskolnikov sees a poor, lean, old mare beaten to death with a crowbar, and we may reflect upon Nietzsche's darkest insights: that pain creates memory, so that the pain is the meaning, and meaning is therefore painful. Dostoevsky was a great visionary and an exuberant storyteller, but there is something paradoxically nihilistic in his narrative visions. The sublime mode asks us to give up easier pleasures for more difficult pleasures, which is altogether an aesthetic request. Dostoevsky belongs not to the sublime genre but to the harsher perspectives of the apocalyptic. He insists that we accept pains that transcend aesthetic limits. His authority at apocalypse is beyond question, but such authority also has its own aesthetic limits.

A.D. NUTTALL

The Intellectual Problem II

W hat then is excluded by our Christian reading of *Crime and Punishment*? I answer: Razumikhin, Svidrigailov and Raskolnikov's failure to repent.

Of these, Razumikhin, Raskolnikov's student friend, is the least important. The problem can be stated very simply. According to the picture we have so far built up, the pre-rational freedom of the existentialist is opposed to Christian love and goodness. But Razumikhin is an existentialist, and he is good.

Many of Razumikhin's sentiments exactly mirror those of the Underground Man. For example, he is angered almost to violence by those who oppose individualism[1] and is himself a resolute opponent of mechanistic socialism.[2] His existentialism can assume a curiously pure and rigorous form in which the academic philosophy of Sartre is partly anticipated. Just as Sartre in his two books on the imagination laid great stress on man's ability to think what *is not* the case, and found in this our unique freedom, so Razumikhin argues that it is through error that we are human, and then adds an ethical corollary: "To go wrong in one's own way is better than to go right in someone else's. In the first case your are a man, in the second you're no better than a bird."[3] Had Raskolnikov or the Underground Man been the speaker of these lines, we would have not "bird" but "insect" in the second

From *Crime and Punishment: Murder as Philosophic Experiment.* © 1978 by A.D. Nuttall.

sentence. The imagery is brightened, it would seem, by the general buoyancy of Razumikhin's character.

But, bright or dark, the ethically revolutionary force of these words is undeniable. W.H. Auden, in an essay,[4] saw this revolution as occurring not just in the minds of stray individuals but in the consciousness of nations. He called it the surrender of *Romanitas*, Rome being for him the embodiment of a civic, essentially public responsibility. The Americans he said, in believing that it was better to do wrong freely than to do right under compulsion had made this crucial surrender. Certainly, applying this lesson of Raskolnikov's own spiritual progress we might be forgiven for seeing in these words the foundation of utter immoralism; better an "authentic" Hitler than an "inauthentic" bourgeois. But then we remember that Razumikhin is not only opposed to mechanistic socialism; he is also, in a manner, opposed to Raskolnikov. Raskolnikov's claim that the *conscience* of the exceptional man could sanction bloodshed shocks and repels[5] Razumikhin. And this surely provides us with the clue we need. Razumikhin's libertarian pronouncements, whatever the degree of formal radicalism they may attain, hold no sting, so to speak, because Razumikhin himself is so incorrigibly kind. His vision of freedom is really a symptom of innocence. It is only because he can hardly conceive of a vicious or cruel use of freedom that he can commend it without reserve. Dounia, who loves Razumikhin and is herself entirely good, sees this. Her first response to his wild imaginings is a mixture of humane assent and intellectual reservation: "Yes, yes ... though I don't agree with you in everything."[6]

Yet it does not seem quite right to conclude that Razumikhin's existentialist extravagance is acceptable only because it is meaningless. Dostoevsky never patronises his own characters in quite that way. There remains an element of attraction in Razumikhin's dream of freedom. We must be content to say that in him the doctrine remains untested.

Where then does the true test come? Who in the book both preaches and practises a genuinely unfettered freedom? Razumikhin may echo Raskolnikov's doctrines but he does so lightly, and we are undisturbed. But the man who haunts Raskolnikov, who mirrors both his thoughts and his worst actions, is Svidrigailov.

Svidrigailov is what is called a "Dostoevskian double"; that is, a figure deliberately parallelling that of the main character, confronting him with an answering image of his own mind. It is sometimes suggested that Dostoevsky, in adopting this device, anticipated the Freudian division of the unified psyche into a dialectical opposition of Ego and Id, conscious and unconscious. This view will scarcely survive an attentive reading of Dostoevsky. The Freudian unconscious is pre-logical, appetitive, and lies "deeper in", so to speak, than the conscious. The Dostoevskian double, conversely, tends to carry to their logical conclusion ideas conceived in the mind of the principal character; like an extra limb, in rational, Cartesian obedience, he executes the dictates of the hero's mind with a consistency which shocks the original conceiver. Thus, in *The Brothers Karamazov* Ivan's double, Smerdyakov, acting on Ivan's proposition, "Everything is permitted", murders their common father, Fyodor Karamazov. The Dostoevskian double is not so much "deeper in" as "further out".

We first hear of Svidrigailov in the letter Raskolnikov receives from his mother near the beginning of the novel. She explains how Dounia, Raskolnikov's sister, has had to leave the Svidrigailov household because the master of the house had conceived a violent passion for her. Dounia's predicament had been the more difficult in that the mistress of the house, Marfa Petrovna, believed that Dounia was herself a willing party to the affair. Even in the sketchy narrative of a letter Svidrigailov already possesses a special potency, which consists in great strength allied with the purest caprice. His behaviour to Dounia is at first sneering and facetious, then passionately sensual and at last (when he shows his wife the letter which clears Dounia of all guilt) almost chivalrous. Some hint of the Dionysiac, pagan power we are to see later at closer quarters is present in the imagery of the letter, with its apparently trivial reference to "the influence of Bacchus".[7] We sense that the manner of Svidrigailov's drunkenness is very different from the manner of Marmeladov's drunkenness. His very forename—Arkady—evokes a world at once golden and pre-Christian. Svidrigailov's past, unlike Raskolnikov's, is not intellectual but military.[8] As the story unfolds he moves closer and closer to us. It is not until the last part that we see his face:

> It was a strange face, like a mask; white and red, with bright red lips, with flaxen beard, and still thick flaxen hair. His eyes were somehow too blue and their expression somehow too heavy and fixed. There was something awfully unpleasant in that handsome face, which looked so wonderfully young for his age.[9]

The description is immensely powerful, though the associations it calls up are fugitive: Santa Claus? Some curly bearded Jupiter painted on a fairground stall? Or (still more remote, but obstinately present to this reader's mind) God the Father from the hand of mad William Blake?

What exactly in the world of fact makes Svidrigailov so transcendently evil is difficult to pin down with certainty. It may well be that this is the source of as much strength as weakness. Dostoevsky in the surviving notebooks for

Crime and Punishment was at one stage much exercised as to how he was to convey the character of Svidrigailov without his novel becoming "unchaste".[10] In the event Dounia's shudder[11] at the mention of his name conveys exactly what is needed. To be sure there is the affair of the serf Philip. Svidrigailov, asked by Raskolnikov whether he believes in ghosts, tells how shortly after the burial of his serf "Filka", he called for his pipe and the man appeared with a hole in the elbow of his coat. Svidrigailov observes, "we had a violent quarrel just before his death".[12] A little later Pulcheria Alexandrovna, Raskolnikov's mother, tells the story to Dounia as she had it from Marfa Petrovna. The story goes that there was indeed a serf called Philip and that he died of ill-treatment (here the story of the ghost begins to take on the atmosphere of Crabbe's *Peter Grimes*). Although Philip killed himself it was "perhaps"[13] Svidrigailov that drove him to it. A similarly powerful suspicion and a similar withholding of final certainty surrounds the rape of the deaf and dumb girl of fifteen who was found hanged in the garret.[14] All this is of course a fairly elementary manipulation of the reader's fears. The indefinitely horrible is always more frightening than the definitely horrible, in fiction at least.

But when we come to Raskolnikov's dreadful dream in which the murder is re-enacted, a higher artistry governs the function in the story of Svidrigailov. Raskolnikov awakens, "but his dream seemed strangely to persist: his door was flung open and a man whom he had never seen stood in the doorway watching him intently." It is his first meeting face to face with Svidrigailov. A friend of mine once described to me the worst dream he ever had. In the dream he was being pursued by something so horrible that years afterwards in recounting the dream he did not dare to describe it. At last, however, his eyes opened and he saw the sunlight from the open window shining on the flowered paper of the bedroom wall. Relief flooded through him. Then the bedroom door opened and the thing that had been chasing him came in. And then he *really* woke up. Dostoevsky's narrative, with its momentary sense of the dream persisting, catches something of the special horror of this experience. My friend believes that he momentarily opened his eyes, registered the appearance of his bedroom, and then fell back into the dream. Raskolnikov's case is in a way the opposite. He really awakes, really sees his room and what is actually standing in the doorway, but finds in what he sees no soothing antidote for nightmare, but instead a further terror.

Indeed Svidrigailov the murderer and rapist is never as frightening as Svidrigailov the watcher and listener. To learn that the whole of Raskolnikov's confession to Sonia was overheard by Svidrigailov is at once disgusting and alarming. For a literary precedent one must turn to *Les Liaisons Dangéreuses*, or even to *Othello*. Our modern term for that which engages the mind in a wholly neutral fashion—"interesting"—is absent from

Shakespeare's vocabulary, but if it had been present, Iago would have used it. Svidrigailov's reaction to what he hears pass between Raskolnikov and Sonia is very Iago-like:

> But all that time Mr Svidrigailov had been standing listening at the door of the empty room ... The conversation had struck him as interesting and remarkable.[15]

Svidrigailov lives the life implied by Raskolnikov's most fundamental theory. He oversteps, innovates, moves in any direction. His life is the endless utterance of a new language. One is tempted to say that he is the better existentialist of the two but the word "existentialist" implies the intellectual acceptance of a theory, and Svidrigailov derives much of his power from the fact that he is unfettered by theory. We have already seen in the Underground Man how this particular sort of existentialism is essentially self-destructive. The theory proposes a pure spontaneity, but no one can be purely spontaneous who acts to demonstrate a theory. Raskolnikov in soliloquy desperately acknowledges that he cannot attain transcendent freedom, that he is, after all, no better than a louse: "... what shows that I am utterly a louse is that ... *I felt beforehand* that I should tell myself so *after* killing her ... The vulgarity! The abjectness!"[16] Raskolnikov is trapped in his own endlessly rationalising consciousness. All the time, both in prospect and retrospect, he is *constructing* his own life as a story, and the whole point about the freedom he desires is that it must not be constructed in this way. Svidrigailov is free from this itch. He is not constantly saying to himself and to others, "Look how unpredictable I am." He lives without casuistry. There is a remarkable moment in the novel when the theorising Raskolnikov attempts to talk philosophy with his unfettered shadow. From Raskolnikov there comes, with all the anguish of an incorrigibly moral soul, a philosophic denial of Christian doctrine: "I don't believe in a future life." We wait for Svidrigailov's answer, expecting ... what? A more radical scepticism still? What we get is infinitely stranger than that, though at the same time entirely appropriate to his nature:

> "And what if there are only spiders there, or something of that sort?" he said suddenly. "He is a madman," thought Raskolnikov. "We always imagine eternity as something beyond our conception, something vast, vast! But why must it be vast? Instead of all that, what if it's one little room, like a bath house in the country, black and grimy and spiders in every corner, and that's all eternity is? I sometimes fancy it like that."[17]

Svidrigailov simply refuses to play the philosophic game; he will not theorise. Instead his reply is almost idiotic, artlessly appalling. In moving from Raskolnikov's words to Svidrigailov's, we leave the universe of reasoned discourse, in which certain concepts are stable, to the mean yet terrible world of a Kafka story. Raskolnikov's answer is interesting: "Can it be you can imagine nothing juster and more comforting than that?" This, from the freethinker!

But if Svidrigailov is as we have described him, what has happened to our picture of *Crime and Punishment* as showing the essential servitude of existential freedom? If we had only Raskolnikov to deal with, that position would be secure. But with the smiling figure of Svidrigailov watching us from the shadows as we watched Raskolnikov in the novel, a different hypothesis presents itself. Raskolnikov reverted to Christian values, not because the other path is intrinsically impassable, but simply because he, personally, lacked the strength to follow it. Doubtless his final submission shows more virtue, more goodness than his rebellion, but then virtue of that kind was never required of the existential hero. The implication is clear: Raskolnikov is an existential failure, and we know this because, stalking behind him through the novel is the living embodiment of existential success.

But, it will be said, Svidrigailov is driven to suicide. Is this freedom? The answer is: perhaps, yes. But we must tread carefully.

Certainly Svidrigailov's final state is a kind of despair. He says to Raskolnikov, "If only I'd been something, a landowner, a father, a cavalry officer, a photographer, a journalist ... I am nothing."[18] He has named indifferently some things which he has in fact been and others which, as far as we know, he has not. But the central intuition is at last the purest, Sartrian existentialism. It is also the centre of his despair. He also fears death.[19] It remains to ask whether Svidrigailov's perception of this dreadful truth diminishes or enhances his heroic stature *seen from the existentialist point of view*. If we take a moment to compare the cold candour of his intelligence at this point with the endless confused moralising of Raskolnikov, we must grant that his stature is if anything enhanced. So with the suicide. Svidrigailov admits to a great fear of death, but when Raskolnikov in prison looked back on the suicide he saw this too as increasing rather than lowering the stature of the suicide.[20] It may be said: Dostoevsky was a Christian; read his journalism; there can be no serious doubt but that Svidrigailov's suicide was intended to be read as a confession of spiritual bankruptcy. But questions of this sort are not so easily settled. Dostoevsky's journalism, certainly, is more doctrinally univocal than his novels. It is also less intelligent, less rich. In the circumstances it is folly to allow the journalism any sort of jurisdiction over the novels, to flatten the ambiguities of the great work into the simplicity of the lesser. In the second place we are confronted here with the special difficulties which arise when the situation is not only ambiguous in itself, but is presented to us under two different systems of interpretation. There is indeed no doubt that by Christian standards Svidrigailov fails. The point is so obvious as to be scarcely worth making. It seems at least possible that by the philosophy he represents he succeeds. At least, he does if his action is free.

Surely, if Dostoevsky wished to make the Christian principle the unquestioned victor in the novel, his opportunity lay here. To show Svidrigailov hunted to his death, and subdued, would have been to show the existentialist principle defeated at its strongest point. But he did not write it in that way.

Let us look first at the part played by imagery. In *Crime and Punishment* we can distinguish two levels at which imagery operates. First there is the high cultural level of scriptural images, highly explicit, exemplified most powerfully in the references to Lazarus. These we have already noticed. Then there is a level of imagery which is much less explicit, but equally potent. This second level is largely concerned with our sense of space. Thus Raskolnikov is repeatedly associated with suffocating, tiny spaces, with cramped living quarters and narrow streets. At one point he compares[21] his confined existence with that of a spider. His words recall Svidrigailov's vision of a horribly reduced eternity. It is as if we have glimpsed, not the sublime Inferno of Dante, but Hell as it actually is. The impression made by this spatial imagery is so intense that it is difficult to remember that St Petersburg (the novel's setting), though it has its share of narrow streets and tenements is also a city of immense squares and noble boulevards. Most English-speaking readers of *Crime and Punishment* come away from the book fully believing that St Petersburg is a city like London, as drawn by Doré. But the careful reader will soon perceive that in fact the effect is not ubiquitous, but is on the contrary carefully reserved for Raskolnikov. Sonia, who might have been expected to lodge in a small room, has in fact an oddly shaped but very large room.[22] It seems as if Dostoevsky felt some fundamental need to differentiate her habitual spatial environment as strongly as possible from Raskolnikov's, as some sort of objective correlative to their respective spiritual conditions. Even the old pawnbroker, wretched herself and a cause of wretchedness in others, lives in a bright sunlit room[23] (the brightness, Raskolnikov surmises, is probably the work of her sister Lizaveta). But although the claustrophobic imagery of *Crime and Punishment* is directed straight to Raskolnikov, others feel it when they draw near him. His mother, Pulcheria Alexandrovna, remarks on leaving his flat, "If he gets out and has a breath of air ... it is fearfully close in his room ... But where is one to get a breath of air here? The very streets here feel like shut-up rooms."[24] Both Svidrigailov and Porfiry, the two watchers of Raskolnikov, observe at different times with an apparent inconsequence that what he most needs is fresh air.[25]

The Christian interpretation of the meaning of this imagery would appear at first to be quite straightforward: existential freedom is really not freedom but servitude. Is there not a delicious (and profound) irony in the moment when Raskolnikov thinks of dropping his plan,[26] and experiences *that* as freedom? On his way to commit the murder, does he not compare his state to that of a man led to execution[27] (a point on which Dostoevsky could speak with special authority)? Did he not feel his "mind clouded"?[28] Just before, when he learned that Alyona was to be alone and that his opportunity was perfect did he not feel, in flat opposition to his grand theory, that his freedom had been taken from him?[29] The case seems marvellously complete. But what, then, of Svidrigailov?

If the lesson of the Raskolnikov spatial imagery is that his crime was the quintessence of un-freedom, what by parity of reasoning are we to make of the suicide of Svidrigailov? The Christian interpretation of *Crime and Punishment*, as we have seen, really needs here a similar bias in the narrative technique. But instead we are given water, space and air. If confinement means servitude, these must imply the purest freedom.

The story of Svidrigailov's suicide begins with him looking very unimpressive. Before he picks up the gun, "a strange smile contorted his face, a pitiful, sad, weak smile, a smile of despair."[30] He goes then to a pleasure garden, and for a while the general atmosphere of meanness is kept up. But, as he rises to leave, the hot night is split by the sound of thunder and torrential rain falls. It is difficult to convey the full force in the novel of this simple change in the weather. This, we know, is air which Raskolnikov will never breathe, and we open our lungs to it in gratitude. The rain soon gives way to a roaring wind and there in the middle of the windy night we see Svidrigailov crossing the bridge between Vassilyevsky Island and the mainland.[31] But Svidrigailov passes out of this great wind into a tiny cramped hotel room.[32] Here we may suppose the alternative imagery of confinement is after all to assert itself; but the image will not hold. It is as if one half of Dostoevsky's mind is struggling to tie down Svidrigailov, but the imagery has developed a life of its own and will not be stilled. The effects which follow are those of nightmare. The hotel room in which he finds himself does not after all enclose him. There is a crack in the wall through which he can see, with preternatural clarity, what is happening in the next room.[33] Svidrigailov lies down to sleep, and the room around him seems to become increasingly frail and insubstantial as he listens with dread to the roaring wind and the trees tossing in the darkness. At last he falls asleep but then awakes abruptly. Now the images of wind and air bifurcate. Svidrigailov in utter horror at all around him imagines a cottage on a summer day with the wind strewing the flowers in the window, but then his imagination escaping his control presents him with the horror of death, the corpse of a girl, lying the middle of this delicious place.[34] He shakes himself free of this unhappy state between dream and reality, crosses the room to the window and flings it wide open. The wind blows in and stings his face, and he becomes aware that there must be a garden beneath the window. And now the imagery begins once more to cohere; what was vertiginous and nauseating a moment before becomes once more invigorating. He hears in the night the boom of the cannon which says that the river is overflowing its banks[35]—overflowing ... overstepping. He determines to go out and to *choose* as the scene of his suicide "a great bush there, drenched with rain, so that as soon as one's shoulder touches it, millions of drops drip on one's head."[36] But one last horror still awaits him. As he leaves his room and finds his way along the dark passage he comes upon a little girl, crying and cold. He comforts her and to warm her lays her in his own bed. Then she turns to him a face of unmistakable lasciviousness. And then he—again?—wakes up, once more in the hotel bed. The special horror of the dream which involves itself with the waking surroundings, formerly applied to Raskolnikov, is here given a further twist as it is used to torture Svidrigailov. Did he then never awake and throw the window open? Was that, too, part of the dream? We cannot tell. Now, at all events, he can really go out. It is now morning and a milky mist is in the air. He steps out and walks till he finds himself outside a great house with a tower and massive gates. Leaning against the gatepost is a man, dressed in a soldier's coat and "Achilles" helmet, with a drowsy, peevish Jewish face. He "challenges" Svidrigailov:

"What do you want here?"
"Nothing brother, good morning," answered Svidrigailov.
"This isn't the place."
"I am going to foreign parts, brother."
"To foreign parts?"
"To America."
"America?"
Svidrigailov took out the revolver and cocked it. Achilles raised his eyebrows.
"I say, this is not the place for such jokes!"
"Why shouldn't it be the place?"
"Because it isn't."

"Well, brother, I don't mind that. It's a good place. When you are asked, you just say he was going, he said, to America."
He put the revolver to his right temple.
"You can't do it here, it's not the place," cried Achilles, rousing himself, his eyes growing bigger and bigger.
Svidrigailov pulled the trigger.[37]

When Raskolnikov killed another, he hardly knew what he was doing; when Svidrigailov kills himself he makes an existential joke. Having ridden out the storm of the night, he is confronted by a sort of parody of his regimental past, a castle which is not really a castle, a sentry who is not exactly a sentry, and a posture of witless intransigence which is a perfectly genuine feature of military life. Dostoevsky himself drops into a style of Victorian facetiousness, calling the man "Achilles" after his helmet. To the reiterated words "This is not the place" Svidrigailov returns enigmatic answers. The man, at this time in the morning anyway, is a simply programmed organism; this is not the place—for what? For whatever Svidrigailov is looking for. For making jokes. For shooting yourself.

The number of jokes is said to be rather small, the number of variations infinite. Svidrigailov says ironically that he is going to America, to the new found land. It is likely enough that part of him is certain, as he speaks, that he is going to the old dark place, the place of the spider, to Hell. The guard says "This is not the way." Svidrigailov's answer is really a variation of the ancient answer *Facilis descensus Averni*: "Easy is the Descent into Hell." These were the words of Sibyl used to Aeneas when he was looking for a way into the dark world of the dead. It is not always remembered that Virgil borrowed the phrase not from Homer but from the comic writer Aristophanes; the phrase, long before Virgil, had begun as a *joke*: "How do I get into Hades?" asks Dionysus in *The Frogs*.[38] "Easy," is the answer, "just jump off that cliff or hang yourself from that tree." "This is not the place," says the guard to Svidrigailov. "Easy," says the crack of the gun as the bullet enters Svidrigailov's skull. They later found in Svidrigailov's notebook a few words in explanation of his suicide; they said that he died in *full possession of his faculties* and no one was to blame for his death.[39]

The contrast with Raskolnikov remains overwhelming. I do not argue that the wind and weather that attend on Svidrigailov's death are uniformly delightful. Manifestly, they carry both relief and terror. I claim only a fundamental antithesis. Heat, confinement and suffocation are one thing; wind, rain and morning mist are another. If the former mean the denial of freedom, the latter must, by the language of images we have learned, mean freedom; freedom with all its horror, but the real thing. We may say of Svidrigailov what was once said of another inhabitant of Hell:

The King's Library

... E parve di costoro
Quegli che vince e non colui che perde.

We now have the material for the existentialist interpretation of *Crime and Punishment*. The breaking of Raskolnikov no longer demonstrates the hollowness of existentialism, but only the weakness of Raskolnikov. The story of *Crime and Punishment* now becomes the story not of a man's descent into hell and rebirth into glory, but of a failure. Raskolnikov tried to be free, but was sucked back into the mire of ethics and all the complex apparatus assembled by the Church for the diminution of humanity. Dostoevsky wrote in the first notebook for *Crime and Punishment* "Sonia and Love broke him."[40]

But what of the language of the Epilogue—"resurrection", "regeneration"? At all this the Existentialist reader will merely smile: "With such goodies the renegades from truth are commonly rewarded." What then of the despair of Svidrigailov? Again the distant smile: "We never said the truth was easy to bear. Our philosophy was not formed to console but to confront. We note only that in Svidrigailov's case the truth is borne and in Raskolnikov's it is not. Svidrigailov kills himself but at least he is the author of his action."

We all know that Dostoevsky, were he a party to this debate, would support the Christian interpretation and attack the existentialist. Yet in a curious way it is the existentialist interpretation which best "preserves the phenomena". The Christian reading is constantly embarrassed—by Razumikhin, by Svidrigailov, but the existentialist reading is utterly unembarrassed. Moreover, the imagery of the book works harder for the existentialist than the Christian. And although the word "existentialist" has been imported into this discussion from a later age, it is obvious that it was always possible to read the novel as the record of a failure.

It is interesting that we possess a critical essay on *Crime and Punishment* by the very Pisarev who held in real life the ferocious opinions maintained by Raskolnikov in his article. True to form, Pisarev sees Raskolnikov's progress away from those views as mere collapse, brought about by economic factors: "... After committing the murder Raskolnikov conducts himself ... like a petty cowardly and weak-nerved impostor for whom a major crime turned out to be beyond his strength."[41] In our own time, the existentialist view, now firmly disengaged from the utilitarian, was forcibly maintained by Middleton Murry, in whose private moral hierarchy the criminal stands appreciably higher than the philanthropist; for example: "In the Underworld Raskolnikov had dreamed of committing crime for its own sake; in the waking world he was one of the thousands who do evil that good may come. He had never for one moment ventured outside the walls of the City of

Good," "He was not even an unsuccessful criminal but an unsuccessful philanthropist." "Svidrigailov is the real hero of the book." "In Dostoevsky's eyes Raskolnikov could never have been more than an incomplete Svidrigailov."[42] Criticism like this can be accused of much, but not, perhaps, of inconsistency.

I have said that Dostoevsky, if asked to choose between the two interpretations before us, would opt for the Christian one. Yet he could not do so without misgivings. The final account of the real relation between existential freedom and Christian love is never clearly set forth. Certainly they are intermittently opposed, and equally certainly at the crude level of plot the hero is lost by one party and gained by the other. But the metaphysical question is unsolved.

Take the case of Porfiry, the police investigator. Porfiry is not, like Svidrigailov, "above" philosophizing. Indeed, he gets pleasure from sharpening his formidable wits in metaphysical discussion (so different, as they say, from our English policemen). When Porfiry talks to Raskolnikov about the article on crime, he lays his finger at once on a weakness in Raskolnikov's case: Should there not be some external definition of the Exceptional Man, since otherwise some poor young fellow might think himself a Mahomet quite erroneously ...?[43] The shaft is well-aimed, since this may well be Raskolnikov's situation. But at the same time, philosophically, a blow is struck for the utilitarian as opposed to the existentialist principle. We saw how the Underground Man confounded his utilitarian opponent by drawing from under him all public means of defining pleasure. Without such means, vacuous caprice is supreme, and, as prediction becomes impossible, so justification in terms of ends and mean's becomes impracticable. Porfiry is thus gently forcing on Raskolnikov the necessity to choose between an arbitrary crime and one that is to be justified in terms of foreseeable consequences. With this question Porfiry strikes a shrewd blow for utilitarianism. Nor is it his last.

For Porfiry definition of one's role is necessary to every human being: "What you need more than anything in life is a definite position."[44] This, as he presents it, is removed by only a hair's breadth from the existentialist position to which it is opposed. The existentialist finds a strange heroism in the resistance maintained by the free individual to encroaching definitions. But there could be no heroism in this if such freedom were not arduous, and such definitions insidiously comforting. Porfiry's case, in a way, consists of a strengthening of these adjectives. Individualist, pre-definitional freedom is not just arduous, it is actually intolerable. Social definition is not just comforting, it is a psychological necessity. This is the foundation of his Socratic method. He attacks the criminal not with blows or proofs, but with the one really unbearable thing, uncertainty. Those Underground Men need only be fed to overflowing with the very indeterminacy they say they think so much of, and they will soon vomit up all their squalid crimes: "Have you seen a butterfly round a candle? That's how he will keep circling and circling round me. Freedom will lose its attractions."[45] One thinks of the course taken by the later literature of existentialism. While a Meursault or a Roquentin may find a certain grim excitement in their supposedly undetermined worlds, it is left to Kafka to show what real indeterminacy does to man. Just as Joseph K in *The Trial* begins by arguing for his innocence but is soon desperate for conviction, so Raskolnikov is filled with fear by the thought that Porfiry thinks him *innocent*.[46] We see Porfiry's technique at work in the superb rhetorical *occupatio* he plays upon Raskolnikov:

> Why, if I had the slightest suspicion of you, should I have acted like that? No, I should first have disarmed your suspicions and not let you see I knew of that fact, should have diverted your attention and suddenly dealt you a knock-down blow ... saying: "And what were you doing, sir, pray, at ten or nearly eleven at the murdered woman's flat and why did you ring the bell and why did you ask about blood? And why did you invite the porters to go with you to the police-station, to the lieutenant?" That's how I ought to have acted if I had a grain of suspicion of you ...[47]

Here we see the weapon of uncertainty in the hands of a master.

At the same time Porfiry professes—but with no great enthusiasm—certain fundamental notions of traditional Russian Christianity. Once again his approach is that of the practical psychologist. Speaking of the workman Nikolay, whose gratuitous "confession" sprang from some religious "need to suffer", Porfiry says, "Suffering, too, is a good thing. Suffer! Maybe Nikolay is right in wanting to suffer."[48]

I think we may say that Dostoevsky hates Porfiry. It might be thought that his commendation of suffering would redeem him in the eyes of his creator. But Porfiry recommends suffering as a doctor might recommend a dose of castor oil. And, more importantly, Dostoevsky's own attitude to suffering is not perhaps as unequivocal as it is often supposed to be. People often speak of Dostoevsky as if his novels were solely taken up with endless orgies of repentance, voluptuous agonies of remorse. Freud in an essay dryly compared Dostoevsky with the barbarians of the great migrations, who "murdered and did penance for it, till penance became an actual technique for enabling murder to be done."[49] But Raskolnikov finds his new life without passing through any vale of contrition. The immemorial pattern of self-prostration is rather part of the background "noise" of the novel. It is the lesser characters, such as Marmeladov, who perform this part. Whenever Raskolnikov attempts it, there is an effect of distortion, something is false, the movement cannot be completed. To Sonia it seems clear as day that if Raskolnikov has committed murder he must "suffer and expiate" his sin, must "stand at the cross-roads, bow down, first kiss the earth which you have defiled and then bow down to all the world and say to all men aloud, 'I am a murderer!' Then God will send you life again." God sent Raskolnikov life again, but not on such terms. True, Raskolnikov does, in a sort of nervous spasm, kneel in the street, but the words "I am a murderer" die on his lips.

This is surely the terrible honesty of the greatest art. Had Dostoevsky been the theological sensationalist he is often described as being, here lay his inevitable climax. But instead he breaks his climax; at the moment of highest expectation everything seeps away into the earth, for no better reason than that anything else would be false. The hunched figure of Raskolnikov on his knees in the mud, utterly lacking the innocent dignity of Sonia, even of Marmeladov, spurious, but pitiably trying at last in the most uncomprehending way to learn—this provides by a kind of deliberate privation of our appetites the most moving moment in the book. The way of prostration and submission is never to be Raskolnikov's.

Even after he has given himself up and is going to his voluntary imprisonment he jibs at all those round him who prate of his need for suffering. In the strangest way they recall Job's comforters in their easy rationalisation of things, and Raskolnikov becomes a Job-like figure in his very resistance to the facile pains held out on every side:

> "They say it is necessary for me to suffer! What is the object of these senseless sufferings? Shall I know any better what they are for, when I am crushed by hardships and idiocy, and weak as an old man after twenty years penal servitude?"[50]

There is a spark of the old Raskolnikov in this, the Raskolnikov who told Sonia that the worst sin she had committed was the destruction of herself.[51] Even if it were not obvious from the tone of the writing, we know from a fragment of external evidence that Dostoevsky was drawn at times to admire the rebel in Raskolnikov; in the manuscript of the novel he scribbled in the margin beside a passage showing just this side of Raskolnikov, "Damn it! That's true in part."[52] Surely it evokes from the reader a deeper sympathy than is ever aroused by the self-crucifixion of a Marmeladov or even a Sonia. Sympathy, and also a kind of relief, like the relief we feel when, in reading the terrible self-lacerating sonnets of Gerard Manley Hopkins, we come upon the unfamiliar beauty of the lines

> My own heart let me more have pity on; let
> Me live to my sad self hereafter kind ...

There is another kind of egotism than the utilitarian, with its own moral claim.

Before he leaves for Siberia Raskolnikov insists[53] that he is not thinking of expiation, and in Siberia he persists in maintaining that his conscience is at rest.[54] Of course in this he is wrong, and half-knows that he is wrong, of that there is no question. What is important is the manner of his correction.

This is done very quietly, without tear-floods or sigh-tempests, indeed with a miraculous simplicity, Raskolnikov falls ill in prison; during his convalescence, Sonia herself falls ill and is unable to visit him. Then, on a bright warm day Raskolnikov is sitting looking at the river when he becomes aware that Sonia has come and sat down beside him. Quite suddenly he weeps and throws his arms round her knees; and the thing has happened. It may be said that this, precisely, is the moment of penitent self-prostration which I have been labouring to withhold from Raskolnikov. But if that is so, why does Raskolnikov make no reference to his crime? The kneeling of Marmeladov is essentially retrospective; it has unmistakable reference to what he has done. Raskolnikov's action, on the other hand, is obscurely prospective.

Roger L. Cox, in his book on Shakespeare and Dostoevsky,[55] seeks to resolve this difficulty by applying to it knowledge gained from Biblical scholarship. We must distinguish, he says, between Paul and John. In the Pauline epistles sin is conceived as a primordial hostile, principle, prior to the individual fallen soul, to be defeated only by rebirth. But in John's Gospel, the sinner is not so much guilty as unhappy, cut off from *light*; sin is posterior to the individual, arising by mere consequence from his initial darkness, that is, his inability to see, believe and love. Paul sees morality in terms of creation, John in terms of revelation. That is why in Shakespeare's *King Lear*, where the morality is Pauline, Lear must be broken before he be remade, while in *Crime and Punishment*, where the morality is Johannine, Raskolnikov need only turn and look up.[56]

It is an attractive thesis. It would seem that the Eastern Church has traditionally stressed John's Gospel where the Western Church has stressed the Pauline Epistles. Moreover the most prominent scriptural reference in *Crime and Punishment*, that to Lazarus, is Johannine. Moreover the general movement of the book is from darkness to light, and from wretchedness to happiness. Lafcadio Hearn observed in 1885 that the mental sufferings of Raskolnikov "are not the sufferings of remorse, but of nervous affection."[57] Somehow the shrewdness of this was always off-key. The reason is that although we do not find Pauline remorse, we do find, persistently, a moral element in Raskolnikov's unhappiness. Hearn wrote from an unconsciously Pauline standpoint: no remorse, no morality. The only conclusion available to him is that Raskolnikov's condition is merely pathological. But it has a further, Johannine dimension: he is a soul in darkness.

But although this account has so much to commend it, it is not completely satisfying. To begin with, the scriptural distinction is perhaps a little too neat. Five minutes with Cruden's *Concordance* is enough to show that Paul is as fond of "light" as John, and "regeneration" no less crucial to John than to Paul. This perhaps is sufficient ground for suspicion, at least. More importantly for our purpose, the substitution of the model of revelation for (re-)creation does not really explain why Raskolnikov should not clearly repent. Light and clarity, surely, should produce not oblivion but articulate acknowledgment. There must be some other impediment.

The truth is that Raskolnikov did what he did in the name of freedom, and neither he nor his creator can bring himself to call that wrong. Raskolnikov, though completely reconciled with Sonia at the end, never quite did things in the way she had wanted. And the suggestion seems to be that, in this, he was wiser than she. The implication that the murder was after all an authentic act of freedom, indefinable, *sui generis* and therefore not to be classified as any sort of sin, survives the conclusion of the book.

Clearly if some inalienable good persists in pure freedom, Dostoevsky is under very great pressure to claim that such freedom is compatible with—perhaps essential to—Christianity. The dim outline of a solution seems to rise before us: if the freedom of a Svidrigailov or a Stavrogin is devilish, might not there be another freedom, a baptised freedom, which God might love? After all, the notion that "everything is permitted"[58] is not confined to the writing of modish freethinkers: remember, "All things are lawful unto me."[59] These are the words of Paul to the Corinthians. It is certain that this thought beckoned Dostoevsky, since so much of his later work is a kind of quest for it.

It will be apparent from what I have just said that I do not believe that *Crime and Punishment,* for all its cogency of formal structure, demonstrates this baptised freedom. Further, even Dostoevsky's last great work, *The Brothers Karamazov,* in which a more sustained onslaught is made upon the problem, does not in my view attain to a solution. No solution is attained because none can be. Dostoevsky was too honest and too intelligent to delude himself in this matter. The example of Kierkegaard notwithstanding, existentialism is incompatible with Christianity. As long as freedom is conceived in existentialist terms it will resist any attempt to baptise it. To develop a notion of freedom as essentially rule-governed and hence both rational and moral—this would be a freedom Christianity could proudly display as one of the brightest jewels in its crown. But existential freedom?

The fundamental principle of Existentialism is that human freedom is prior to any system, and that must include any system *of values*. This leaves freedom itself as the sole absolute value. It is equally essential to Christianity that God, and therefore good (which comprehends far more than mere freedom) is prior to man. What God hath put asunder let no man try to join.

But, it will be said, did not Dostoevsky succeed in doing exactly this at the end of his life in the strange story which Ivan tells his brother in *The Brothers Karamazov*—the story of the Grand Inquisitor?

The Brothers Karamazov are four, and three of them can be crudely characterised with the terms we have acquired in analysing *Crime and Punishment*: Alyosha is the figure of Christian love and submission; Ivan (like Raskolnikov) is a sort of utilitarian nihilist; Dmitri is a figure of turbulent will and appetite and small reflection (a little like Svidrigailov but much more humane) and finally there is Smerdyakov, who is like nothing else on earth and whose portrait will not be attempted here. Ivan's story tells how Christ appeared on earth in sixteenth century Seville, where, the day before, nearly a hundred heretics had been burned by the Inquisition. Christ is recognized by the people in the street; he gives sight to a blind man and life to a dead child. The Grand Inquisitor, passing, observes all this and promptly arrests Christ. That same night the Inquisitor visits his prisoner in the darkness of his cell, and tells him that he is to be burned; whether or not he is the true Christ, the point is the same; the authority of Rome has at last learned to tame the freedom which Christ bequeathed to man. It has laboured to take away this freedom, not in order to oppress but in order to make men happy. There is only one motive which can justify a second crucifixion and the *auto da fé*, and that is the knowledge that by this means millions will in the end be relieved of anguish and be comforted. If Christ has come back, it can only be, says the Grand Inquisitor, to meddle with this work of loving kindness, and therefore if is the Inquisitor's duty to destroy Christ, even if he really is the son of God. The Inquisitor, as Ivan explains to Alyosha, is not speaking ironically. He means every word. As Christ remains silent he develops his case at greater length, but does nothing to modify its essence. Christ confers freedom, which is endless pain; the Church, through, a miracle, mystery and authority, confers happiness. Christ offered man spiritual bread, which would be fatuous were it not also cruel; for man is frail, and what is offered as a priceless gift would be to him nothing but a burden too heavy to lift. Real love listens to his cries, and gives him the earthly bread he asks for. "Respecting him less, thou wouldst have asked less of him. That would have been more like love, for his burden would have been lighter."[60]

The Inquisitor talks on, and the reader notices how there is less and less of the chapter left and wonders what words Christ will be given for his reply. But Christ never speaks. Instead he simply kisses the aged Inquisitor and goes out of the cell into the dark alleys of the town. Most readers feel that the kiss, the action of love in torment, simply transcends everything the Inquisitor has said, and turns it to dust and ashes. Alyosha, the monkish brother, is eager to take it so, but it is Ivan's story, and Ivan is of the party of the Inquisitor. And indeed the Inquisitor stands firm, even under the last, most most terrible temptation of Christ's love. "And the old man?" asks Alyosha. "The kiss glows in his heart, but the old man adheres to his idea," says Ivan.[61]

It will be noticed that in this story Dostoevsky is working from his habitual base: an opposition of existentialism and utilitarianism. Moreover Christ is now firmly advanced as the figure of freedom. Meanwhile the Grand Inquisitor, however much it might surprise Jeremy Bentham, is a utilitarian. In this strange experiment with the limits of conception, Dostoevsky proceeds by a method of deliberate intellectual trauma. Thus, he takes as his emblem of benevolence a figure who for most people would be an incarnation of cruelty; then with a fine freedom of appropriation he presents the Roman Catholic Church as an equivalent to socialism. When the reader's mind has recovered from these assaults it is in a fit state to survey the meaning of *The Grand Inquisitor*. Certainly, for purely historical reasons, the second hurdle is specially high for Englishmen. The first English socialists were dreamy, backward-looking men, much less interested in the possibilities of totalitarian power than in the tapestries and sculpture of the middle ages—men like Ruskin and Morris. At every possible point the hard economic doctrine was qualified by an insular liberalism. But Dostoevsky lived in what was to be the country of Stalin. Nor is there anything merely wilful in ascribing benevolence to the Inquisitor. As we have seen, it is an essential part of the calculus by which ends justify means. Even the burning of a hundred human beings can be justified, as anything less than an infinity of suffering can be justified. If we ask what justifies it, the answer is, "Whatever it takes;" that is, however much consequent happiness is necessary to tip the scale.

It might be objected that by transposing utilitarianism to a religious context Dostoevsky has deprived his argument of any relevance to Bentham.

Certainly, religious utilitarianism has existed, as we shall realise if we recall Leslie Stephens' words: "Bentham is Paley *minus* a belief in hell-fire. But Bentham, in another sense, is Paley *plus* a profound belief in himself."[62] Indeed Paley (perhaps the most complacent theologian the eighteenth century produced), most ingenuously affirmed the ethics of the old hymn:

> Whatever, Lord, we lend to Thee,
> Repaid a thousandfold shall be,
> Then gladly will we give to Thee.[63]

Paley's definition of virtue has become famous: it is "the doing good to mankind, in obedience to the will of God, and for the sake of ever-lasting happiness."[64] For this doctrine Bentham had nothing but contempt. For according to Benthamite utilitarianism God, as a source of ethical imperatives, becomes a dispensable hypothesis; he, like everyone else, will simply desire the greatest happiness of the greatest number.[65] And of Louis XIV he says this:

> There are certain errors, in matters of belief to which all mankind are prone: and for these errors in judgment, it is the determination of a Being of infinite benevolence, to punish them with a variety of torments. But from these errors the legislator himself is necessarily free ... such were the motives which led Lewis XIVth into those coercive measures which he took for the conversion of heretics and the confirmation of true believers. The groundwork, pure sympathy and loving-kindness: the superstructure, all the miseries which the most determined malevolence could have devised.[66]

It might be said that the difference between Louis XIV and Bentham is that the Frenchman believed in heaven. But Bentham, even if he conceded the existence of heaven, would still have strong criticism of the omnipotent God who commanded suffering as the price of entry. Thus it would seem Bentham and the Grand Inquisitor belong to opposite factions.

But look again. The resemblance between the Inquisitor and Louis XIV is superficial. Both burn heretics, but the Inquisitor acts from the motives, not of a Paley, but, strange as it may seem, of a true Benthamite. The Inquisitor is no eschatological utilitarian; his conception of happiness takes no account of Heaven or Hell, but is instead political, humanitarian, naturalist:

> There will be thousands of millions of happy babes, and a
> hundred thousand sufferers who have taken upon themselves the
> curse of the knowledge of good and evil in Thy name, and
> beyond the grave they will find nothing but death.[67]

The Inquisitor sees himself as promoting the happiness not of those who
burn but of those who survive. He sees beyond the flames, not the Heavenly
City, but the ideal commonwealth.[68]

But if we ask "Does the Inquisitor believe in God?" we feel a certain
discomfort, much like that provoked by modern assertions that "God is
dead". Does "God is dead" mean "God used to exist but does no longer", or
"Men have found out that belief in God in groundless" or "The concept of
God has ceased to be culturally important"? It is my experience that people
who use this phrase often mean all three, without any clear awareness of the
difference between them. Part of the eerie quality of *The Grand Inquisitor*
turns on a sense of religious schizophrenia in the Inquisitor himself. On
behalf of his flock, he is an atheist, but in his inmost heart he knows that God
is there, and is thus able to recognize Christ when he comes. Immediately
after his denial of the life to come, his tone in addressing Christ becomes
almost conspiratorial:

> But we shall keep the secret, and for their happiness we shall
> allure them with the reward of heaven and eternity. Though if
> there were anything in the other world, it certainly would not be
> for such as they.[69]

An invisible line is drawn between the multitude and the strong governor. In
doing this, the Inquisitor is, of course, only doing what Chernyshevsky and
Pisarev did, but now the whole character of utilitarian elitism is transformed
by an irony which could scarcely be exceeded. The implication is not far to
seek that heaven and hell, though irrelevant to *them*, might be relevant to *us*,
the governors, the responsible ones. The Inquisitor knows that God wants
his creatures to be free and, since freedom is incompatible with happiness,
that God does not want his creatures to be happy. Thus to make them happy
involves, for those who are so unfortunate as to know the real constitution of
things, a transgression against the law of God. The Inquisitor so loved the
world that he took upon himself the burden of this transgression. Perhaps, in
order that the weak might suffer no longer, he was willing to send himself to
hell. I once heard a man say that every major figure in Dostoevsky turns into
a Christ figure at some point. It remains shaking to find the principle
extended even to the figure of anti-Christ himself.

Of course Dostoevsky does not make the point fully explicit. Ivan actually tells Alyosha, in answer to a question, that the Inquisitor does not really believe in God, but immediately goes on to describe his unbelief, not as a simple want of conviction, but as a sort of renunciation,[70] and the Inquisitor himself is allowed one unmistakable echo of the Gospel: "the Punishment for these sins we take upon ourselves."[71] The question is thus raised, and is scarcely dispelled by the Inquisitor's defiance of God's judgement a few sentences later.

At the end of the story, the Inquisitor drives Christ out into the streets. What if he had done as he threatened at the beginning of the story, and burned Christ? In that case the crucifixion would have happened a second time, but behind it a larger and more terrible crucifixion would loom, where the tortured figure would not be that of Christ but of the Inquisitor. Christ so loved the world that he suffered death on the cross that man might be free, and live. The Inquisitor so loved the world that he suffered an eternity of hell that men might be happy. These bizarre speculations belong to the penumbra of *The Grand Inquisitor* rather than the work itself, but no great labour is required to raise them.

But if the Inquisitor is a naturalist, Christ is if anything more of a naturalist than he. The Inquisitor looks forward to the perfect state. Christ is confined (and liberated) by the here and now. The whole of *The Brothers Karamazov*—indeed the whole of Dostoevsky's oeuvre—makes it clear that there is one line of Christian apologetics which he cannot touch; and that is the notion that such little evils as come within man's purview will be lavishly made good in the next world. This is the theology of Paley, and it is too closely akin to the philosophy of the Inquisitor to be usable. The objection to the Inquisitor is not that the pleasures he offers are transient, or fatal to some larger bliss. It is, simply, that he sets a tranquil happiness above anguished freedom. To such a theology as Dostoevsky's, the so-called Problem of Evil (setting aside the suffering of children and animals) is no problem at all. Heaven, on the other hand, so eagerly seized by the eighteenth century as the place where anomalies might be straightened and losses turned to gains, is to Dostoevsky a positive embarrassment. No Christian writer of comparable stature has placed so little emphasis on the next world. Dostoevsky so excels at showing how the best kind of pity and charity can emerge only from a background of the blackest degradation, and his entire ethical outlook is so firmly rooted in this insight, that in the end his Christianity can absorb almost anything but harmony. True, the hero of Dostoevsky's last story, "The Dream of a Ridiculous Man", is a sort of Adam unparadised who preaches to uncomprehending listeners the glories of the harmonious Eden he has known. But this seeming simplicity is swiftly dissolved. The religion of the unfallen is described in a style which comes close to burlesque: they live in "oneness with the whole of the universe".[72] The hero is able to praise them only from afar; when he was among them his function was to introduce suffering and corruption, and it is at this point that Dostoevsky's imagery associates him not with Satan but with Christ. By the time Dostoevsky had completed his labours, the slums of St Petersburg were to him more compatible than the Paradiso with the divine love. When, in *The Possessed*, old Verkhovensky goes on his strange last pilgrimage, he meets a priest, who smoothly expatiates on eternal bliss as a reward for righteousness; Verkhovensky politely dissents: eternity is valuable to him not as a source of happiness but as an opportunity to love Gpf endlessly.[73] In the same novel, in the mouth of the half-crazed Kirilov, the very language of eternity is deprived of its reference to a future beyond death and applied instead to the present:

> "You've begun to believe in future eternal life?"
> "No, no! in a future eternal life, but in eternal life here."[74]

Again, it is Berdyaev who shows by his terminology that he understands Dostoevsky's alignment of concepts: "We need not, anyhow, suppose that Dostoievsky looked at the question from the over-simple and utilitarian point of view that in eternal life evil will be punished and good rewarded".[75] The idea of religious utilitarianism is obviously no stranger to him.

Thus a picture of Dostoevsky's "baptised existentialism" begins to emerge. God is a loving personality who confers freedom, not rule. There is therefore no moral *law*, and no system of sanctions. But not everyone will agree with this.

For example, Edward Wasiolek, in his *Dostoevsky: the Major Fiction*, argues that the brothers Karamazov in rejecting their father reject God.[76] Wasiolek works through a sort of inverted Freudianism: instead of God being a sort of after-image of one's father, the father-figure is a symbol of God. But Freud, whether you stand him on his head or his feet, is the last man to enlist as an interpreter of Dostoevsky. Freud is anti-Dostoevsky for the same reasons that make him anti-existentialist: he believes that human nature has a discoverable rationale; he approaches the soul with the apparatus of nineteenth century scientific determinism; his conception of the pleasure principle and his account of the evolution of society in *Civilization and its Discontents* proclaim him a member of the utilitarian tradition, And, in particular, Freud's Oedipal account of the murder of the father in *The Brothers Karamazov* is incredible partly because of the contemptible character of Feodor Karamazov and partly because of the absence from the novel of a Jocasta-figure.

Thus Wasiolek's thesis does not fit the book. The father is a tyrant, whereas the God of Alyosha and Father Zossima is essentially other-than-tyrannical. It may be that the God conceived by Ivan is a tyrant but this view, we are given to understand, is the consequence of an infected understanding. It is a great irony in Ivan's character that he rejects the tyranny of God only to replace it with the utilitarian tyranny of the Grand Inquisitor. To be sure, Ivan may sometimes fall short of a full intellectual consistency. He claims that nothing God did could ever justify the torturing of a child. Of course, the fact that he is talking about God in part excuses him, for if we grant that God is omnipotent the justification of the means by the end collapses. But in general every utilitarian must grant that the torturing of a child may be justifiable. However that may be, Ivan's general ethical position is sufficiently clear. His imprisonment within a series of tyrannies derives from his fundamental notion of right as a law, authoritatively pronounced, enforced by sanctions: *ius quia iussum non quia iustum*. Hence it is Ivan who says that if God is dead then everything is permitted.[77] It is a sentiment which strikes one half of mankind with all the force of Euclidian logic, while to the other half it is simply meaningless. Ivan belongs with those thinkers of the past who held that actions were right because God commanded them, and not that God commanded them because they were right. Ivan is a spiritual descendant of Hobbes for whom ethical statements were meaningless unless traceable to a proper authority.

And indeed this makes very good sense if we consider the genealogical tree of utilitarianism. Hobbes (whose appetitive state of nature is organized by a supervening law of group interest) begat Hume (or part of Hume), Hume begat Bentham, Bentham begat Darwin who in turn begat Freud, whose appetitive state of nature is curbed and organized, like Hobbes's, by the law of the group. But Dostoevsky (for the weight of his book is against Ivan: he has to outgrow his false ideals) belongs by implication to the other tradition; he belongs with those who feel that too complete a system of sanctions deprives moral action of its proper disinterestedness, of its proper spontaneity; his English allies, surprising as it may seem, are the Cambridge Platonists, especially Cudworth, who hated[78] the Hobbist reduction of morality to a set of commands, and Sir Thomas Browne who was unwilling to believe that a man could be "scared into Heaven"[79] by the threat of hell fire. For those who cannot believe that a similar theology underlies the fire and ice of Dostoevsky's novels and the lukewarm style of Cudworth, there is small comfort. For I have a yet more improbable comparison to propose: Dostoevsky in some ways resembles Matthew Arnold—that is, the Matthew Arnold who wrote *Literature and Dogma*. Arnold followed such Cambridge Platonists as John Smith in transposing religious language about Heaven,

Hell and the Devil into naturalistic, moral terms. Indeed Smith's observation that "When we say that the devil is continually busy with us, I mean ... that spirit of apostasy which is lodged in all men's natures" was a favourite of Arnold's; he quoted it in his essay, "A Psychological Parallel."[80] Arnold himself reduced God to "the enduring power, not ourselves, that makes for righteousness."[81] He rejected all insistence on a future life as *Aberglaube*, "extra-belief", and delighted in the text, "The kingdom of God is within you."[82] What links Dostoevsky with Arnold and what separates him from a superficially similar writer like Graham Greene is his naturalism. In Green morality is less real than magic; God's body melting on the tongue under the material accident of bread is more than any merely human pity or love. In Arnold what is real is the mystery of moral experience, the purity or pollution of the human heart. But to place Dostoevsky in such a tradition is to give him companions who would scarcely be to his liking. It is the inner logic of his theology which points towards naturalism, and indeed for a very good reason. Dostoevsky felt a strong compulsion to blur the differences between the theology of Ivan and that of Alyosha. Thus he makes the sage Zossima assent to the logic of Ivan's position while doubting his premise.[83] The reason (doubtless here clearly perceived by Dostoevsky) is that Alyosha's philosophy leads to atheism rather more easily than does Ivan's.

The real purpose of my comparison with Arnold was to show the fundamental tendency of that school of thought which refuses to derive ethics from the commands of a pre-moral deity. The tendency is, as I have hinted, atheism. Admittedly Arnold claimed that in *Literature and Dogma* he had preserved true Christianity, but a man cannot pray to a shared moral impulse. The poems, *Dover Beach* and *The Scholar Gypsy*, show that Arnold, at a deeper level of his personality, was well aware of this. We may reflect that, as there is little about Heaven or Hell in the pages of Dostoevsky, so there is little praying. God is in the freedom, in the movements of pity and submission, within the human situations, and seldom outside them. He is almost entirely immanent, hardly at all transcendent. But a God who is wholly immanent is no longer a God. Dostoevsky's God is absorbed in man and as a result loses his power to command. Doubtless Dostoevsky himself would resist this account. Nevertheless it flows naturally from the inner logic of his ideas. The Cambridge Platonists likewise thought themselves—and, in a sense, were—good Christians. But in choosing to say that God ordered things because they were right, they made ethics prior to God, which is ultimately to make God morally dispensable. The determining God of Calvin[84] may have been tyrannical but he was very much *there*. When God no longer legislates, he becomes a secondary being, at first like ourselves and at last like the best part of ourselves.

Nevertheless, if morality is conceived as a series of authoritative commands the mind will naturally seek the authority behind them. The model of the imperative suggests a logical basis for belief in God. An imperative implies an imperator. But the believer in an open morality is under no such logical pressure to believe. Some pages back I suggested that Christianity and existentialism could never be reconciled since Christianity entails a belief in certain ethical absolutes, prior to our merely human choices. It then looked for a time as if *The Brothers Karamazov* had succeeded in resolving this opposition by locating God, not in the coercive law but in man's very freedom. But this resolution is spurious. For why should *freedom* need ontological support from a God standing behind it? It is all very well to say: "You are familiar with the idea of God impressing his will on the world from above; well, I have merely transferred his point of contact with Nature from the sphere of law to the sphere of pure freedom." But the reasons which made God an urgent necessity at his original "point of contact" are simply absent in the second. The sentinel has been moved to a position where his services are no longer needed. One is reminded of Jean Paul Sartre's advice to the young man who could not decide whether to fight for the free French, or to look after his aged mother. Sartre with all the authority of a sage told him the answer prescribed by existentialism: "Choose!"[85] A God who stands behind our freedom is scarcely more useful. For the whole point about freedom is that it is something we call do for ourselves.

Thus Dostoevsky, in supporting the open ethics of Alyosha against the closed ethics of Ivan, did not preserve Christianity but lost it. The whole history of modern theology implies that if God is not a tyrant, he is little better than an ethical mist. Those who reject the stern Father end by worshipping the fact that love is a good thing.[86]

But Dostoevsky never explicitly isolated the concept of an open morality that was nonetheless a morality. He was thus never able to frame a connexion between two insights, both of which seemed to him of enormous power, and yet to be formally contradictory. The first was that everything was permitted. It was essential to Dostoevsky's existentialism that he should grant this, though in a sense different from Ivan's. For Ivan, if God existed, many things were forbidden. But Ivan's great error lay in not seeing that God is the author of freedom, not rule. Therefore, all things are permitted, and it is God who permits them (and here we note that a God who exists to permit you to do the things you would have done anyway is hardly going to be an *urgent* presence). But the second insight which Dostoevsky found inescapable was that certain actions were intrinsically and obviously vile or glorious. However much one prates of freedom one discovers by experiment that there are certain things one must not do. If Dostoevsky had made a clear separation between open and closed morality, he might have gone far towards resolving this contradiction; he might have argued that although nothing is actually *forbidden*, and although one is entirely free to choose, certain actions remain morally wrong, so that to choose them is to choose wrongly. After all, the fact that not all choices are correct hardly implies that there is no such thing as choice. But if he had followed out this line of argument it would have entailed a drastic modification of his existentialist conception of freedom.

Thus the long story of Dostoevsky's struggle to rescue freedom from the godless remains without an ending. It would be easy to fake a conclusion but to do so would be an insult to Dostoevsky, whose love of goodness was always joined with an equal love of truth.

NOTES

1. *Ibid.*, III.i, pp. 178–179.
2. *Ibid.*, II.v. p. 277.
3. *Ibid.*, III.i, p. 179.
4. His introduction to Henry James, *The American Scene*, New York. 1946.
5. *Ibid.*, III.v, p. 234.
6. *Ibid.*, III.i, p. 179.
7. *Ibid.*, I.iii, p. 28.
8. *Ibid.*, I.iii, p. 28.
9. *Ibid.*, VI.iii, p. 412.
10. See for example *The Notebooks for Crime and Punishment*, ed, and trans. by E. Wasiolek, Chicago and London, 1967, p. 194.
11. *Crime and Punishment*, III.iii, p. 202.
12. *Ibid.*, IV.i, p. 255.
13. *Ibid.*, IV.ii, p. 264.
14. *Ibid.*, IV.ii, p. 264.
15. *Ibid.*, IV.iv, p. 293.
16. *Ibid.*, III.vi, p. 244.
17. *Ibid.*, IV.i, p. 256.
18. *Ibid.*, VI.iii, p. 414.
19. *Ibid.*, VI.iii, p. 415.
20. *Ibid.*, Epilogue, ii, p. 477.
21. *Ibid.*, V.iv., p, 367.
22. *Ibid.*, IV.iv., p. 279.
23 *Ibid.*, I.i, p. 5.
24. *Ibid.*, III.iv, p. 214.
25. Svidrigailov at VI.i, p. 387. Porfiry at VI.ii, p. 405.
26. *Ibid.*, I.v, p. 55.
27. *Ibid.*, I.vi, p. 67.
28. *Ibid.*, I.vi, p. 68.
29. *Ibid.*, I.v, p. 57.
30. *Ibid.*, VI.v, p. 439.
31. *Ibid.*, VI.vi, p. 443.

32. *Ibid.*, VI.vi, p. 444.

33. *Ibid.*, VI.vi, p. 444.

34. *Ibid.*, VI.vi, p. 447.

35. *Ibid.*, VI.vi, p. 447.

36. *Ibid.*, VI.vi, p. 448.

37. *Ibid.*, VI.vi, pp. 450–451.

38. 118–122.

39. *Crime and Punishment*, VI.viii, p. 467.

40. *The Notebooks for Crime and Punishment*, ed. and trans. by E. Wasiolek, Chicago and London, 1967, p. 67.

41. "Struggle for Life," in *Crime and Punishment and the Critics*, ed. E. Wasiolek, Belmont, California. 1961. p. 136.

42. *Crime and Punishment and the Critics, seriatim*, pp. 48, 47. 49, 53.

43. *Crime and Punishment*, III.v, pp. 232, 234.

44. *Ibid.*, VI.ii, p. 406.

45. *Ibid.*, IV.v, p. 301.

46. *Ibid.*, VI.i, p. 392.

47. *Ibid.*, IV.v, p. 307.

48. *Ibid.*, VI.ii, p. 405.

49. "Dostoevsky and Parricide", in *The Collected Psychological Works*, ed. J. Strachey, vol. XXI, 1961, p. 177.

50. *Ibid.*, VI.vii, p. 458.

51. *Ibid.*, IV.iv, p. 285.

52. *The Notebooks for Crime and Punishment*, ed. and trans. Wasiolek, p. 58.

53. *Crime and Punishment*, VI.vii, p. 457.

54. *Ibid.*, Epilogue, ii, p. 477.

55. *Between Earth and Heaven: Shakespeare, Dostoevsky and the Meaning of Christian Tragedy*, New York, 1969.

56. *Op. cit.*, pp. 30–36.

57. "A Terrible Novel", in *Crime and Punishment and the Critics*, ed. Wasiolek, p. 34.

58. *Crime and Punishment*, III.vi, p. 243. VI.v, p. 434.

59. I Corinthians, vi. 12.

60. *The Brothers Karamazov*, p. 263.

61. *Ibid.*, p. 270.

62. *History of English Thought in the Eighteenth Century*, vol. II, p. 106.

63. Quoted in Lewis Carroll, *Silvie and Bruno*, 1889, chap. XIX, p. 276; in *The Complete Works of Lewis Carroll*, the Nonesuch Edition (n.d.) p. 396.

64. *Moral Philosophy*, Lvii, in *The Works of William Paley*, D.D., 1838, vol. III, p. 20. Cf *Evidences of Christianity*, II.ii, *Works*, vol. II, pp. 156 ff.

65. See *Principles*, p. 125.

66. *Ibid.*, pp. 320–321.

67. *The Brothers Karamazov*, V.v, p. 267.

68. In his secularising of the Christian eschatology, the Inquisitor is a true son of the Enlightenment; see C.L. Becker, *The Heavenly City of the Eighteenth Century Philosophers*, New Haven, 1932.

69. *The Brothers Karamazov*, V.v, p. 267.

70. *Ibid.*, p. 269.

71. *Ibid.*, pp. 266–267.

72. In *An Honest Thief and Other Stories*, trans. C. Garnett, 1919., p. 397.

73. *Op. cit*, trans. C. Garnett, 1914, p. 603. In David Magarshack's Penguin translation (1953) the point is obscured.

32   A.D. Nuttall

74. *Ibid.*, p. 213.

75. *Dostoevsky*, p. 105.

76. *Op. Cit.*, Cambridge, Mass., 1964, pp. 149–151.

77. *The Brothers Karamazov*, V.v, in Constance Garnett's translation. *Everyman*, 1927, vol. I, p. 270.

78. See his *Treatise concerning Eternal and Immutable Morality*. The crucial section is given in L.H. Selby-Bigge, *British Moralists*, New York, 1965, §813–815. See also A.N. Prior, *Logic and the Basis of Ethics*, 1949, pp. 13–25.

79. *Religio Medici and Other Works*, ed. L.C. Martin, 1964. Liii, p. 49.

80. In his *Last essays on Church and Religion*, 1903, pp. 18–19.

81. *Literature and Dogma*, first published 1873, the 1924 impression of the edn. of 1909, p. 43.

82. Luke, xvii.21; see *Literature and Dogma*, p. 116.

83. *The Brothers Karamazov*, p. 66.

84. Calvin seems sometimes to have hesitated over the idea of God as the source rather than the servant of morality. "We do not imagine God to be lawless (*exlegem*)", he says, but on the contrary "the will of God... is the supreme standard of perfection" (*Institutes of the Christian Church*, III, xxiii. 2; in the translation of H. Beveridge, Edinburgh, 1863, vol. II, pp. 227–228). It is a sad piece of reasoning; God is not above the law, since his will sets the standard of all law. The question of priority is merely evaded.

85. *L'Existentialisme est un Humanisme*, Paris, 1952, p. 47.

86. I have said nothing about the strain in *The Brothers Karamazov*, which suggests that Christ is in some way the antithesis of futile, merely human Freedom. In fact the matter is fairly simple. These passages are about the discovery by the would-be existentialist of moral absolutes. They thus constitute a qualification to Dostoevsky's existentialism without really restoring traditional supernaturalist Christianity. *A fortiori* they have nothing to offer for the reconciliation of Christianity and existentialism.

MIKHAIL BAKHTIN

Characteristics of Genre and Plot Composition in Dostoevsky's Works

We must now move on to the problem of carnival and the carnivalization of literature, already mentioned by us earlier.

The problem of *carnival* (in the sense of the sum total of all diverse festivities, rituals and forms of a carnival type)—its essence, its deep roots in the primordial order and the primordial thinking of man, its development under conditions of class society, its extraordinary life force and its undying fascination—is one of the most complex and most interesting problems in the history of culture. We cannot, of course, do justice to it here. What interests us here is essentially only the problem of carnivalization, that is, the determining influence of carnival on literature and more precisely on literary genre.

Carnival itself (we repeat:, in the sense of a sum total of all diverse festivities of the carnival type) is not, of course, a literary phenomenon. It is *syncretic pageantry* of a ritualistic sort. As a form it is very complex and varied, giving rise, on a general carnivalistic base, to diverse variants and nuances depending upon the epoch, the people, the individual festivity. Carnival has worked out an entire language of symbolic concretely sensuous forms—from large and complex mass actions to individual carnivalistic gestures. This language, in a differentiated and even (as in any language) articulate way, gave expression to a unified (but complex) carnival sense of the world,

From *Problems of Dostoevsky's Poetics*. © 1984 by the University of Minnesota.

permeating all its forms. This language cannot be translated in any full or adequate way into a verbal language, and much less into a language of abstract concepts, but it is amenable to a certain transposition into a language of artistic images that has something in common with its concretely sensuous nature; that is, it can be transposed into the language of literature. We are calling this transposition of carnival into the language of literature the carnivalization of literature. From the vantage point of this transposition, we will isolate and examine individual aspects and characteristic features of carnival.

Carnival is a pageant without footlights and without a division into performers and spectators. In carnival everyone is an active participant, everyone communes in the carnival act. Carnival is not contemplated and, strictly speaking, not even performed; its participants *live* in it, they live by its laws as long as those laws are in effect; that is, they live a *carnivalistic life*. Because carnivalistic life is life drawn out of its *usual* rut, it is to some extent "life turned inside out," "the reverse side of the world" ("*monde à l'envers*").

The laws, prohibitions, and restrictions that determine the structure and order of ordinary, that is noncarnival, life are suspended during carnival: what is suspended first of all is hierarchical structure and all the forms of terror, reverence, piety, and etiquette connected with it that is, everything resulting from socio-hierarchical inequality or any other form of inequality among people (including age). All *distance* between people is suspended, and a special carnival category goes into effect: *free and familiar contact among people*. This is a very important aspect of a carnival sense of the world. People who in life are separated by impenetrable hierarchical barriers enter into free familiar contact on the carnival square. The category of familiar contact is also responsible for the special way mass actions are organized, and for free carnival gesticulation, and for the outspoken carnivalistic word.

Carnival is the place for working out, in a concretely sensuous, half-real and half-play-acted form, a *new mode of interrelationship between individuals*, counterposed to the all-powerful socio-hierarchical relationships of noncarnival life. The behavior, gesture, and discourse of a person are freed from the authority of all hierarchical positions (social estate, rank, age, property) defining them totally in noncarnival life, and thus from the vantage point of noncarnival life become eccentric and inappropriate. *Eccentricity* is a special category of the carnival sense of the world, organically connected with the category of familiar contact; it permits—in concretely sensuous form—the latent sides of human nature to reveal and express themselves.

Linked with familiarization is a third category of the carnival sense of the world: *carnivalistic mésalliances*. A free and familiar attitude spreads over everything: over all values, thoughts, phenomena, and things. All things that were once self-enclosed, disunified, distanced from one another by a noncarnivalistic hierarchical worldview are drawn into carnivalistic contacts and combinations. Carnival brings together, unifies, weds, and combines the sacred with the profane, the lofty with the low, the great with the insignificant, the wise with the stupid.

Connected with this is yet a fourth carnivalistic category, *profanation*: carnivalistic blasphemies, a whole system of carnivalistic debasings and bringings down to earth, carnivalistic obscenities linked with the reproductive power of the earth and the body, carnivalistic parodies on sacred texts and sayings, etc.

These carnivalistic categories are not *abstract thoughts* about equality and freedom, the interrelatedness of all things or the unity of opposites. No, these are concretely sensuous ritual-pageant "thoughts" experienced and played out in the form of life itself, "thoughts" that had coalesced and survived for thousands of years among the broadest masses of European mankind. This is why they were able to exercise such an immense *formal, genre-shaping* influence on literature.

These carnival categories, and above all the category of free familiarization of man and the world, were over thousands of years transposed into literature, particularly into the dialogic line of development in novelistic prose. Familiarization facilitated the destruction of epic and tragic distance and the transfer of all represented material to a zone of familiar contact; it was reflected significantly in the organization of plot and plot situations, it determined that special familiarity of the author's position with regard to his characters (impossible in the higher genres); it introduced the logic of mésalliances and profanatory debasings; finally, it exercised a powerful transforming influence on the very verbal style of literature. All this already shows up quite clearly in the menippea. We shall return to this later, but first we must touch upon several other aspects of carnival, most importantly *carnivalistic acts*.

The primary carnivalistic act is the *mock crowning and subsequent decrowning of the carnival king*. This ritual is encountered in one form or another in all festivities of the carnival type: in the most elaborately worked out forms—the saturnalia, the European carnival and festival of fools (in the latter, mock priests, bishops or popes, depending on the rank of the church, were chosen in place of a king); in a less elaborated form, all other festivities of this type, right down to festival banquets with their election of short-lived kings and queens of the festival.

Under this ritual act of decrowning a king lies the very core of the carnival sense of the world—*the pathos of shifts and changes, of death and renewal*. Carnival is the festival of all-annihilating and all-renewing time.

Thus might one express the basic concept of carnival. But we emphasize again: this is not an abstract thought but a living sense of the world, expressed in the concretely sensuous forms (either experienced or play-acted) of the ritual act.

Crowning/decrowning is a dualistic ambivalent ritual, expressing the inevitability and at the same time the creative power of the shift-and-renewal, the *joyful relativity* of all structure and order, of all authority and all (hierarchical) position. Crowning already contains the idea of immanent decrowning: it is ambivalent from the very start. And he who is crowned is the antipode of a real king, a slave or a jester; this act, as it were, opens and sanctifies the inside–out world of carnival. In the ritual of crowning all aspects of the actual ceremony—the symbols of authority that are handed over to the newly crowned king and the clothing in which he is dressed—all become ambivalent and acquire a veneer of joyful relativity; they become almost stage props (although these are ritual stage props); their symbolic meaning becomes two-leveled (as real symbols of power, that is in the noncarnival world, they are single-leveled, absolute, heavy, and monolithically serious). From the very beginning, a decrowning glimmers through the crowning. And all carnivalistic symbols are of such a sort: they always include within themselves a perspective of negation (death) or vice versa. Birth is fraught with death, and death with new birth.

The ritual of decrowning completes, as it were, the coronation and is inseparable from it (I repeat: this is a dualistic ritual). And through it, a new crowning already glimmers. Carnival celebrates the shift itself, the very process of replaceability, and not the precise item that is replaced. Carnival is, so to speak, functional and not substantive. It absolutizes nothing, but rather proclaims the joyful relativity of everything. The ceremonial of the ritual of decrowning is counterposed to the ritual of crowning: regal vestments are stripped off the decrowned king, his crown is removed, the other symbols of authority are taken away, he is ridiculed and beaten. All the symbolic aspects of this ceremonial of decrowning acquire a second and positive level of meaning—it is not naked, absolute negation and destruction (absolute negation, like absolute affirmation, is unknown to carnival). Moreover, precisely in this ritual of decrowning does there emerge with special clarity the carnival pathos of shifts and renewals, the image of constructive death. Thus the ritual of decrowning has been the ritual most often transposed into literature. But, we repeat, crowning and decrowning are inseparable, they are dualistic and pass one into the other; in any absolute dissociation they would completely lose their carnivalistic sense.

The carnivalistic act of crowning/decrowning is, of course, permeated with carnival categories (with the logic of the carnival world): free and familiar contact (this is very clearly manifest in decrowning), carnivalistic mésalliances (slave–king), profanation (playing with the symbols of higher authority), and so on.

We shall not dwell here on the details of the crowning–decrowning ritual (although they are very interesting), nor on its diverse variations from epoch to epoch and in the various festivities of the carnival type. Nor shall we analyze the various accessory rituals of carnival, for example, disguise— that is, carnivalistic shifts of clothing and of positions and destinies in life; nor carnival mystifications, bloodless carnival wars, verbal agons[G] and cursing matches, exchanges of gifts (abundance as an aspect of carnivalistic utopia), and so on. These rituals too were transposed into literature, imparting symbolic depth and ambivalence to the corresponding plots and plot situations, imparting a joyful relativity, carnival levity and rapidity of change.

But of course an extraordinarily great influence on literary-artistic thinking was exercised by the ritual of crowning/decrowning. This ritual determined a special *decrowning type* of structure for artistic images and whole works, one in which the decrowning was essentially ambivalent and two-leveled. If carnivalistic ambivalence should happen to be extinguished in these images of decrowning, they degenerated into a purely negative *exposé* of a moral or socio-political sort, they became single-leveled, lost their artistic character, and were transformed into naked journalism.

We must consider again in more detail the ambivalent nature of carnival images. All the images of carnival are dualistic; they unite within themselves both poles of change and crisis: birth and death (the image of pregnant death), blessing and curse (benedictory carnival curses which call simultaneously for death and rebirth), praise and abuse, youth and old age, top and bottom, face and backside, stupidity and wisdom. Very characteristic for carnival thinking is paired images, chosen for their contrast (high/low, fat/thin, etc.) or for their similarity (doubles/twins). Also characteristic is the utilization of things in reverse: putting clothes on inside out (or wrong side out), trousers on the head, dishes in place of headgear, the use of household utensils as weapons, and so forth. This is a special instance of the carnival category of *eccentricity*, the violation of the usual and the generally accepted, life drawn out of its usual rut.

Deeply ambivalent also is the image of *fire* in carnival. it is a fire that simultaneously destroys and renews the world. In European carnivals there was almost always a special structure (usually a vehicle adorned with all

---

G. Agon: in Greek, "contest." An agon is that part of a Greek drama in which two protagonists, each aided by half of the chorus, engage in verbal conflict.

possible sorts of gaudy carnival trash) called "hell," and at the close of
carnival this "hell" was triumphantly set on fire (sometimes this carnival
"hell" was ambivalently linked with a horn of plenty). Characteristic is the
ritual of "moccoli" in Roman carnival: each participant in the carnival carried
a lighted candle ("a candle stub"), and each tried to put out another's candle
with the cry "Sia ammazzato!" ("Death to thee!"). In his famous description
of Roman carnival (in *Italienische Reise*)[H] Goethe, striving to uncover the
deeper meaning behind carnival images, relates a profoundly symbolic little
scene: during "moccoli" a boy puts out his father's candle with the cheerful
carnival cry: "Sia ammazzato il Signore Padre!" [that is, "death to thee,
Signor Father!"]

Deeply ambivalent also is carnival *laughter* itself. Genetically it is linked
with the most ancient forms of ritual laughter. Ritual laughter was always
directed toward something higher: the sun (the highest god), other gods, the
highest earthly authority were put to shame and ridiculed to force them to
renew themselves. All forms of ritual laughter were linked with death and
rebirth, with the reproductive act, with symbols of the reproductive force.
Ritual laughter was a reaction to *crises* in the life of the sun (solstices), crises
in the life of a deity, in the life of the world and of man (funeral laughter). In
it, ridicule was fused with rejoicing.

This ancient ritualistic practice of directing laughter toward something
higher (a deity or authority) defined the privileges of laughter in antiquity
and in the Middle Ages. Much was permitted in the form of laughter that was
impermissible in serious form. In the Middle Ages, under cover of the
legitimized license of laughter, "parodia sacra" became possible—that is,
parody of sacred texts and rituals.

Carnivalistic laughter likewise is directed toward something higher—
toward a shift of authorities and truths, a shift of world orders. Laughter
embraces both poles of change, it deals with the very process of change, with
crisis itself. Combined in the act of carnival laughter are death and rebirth,
negation (a smirk) and affirmation (rejoicing laughter). This is a profoundly
universal laughter, a laughter that contains a whole outlook on the world.
Such is the specific quality of ambivalent carnival laughter.

In connection with laughter we shall touch upon one more question—
the carnivalistic nature of *parody*. Parody, as we have already noted, is an
integral element in Menippean satire and in all carnivalized genres in
general. To the pure genres (epic, tragedy) parody is organically alien; to the

---

H. J.W. Goethe, *Italian Journey*, trans. W. H. Auden and Elizabeth Mayer (London: Collins,
1962). See Part Three (January 1788), "The Roman Carnival," and especially the section
"Moccoli," pp. 467–69.

carnivalized genres it is, on the contrary, organically inherent. In antiquity, parody was inseparably linked to a carnival sense of the world. Parodying is the creation of a *decrowning double*; it is that same "world turned inside out." For this reason parody is ambivalent. Antiquity parodied essentially everything: the satyr drama, for example, was originally the parodic and laughing aspect of the tragic trilogy that preceded it. Parody here was not, of course, a naked rejection of the parodied object. Everything has its parody, that is, its laughing aspect, for everything is reborn and renewed through death. In Rome, parody was an obligatory aspect of funeral as well as of triumphant laughter (both were of course rituals of the carnivalistic type). In carnival, parodying was employed very widely, in diverse forms and degrees: various images (for example, carnival pairs of various sorts) parodied one another variously and from various points of view; it was like an entire system of crooked mirrors, elongating, diminishing, distorting in various directions and to various degrees.

Parodying doubles have become a rather common phenomenon in carnivalized literature. They find especially vivid, expression in Dostoevsky—almost every one of the leading heroes of his novels has several doubles who parody him in various ways: for Raskolnikov there are Svidrigailov, Luzhin, and Lebeziatnikov; for Stavrogin—Peter Verkhovensky, Shatov, and Kirillov; for Ivan Karamazov—Smerdyakov, the devil, Rakitin. In each of them (that is, in each of the doubles) the hero dies (that is, is negated) in order to be renewed (that is, in order to be purified and to rise above himself).

In the narrowly formal literary parody of modern times, the connection with a carnival sense of the world is almost entirely broken. But in the parodies of the Renaissance (in Erasmus, Rabelais, and others) the carnival fire still burned: parody was ambivalent and sensed its bond with death/renewal. Thus could be born in the bosom of parody one of the greatest and at the same time most carnivalistic novels of world literature: Cervantes' *Don Quixote*. Here is how Dostoevsky assessed that novel: "There is nothing in the world more profound and powerful than this work. It is the ultimate and greatest word yet uttered by human thought, it is the most bitter irony that a man could express, and if the world should end and people were asked there, somewhere, 'Well, did you understand your life on earth and what conclusions have you drawn from it?' a person could silently point to Don Quixote: 'Here is my conclusion about life, can you judge me for it?'"[I]

I. The comment on Quixote occurs in *The Diary of a Writer*, 1876, March, Ch. II, 1: "Don Carlos and Sir Watkin. Again, Symptoms of 'the Beginning of the End,'" p. 260.

It is characteristic that Dostoevsky structures his evaluation of *Don Quixote* in the form of a typical "threshold dialogue."

To conclude our analysis of carnival (from the vantage point of carnivalized literature), a few words about the carnival square.

The main arena for carnival acts was the square and the streets adjoining it. To be sure, carnival also invaded the home; in essence it was limited in time only and not in space; carnival knows neither stage nor footlights. But the central arena could only be the square, for by its very idea carnival *belongs to the whole people*, it is *universal*, *everyone* must participate in its familiar contact. The public square was the symbol of communal performance. The carnival square—the square of carnival acts—acquired an additional symbolic overtone that broadened and deepened it. In carnivalized literature the square, as a setting for the action of the plot, becomes two-leveled and ambivalent: it is as if there glimmered through the actual square the carnival square of free familiar contact and communal performances of crowning and decrowning. Other places of action as well (provided they are realistically motivated by the plot, of course) can, if they become meeting- and contact-points for heterogeneous people—streets, taverns, roads, bathhouses, decks of ships, and so on—take on this additional carnival-square significance (for all the naturalistic qualities of the representation, the universal symbol-system of carnival is in no danger of naturalism).

Festivities of the carnival type occupied an enormous place in the life of the broadest masses of the people in ancient times—in Greek and even more in Roman life, where the central (but not the sole) festival of the carnival type was the *saturnalia*. These festivals had no less (and perhaps, even more) significance in medieval Europe and during the Renaissance, where they were in part a direct living continuation of Roman saturnalia. In the realm of carnivalistic folk culture there was no break in tradition between antiquity and the Middle Ages. In all epochs of their development, festivities of the carnival type have exercised an enormous influence—as yet insufficiently appreciated and researched—on the development of culture as a whole, including literature, several of whose genres and movements have undergone a particularly intense carnivalization. In the ancient period, early Attic comedy and the entire realm of the serio-comical was subjected to a particularly powerful carnivalization. in Rome, the many diverse varieties of satire and epigram were linked, and were designed to be linked, with the saturnalia; they were either written for saturnalia, or at least were created under cover of that legitimized carnival license enjoyed by the festival (all of Martial's* work, for example, was directly connected with the saturnalia).

In the Middle Ages the vast comic and parodic literature in vernacular languages and in Latin was, one way or another, connected with festivals of the carnival type—with carnival proper, with the "Festival of Fools," with free "paschal laughter" (*risus paschalis*), and so forth. Essentially every church holiday in the Middle Ages had its carnivalistic side, the side facing the public square (especially those holidays like Corpus Christi). Many national festivities, such as the bullfight, for example, were of a clearly expressed carnivalistic character. A carnival atmosphere reigned during the days of a fair, on the festival of the harvesting of grapes, on the performance days of miracle plays, mystery plays, *soties*[J] and so forth; the entire theatrical life of the Middle Ages was carnivalistic. The large cities of the late Middle Ages (such cities as Rome, Naples, Venice, Paris, Lyon, Nuremberg, Cologne) lived a full carnival life on the average of three months out of the year (and sometimes more). It could be said (with certain reservations, of course) that a person of the Middle Ages lived, as it were, *two lives*: one was the *official* life, monolithically serious and gloomy, subjugated to a strict hierarchical order, full of terror, dogmatism, reverence, and piety; the other was the *life of the carnival square*, free and unrestricted, full of ambivalent laughter, blasphemy, the profanation of everything sacred, full of debasing and obscenities, familiar contact with everyone and everything. Both these lives were legitimate, but separated by strict temporal boundaries.

Without taking into account the alternation and mutual estrangement of these two systems of life and thought (the official and the carnivalistic), one cannot understand correctly the peculiar nature of medieval man's cultural consciousness, and cannot make sense of many phenomena in medieval literature—such as, for example, the "parodia sacra."[6]

This epoch also witnessed the carnivalization of the *speech life* of European peoples: whole layers of language, the so-called *familiar speech of the public square*, were permeated with a carnival sense of the world; there came into being an enormous fund of unrestrained carnivalistic gesticulations. The familiar speech of all European peoples is to this day filled with relics of carnival, especially speech of abuse and ridicule; the symbol-system of carnival also fills the abusive, ridiculing gesticulations of today.

During the Renaissance, one could say that the primordial elements of carnival swept away many barriers and invaded many realms of official life and worldview. Most importantly, they took possession of all the genres of high literature and transformed them fundamentally. There occurred a deep and almost total carnivalization of all artistic literature. The carnival sense of the world, with its categories, its carnival laughter, its symbol-system of

---

J. *Soties*: French satirical farces of the medieval period, in which actors (in fool's costume) ridiculed social manners and political events.

carnival acts of crowning/decrowning, of shifts and disguises, carnival ambivalence and all the overtones of the unrestrained carnival word—familiar, cynically frank, eccentric, eulogistic-abusive and so on—penetrated deeply into almost all genres of artistic literature. On the basis of this carnival sense of the world, the complex forms of the Renaissance worldview came into being. Even antiquity, as assimilated by the humanists of the epoch, was to a certain extent refracted through the prism of the carnival sense of the world. The Renaissance is the high point of carnival life.[7] Thereafter begins its decline.

Beginning with the seventeenth century, folk-carnival life is on the wane: it almost loses touch with communal performance, its specific weight in the life of people is sharply reduced, its forms are impoverished, made petty and less complex. As early as the Renaissance a *festive court masquerade* culture begins to develop, having absorbed into itself a whole series of carnivalistic forms and symbols (mostly of an externally decorative sort). Later there begins to develop a broader line of festivities and entertainments (no longer limited to the court) which we might call the *masquerade line* of development; it preserved in itself a bit of the license and some faint reflections of the carnival sense of the world. Many carnival forms were completely cut off from their folk base and left the public square to enter this chamber masquerade line, which exists even today. Many ancient forms of carnival were preserved and continue to live and renew themselves in the *farcical* comic antics of the public square, and also in the *circus*. Certain elements of carnival are also preserved in the life of the theater and spectacle in modern times. It is characteristic that the subculture of the theater has even retained something of carnivalistic license, the carnivalistic sense of the world, the fascination of carnival; this was very well illustrated by Goethe in *Wilhelm Meisters Lehrjahre*, and for our time by Nemirovich-Danchenko* in his memoirs.[K] Something of the carnival atmosphere is retained, under certain conditions, among the so-called bohemians, but here in most cases we are dealing with the degradation and trivialization of the carnival sense of the world (there is, for example, not a grain of that carnival spirit of communal performance).

Alongside these later branchings from the basic carnival trunk—branchings that had emaciated the trunk—there continued and still continues to exist a public-square carnival in the proper sense, as well as other festivities of the carnivalistic type, but they have lost their former significance and their former wealth of forms and symbols.

K. See, in English, Vladimir Ivanovich Nemirovich-Danchenko, *My Life in the Russian Theatre*, trans. John Cournos (Boston: Little, Brown & Co., 1936).

As a consequence, there occurred a deterioration and dissipation of carnival and the carnival sense of the world; it lost that authentic sense of a communal performance on the public square. And thus a change also occurred in the nature of the carnivalization of literature. Until the second half of the seventeenth century, people were *direct participants* in carnivalistic acts and in a carnival sense of the world; they still *lived* in carnival, that is, carnival was one of the forms of life itself. Therefore carnivalization was experienced as something unmediated (several genres in fact directly serviced carnival). *The source of carnivalization was carnival itself*. in addition, carnivalization had genre-shaping significance; that is, it determined not only the content but also the very generic foundations of a work. From the second half of the seventeenth century on, carnival almost completely ceases to be a direct source of carnivalization, ceding its place to the influence of already carnivalized literature; in this way carnivalization becomes a purely literary tradition. Thus in Sorel* and Scarron* we already observe, alongside the direct influence of carnival, the powerful effect of the carnivalized literature of the Renaissance (primarily Rabelais and Cervantes), and this latter influence predominates. Carnivalization, consequently, is already becoming a literary and generic tradition. Carnival elements in this literature—already cut off from their direct source, carnival—change their appearance somewhat and are reconceptualized.

It is of course true that carnival in the proper sense as well as other festivities of the carnival type (bullfights, for example), the masquerade line, farcical street antics, and other forms of carnivalistic folklore continue to exercise a certain direct influence on literature even to this day. But in the majority of cases this influence is limited to the content of works and does not touch their generic foundation; that is, it is deprived of any genre-shaping power.

We can now return to the carnivalization of genres within the realm of the serio-comical—a realm whose very name already sounds ambivalent, after the manner of carnival.

The carnivalistic base of the Socratic dialogue, despite its very complicated form and philosophical depth, is beyond any doubt. Folk-carnival "debates" between life and death, darkness and light, winter and summer, etc., permeated with the pathos of change and the joyful relativity of all things, debates which did not permit thought to stop and congeal in one-sided seriousness or in a stupid fetish for definition or singleness of meaning—all this lay at the base of the original core of the genre. This distinguishes the Socratic dialogue from the purely rhetorical dialogue as well as from the tragic dialogue; but this carnivalistic base also brings Socratic dialogue close in several respects to the agons of ancient Attic comedy and to the mimes of Sophron (there have even been attempts to reconstruct the mimes of Sophron after certain Platonic dialogues). The Socratic discovery of the dialogic nature of thought, of truth itself, presumes a carnivalistic familiarization of relations among people who have entered the dialogue, it presumes the abolition of all distance between them; moreover, it presumes a familiarizing of attitudes toward the object of thought itself, however lofty and important, and toward truth itself. Several of Plato's dialogues are constructed along the lines of a carnival crowning/decrowning. Characteristic for a Socratic dialogue are unrestrained mésalliances of thoughts and images. "Socratic irony" is reduced carnival laughter.

The image of Socrates himself is of an ambivalent sort—a combination of beauty and ugliness (see the characterization of him by Alcibiades in Plato's *Symposium*); Socrates' own characterizations of himself as a "pander" and "midwife" are also constructed in the spirit of carnival debasings. And the personal life of Socrates was itself surrounded by carnivalistic legends (for example, his relationship with his wife Xanthippe). Carnivalistic legends in general are profoundly different from traditional heroicizing epic legends: carnivalistic ends debase the hero and bring him down to earth, they make him familiar, bring him close, humanize him; ambivalent carnival laughter burns away all that is stilted and stiff, but in no way destroys the heroic core of the image. It should be pointed out that novelistic images of heroes (Gargantua, Eulenspiegel, Don Quixote, Faust, Simplicissimus and others) also coalesced in the atmosphere of carnivalistic legends.

The carnivalistic nature of the menippea is even more pronounced. Carnivalization permeates both its external layers and its deepest core. Certain menippea directly portray festivals of the carnival type (Roman festivals are depicted in two of Varro's satires, for example; in one menippea by Julian the Apostate, there is a depiction of the celebration of saturnalia on Olympus). This is a purely external (so to speak, thematic) connection, but it too is characteristic. More essential is the carnivalistic treatment of the three planes of the menippea; Olympus, the nether world, and earth. The representation of Olympus is clearly carnivalistic: free familiarization, scandals and eccentricities, crownings and decrownings are characteristic for the Olympus of the menippea. Olympus is, as it were, transformed into a carnival square (as, for example, in Lucian's *Juppiter tragoedus*). Olympian scenes are sometimes presented as carnivalistic debasings and bringings-down-to-earth (also in Lucian). Still more interesting is the consistent carnivalization of the nether world. The nether world equalizes representatives of all earthly positions in life; there the emperor and the slave, the rich man and the beggar come together on equal terms and enter into familiar contact; death decrowns all who have been crowned in life. Representation of the nether world often applied the carnivalistic logic of "a world upside down": an emperor in the nether world becomes a slave, a slave an emperor, and so forth. The carnivalized nether world of the menippea determined the medieval tradition of representations of *joyful bell*, a tradition which found its culmination in Rabelais. Characteristic for this medieval tradition is a deliberate confusion of the ancient nether world and Christian hell. In the mystery plays, hell and devils (in the "diableries") are also consistently carnivalized.

The earthly plane in the menippea is also carnivalized: behind almost all scenes and events of real life, most of which are portrayed in a naturalistic manner, there glimmers more or less distinctly the carnival square with its specific carnivalistic logic of familiar contacts, mésalliances, disguises and mystifications, contrasting paired images, scandals, crownings/decrownings, and so forth. Behind all the slum-naturalism scenes of the *Satyricon*, more or less distinctly, the carnival square is glimmering. And in fact the very plot of the *Satyricon* is thoroughly carnivalized. We notice the same thing in Apuleius' *Metamorphoses (The Golden Ass)*. Sometimes carnivalization lies buried at deeper levels and permits us to speak only of *carnivalistic overtones* to individual images and events. But sometimes it surfaces, for example in the purely carnivalistic episode of the supposed murder *on the threshold*, when instead of humans Lucius stabs wineskins filled with wine, mistaking the wine for blood, and in the subsequent scene of carnival mystification surrounding his trial. Carnivalistic overtones are heard even in a menippea of so serious a tone as Boethius' *De Consolatione Philosophiae*.

Carnivalization even penetrates the deepest philosophical and dialogic core of the menippea. Characteristic for the genre, as we have seen, is a naked posing of ultimate questions on life and death, a universalism of the most extreme sort (personal problems and elaborate philosophical argumentation are unknown to it). Carnivalistic thought also lives in the realm of ultimate questions, but it gives them no abstractly philosophical or religiously dogmatic resolution; it plays them out in the concretely sensuous form of carnivalistic acts and images. Thus carnivalization made possible the transfer of ultimate questions from the abstractly philosophical sphere, through a carnival sense of the world, to the concretely sensuous plane of images and events—which are, in keeping with the spirit of carnival, dynamic, diverse and vivid. A carnival sense of the world also made it possible to "deck out philosophy in the motley dress of a hetaera." A carnival sense of the world is the drive-shaft between the *idea* and the *artistic image of adventure*. A vivid example of this in European literature of modern times are the philosophical novellas of Voltaire, with their universalism of ideas, their carnivalistic dynamism and motley colors (*Candide*, for example); in very graphic form these novellas reveal the traditions of the menippea and carnivalization.

Carnivalization thus penetrates to the very philosophical core of the menippea.

The following conclusion can now be drawn. We have uncovered in the menippea a striking combination of what would seem to be absolutely heterogeneous and incompatible elements: philosophical dialogue, adventure and fantasticality, slum naturalism, utopia, and so forth. We can now say that the clamping principle that bound all these heterogeneous elements into the organic whole of a genre, a principle of extraordinary strength and tenacity, was carnival and a carnival sense of the world. in the subsequent development of European literature as well, carnivalization constantly assisted in the destruction of all barriers between genres, between self-enclosed systems of thought, between various styles, etc.; it destroyed any attempt on the part of genres and styles to isolate themselves or ignore one another; it brought closer what was distant and united what had been sundered. This has been the great function of carnivalization in the history of literature.

Now a few words about the menippea and carnivalization on Christian soil.

The menippea and kindred genres developing within its orbit exercised a defining influence on emerging ancient Christian literature—Greek, Roman, and Byzantine.

The basic narrative genres of ancient Christian literature—"Gospels," "Acts of the Apostles," "Apocalypse," and "Lives of Saints and Martyrs"—are linked with an ancient aretology which in the first centuries A.D. developed within the orbit of the menippea. In the Christian genres this influence was sharply increased, especially at the expense of the *dialogic element* of the menippea. In these genres, and especially in the numerous "Gospels" and "Acts," the classical Christian dialogic syncrises are worked out: that of the tempted (Christ or a righteous man) with the tempter, the believer with the nonbeliever, the righteous man with the sinner, the beggar with the rich man, the follower of Christ with the Pharisee, the apostle (the Christian) with the heathen, and so forth. These syncrises are familiar to everyone through the canonical Gospels and Acts. The corresponding anacrises are also developed (that is, provocation through discourse or plot situation).

In the Christian genres as in the menippea, enormous organizing significance is allotted to the *testing of an idea and its carrier*, testing by means of temptations and martyrdom (especially, of course, in the hagiographic genre). As in the menippea, rulers, rich men, thieves, beggars, hetaerae come together here on equal terms on a single, fundamentally dialogized plane. Here, as in the menippea, considerable importance is given to dream visions, insanity, obsessions of all sorts. And finally, Christian narrative literature also absorbed into itself kindred genres: the symposium (the gospel meals) and the soliloquy.

Christian narrative literature (independently of the influence of carnivalized menippea) was also subjected to direct carnivalization. It is enough to recall the scene of crowning and decrowning the "King of the Jews" in the canonical Gospels. But carnivalization is even more powerfully present in apocryphal Christian literature.

Thus ancient Christian narrative literature (including that which was canonized) is also permeated by elements of the menippea and carnivalization.[8]

These are the ancient sources, the "origins" (the "archaic portion") of that generic tradition, one of whose high peaks was to be the work of Dostoevsky. These "origins" are preserved, in a renewed form, in his work.

But Dostoevsky is separated from these sources by two thousand years, during which time the generic tradition continued to develop, to become more complex, to change its shape and be reconceptualized (while preserving throughout its unity and continuity). A few words now on the further development of the menippea.

We have seen that on ancient soil, including the earliest Christian period, the menippea already manifested an extraordinary "protean" capacity for changing its external form (while preserving its inner generic essence), a capacity to grow into whole novels, to combine with kindred genres, to infiltrate other large genres (for example, the Greek and ancient Christian novel). This capacity manifests itself in the subsequent development of the menippea, in the Middle Ages as well as in modern times.

During the Middle Ages, certain generic features of the menippea continue to live and be renewed in several genres of Latin ecclesiastical literature, directly continuing the tradition of ancient Christian literature, especially in certain varieties of hagiographic literature. in more free and original form the menippea lives on in such dialogized and carnivalized medieval genres as "arguments," "debates," ambivalent "panegyrics" (*desputaisons*, *dits*, *débats*),[L] morality and miracle plays, and in the later Middle Ages mystery plays and *soties*. Menippean elements are felt in the intensely carnivalized parodic and semi-parodic literature of the Middle Ages: in

---

L. In medieval literature, the *dit* is a flexible verse composition, either descriptive or didactic. The *débat* is a didactic *dit* in the form of a dialogue, often between personifications (of the seasons, etc.) and frequently on religious themes.

parodic visions from beyond the grave, in parodic "Gospel readings," and so forth. And finally, as a very important moment in the development of this generic tradition, there is the novelistic literature of the Middle Ages and the early Renaissance—a literature thoroughly permeated with elements of the carnivalized menippea.[9]

The entire medieval development of the menippea is permeated with elements of *local* carnival folklore and reflects the specific features characteristic of various periods in the Middle Ages.

During the Renaissance—an epoch of deep and almost complete carnivalization of literature and worldview—the menippea infiltrates all the large genres of the epoch (the works of Rabelais, Cervantes, Grimmelshausen* and others); there develop at the same time diverse Renaissance forms of the menippea, in most cases combining ancient and medieval traditions of the genre: Des Périers' *Cymbalum mundi*, Erasmus' *The Praise of Folly*, *Novelas ejemplares* of Cervantes, *Satyre Ménippée de la vertu du Catholicon d'Espagne* (1594, one of the greatest political satires of world literature), the satires of Grimmelshausen, Quevedo, and others.

In modern times, while infiltrating deep into other carnivalized genres, the menippea continues its own independent development, in diverse variants and under diverse names: the "Lucianic dialogue," "dialogues of the dead" (varieties in which ancient traditions predominate), the "philosophical tale" (a variety of menippea characteristic for the Enlightenment), the "fantastic story" and "philosophical fairy tale" (forms characteristic for Romanticism—Hoffmann, for example), and others. Here it should be noted that in modern times the generic characteristics of the menippea have been used by various literary movements and creative methods, renewing them, of course, in a variety of ways. Thus, for example, the rationalistic "philosophical tale" of Voltaire and the romantic "philosophical fairy tale" of Hoffmann share common generic features of the menippea and are equally intensely carnivalized, for all the profound differences in artistic intention, the content of their ideas, and, of course, their individuality as creative works of art (it suffices to contrast, for example, *Micromégas* with *Klein Zaches*). It must be said that the menippea has been, in the literature of modern times, the primary conduit for the most concentrated and vivid forms of carnivalization.

In conclusion we consider it necessary to emphasize that the generic label "menippea," like all other generic labels—"epic," "tragedy," "idyll," etc,—is, when applied to the literature of modern times, a means of designating the *essence of a genre*, and not any specific genre canon (as in antiquity).[10]

With this we conclude our digression into the realm of the history of genres and return to Dostoevsky (although throughout this entire digression we have not for a single moment lost sight of him).

We already noted in the course of our digression that the characterization we offered of the menippea and its kindred genres also applies, and almost in its entirety, to the generic features of Dostoevsky's work. We must now illustrate this concretely with an analysis of several of his works that are *key* from the generic standpoint.

Two "fantastic stories" of the late Dostoevsky—"Bobok" (1873) and "The Dream of a Ridiculous Man" (1877)—may be called menippea almost in the strict ancient sense of the term, so precisely and fully manifest in them are the classical characteristic features of the genre. A number of other works ("Notes from Underground," "A Meek One," and others) constitute variants, freer and more distant from the ancient models, of the same generic essence. Finally, the menippea infiltrates all of Dostoevsky's larger works, especially his five mature novels, and infiltrates, moreover, precisely the most fundamental and decisive aspects of the novels. Therefore we can say outright that the menippea essentially sets the tone for Dostoevsky's entire work.

We would hardly be mistaken in saying that "Bobok," in all its depth and boldness, is one of the greatest menippea in all word literature. But the depth of its content will not detain us here; here we are interested only in the particular generic characteristics of the work.

Characteristic first of all is the image of the narrator and the *tone* of his story. The narrator—a "certain person"[11]—is on the *threshold* of insanity (delirium tremens). But that aside, he is already a person *not like everyone else*; that is, he is one who has deviated from the general norm, who has fallen out of life's usual rut, who is despised by everyone and who himself despises everyone—that is, we have before us a new variety of the "underground man." His tone is unstable, equivocal, full of muffled ambivalence, with elements of infernal buffoonery (similar to the devils of mystery plays). Despite the external form of short, "choppy" categorical sentences, he conceals his final word, evades it. He himself quotes a characterization of his style, given by a friend:

> "Your style is changing," he said; "it is choppy: you chop and chop—and then a parenthesis, then a parenthesis in the parenthesis, then you stick in something else in brackets, then you begin chopping and chopping again." [*SS* X, 343]

His speech is internally dialogized and shot through with polemic. The story in fact begins directly on a polemic with one Semyon Ardalionovich, who has accused him of being a drunkard. He also polemicizes with the editors who refuse to print his words (he is an unrecognized author), and with the contemporary public not capable of understanding humor; in fact he polemicizes with all of his contemporaries. And later, when the main action of the story unfolds, he indignantly polemicizes with "contemporary corpses." Such is the dialogized and equivocal verbal style and tone of the story, so typical of the menippea.

At the beginning of the story there is discussion on a theme typical for the carnivalized menippea: the relativity and ambivalence of reason and madness, intelligence and stupidity. Then follows the description of a cemetery and a funeral.

The entire description is permeated with a markedly *familiar* and *profaning* attitude toward the cemetery, the funeral, the cemetery clergy, the deceased, the very "sacrament of death" itself. The entire description is built on oxymoronic combinations and carnivalistic mésalliances; it is full of *debasing* and *bringings-down-to-earth*, full of the *symbol-system* of carnival and at the same time a crude naturalism.

Here are some typical excerpts:

> I went out in search of *diversion*, I hit upon a *funeral*.... It's been twenty-five years, I think, since I was at the cemetery; *what a wretched place*!
>
> To begin with, the *odor*. About fifteen corpses *arrived. Shrouds at various prices*; there were even two catafalques.
>
> One was a general's and one some lady's. There were many *mourners*, a great deal of feigned mourning and a great deal of *open gaiety*. The clergy have nothing to complain of; it brings them a good *income*. But the *odor*, the *odor*. I should not like to be in *the holy orders* here. [A profanatory pun typical for the genre.][M]
>
> I kept glancing at the faces of the dead cautiously, distrusting my impressionability. Some had a mild expression, some looked unpleasant. As a rule the *smiles* were disagreeable, and in some cases very much so ... I went out while the *service* was going on and strolled *outside the gates*. Close by was an almshouse, and a

---

M. The Russian root *dukh* ["animus"] is found in the Russian words for breath, air, spirit, and odor. The pun to which Bakhtin refers here is Dostoevsky's juxtaposition of *dukh* (odor) with *dukhovnoe litso* (spiritual personage or member of the clergy). There is an additional pun on *dokhody* (income) and perhaps a hidden one on *dokhnut'* (to die, as an animal dies; to croak).

little further off there was a *restaurant*. It was not a bad little restaurant: one could have a snack and everything. There were lots of the *mourners* there. I noticed a great deal of *gaiety* and *genuine heartiness. I had something to eat and drink*. [*SS* X, 343–44]

We have italicized the most striking overtones of familiarization and profanation, the oxymoronic combinations, the mésalliances, bringings-down-to-earth, naturalism and symbolic elements. We see that the text is very strongly saturated with them. Before us is a somewhat condensed model for the style of a carnivalized menippea. We recall the symbolic significance of the ambivalent combination: death—laughter (here, gaiety)—feasting (here, I had something to eat and drink").

This is followed by a short and vacillating meditation by the narrator, who has sat down on a gravestone, on the theme of *wonder* and *respect*, which his contemporaries have rejected. This meditation is important for an understanding of the author's conception. And then follows this simultaneously naturalistic and symbolic detail:

A half-eaten sandwich was lying on the tombstone near me; stupid and inappropriate. I threw it on the ground, as it was not bread but only a sandwich. Though I believe it is not a sin to throw bread on the earth, but only on the floor. I must look it up in Suvorin's calendar. [*SS* X, 345]

This particularly naturalistic and profaning detail—a half-eaten sandwich on the grave—gives us occasion to touch on a symbolic attribute of the carnival type: throwing bread on the ground is permitted, for that is sowing, fructification; throwing it on the floor is forbidden, for that is barren soil.

Further on begins development of the fantastic plot, which creates an *anacrisis* of extraordinary power (Dostoevsky is a great master of the anacrisis). The narrator listens in on a conversation of the dead beneath the earth. It so happens that their lives in the grave continue for a certain time. The deceased philosopher *Platon* Nikolaevich (an allusion to the Socratic dialogue) explained it in this way;

"He [Platon Nikolaevich-M. B.] explains this by a very simple fact, namely that when we were living on the surface we mistakenly thought that death there was death. The body revives, as it were, here; the remains of life are concentrated, but only in consciousness. I don't know how to express it, but life goes on, as it were, by inertia. In his opinion everything is concentrated somewhere in consciousness and goes on for two or three months ... sometimes even for half a year.... There is one here, for instance, who is almost completely decomposed, but once every six weeks he suddenly utters one word, quite senseless of course, about some *bobok*, 'Bobok bobok,' but even in him, that means, life is still glimmering with an imperceptible spark ..." [*SS* X, 354]

This creates an extraordinary situation: the *final life of the consciousness* (the two or three months before it falls asleep forever), freed from all the conditions, positions, obligations, and laws of ordinary life, as it were a *life outside of life*. And how will it be used by the "contemporary corpses"? As anacrisis, provoking the consciousnesses of the corpses to reveal themselves with *full*, absolutely unlimited *freedom*. And reveal themselves they do.

What unfolds is the typical carnivalized nether world of the menippea: a rather motley crew of corpses which cannot immediately liberate themselves from their earthly hierarchical positions and relationships, giving rise to comic conflicts, abuse, and scandals; on the other hand, liberties of the carnival type, the awareness of a complete absence of responsibility, open graveyard eroticism, laughter in the coffins ("... the general's *corpse* shook with agreeable *laughter*"), and so on. The marked carnivalistic tone of this paradoxical "life outside of life" is set from the very beginning, with a game of cards being played in the grave on which the narrator sits (it is of course a make-believe game, played "by heart"). All these are typical traits of the genre.

The "king" of this carnival of the dead is a "scoundrel of pseudo-high society" (as he characterizes himself), one baron Klinevich. We will quote his words, which cast much light on the anacrisis and its use. Having dispensed with the moral interpretations of the philosopher Platon Nikolaevich (paraphrased by Lebezyatnikov), Klinevich declares:

"Enough; all the rest of it, I am sure, is nonsense. The great thing is that we have two or three months more of life and then— bobok! I propose to spend these two months as agreeably as possible, and so to arrange everything on a new basis. Gentlemen! *I propose to cast aside all shame*."

Once he obtains the general approval of the dead, he develops his thought somewhat further along these lines:

Though meanwhile I *don't want us to be telling lies*. That's all I care about, for that is one thing that matters. *One cannot exist on the surface without lying, for life and lying are synonymous,* but here we will *amuse ourselves* by not lying. Hang it all, the *grave* has some value after all! *We'll all tell our stories aloud, and we won't be ashamed of anything.* First of all I'll tell you about myself. I am one of the predatory kind, you know. *All that was bound and held in check by rotten cords up there on the surface.* Away with cords and let us spend these two months in *shameless truthfulness! Let us strip and go naked!*"

"Let us go naked, naked!" cried all the voices. [*SS* X, 355–56]

This dialogue of dead people was unexpectedly interrupted in a carnival manner:

> And here I suddenly *sneezed.* It happened suddenly and unintentionally, but the effect was striking: all became as silent as a *grave,* it all vanished like a dream. A real silence of the tomb set in.

I shall also quote the narrator's concluding comments, which are interesting for their tone:

> No, that I cannot admit, no, I really cannot! It's not bobok that bothers me (so it did turn out to be bobok!).
> Depravity in such a place, depravity of the last aspirations, depravity of sodden and rotten corpses—and not even sparing the *last moments of consciousness!* Those moments have been granted, vouchsafed to them, and ... and, worst of all, in such a place! No, that I cannot admit. [*SS* X, 357–58]

Here the almost pure words and intonations of a completely different voice, that is, the author's voice, break in on the narrator's speech; they break in, but then are immediately broken off on the word "and ...".

The ending of the story is journalistic, feuilletonistic:

> I shall take it to the *Citizen;* the editor there has had his portrait exhibited too. Maybe he will print it.

Such is Dostoevsky's almost classical menippea. The genre is sustained with remarkable integrity. One could even say that the genre of the menippea reveals here its greatest potential, realizes its maximum. Least of all is this a *stylization* of a defunct genre. On the contrary, in Dostoevsky's piece the genre of the menippea *continues to live* its full generic life. For the life of a genre consists in its constant rebirths and renewals in *original* works. Dostoevsky's "Bobok" is, of course, profoundly original. Dostoevsky was not writing a parody on the genre; he was using it in its straightforward sense. However, it should be noted that the menippea—and this includes also its oldest antique forms—to some extent always parodies itself. That is one of the generic characteristics of the menippea. This element of self-parody is one of the reasons for the extraordinary vitality of the genre.

Here we must touch upon the question of Dostoevsky's possible generic sources. The essence of every genre is realized and revealed in all its fullness only in the diverse variations that arise throughout a given genre's historical development. The more accessible all these variants are to the artist, the more richly and flexibly will he command the language of the given genre (for the language of a genre is concrete and historical).

Dostoevsky understood subtly and well all the generic possibilities of the menippea. He possessed an extraordinarily deep and well-differentiated feeling for this genre. To trace all of Dostoevsky's possible contacts with different varieties of the menippea would be a very important task, both for a deeper understanding of the generic characteristics of his works and for a more complete idea of the development of the generic tradition itself, before Dostoevsky.

Dostoevsky was linked with varieties of the ancient menippea most directly and intimately through ancient Christian literature (that is, through the Gospels, the Apocalypse, the Lives of Saints, and so on). But he was doubtless also familiar with the classic models of the ancient menippea. It is very likely that he knew Lucian's menippea *Menippus, or a Journey to the Kingdom of the Dead*, as well as his *Dialogues of the Dead* (a group of small-scale dialogic satires). These works illustrate various types of *behavior of dead people* under the conditions of the Kingdom beyond the Grave, that is, in the carnivalized nether world. It should be pointed out that Lucian—"the Voltaire of antiquity"—was widely known in Russia beginning with the eighteenth century[12] and inspired numerous imitations, and the generic situation of "meetings beyond the grave" became a common one in literature, right down to the level of school exercises.

Dostoevsky was quite possibly also acquainted with Seneca's menippea *Apocolocyntosis*. We find in Dostoevsky three aspects that recall that satire. (1) The "open gaiety" of the mourners at the cemetery in Dostoevsky is, perhaps, evoked by an episode in Seneca: Claudius, flying from Olympus to the nether world via Earth, comes upon his own funeral on Earth and satisfies himself that all the mourners are very cheerful (except the contentious ones); (2) the make-believe game of cards, played "by heart," is perhaps evoked by Claudius' game of dice in the nether world, which is also make-believe (the dice tumble out before they are thrown); (3) the naturalistic decrowning of death in Dostoevsky recalls an even cruder depiction of the death of Claudius, who dies (gives up the ghost) at the moment of defecation.[13]

There is no doubt about Dostoevsky's familiarity—more or less intimate—with other ancient works of the genre: *The Satyricon*, *The Golden Ass*, and others.[14]

Dostoevsky's European generic sources, those that might have revealed for him the richness and diversity of the menippea, are very numerous and heterogeneous. He probably knew Boileau's literary-polemical menippea *Dialogue des héros de romans*, and perhaps also Goethe's literary-polemical satire *Götter, Helden und Wieland*. He was probably familiar with the "dialogues of the dead" of Fénelon and Fontenelle (Dostoevsky had an excellent knowledge of French literature). All these satires are linked through their depiction of the kingdom beyond the grave, and all of them externally sustain the ancient (predominantly Lucianic) form of the genre.

Of fundamental significance for understanding Dostoevsky's generic traditions are the menippea of Diderot, free in their external form but typical in their generic essence. Of course the tone and style of telling in Diderot (sometimes in the spirit of eighteenth-century erotic literature) differs from Dostoevsky. In *Le neveu de Rameau* (also in essence a menippea, but without the fantastic element) the motif of extremely frank confessions without a single grain of remorse recalls "Bobok." And the very image of Rameau's nephew, an openly "rapacious type," who like Klinevich considers social morality "rotten cords" and who recognizes only the "shameless truth," recalls the image of Klinevich.

Dostoevsky was acquainted with another variety of the free menippea through Voltaire's *Contes philosophiques*.[N] This type of menippea was very close to certain sides of his own creative talent (Dostoevsky even had a plan to write the "Russian Candide").

We should keep in mind the enormous significance for Dostoevsky of the *dialogic culture* of Voltaire and Diderot, which had its roots in the Socratic dialogue, the ancient menippea, and somewhat in the diatribe and the soliloquy.

Another type of free menippea, with a fantastic and fairy-tale element, was represented in the work of Hoffmann, who already exercised a significant influence on the early Dostoevsky. Dostoevsky's attention was also

---

N. A "conte" is a short fictitious narrative, often didactic, relying on wit, allegory, or titillation to attract the reader and drive home the moral. it was a popular eighteenth-century form, Voltaire's *Candide* is perhaps the most famous example.

attracted by the tales of Edgar Allan Poe, close in essence to the menippea. In his prefatory note "Three Tales of Edgar Poe," Dostoevsky quite correctly noted the characteristics of that writer, so similar to his own:

"He almost always takes the most extraordinary reality, *places his hero in the most extraordinary external or psychological position*, and with what power of penetration, with what stunning accuracy does he tell the story of the state of that person's soul!"[15]

To be sure, this definition singles out only one aspect of the menippea—the creation of an extraordinary plot situation, that is, a provocative anacrisis—but precisely this aspect was consistently singled out by Dostoevsky himself as the major distinguishing feature of his own creative method.

Our survey (far from complete) of Dostoevsky's generic sources indicates that he knew, or could have known, diverse variants of the menippea, a genre of very rich and plastic possibilities, extraordinarily well-suited for penetrating into the "depths of the human soul" and for a keen and naked posing of "ultimate questions."

The story "Bobok" demonstrates to what an extent the generic essence of the menippea answered to all the fundamental creative aspirations of Dostoevsky. From the generic standpoint, this story is one of his key works.

Let us attend first to the following observation. Little "Bobok"—one of Dostoevsky's shortest plotted stories—is almost a microcosm of his entire creative output. Very many, and including the most important, ideas, themes and images of his work—both preceding and following "Bobok"—appear here in extremely keen and naked form: the idea that "everything is permitted" if there is no God and no immortality for the soul (one of the leading idea-images of his work); the related theme of confession without repentance and of "shameless truth," which runs through all of Dostoevsky's work beginning with *Notes from Underground*; the theme of the final moments of consciousness (connected in other works with the themes of capital punishment and suicide); the theme of a consciousness on the brink of insanity; the theme of sensuality, penetrating the highest spheres of consciousness and thought; the theme of the total "inappropriateness" and "unseemliness" of life cut off from its folk roots and from the people's faith, and so on—all these themes and ideas, in condensed and naked form, are fitted into the seemingly narrow confines of this story.

The leading images of the story (there are not, to be sure, many of them) also recall other images in Dostoevsky's work: Klinevich in a simplified and intensified form repeats Prince Valkovsky, Svidrigailov, and Fyodor Pavlovich; the narrator ("a certain person") is a variant of the Underground Man; General Pervoedov[16] is also somewhat familiar to us, as are the sensual old official who had squandered a huge sum of public funds earmarked "for widows and orphans," the sycophant Lebezyatnikov, and the engineer and believer in progress who wishes to "arrange life down here on a rational basis."

A special place among the dead is occupied by *"prostoliudin"* (a "simpleman," a well-to-do shopkeeper); he alone has preserved a bond with the common people and their faith, and thus behaves properly even in the grave, accepts death as a sacrament, interprets what is going on around him (among the debauched dead) as "a visitation of tribulations upon their souls," impatiently awaits the *sorokoviny*[O] ("May our forty days pass quickly, then I shall hear tearful voices over my head, my wife's lament and my children's soft weeping ..."). The seemliness and highly reverent style of speech of this "simpleman," juxtaposed to the impropriety and familiar cynicism of all the others (both living and dead), anticipate in part the future image of the pilgrim Makar Dolgoruky, although here, under conditions of the menippea, the "seemly" simpleman is presented with a slight overtone of comicality, as if he were somewhat inappropriate.

In addition, the carnivalized nether world of "Bobok" is *internally* profoundly resonant with those scenes of scandal and catastrophe that have such crucial significance in almost all of Dostoevsky's works. These scenes, usually taking place in drawing rooms, are of course considerably more complex, more motley, more full of carnivalized contrasts, abrupt mésalliances and eccentricities, fundamental crownings and decrownings, but their inner essence is analogous: the "rotten cords" of the official and personal lie are snapped (or at) least weakened for the moment), and human souls are laid bare, either terrible souls as in the nether world, or else bright and pure ones. People appear for a moment outside the usual conditions of their lives, on the carnival square or in the nether world, and there opens up another—more genuine—sense of themselves and of their relationships to one another.

Of such a sort, for example, is the famous scene at Nastasya Filippovna's name-day party (*The Idiot*). Here there are also external resonances with "Bobok": Ferdyshchenko (a petty mystery-play devil) proposes a *petit-jeu*—everyone is to tell the worst action of his life (cf. Klinevich's proposal: "We'll all tell our stories aloud, and we won't be ashamed of anything"). To be sure, the stories that are told do not justify Ferdyshchenko's expectations, but this *petit-jeu* helps prepare the way for that carnival-square atmosphere in which abrupt carnivalistic changes in the fates and appearances of people can occur, where cynical calculations are exposed,

---

O. *Sorokoviny*: a commemorative service in the Orthodox Church forty days after a death.

where Nastasya Filippovna's familiar and decrowning speech can take on the sound of the carnival square. We are not concerned here, of course, with the profound moral-psychological and social meaning of this scene—what interests us is precisely its generic aspect, those *carnivalistic overtones* that sound in almost every image and word (however realistic and motivated), and that second plane of the carnival square (and the carnivalized nether world) which, as it were, glimmers through the actual fabric of the scene.

One could also mention the sharply carnivalized scene of scandals and decrownings at the funeral feast for Marmeladov (in *Crime and Punishment*). Or the even more complicated scene in Varvara Petrovna Stavrogina's grand drawing room in *The Possessed*, with the part played by the mad lame girl, the entry of her brother Captain Lebyadkin, the first appearance of the "devil" Pyotr Verkhovensky, the triumphant eccentricity of Varvara Petrovna, the exposure and banishment of Stepan Trofimovich, Liza's hysterics and fainting fit, Shatov's slap in Stavrogin's face, and so on. Here everything is unexpected, out of place, incompatible and impermissible if judged by life's ordinary, "normal" course. It is absolutely impossible to imagine such a scene in, say, a novel by Leo Tolstoy or Turgenev. This is no grand drawing room, it is the public square with all the specific logic of carnivalized public-square life. And finally one must mention the extraordinarily vivid carnivalistic-menippean coloration of the scandal scene in Father Zosima's cell (*The Brothers Karamazov*).

These scandal scenes—and they occupy a very important place in Dostoevsky's works—almost always met with negative criticism from his contemporaries,[17] and continue to do so today. They seemed then, and still seem today, improbable in terms of life and unjustified in terms of art. They were often explained by the author's fondness for purely external and false effects. But in fact these scenes are in the spirit and the style of Dostoevsky's whole work. And they are deeply organic, there is nothing contrived in them—in their entirety as well as *in each detail* they are a result of that consistent artistic logic of carnivalistic acts and categories characterized above—and absorbed over the centuries into the carnivalized line of artistic prose. At their base lies a profound carnivalistic sense of the world, which gives meaning to and unites all the seemingly absurd and unexpected things in these scenes and creates their artistic truth.

"Bobok," thanks to its *fantastic* plot, can present this carnival logic in a somewhat simplified form (as required by the genre), and yet keenly and nakedly, and can therefore serve as a sort of commentary to more complicated but analogous phenomena in Dostoevsky's work.

In the story "Bobok," rays issuing from preceding and subsequent works of Dostoevsky come to a focus. "Bobok" could become such a focus precisely because it is a menippea. All aspects of Dostoevsky's creativity feel in their element here. The narrow framework of that story, as we see, has turned out to be quite spacious indeed.

We remember that the menippea is the *universal genre* of *ultimate questions*. Its action takes place not only in the "here" and the "now," but throughout the world and for all eternity: on earth, in the nether world, and in heaven. In Dostoevsky the menippea is brought close to the mystery play. The mystery play is, after all, nothing other than a modified medieval dramatic variant of the menippea. In Dostoevsky, the participants in the act stand *on the threshold* (on the threshold of life and death, falsehood and truth, sanity and insanity). And they are presented here as *voices*, ringing out, speaking out "before earth and heaven." The central figurative idea here is also that of the mystery play (to be sure, in the spirit of the Eleusinian mysteries): "contemporary dead men" are as sterile seed, cast on the ground, but capable neither of dying (that is, of being cleansed of themselves, of rising above themselves), nor of being renewed (that is, of bearing fruit).

The second key work from the generic standpoint is Dostoevsky's "Dream of a Ridiculous Man" (1877).

In its generic essence this work can also be traced to the menippea, but to different varieties of it: to the "dream satire" and to "fantastic journeys" containing a utopian element. In the subsequent development of the menippea, these two varieties are often combined.

The dream, as something with its own (nonepic) artistic interpretation, first entered European literature, as we have said, in the genre of Menippean satire (and in the realm of the serio-comical in general). Dreams in the epic did not destroy the unity of a represented life and did not create a second plane; they also did not destroy the *simple* integrity of the hero's image. The dream was not counterposed to ordinary life as *another* possible life. Such an opposition (from one or another viewpoint) appears for the first time in the menippea. The dream is introduced there precisely as the *possibility* of a completely different life, a life organized according to laws different from those governing ordinary life (sometimes directly as an "inside–out world"). The life seen in the dream makes ordinary life seem strange, forces one to understand and evaluate ordinary life in a new way (in the light of another glimpsed possibility). The person in a dream becomes another person, reveals in himself new possibilities (both worse and better), tests himself and verifies himself by means of the dream. Sometimes the dream is constructed directly as a crowning/decrowning of the person in life.

Thus an extraordinary situation is created in the dream quite impossible in ordinary life, a situation that serves here the same purpose it serves in the menippea—the testing of an idea and the man of an idea.

The traditional way of using menippean dreams in art continues to live on in the subsequent development of European literature, in diverse variations and with diverse nuances: in the "dream visions" of medieval literature, in the grotesque satires of the sixteenth and seventeenth centuries (especially vividly in Quevedo and Grimmelshausen), in its fairytale-symbolic use by the Romantics (including the highly original dream lyrics of Heinrich Heine), in its psychological and socio-historical application in realistic novels (in George Sand and Chernyshevsky). Special note should be made of the important variation known as *crisis dreams*, which lead a person to rebirth and renewal (the crisis variant was used in dramaturgy as well: in Shakespeare, Calderón, and in the nineteenth century in Grillparzer).

Dostoevsky made very wide use of the artistic possibilities of the dream in almost all its variations and nuances. Indeed, in all of European literature there is no writer for whom dreams play such a large and crucial role as Dostoevsky. We recall the dreams of Raskolnikov, of Svidrigailov, Myshkin, Ippolit, the Adolescent, Versilov, Alyosha and Dmitry Karamazov, and the role which they play in realizing the ideational design of their respective novels. Predominant in Dostoevsky is the crisis variation of the dream. To such a type belongs the dream of the "ridiculous man."

Concerning the generic variety of "fantastic journeys" used in "The Dream of a Ridiculous Man," Dostoevsky may have been acquainted with Cyrano de Bergerac's work *Histoire comique des états et empires de la Lune* [Comical History of the States and Empires of the Moon] (1647–50).* This is a description of an earthly paradise on the moon, from which the narrator has been banished for disrespectfulness. He is accompanied on his journey about the moon by the "demon of Socrates," thus permitting the author to introduce a philosophical element (in the spirit of Gassendi's* materialism). In its external form de Bergerac's work is an entire philosophical-fantastic novel.

Also interesting is Grimmelshausen's menippea *Der fliegende Wandersmann nach dem Monde* (c. 1659), which shares a common source with Cyrano de Bergerac's work. Here the utopian element is of foremost importance. There is a description of the extraordinary purity and truthfulness of the Moon's inhabitants; they know no vices, no crimes, no falsehood; in their country it is eternal spring, they live a long time and greet death with cheerful feasting amid a circle of friends. Children born with evil tendencies are sent off to Earth to prevent them from corrupting society. The precise date of the hero's arrival on the moon is indicated (just as the date of the dream is given in Dostoevsky).

Dostoevsky was undoubtedly familiar with Voltaire's menippea *Micromégas*, belonging to the same fantastic line in the development of the menippea, the line that estranges earthly reality.

In "The Dream of a Ridiculous Man" we are struck, first of all, by the maximal universalism of this work and at the same time by its maximal terseness, its remarkable artistic and philosophical laconicism. There is no developed discursive argumentation in it whatsoever. There is clear evidence here of Dostoevsky's extraordinary capacity to *see and feel an idea*, a trait we mentioned in the previous chapter. We have before us an authentic *artist of the idea*.

"The Dream of a Ridiculous Man" presents us with a full and complete synthesis of the universalism of the menippea—a genre of ultimate questions of worldview—with the universalism of the medieval mystery play portraying the fate of mankind: earthly paradise, the Fall, redemption. In "The Dream of a Ridiculous Man" this internal kinship between the two genres emerges very clearly; the genres are, of course, also akin to each other historically and genetically. But from the generic standpoint, the ancient type of menippea is dominant here. And in general what dominates in "The Dream of a Ridiculous Man" is not the Christian but the ancient spirit.

In its style and composition, "The Dream of a Ridiculous Man" differs rather significantly from "Bobok": it contains crucial elements of the diatribe, the confession, and the sermon. Such a complex of genres is in general characteristic of Dostoevsky's work.

The central part of the work is the story of a dream vision. Here we are given a splendid character-sketch, so to speak, of the peculiar compositional nature of the dream:

> ... everything was happening the way it usually happens in dreams when you leap over space and time, over all laws of life and reason, and only pause where your heart's desire bids you pause. [*SS* X, 429]

This is in fact a completely true characterization of the compositional method used for constructing a fantastic menippea. And, with certain limitations and reservations, these characteristics can be applied to Dostoevsky's entire creative method as well. In his works Dostoevsky makes almost no use of relatively uninterrupted historical or biographical time, that is, of strictly epic time; he "leaps over" it, he concentrates action at *points of crisis, at turning points and catastrophes*, when the inner significance of a moment is equal to a "billion years," that is, when the moment loses its temporal restrictiveness. In essence he leaps over space as well, and concentrates action in two "points" only: on the *threshold* (in doorways, entrance ways, on staircases, in corridors, and so forth), where the crisis and the turning point occur, or on the *public square*, whose substitute is usually the drawing room (the hall, the dining room), where the catastrophe, the scandal take place. Precisely this is his artistic conception of time and space. He often leaps over elementary empirical norms of verisimilitude and superficial rational logic as well. This is why he finds the genre of the menippea so congenial.

These words of the Ridiculous Man are also characteristic for the artistic method of Dostoevsky, as an artist of the idea:

> I have seen the truth, it was not a figment of my imagination or my mind, have seen it, seen it, and its living image has taken hold of my soul for ever. [*SS* X, 440]

In its subject matter "The Dream of a Ridiculous Man" is practically a complete encyclopedia of Dostoevsky's most important themes, and at the same time all these themes, as well as the means for elaborating them in art, are very characteristic of the carnivalized genre of the menippea. We shall pause on several of them.

1. In the central figure of the Ridiculous Man there are clear traces of the *ambivalent*—serio-comical—image of the "wise fool" and "tragic clown" of carnivalized literature. But such ambivalence—to be sure, usually in more muffled form—is characteristic for all of Dostoevsky's heroes. It might be said that Dostoevsky's mode of artistic thinking could not imagine anything in the slightest way humanly significant that did not have certain elements of *eccentricity* (in all its diverse variations). This is revealed most clearly in the image of Myshkin. But in all other major Dostoevskian heroes—in Raskolnikov, Stavrogin, Versilov, Ivan Karamazov—there is always "something ridiculous," although in a more or less reduced form.

We repeat: Dostoevsky, as an artist, could not imagine human significance as a *single-toned* thing. In the preface to *The Brothers Karamazov* ("From the Author") he even makes a case for the special and vital *historical* importance of eccentricity:

> For not only is an eccentric "not always" an isolated case and an exception, but, on the contrary, it happens sometimes that such a person, I dare say, carries within himself the very heart of the whole, and the rest of the men of his epoch have for some reason been temporarily torn from it, as if by a gust of wind ... [*SS* IX, 9]

In the image of the Ridiculous Man this ambivalence is, in keeping with the spirit of the menippea, laid bare and emphasized.

Also very characteristic for Dostoevsky is the *fullness of self-consciousness* in the Ridiculous Man: he himself knows better than anyone that he is ridiculous ("... of all the people in the world, I knew best how ridiculous I was ..."). When he begins to preach *paradise* on earth, he himself understands perfectly that it can never be realized: "I shall go further: let it never, never come true, let paradise never be (after all, I do realize that!), I shall anyway go and spread the word" [*SS* X, 441]. This is an eccentric who is keenly conscious of both himself and everything else; there is not a grain of naiveté in him; it is impossible to finalize him (since there is nothing located external to his consciousness).

2. The story opens with a theme most typical for the menippea, the theme of a person who is *alone* in his knowledge of the truth and who is therefore ridiculed by everyone else as a madman. Here is that splendid opening:

> I am a ridiculous man. They call me a madman now. That would be a promotion, if it were not that I remain as ridiculous to them as ever. But I no longer mind—they are all dear to me now, even when they are laughing at me—indeed, something endears them to me particularly then. I would laugh with them—not at myself, that is, but because I love them—I would laugh if I did not feel so sad watching them. What saddens me is that they do not know the Truth, and I do. Oh, how hard it is to be the only one to know the Truth! But they will not understand this. No, they will not. [*SS* X, 420]

This is the typical position of the wise man in the menippea (Diogenes, Menippus, or Democritus from the "Hippocratic novel"): the carrier of truth vis-à-vis all other people who consider the truth either insanity or stupidity; but here this position is, when compared with the ancient menippea, both more complicated and more profound. At the same time this position is, in different variations and with various nuances, characteristic for all of Dostoevsky's major heroes from Raskolnikov to Ivan Karamazov: being possessed by their "truth" defines their relationship to other people and creates the special sort of loneliness these heroes know.

3. Further along in the story there appears a theme very characteristic for the menippea of the Cynics and the Stoics, the theme of absolute indifference to everything in the world:

> ... that hopeless sadness that was mounting in my soul about something that was infinitely greater than myself: this something was a mounting conviction that **nothing mattered**. I had begun

to suspect this long ago, but positive conviction came to me all at once, one day last year. I suddenly knew that **I would not have cared** if the world existed at all or if there was nothing anywhere. I began to know and feel with all my being that **nothing in my lifetime had existed**. [*SS* X, 421]

This universal indifference and the premonition of nonexistence leads the Ridiculous Man to thoughts of suicide. Before us is one of Dostoevsky's numerous variations on the theme of Kirillov.

4. There follows the theme of the final hours of life before suicide (one of Dostoevsky's major themes). Here this theme—in keeping with the spirit of the menippea—is laid bare and intensified.

After the Ridiculous Man makes the final decision to kill himself, he meets a little girl on the street who begs him to help her. The Ridiculous Man shoves her away rudely, since he already feels himself to be outside all norms and obligations of human life (like the dead in "Bobok"). Here are his reflections:

But if I was going to kill myself in a couple of hours from then, why should I be concerned with the girl and what did I care for shame or anything else in the world? ... Why, the reason I had stamped my feet and shouted so brutally at the poor child was to assert that "far from feeling pity, I could even afford to do something inhumanly vile now, because two hours hence everything would be snuffed out."

This is moral experimentation, characteristic for the genre of the menippea and no less characteristic of Dostoevsky's work. Further along the reflections continue:

For instance, a strange notion like this occurred to me: supposing I had once lived on the moon or Mars and had committed there the foulest and most shameful deed imaginable, and had been put to such shame and disgrace as can be experienced and imagined only sometimes in dreams, in nightmares, and supposing I later found myself on the earth, with the crime committed on that other planet alive in my consciousness and, moreover, knowing there was no return for me, ever, under any circumstances— would **I have cared** or not as I gazed at the moon from this earth? Would I have felt shame for that deed or not? [*SS* X, 425–26]

In a conversation with Kirillov, Stavrogin puts to himself an absolutely analogous "experimental" question about an act on the moon [*SS* VII, 250; *The Possessed*, Part Two, ch. 1, 5]. All this is the familiar problematic posed by Ippolit (*The Idiot*), Kirillov (*The Possessed*), by the graveside shamelessness in "Bobok." In fact they are all merely various facets of a leading theme of all Dostoevsky's work, the theme that "all is permitted" (in a world where there is no God and no immortality of the soul) and, linked with it, the theme of ethical solipsism.

5. Further on there unfolds the central (and one might say genre-shaping) *theme of the crisis dream*; more precisely, it is the theme of a man's rebirth and renewal through a dream vision, permitting him *to see* "with his own eyes" the possibility of an entirely different human life on earth.

> Yes, I dreamed that dream then, my 3rd of November dream! They all tease me now, telling me it was nothing but a dream. But surely it makes no difference whether it was a dream or not since it did reveal the Truth to me. Because if you have come to know it once and to see it, you will know it is the Truth and that there neither is nor can be any other, whether you are dreaming or awake. Very well, it was a dream—let it be a dream, but the fact remains that this real life which you so extol I was going to snuff out by suicide, whereas my dream, my dream—oh, it revealed to me another life, a great, renewed and powerful life! [*SS* X, 427]

6. In the "dream" itself there is detailed development of the utopian theme of heaven on earth, experienced by the Ridiculous Man and seen with his own eyes on a distant unknown star. The very description of this earthly paradise is sustained in the spirit of the ancient Golden Age, and is thus thoroughly permeated with a carnival sense of the world. The portrayal of this earthly paradise recalls in many ways Versilov's dream (*The Adolescent*). Very characteristic here is the purely carnivalistic faith professed by the Ridiculous Man in the unity of mankind's aspirations and in the goodness of human nature:

> And yet everyone is going towards the same thing, at least all strive for the same thing, all—*from the wise man to the meanest wretch*—only all follow different paths. It's an old truth, but here's something new: I cannot flounder too badly, you know. Because *I have seen the Truth, I have seen it* and I know that people can be beautiful and happy without losing their ability to dwell on this earth. I cannot and will not believe that evil is man's natural state. [*SS* X, 440]

We emphasize again that truth, according to Dostoevsky, can only be the subject of a living vision, not of abstract understanding,

7. At the end of the story there sounds a theme very characteristic for Dostoevsky, the theme of the *instantaneous* transformation of life into paradise (it finds its most profound expression in *The Brothers Karamazov*):

> And yet it could be done so simply: in a single day, in a **single hour** everything would be settled! One should love others as one loves oneself, that is the main thing, that is all, nothing else, absolutely nothing else is needed, and then one would instantly know how to go about it. [*SS* X, 441]

8. We note also the theme of the mistreated little girl, which runs through a series of Dostoevsky's works: we meet her in *The Insulted and the Injured* (Nelly), in Svidrigailov's dream before his suicide, in "Stavrogin's Confession," in "The Eternal Husband" (Liza); the theme of the suffering child is one of the leading themes in *The Brothers Karamazov* (the images of suffering children in the chapter "Rebellion," the image of Ilyushechka, "the babe weeping" in Dmitri's dream).

9. Also present here are elements of slum naturalism: the debauched captain begging for alms on Nevsky Prospect (the image is familiar to us from *The Idiot* and *The Adolescent*), drunkenness, a card game and fighting in the room next door to the little closet where the Ridiculous Man has spent his sleepless nights in the Voltairian armchair, absorbed in solving ultimate questions, and where he dreams his dream about the fate of mankind.

Of course we have not exhausted all the themes in "The Dream of a Ridiculous Man," but even these are sufficient to demonstrate the enormous ideational spaciousness of this particular variety of the menippea and its suitability to Dostoevsky's subject matter.

In "The Dream of a Ridiculous Man" there are no compositionally expressed dialogues (except one half-expressed dialogue with the "unknown being"), but the narrator's entire speech is permeated with interior dialogue: all words are addressed to himself, to the universe, to his creator,[18] to all people. And here, as in a mystery play, the word rings out before heaven and before earth, that is, before the entire world.

Such are the two key works of Dostoevsky that reveal most clearly the generic essence of his creative work, one with great affinity for the menippea and genres kindred to it.

We have offered our analyses of "Bobok" and "The Dream of a Ridiculous Man" from the vantage point of an historical poetics of genre. Of primary interest to us has been the way in which these works manifest the generic essence of the menippea. But at the same time we have tried to show how the traditional features of the genre are organically combined, in Dostoevsky's use of them, with an individual uniqueness and profundity.

We shall touch on several other works of his which are also in their essence close to the menippea, but of a somewhat different type and without the direct fantastic element.

One of the best examples is the story "A Meek One." Here the sharp plot-line anacrisis characteristic for the genre, with its abrupt contrasts, its mésalliances and moral experimentation, is formulated as a soliloquy. The hero of the tale says of himself: "I am a past master at speaking silently, I have spent a lifetime speaking in silence and I have lived through whole dramas by myself and in silence." The image of the hero is revealed precisely through this dialogic relationship to his own self. And he remains almost until the very end by himself, in utter loneliness and hopeless despair. He does not acknowledge any higher judgment on himself. He generalizes from his own loneliness, universalizes it as the ultimate loneliness of the entire human race:

> Stagnation! Nature! Men are alone on earth—that's the horror!
> ... Everything is dead, and the dead are everywhere. Men are alone, and around them is silence—that is the earth!

Another work close in its essence to the menippea is *Notes from Underground* (1864). It is constructed as a diatribe (a conversation with an absent interlocutor), saturated with overt and hidden polemic, and contains important elements of the confession. A story with an acute anacrisis is introduced into the second part. In *Notes from Underground* we also find other familiar signs of the menippea: abrupt dialogic syncrises, familiarization and profanation, slum naturalism, and so on. This work too is characterized by an extraordinary ideational spaciousness, almost all the themes and ideas of Dostoevsky's subsequent work are outlined here in simplified and stripped-down form. The verbal style of this work will be dealt with in the following chapter.

We shall touch upon one more work of Dostoevsky with a very characteristic title: "A Nasty Story" (1862).[P] This *deeply carnivalized* story is also close to the menippea (but of the Varronian type). Serving as plot-center for the ideas is an argument among three generals at a name-day party. Afterwards the hero of the story (one of the three), in order to test his liberal-

---

P. "*Skvernyi anekdot*," The story is variously translated into English as "An Unpleasant Predicament," "A Most Unfortunate Incident," "A Nasty Predicament."

humanistic idea, drops in on the wedding feast of one of his lowliest subordinates—where, due to inexperience (he is a nondrinker), he gets thoroughly drunk. Everything is built on the extreme *inappropriateness* and *scandalous nature* of all that occurs. Everything is full of sharp carnivalistic contrasts, mésalliances, ambivalence, debasing, and decrownings. There is also an element here of rather cruel moral experimentation. We are not, of course, concerned here with the profound social and philosophical idea present in this work, which even today is not adequately appreciated. The tone of the story is deliberately unsteady, ambiguous and mocking, permeated with elements of hidden socio-political and literary polemic.

Elements of the menippea can be found in all early (that is, pre-exile) works of Dostoevsky (influenced for the most part by the generic traditions of Gogol and Hoffmann).

The menippea, as we have said, also infiltrates Dostoevsky's novels. We shall cite only the most essential instances (without any particular supporting argumentation).

In *Crime and Punishment*, the famous scene of Raskolnikov's first visit to Sonya (with the reading of the Gospel) is an almost perfect Christianized menippea: sharp dialogic syncrises (faith vs. lack of faith, meekness vs. pride), sharp anacrisis, oxymoronic combinations (the thinker-criminal, the prostitute-righteous woman), a naked statement of ultimate questions and a reading of the Gospels in a slum setting. Raskolnikov's dreams are also menippea, as is Svidrigailov's dream before his suicide.

In *The Idiot*, Ippolit's confession ("An Essential Explanation") is a menippea, framed by a carnivalized scene of dialogue on Prince Myshkin's terrace and ending with Ippolit's attempted suicide. In *The Possessed* it is Stavrogin's confession, together with the dialogue between Stavrogin and Tikhon which frames it. In *The Adolescent* it is Versilov's dream.

In *The Brothers Karamazov* there is a remarkable menippea in the conversation between Ivan and Alyosha in "Metropolis" tavern on the market square of a godforsaken provincial town. Here, to the sounds of the tavern organ, the clacking of billiard balls and uncorking of beer bottles, monk and atheist solve ultimate universal questions. Into this Menippean satire a second satire is inserted—"The Legend of the Grand Inquisitor," which has its own independent significance and is constructed on the syncrisis in the Gospels between Christ and the Devil.[19] Both these interconnected Menippean satires are among the most profound artistic and philosophical works of all world literature. And finally, there is an equally profound menippea in the conversation between Ivan Karamazov and the devil (the chapter: "The Devil. Ivan Fyodorovich's Nightmare").

Of course, all these menippea are subordinated to the polyphonic design of the novelistic whole encompassing them, are determined by it and are inseparable from it.

But in addition to these relatively independent and relatively finalized menippea, all of Dostoevsky's novels are permeated with menippean elements, and with elements of other kindred genres as well—the Socratic dialogue, the diatribe, the soliloquy, the confession. Of course these genres all reached Dostoevsky after thousands of years of intense development, but throughout all changes they retained their generic essence. Sharp dialogic syncrises, extraordinary and provocative plot situations, crises and turning points and moral experimentation, catastrophes and scandals, contrasts and oxymoronic combinations are what determine the entire plot and compositional structure of Dostoevsky's novels.

Without further thorough research into the essence of the menippea and other kindred genres, without research into the history of these genres and their diverse varieties in the literatures of modern times, it is impossible to arrive at a correct historico-genetic explanation of the generic characteristics of Dostoevsky's works (and not only Dostoevsky's works; the problem is of much broader significance).

Analyzing the generic characteristics of the menippea in Dostoevsky, we simultaneously uncovered in it elements of carnivalization. And this is fully understandable, since the menippea is a profoundly carnivalized genre. But the phenomenon of carnivalization in Dostoevsky's work is of course much broader than the menippea; it has additional generic sources and therefore requires special attention.

To say that carnival and its later derivatives (the masquerade line of development, the farcical street comedy, and so on) exercised a direct and vital influence on Dostoevsky is difficult (although real experiences of a carnival type did certainly exist in his life).[20] Carnivalization acted on him, as on the majority of other eighteenth- and nineteenth-century writers, primarily as a literary and generic tradition whose extraliterary source, that is, carnival proper, was perhaps not even perceived by him in any clearly precise way.

But over the long course of centuries carnival, its forms and symbols, and above all a carnival sense of the world, seeped into many literary genres, merged with their features, shaped them, became somehow inseparable from them. Carnival was, as it were, *reincarnated in literature*, and precisely into one specific and vigorous line of its development. Carnival forms, transposed into the language of literature, became a *powerful means* for comprehending life in art, they became a special language whose words and forms possess an extraordinary capacity for *symbolic* generalization, that is, for *generalization in depth*. Many essential sides of life, or more precisely its *layers* (and often the most profound), can be located, comprehended, and expressed only with the help of this language.

In order to master this language, that is, in order to attach himself to the carnivalistic generic tradition in literature, a writer need not know all the links and all the branchings of that tradition. A genre possesses its own organic logic which can to a certain extent be understood and creatively assimilated on the basis of a few generic models, even fragments. *But the logic of genre is not an abstract logic.* Each new variety, each new work of a given genre always enriches it in some way, aids in perfecting the language of the genre. For this reason it is important to know the possible generic sources of a given author, the literary and generic atmosphere in which his creative work was realized. The more complete and concrete our knowledge of an artist's *generic contacts*, the deeper can we penetrate the peculiar features of his generic form and the more correctly can we understand the interrelationship, within it, of tradition and innovation.

All this obliges us—insofar as we are touching here upon questions of *historical* poetics—to characterize at least those basic links in the carnivalistic generic tradition with which Dostoevsky was directly or indirectly connected and which defined the generic atmosphere of his work, in many ways so fundamentally different from the generic atmosphere of Turgenev, Goncharov, or Leo Tolstoy.

One basic source of carnivalization for literature of the seventeenth, eighteenth and nineteenth centuries was the writers of the Renaissance— above all Boccaccio, Rabelais, Shakespeare, Cervantes, and Grimmelshausen.[21] Another such source was the early picaresque novel (directly carnivalized). An additional source of carnivalization for the writers of these centuries was, of course, the carnivalized literature of antiquity (including Menippean satire) and of the Middle Ages.

All the above-named basic sources for the carnivalization of European literature were very well known to Dostoevsky, except, perhaps, Grimmelshausen and the early picaresque novel. But the characteristic features of this type of novel were familiar to him from Lesage's *Gil Blas*, and he took an intense interest in them. The picaresque novel portrayed life drawn out of its ordinary and (as it were) legitimized rut, it decrowned all hierarchical positions people might hold, and played with these positions; it was filled with sudden shifts, changes and mystifications, it perceived the entire represented world in a zone of familiar contact. As concerns Renaissance literature, its direct influence on Dostoevsky was considerable (especially Shakespeare and Cervantes). We are speaking here not of the influence of individual themes, ideas, or images, but rather of the deeper influence of *a carnival sense of the world itself*, that is, the influence of the very forms for visualizing the world and man, and that truly *godlike freedom* in approaching them which is manifest not in the individual thoughts, images, and external devices of construction, but in these writers' work as a *whole*.

The literature of the eighteenth century was of essential importance for Dostoevsky's assimilation of the carnival tradition, and above all Voltaire and Diderot. Characteristic for both was a combination of carnivalization with high dialogic culture, culture raised on antiquity and on the dialogues of the Renaissance. Here Dostoevsky found an organic combination of carnivalization with the rationalistic philosophical idea, and, in part, with the social theme.

The combination of carnivalization with the adventure plot and with pressing social themes of the day was found by Dostoevsky in the social-adventure novels of the nineteenth century, primarily in Frédéric Soulié and Eugène Sue (also somewhat in Dumas fils and in Paul de Kock). Carnivalization in these authors is of a more external sort: it is manifested in the plot, in external carnivalistic antitheses and contrasts, in abrupt changes of fate, in mystifications, and so on. A deep and free carnival sense of the world is almost entirely absent. The most essential feature in these novels is an application of carnivalization to the portrayal of contemporary reality and contemporary everyday life; *everyday life* is drawn into the carnivalized action of the plot; the ordinary and constant is combined with the extraordinary and changeable.

A more profound assimilation of the carnival tradition Dostoevsky found in Balzac, George Sand, and Victor Hugo. Here there are considerably fewer external manifestations of carnivalization, but there is a deeper carnival sense of the world, and, most importantly, carnivalization permeates the very construction of the major strong characters and the development of the passions. The carnivalization of passion is evidenced first and foremost in its ambivalence: love is combined with hatred, avarice with selflessness, ambition with self-abasement, and so forth.

A combination of carnivalization with a sentimental perception of life was found by Dostoevsky in Sterne and Dickens.

Finally, the combination of carnivalization with an idea of the romantic type (rather than a rationalistic idea, as in Voltaire and Diderot) Dostoevsky found in Edgar Allan Poe and even more in Hoffmann.

A special place is held by Russian tradition. In addition to Gogol, mention must be made here of the huge influence exercised on Dostoevsky by the most carnivalized works of Pushkin: *Boris Godunov*, *The Tales of Belkin*, the *Little Tragedies* and *The Queen of Spades*.

Our brief survey of the sources of carnivalization does not pretend in any way to be complete. For our purposes it was important to trace only the basic lines of the tradition. We emphasize again that we are not interested in the influence of separate individual authors, individual works, individual themes, ideas, images—what interests us is precisely the influence of the *generic tradition itself* which was transmitted through the particular authors. Throughout this process the tradition is reborn and renewed in each of them in its own way, that is, in a unique and unrepeatable way. This constitutes the life of the tradition. What interests us—we use a comparison here—is the discourse of a *language*, and not its *individual use* in a particular *unrepeatable context*, although, of course, the one cannot exist without the other, it is certainly possible to study individual influences as well, that is, the influence of one individual writer on another (for example, Balzac on Dostoevsky), but this is already a special task and one which we do not set for ourselves here. We are interested only in the tradition itself.

In Dostoevsky's work too, of course, the carnivalistic tradition is reborn in a new way: it takes on its own meaning, combines with other artistic elements, furthers its own particular artistic goals, precisely those goals that we have tried to point out in the preceding chapters. Carnivalization is combined organically with all the other characteristics of the polyphonic novel.

Before moving on to an analysis of the elements of carnivalization in Dostoevsky (we shall concentrate on a few works only), we must first touch upon two additional questions.

To understand correctly the problem of carnivalization, one must dispense with the oversimplified understanding of carnival found in the *masquerade* line of modern times, and even more with a vulgar bohemian understanding of carnival. Carnival is past millennia's way of sensing the world as one great communal performance. This sense of the world, liberating one from fear, bringing the world maximally close to a person and bringing one person maximally close to another (everything is drawn into the zone of free familiar contact), with its joy at change and its joyful relativity, is opposed to that one-sided and gloomy official seriousness which is dogmatic and hostile to evolution and change, which seeks to absolutize a given condition of existence or a given social order. From precisely that sort of seriousness did the carnival sense of the world liberate man. But there is not a grain of nihilism in it, nor a grain of empty frivolity or vulgar bohemian individualism.

One must also dispense with that narrow theatrical-pageantry concept of carnival, so very characteristic of modern times.

For a proper understanding of carnival, one must take it at its *origins* and at its *peaks*, that is, in antiquity, in the Middle Ages and finally in the Renaissance.[22]

The second question concerns literary movements. Carnivalization, once it has penetrated and to a certain extent determined the structure of a genre, can be used by various movements and creative methods. It is quite wrong to see it as no more than a specific characteristic of Romanticism. In fact, every movement, and creative method interprets and renews it in its own way. To be persuaded of this, it is enough to contrast carnivalization in Voltaire (Enlightenment realism), the early Tieck (Romanticism), Balzac (critical realism), and Ponson du Terrail (pure adventure). The degree of carnivalization in each of the above authors is almost identical, but each is subordinated to its own special artistic tasks (connected with its literary movement) and therefore each "sounds" differently (we are not speaking here of the individual characteristics of these writers). At the same time the presence of carnivalization defines them as belonging to one and the same *generic* tradition and creates, from the point of view of a poetics, a very *fundamental common ground* between them (we repeat, even given all the differences in literary movement, individual personality and artistic merit).

In "Petersburg Visions in Verse and Prose" (1861) Dostoevsky recalls the unique and vivid carnival sense of life experienced by him at the very beginning of his career as a writer. This was above all a special sense of Petersburg, with all its sharp social contrasts, as "a fantastic magical daydream," as "dream," as something standing on the boundary between reality and fantastic invention. An analogous carnival sense of a great city (Paris) can be found in Balzac, Sue, Soulié, and others, but not as strong or as deep as it is in Dostoevsky; the sources of this tradition go back to the ancient menippea (Varro, Lucian). Building on this sense of the city and the city crowd, Dostoevsky proceeds to give a sharply carnivalized picture of the emergence of his own first literary projects, including a plan for *Poor Folk*:

> And I began to look around and suddenly I saw some strange faces. They were all strange, queer, totally prosaic figures, in no way a Don Carlos or a Posa, nothing more than titular counselors, but at the same time they somehow seemed to be fantastic titular counselors. Someone *grimaced* in front of me, hiding behind that *fantastic crowd*, and *jerked at some strings and springs*, and these *puppets* moved, and he guffawed, how he guffawed! And then another story occurred to me, in some dark corners, some titular heart, honest and pure, moral and loyal to the authorities, and alongside it some little girl, mistreated and melancholy, and this whole story rent my heart deeply. And if one could gather together that whole crowd which I dreamed of then, it would make a wonderful *masquerade* ...[23]

In this way, according to Dostoevsky's own reminiscences, his creative art was born—born, as it were, out of a vivid carnival vision of life ("I call the feeling I had on the Neva a vision," Dostoevsky tells us). Here we have the characteristic accessories of a carnival complex: guffaw and tragedy, a clown, comical street farces, a crowd of masqueraders. But the most important thing here, of course, is that very carnival sense of the world, which thoroughly permeates "Petersburg Dreams." In its generic essence this work is a variety of carnivalized menippea. One should emphasize the central *guffaw* accompanying the vision. We shall see further that Dostoevsky's entire work is in fact permeated with it, though in a reduced form.

The carnivalization of Dostoevsky's early work will not be dealt with in detail. We shall examine only certain elements of carnivalization in some of the individual works published after his exile. Here we set ourselves a limited task—to prove the presence of carnivalization and to uncover its basic functions in Dostoevsky. A deeper and fuller study of the problem, based on all of Dostoevsky's work, is beyond the limits of the present book.

The first work of the second period—"Uncle's Dream"—is remarkable for its vividly expressed, but somewhat simplified and *external*, carnivalization. At its center lies a scandal-catastrophe with a double decrowning—of Moskaleva and the prince. Even the very tone of the story told by Mordasov's chronicler is ambivalent: there is an ironic glorification of Moskaleva, that is, a carnivalistic fusion of praise and abuse.[24]

The scene of the scandal and decrowning of the prince—the carnival king, or more accurately the carnival bridegroom—is consistently portrayed as a *tearing to pieces*, as a typical carnivalistic "sacrificial" dismemberment into parts:

> "... If I'm a tub, then you are a *one-legged cripple!*"
>
> "Me—one-legged—"
>
> "Yes, yes, one-legged and *toothless* into the bargain, that's what you are!"
>
> "And one-eyed, too!" shouted Marya Alexandrovna.
>
> "You have a corset instead of ribs," added Natalya Dmitriyevna.
>
> "Your *face* is on springs!"
>
> "You have no *hair* of your own!"
>
> "And the old fool's *moustache* is artificial, too," screeched Marya Alexandrovna.
>
> "At least leave me my *nose*, Marya Alexandrovna!" cried the Prince, flabbergasted by such unexpected *revelations*....
>
> "Good God," said the unfortunate Prince, "... take me away, my good fellow, take me away, or they'll *tear me to pieces* ..." [*SS* II, 398–99]

We have here a typical "carnival anatomy"—an enumeration of the parts of the dismembered body. Such "enumerations" were a widespread comic device in the carnivalized literature of the Renaissance (it is met very often in Rabelais, and in a somewhat less developed form in Cervantes).

The role of a decrowned carnival king was also played by the heroine of the tale, Mary Alexandrovna Moskaleva:

> The guests dispersed with squeals and abuse, and Marya Alexandrovna was at last alone amidst the ruins and fragments of her former glory. Alas! Power, glory, distinction—all had vanished in a single evening. [*SS* 11, 399]

But after the scene of the *comic* decrowning of the *old* bridegroom, the prince, there follows a *paired* scene of the tragic self-decrowning and death of the young bridegroom, the schoolteacher Vasya. Such a *pairing* of scenes (and individual images) that reflect one another or shine through one another—one given in the comic plane and the other in the tragic (as in this instance) or one on a lofty and the other on a low plane, or one affirming, the other repudiating, and so forth—is characteristic of Dostoevsky; taken together, these paired scenes create an ambivalent whole. It is evidence of an even deeper influence of the carnival sense of the world. To be sure, in "Uncle's Dream" this characteristic is still expressed somewhat externally.

Carnivalization is much deeper and more substantial in the tale *The Village of Stepanchikovo and its Inhabitants*,Q although here, too, there is still much that is external. All life in Stepanchikovo is concentrated around Foma Fomich Opiskin, former *hanger-on* and *buffoon*, who has become the *unlimited despot* on Colonel Rostanev's estate; that is, all life is concentrated around a *carnival king*. Thus all life in the village of Stepanchikovo assumes a carnivalistic character, vividly expressed. This is life that has left its normal rut, almost a "world turned inside out."

And it cannot be otherwise, insofar as the tone is set by a carnival king—Foma Fomich. All the other characters, participants in this life, take on carnival coloration as well: the *mad* rich lady Tatyana Ivanovna, suffering from an erotic mania for falling in love (in the banal-romantic style) and who is at the same time the purest and kindest of souls; the *mad wife of the general* with her adoration and cult of Foma; the little *fool* Falalei with his persistent dream about the white bull and his KamarinskayaR; the *mad lackey* Vidoplyasov, who is constantly changing his name to one more noble—such

---

Q. One of Dostoevsky's early post-exile works (1859); translated by Constance Garnett as "The Friend of the Family."

R. "Kamarinskaya," native Russian dance, made famous by Glinka's orchestral fantasy of the same name (1848).

as "Tantsev," "Esbuketov" (this he must do because the house servants find an indecent rhyme for each new name); the *old man* Gavrila, who is forced in his old age to study French; the malicious *buffoon* Ezhevikin; the "*progressive*" *fool* Obnoskin who dreams of a wealthy bride; the *bankrupt hussar* Mizinchikov; the *eccentric* Bakhcheev, and others too. These are all people who for one reason or another have left the normal rut of life, who are denied the position in life normal and appropriate for them. The entire action of the tale is an uninterrupted series of scandals, eccentric escapades, mystifications, decrownings and crownings. The work is saturated with parodies and semiparodies, including a parody on Gogol's *Selected Passages from a Correspondence with Friends*; these parodies are organically linked with the carnival atmosphere of the tale as a whole.

Carnivalization allows Dostoevsky to glimpse and bring to life aspects in the character and behavior of people which in the normal course of life could not have revealed themselves. Especially deeply carnivalized is the character of Foma Fomich: he does not coincide with himself, he is not equal to himself, he cannot be given a monosemantic finalizing definition, and he anticipates in many ways the future heroes of Dostoevsky. He is, incidentally, presented in a carnivalistic contrasting pair with Colonel Rostanev.

We have concentrated on carnivalization in two works of Dostoevsky's second period because there it is more or less external and consequently very visible, obvious to all. In subsequent works carnivalization recedes into the deeper levels and its nature changes. In particular, the comic aspect, here rather loud, is later muffled and reduced almost to the minimum. We must treat this point in somewhat more detail.

We have already made reference to the phenomenon of reduced laughter, so important in world literature. Laughter is a specific aesthetic relationship to reality, but not one that can be translated into logical language; that is, it is a specific means for artistically visualizing and comprehending reality and, consequently, a specific means for structuring an artistic image, plot, or genre. Enormous creative, and therefore genre-shaping, power was possessed by ambivalent carnivalistic laughter. This laughter could grasp and comprehend a phenomenon in the process of change and transition, it could fix in a phenomenon both poles of its evolution in their uninterrupted and creative renewing changeability: in death birth is foreseen and in birth death, in victory defeat and in defeat victory, in crowning a decrowning. Carnival laughter does not permit a single one of these aspects of change to be absolutized or to congeal in one-sided seriousness,

When we say that birth is "foreseen" in death, we inevitably make logical, and thus somewhat distort, carnival ambivalence: for in so doing we sever death from birth and distance them somewhat from each other. In living carnival images, death itself is pregnant and gives birth, and the mother's womb giving birth becomes a grave. Precisely such images are produced by creative ambivalent carnival laughter, in which mockery and triumph, praise and abuse are inseparably fused.

When the images of carnival and carnivalistic laughter are transposed into literature, they are transformed to a greater or lesser degree in keeping with specific artistic and literary tasks. But regardless of the degree or nature of the transformation, ambivalence and laughter remain in the carnivalized image. Under certain conditions and in certain genres, however, laughter can be reduced. It continues to determine the structure of the image, but it itself is muffled down to the minimum: we see, as it were, the track left by laughter in the structure of represented reality, but the laughter itself we do not hear. Thus in Plato's Socratic dialogues (of the first period) laughter is reduced (although not entirely), but it remains in the structure of the image of the major hero (Socrates), in the methods for carrying on the dialogue, and— most importantly—in authentic (not rhetorical) dialogicality itself, immersing thought itself in the joyful relativity of evolving existence and not permitting it to congeal in abstractly dogmatic (monologic) ossification. But here and there in the dialogues of the early period laughter goes beyond the structure of the image and, so to speak, bursts out in a loud register. In the dialogues of the later period, laughter is reduced to a minimum.

In the literature of the Renaissance, laughter is generally not reduced, but certain gradations of "volume" do, of course, exist even here. In Rabelais, for example, it rings out loudly, as is fitting on a public square. In Cervantes there is no longer that public-square intensity of sound, although in the first book of *Don Quixote* laughter is still quite loud, and in the second it is significantly (when compared with the first) reduced. This reduction is also linked with certain changes in the structure of the major hero's image, and with changes in the plot.

In carnivalized literature of the eighteenth and nineteenth centuries, laughter is as a rule considerably muffled—to the level of irony, humor, and other forms of reduced laughter.

Let us return to reduced laughter in Dostoevsky. In the first two works of the second period, as we have said, laughter can still be distinctly heard, for elements of carnival ambivalence are of course still preserved in it.[25] But in Dostoevsky's subsequent great novels, laughter is reduced almost to the minimum (especially in *Crime and Punishment*). In all his novels, however, we find a trace of that ambivalent laughter, absorbed by Dostoevsky together with the generic tradition of carnivalization, performing its work of artistically organizing and illuminating the world. We find such traces in the structure of images, in numerous plot situations, and in certain characteristics of verbal style. But the most important—one could say, the decisive—expression of reduced laughter is to be found in the ultimate position of the author. This position excludes all one-sided or dogmatic seriousness and does not permit any single point of view, any single polar extreme of life or of thought, to be absolutized. All one-sided seriousness (of life and thought), all one-sided pathos is handed over to the heroes, but the author, who causes them all to collide in the "great dialogue" of the novel, leaves that dialogue open and puts no finalizing period at the end.

It should be pointed out that the carnival sense of the world also knows no period, and is, in fact, hostile to any sort of *conclusive conclusion*: all endings are merely new beginnings; carnival images are reborn again and again.

Certain scholars (Vyacheslav Ivanov,[S] Komarovich) apply to Dostoevsky's works the ancient (Aristotelian) term "catharsis" (purification). if this term is understood in a very broad sense, then one can agree with it (without catharsis in the broad sense there is no art at all). But tragic catharsis (in the Aristotelian sense) is not applicable to Dostoevsky. The catharsis that finalizes Dostoevsky's novels might be—of course inadequately and somewhat rationalistically—expressed in this way: *nothing conclusive has yet taken place in the world, the ultimate word of the world and about the world has not yet been spoken, the world is open and free, everything is still in the future and will always be in the future.*

But this is, after all, also the *purifying sense* of ambivalent laughter.

It would not, perhaps, be superfluous to emphasize again that we speak here of Dostoevsky the artist. Dostoevsky the journalist was by no means a stranger to cramped and one-sided seriousness, to dogmatism, even to eschatology. But these ideas of the journalist, once introduced into the novel, become there merely one of the embodied voices of an unfinalized and open dialogue.

In Dostoevsky's novels, everything is directed toward that unspoken and as yet unpredetermined *"new word,"* everything waits tensely on that word, and the *author* does not block its path with his own one-sided and monosemantic seriousness.

Reduced laughter in carnivalized literature by no means excludes the possibility of somber colors within a work. For this reason the somber coloration of Dostoevsky's works should not confuse us: it is not their final word.

S. in English, see Vyacheslav Ivanov, *Freedom and the Tragic Life: A Study in Dostoevsky*, pp. 12–14.

Sometimes in Dostoevsky's novels reduced laughter rises to the surface, especially in those places where a narrator or a chronicler is introduced whose story is almost always constructed in parodic-ironic ambivalent tones (for example, the ambivalent glorification of Stepan Trofimovich in *The Possessed*, very close in tone to the glorification of Moskaleva in "Uncle's Dream"). This laughter comes to the fore in open or half-concealed parodies that are scattered throughout all of Dostoevsky's novels.[26]

We shall pause on several other characteristics of carnivalization in Dostoevsky's novels.

Carnivalization is not an external and immobile schema which is imposed upon ready-made content; it is, rather, an extraordinarily flexible form of artistic visualization, a peculiar sort of heuristic principle making possible the discovery of new and as yet unseen things. By *relativizing* all that was externally stable, set and ready-made, carnivalization with its pathos of change and renewal permitted Dostoevsky to penetrate into the deepest layers of man and human relationships. It proved remarkably productive as a means for capturing in art the developing relationships under capitalism, at a time when previous forms of life, moral principles and beliefs were being turned into "rotten cords" and the previously concealed, ambivalent, and unfinalized nature of man and human *thought* was being nakedly exposed. Not only people and their actions but even *ideas* had broken out of their self-enclosed hierarchical nesting places and had begun to collide in the familiar contact of "absolute" (that is, completely unlimited) dialogue. Capitalism, similar to that "pander" Socrates on the market square of Athens, brings together people and ideas. In all of Dostoevsky's novels, beginning with *Crime and Punishment*, there is a consistent *carnivalization* of dialogue.

We find other instances of carnivalization in *Crime and Punishment*. Everything in this novel—the fates of people, their experiences and ideas—is pushed to its boundaries, everything is prepared, as it were, to pass over into its opposite (but not, of course, in the abstractly dialectical sense), everything is taken to the extreme, to its outermost limit. There is nothing in the novel that could become stabilized, nothing that could justifiably relax within itself, enter the ordinary flow of biographical time and develop in it (the possibility of such a development for Razumikhin and Dounia is only indicated by Dostoevsky at the end of the novel, but of course he does not show it: such life lies outside his artistic world). Everything requires change and rebirth. Everything is shown in a moment of unfinalized transition.

It is characteristic that the very setting for the action of the novel—*Petersburg* (its role in the novel is enormous)—is on the borderline between existence and nonexistence, reality and phantasmagoria, always on the verge of dissipating like the fog and vanishing. Petersburg too is devoid, as it were, of any internal grounds for justifiable stabilization; it too is on the threshold.[27]

The sources of carnivalization for *Crime and Punishment* are no longer provided by Gogol. We feel here in part a Balzacian type of carnivalization, and in part elements of the social-adventure novel (Soulié and Sue). But perhaps the most vital and profound source of carnivalization for this novel was Pushkin's "Queen of Spades."

We shall pause for analysis on only one small episode of the novel, which will permit us to investigate several important characteristics of carnivalization in Dostoevsky, and at the same time clarify our claim concerning Pushkin's influence.

After the first meeting with Porfiry and the appearance of the mysterious artisan with his one word, "Murderer!", Raskolnikov has a *dream* in which he *again* commits the murder of the old woman. We quote the end of this dream:

> He stood over her. "She is afraid," he thought. He stealthily took the axe from the noose and struck her one blow, then another on the skull. But strange to say she did not stir, as though she were made of wood. He was frightened, bent down nearer and tried to look at her; but she, too, bent her head lower. He bent right down to the ground and peeped up into her face from below, he peeped and turned cold with horror; the old woman was sitting and *laughing, shaking with noiseless laughter*, doing her utmost that he should not hear it. Suddenly he fancied that the door from the bedroom was opened a little and that there was *laughter* and whispering within. He was overcome with frenzy and he began hitting the old woman on the head with all his force, but at every blow of the axe and the *laughter* and whispering from the bedroom *grew louder* and the old woman was simply shaking with mirth. He was rushing away, but the *passage was full of people, the doors* of the flats stood open and *on the landing, on the stairs* and everywhere below there were people, rows of heads, *all looking*, but huddled together in silence and expectation. Something gripped his heart, his legs were rooted to the spot, they would not move.... He tried to scream and woke up. [*SS* V, 288; *Crime and Punishment*, Part III, ch. 6]

Several points are of interest here.

1. The first point is already familiar to us: the fantastic logic of dreams

employed here by Dostoevsky. We recall his words: "... *you leap over* space and time, *over all laws of life and reason*, and only pause where your *heart's desire* bids you pause" ("Dream of a Ridiculous Man"). This same dream logic made it possible to create here the image of a *laughing murdered old woman, to combine laughter with death and murder*. But this is also made possible by the ambivalent logic of carnival. Before us is a typical carnival combination.

The image of the laughing old woman in Dostoevsky echoes Pushkin's image of the old Countess winking from the coffin, and the winking Queen of Spades on the card (the Queen of Spades is, incidentally, a *carnival double* of the old Countess). We have here a *fundamental resonance* between two images and not a chance external similarity, for it occurs against the background of a general resonance between these two works ("The Queen of Spades" and *Crime and Punishment*). This is a resonance both in the atmosphere of images and in the basic content of ideas: "Napoleonism" on the specific terrain of early Russian capitalism. In both works this concretely historical phenomenon receives a second *carnivalistic plane*, one which recedes into infinite semantic space. The motivation for these two echoing images (the laughing dead woman) is also similar: in Pushkin it is *insanity*, in Dostoevsky, the *delirious dream*.

2. In Raskolnikov's dream it is not only the murdered woman who laughs (in the dream, to be sure, it proves impossible to murder her). Other people are also laughing, elsewhere in the apartment, in the bedroom, and they laugh louder and louder. Then a crowd appears, a multitude of people on the *stairway* and *down below* as well, and in relation to this crowd passing *below*, Raskolnikov is located at the *top of the stairs*. Before us is the image of communal ridicule on the public square decrowning a carnival king-pretender. The public square is a symbol of the communal performance, and at the end of the novel, Raskolnikov, before going to give himself up at the police station, comes out on the square and bows low to the earth before the whole people. This communal decrowning, which "came to Raskolnikov's heart" in a dream, has no *direct* echo in the "The Queen of Spades," but a distant echo is nevertheless there; Hermann's fainting spell in the presence of the people at the Countess' grave. A fuller echo of Raskolnikov's dream can be found in another of Pushkin's works, *Boris Godunov*. We have in mind the thrice-recurring prophetic *dream* of the Pretender (the scene in the cell of Chudovo Monastery);

> I dreamed I climbed a *crooked stair* that led
> Up to a tower, and there upon that *height*
> I stood, where Moscow like an ant hill lay
> *Under* my feet, and in the *marketplace*

The *people* stared and pointed at me *laughing*;
I felt *ashamed, a trembling overcame me,*
I fell headfirst, and in that fall I woke.[T]

Here is the same carnival logic of self-appointed *elevation*, the communal act of comic *decrowning on the public square*, and a falling *downward*.

3. In Raskolnikov's dream, *space* assumes additional significance in the overall symbol-system of carnival. *Up*, *down*, the *stairway*, the *threshold*, the *foyer*, the *landing* take on the meaning of a "point" where *crisis*, radical change, an unexpected turn of fate takes place, where decisions are made, where the forbidden line is overstepped, where one is renewed or perishes.

Action in Dostoevsky's works occurs primarily at these points. The interior spaces of a house or of rooms, spaces distant from the boundaries, that is from the threshold, are almost never used by Dostoevsky, except of course for scenes of scandals and decrownings, when interior space (the drawing room or the hall) becomes a substitute for the public square. Dostoevsky "leaps over" all that is comfortably habitable, well-arranged and stable, all that is far from the threshold, because the life that he portrays does not take place in that sort of space. Dostoevsky was least of all an estate-home-room-apartment-family writer. In comfortably habitable interior space, far from the threshold, people live a biographical life in biographical time: they are born, they pass through childhood and youth, they marry, give birth to children, die. This biographical time Dostoevsky also "leaps over." On the threshold and on the square the only time possible is *crisis time*, in which a *moment* is equal to years, decades, even to a "billion years" (as in "The Dream of a Ridiculous Man"). If we now turn from Raskolnikov's *dream* to what happens in the waking life of the novel, we will be persuaded that the threshold and its substitutes are the fundamental "points" of action in the novel.

First of all, Raskolnikov lives, in essence, on a threshold: his narrow room, a "coffin" (a carnival symbol here) opens directly onto the *landing of the staircase*, and he never locks his door, even when he goes out (that is, his room is unenclosed interior space). In this "coffin" it is impossible to live a biographical life—here one can experience only crisis, make ultimate decisions, die or be reborn (as in the coffins of "Bobok" or the coffin of the Ridiculous Man). Marmeladov's family lives on the threshold as well, in a walk-through room leading directly onto a staircase (here, on the threshold, while bringing home the drunken Marmeladov, Raskolnikov meets the members of the family for the first time). Raskolnikov experiences terrible

---

T. Translation by Paul Schmidt in his *Meyerbold at Work* (Austin: U. of Texas Press, 1980), p. 85.

moments at the threshold of the murdered pawnbroker's when, on the other side of the door, on the stairway landing, her visitors stand and tug at the bell. It is to this place that he returns and himself rings the bell, in order to relive those moments. The scene of his half-confession to Razumikhin takes place on the threshold in the corridor by a lamp, without words, only in glances. On the threshold, near the doors leading to a neighboring apartment, his conversations with Sonya occur (with Svidrigailov eavesdropping on the other side of the door). There is certainly no need to enumerate further all the "acts" that take place on the threshold, near the threshold, or that are permeated with the living sensation of threshold in this novel.

The threshold, the foyer, the corridor, the landing, the stairway, its steps, doors opening onto the stairway, gates to front and back yards, and beyond these, the city: squares, streets, façades, taverns, dens, bridges, gutters. This is the space of the novel. And in fact absolutely nothing here ever loses touch with the threshold, there is no interior of drawing rooms, dining rooms, halls, studios, bedrooms where biographical life unfolds and where events take place in the novels of writers such as Turgenev, Tolstoy, and Goncharov. Of course, we can uncover just such an organization of space in Dostoevsky's other works as well.

NOTES

6. Two lives—the official and the carnivalistic—also existed in the ancient world, but there was never such a sharp break between them (especially in Greece).

7. My work *Rabelais and the Folk Culture of the Middle Ages and the Renaissance* (1940), at the present time [1963] being prepared for publication, is devoted to the carnivalistic folk culture of the Middle Ages and the Renaissance. It provides a special bibliography on the question. [Bakhtin's book on Rabelais, submitted as a doctoral dissertation in 1940, was not published until 1965. It exists in English as Mikhail Bakhtin, *Rabelais and His World*, trans. Hélène Iswolsky (Cambridge, MA: MIT Press, 1968).]

8. Dostoevsky was very familiar not only with canonical Christian literature, but with the apocrypha as well.

9. Mention must be made here of the enormous influence exerted by the novella "The Widow of Ephesus" (from the *Satyricon*) on the Middle Ages and the Renaissance. This inserted novella is one of the greatest menippea of antiquity. [See Bakhtin's extensive analysis in "Forms of Time and Chronotope in the Novel," *The Dialogic Imagination*, pp. 221–24.]

10. The application of such terms as "epic," "tragedy," "idyll" to modern literature has become generally accepted and customary, and we are not in the least confused when *War and Peace* is called an epic, *Boris Godunov* a tragedy, "Old-World Landowners" an idyll. But the generic term "menippea" is not customary (especially in our literary scholarship), and therefore its application to works of modern literature (Dostoevsky, for example), may seem somewhat strange and strained.

11. In *Diary of a Writer* he appears again in "A Certain Person's Half-letter." [See *The Diary of a Writer*, 1873, pp. 65–74.]

12. In the eighteenth century, *Dialogues of the Dead* were written by Sumarokov and even by A. V. Suvorov, the future Field Commander (see his *Razgovor v tsarstve mertvykh mezhdu Aleksandrom Makedonskim i Gerostratom* [A Conversation in the Kingdom of the Dead Between Alexander the Great and Herostratus], 1755).

13. it is true that juxtapositions of this sort cannot decisively prove anything. All these similar elements could have been engendered by the logic of the genre itself, particularly by the logic of carnivalistic decrownings, debasings, and mésalliances.

14. The possibility cannot be discounted, although it is doubtful, that Dostoevsky was familiar with the satires of Varro. A complete scholarly edition of Varro's fragments was published in 1965 (Riese, *Varronis Saturarum Menippearum relinquiae*, Leipzig, 1865). The book aroused interest beyond the narrow philological circles, and Dostoevsky might have pined a secondhand acquaintance of it during his stay abroad, or perhaps through his Russian philologist friends.

15. *PS* XIII, 523. [The note was published in Dostoevsky's journal *Vremia* (Time) in January, 1861, as an editor's foreword to a Russian translation of three Poe stories ("The Black Cat," "The Tell-tale Heart," "The Devil in the Belfry"). Contrasting Poe and Hoffmann, Dostoevsky distinguishes between two types of fantasticality: the direct reproduction of the otherworldly realm, and—more his own practice—an indirect, external and "materialized" form of fantasticality that functions as a literary device, and as a principle for structuring the plot or image. The Russian text can be found in *F. M. Dostoevskii ob iskusstve* (Moscow: Iskusstvo, 1973), pp. 114–17.]

16. General Pervoedov ["he who eats first"] even in the grave could not renounce the consciousness of his general's dignity, and in the name of that dignity he categorically protests against Klinevich's proposal ("to cease to be ashamed"), announcing, "I have served my monarch." In *The Possessed* there is an analogous situation, but on the real-life earthly plane: General Drozdov, finding himself among nihilists, for whom the very word "general" is a word of abuse, defends his dignity as a general with the very same words. Both episodes are handled in a comic way.

17. Even from such well-meaning and competent contemporaries as A. N. Maikov.*

18. "And suddenly I called out, not with my voice for I could not move, but with the whole of my being, to the master of all that was befalling me" [*SS* X, 428].

19. On the generic and thematic sources of the "Legend of the Grand Inquisitor" (*Histoire de Jenni, ou L'Athée et le Sage* of Voltaire, Victor Hugo's *Le Christe au Vatican*), see the works of L. P. Grossman.

20. Gogol was still subject to the direct and vital influence of Ukrainian carnivalistic folklore.

21. Grimmelshausen is already beyond the limits of the Renaissance, but his work reflects the deep and direct influence of carnival no less than does the work of Shakespeare and Cervantes.

22. It cannot be denied, of course, that a certain degree of special fascination is inherent in all contemporary forms of carnivalistic life. It is enough to name *Hemingway*, whose work, on the whole deeply carnivalized, was strongly influenced by contemporary forms and festivals of a carnival type (especially the bullfight). He had a very keen ear for everything carnivalistic in contemporary life.

23. *PS* XIII, pp. 158–59. ["Petersburg Dreams in Verse and Prose" was published as a feuilleton in Dostoevsky's journal *Vremia* (*Time*) in 1861.]

24. Here the model for Dostoevsky was Gogol, namely the ambivalent tone of "The Story about how Ivan Ivanovich Quarreled with Ivan Nikiforovich."

25. During this period Dostoevsky was working on a large comic epic, of which "Uncle's Dream" is an episode (according to his own statement in a letter). As far as we know, Dostoevsky never subsequently returned to a plan for a large, purely comic work.

26. Thomas Mann's novel *Doktor Faustus*, which reflects the powerful influence of breaking through to the surface, especially in the narrator Zeitblom's story. Thomas Mann himself, in his history of the creation of the novel, writes of it this way: "Therefore I must introduce as much jesting, as much ridicule of the biographer, as much *anti-self-important mockery as possible*—as much of that as was humanly possible!" (T. Mann, "Istoriia *Doktora Faustusa*. Roman odnogo romana," *Sobranie sochinenii* [The History of Doktor Faustus. The Novel of a Novel, Collected Works] (Moscow: Golitizdat, 1960], vol. 9, p. 224). Reduced laughter, primarily of the parodic type, is in general characteristic of all of Mann's work. In comparing his style with that of Bruno Frank, Mann makes a very characteristic admission: "He [that is, B. Frank—M. B.] uses the humanistic narrative style of Zeitblom with *complete seriousness* as his own: In *matters of style I really no longer admit anything but parody*" (ibid., p. 235). It should be pointed out that Thomas Mann's work is profoundly carnivalized. Carnivalization occurs in most vivid external form in Mann's novel *Die Bekenntnisse des Hochstaplers Felix Krull* (where Professor Kuckuck becomes the mouthpiece for a sort of philosophy of carnival and carnival ambivalence). [See, in English, Mann's discussion of Zeitblom as narrator in Thomas Mann, *The Story of a Novel: The Genesis of Doctor Faustus*, trans. Richard and Clara Winston (New York: Knopf, 1961). The passages Bakhtin cites occur on p. 38 and 54.]

27. A carnivalized sense of Petersburg first appears in Dostoevsky in his novella *A Faint Heart* (1847), and was later powerfully developed, in ways applicable to all of Dostoevsky's early works, in "Petersburg Visions in Verse and Prose."

HARRIET MURAV

Crime and Punishment: *Psychology on Trial*

In his journal *Time* during 1861 and 1862, Dostoevsky included a series of transcripts of some of the more sensational French criminal proceedings from several prior decades. One of these was the trial of a thief and murderer named Lacenaire. In his introductory remarks, Dostoevsky told his readers that he considered the trial more interesting than anything that could be found in novels. During the trial, Lacenaire said that there were times in life when there was no other way out for him other than suicide or crime. When asked why he did not kill himself, Lacenaire replied that when he asked himself whether he was "his own victim" or the victim of society, he came to the conclusion that he was the latter. Lacenaire said that he felt some pity for his victims but that they were "predestined to perish," for he had decided "to go against everyone."

Lacenaire's trial took place in 1835. Dostoevsky published the transcript almost 30 years later. For him, the time lag was unimportant. Lacenaire, the self-styled victim of society, whose crime was a form of protest, and whose victims were sacrifices for a cause, seemed to Dostoevsky to embody the ideas and opinions of the immediate moment. But there is more. The transcript of the trial has great interest for Dostoevsky not only for its content but for its form. He suggests that the transcript, with its straightforward questions and answers, more truthfully captured the criminal's dark and enigmatic personality than any work of literary fiction.

From *Holy Foolishness: Dostoevsky's Novels & the Poetics of Cultural Critique.* © 1992 by the Board of Trustees of the Leland Stanford Junior University.

That is, any literary work until *Crime and Punishment*. With the creation of Raskolnikov, Dostoevsky outdoes the trial transcript of Lacenaire, which he had likened to a "daguerreotype" of a "phenomenal personality" (*PSS* 19:89–90). Nineteenth-century readers of *Crime and Punishment* were struck by the graphic description of its criminal hero. In 1884, for example, Dr. V. Chizh, who was prominent in the field of experimental psychology, wrote that the "veracity and detail" of Dostoevsky's descriptions were "worthy of the best natural scientist" ("Dostoevskii kak psikhopatolog," pp. 117–18). Dostoevsky had, according to some of his contemporaries, produced in *Crime and Punishment* a scientifically accurate study in psychopathology. Indeed, for the time of its publication to the present, *Crime and Punishment* (and all of Dostoevsky's other fiction) has been read for its masterful psychological analysis.[1] In this chapter I will suggest a different approach, first by showing how the novel provides a critique of the scientific psychology of its time, and second by showing how the novel offers, as an alternative to science, what I will call the discourse of holy foolishness.

In a letter written in 1865 to the editor of the journal *The Russian Messenger*, Dostoevsky described his plans for a new novel, which was to be a "psychological account of a crime." The crime, as we will see, borrows some of its ideological basis from Lacenaire. Dostoevsky writes in his letter:

> A young man ... living in extreme poverty, from the immaturity
> and instability of his thinking, having given in to a certain strange
> half-baked ideas, which are part of the atmosphere, decided to
> extricate himself from his miserable position at once. He decided
> to murder an old woman ... who lent money for interest. The old
> woman is stupid, deaf, greedy ..... "She's not good for anything,"
> "what does she live for? "Such questions bewilder the young man.
> He decides to kill the old woman and rob her. [*PSS* 28.2: 136]

Dostoevsky was to make several important changes in the final version of the novel, enhancing the ideological motivation for the crime and emphasizing the "half-baked ideas" that are so characteristic of the atmosphere of the time. These include the rational utilitarianism advocated by Chernyshevskii and others, the utopian Socialism of the 1840's that Dostoevsky had himself been fascinated by, and the new social theories that correlated the external environment with criminality.[2] But *Crime and Punishment* should not be seen primarily as a document that records the social history of its time. In recapitulating these ideas in *Crime and Punishment*, Dostoevsky, as I will show, renders them problematic. Bakhtin says, as we have seen, that the novel relativizes and parodies the languages of Its time. Ultimately, *Crime and Punishment* unravels what these "languages" have to say about Raskolnikov's crime. Just as the holy fool's efforts to imitate the incarnate God challenge the norms of the dominant culture of his time, so, too, Dostoevsky's writing challenges the new normative scientism of the nineteenth century.

A Normal Society and the "New Word" of the Criminal

One offshoot of this new scientistic discourse was the notion that crime is a protest against a victimizing environment. We hear about this idea during a conversation among Raskolnikov, Razumikhin, his bumbling but well-intentioned friend, and the court investigator, Porfirii Petrovich. Razumikhin explains that the view of the socialists is that "crime is a protest against the abnormality of the social structure—and only that and nothing more" (*PSS* 6: 196, *CP* 3.5). Razumikhin says that the socialists hoped to solve all of mankind's problems by leaping over "living history" in order to arrive at a mathematically perfect solution, which he characterizes as nothing more than the correct arrangements of the corridors and rooms in the phalansteries—a reference to the communal living arrangements designed by the utopian socialist and mathematician Charles Fourier.

As a member of the Petrashevskii circle in the 1840's, Dostoevsky had become familiar with the ideas of Fourier and his disciples.[3] He had no doubt become familiar with Butashevich-Petrashevskii's *Pocket Dictionary of Words*, a radical philosophical tract in the form of a dictionary, published in 1841 and 1846. The entry for "the normal condition" (*normal'noe sostoianie*) contains a whole treatise about the relation between the individual and the environment and the need to reconstruct society along more "normal lines." In this little treatise, and in Razumikhin's use of the term "abnormality," we see the way in which the language of disease has become assimilated into moral and political discourse.

Petrashevskii wrote that in "the most recent philosophical theories," the normal condition is a technical term that signifies "the normality of the development of society and mankind." His conception of a "normally developed individual" is one in whom all the passions are harmoniously developed" (*Karmannnyi slovar' inostrannykh slov*, p. 250). The notion of the harmonious reconciliation of the passions and of their importance for the "normal condition" of the individual is derived from Fourier, who saw in human passion a force akin to the universal, nonorganic force of attraction, that is, gravity.[4] In *Crime and Punishment*, it is the medical student Zametin who remarks to Raskolnikov's sister that there are very few "harmonious individuals in the world."

Petrashevskii goes on to say that such normal development depends less on the individual than on society, which must provide him with the minimum necessary for his existence. The normal condition can be said to have been achieved only when "the spirit of unity pervades; and everything that is considered oppressive and repulsive is transformed into a source of the immediate enjoyment of life" (Petrashevskii, p. 250). For Petrashevskii, the normal condition is an ideal one, in which both the individual and society are in a state of harmony. Once society is reconstructed normally, all the sources of conflict, both internal (the struggle between reason and passion) and external (the conflicts between various members of society) will be removed, and unity will be achieved. The reform of human nature is to be brought about by the reorganization of society as a whole. In *Crime and Punishment*, Fourier is quoted only to be parodied. Lebeziatnikov says that Sonia Marmeladova's prostitution is a protest against "the structure of society" (*PSS* 6: 283).

In *Crime and Punishment*, the veiled reference to Petrashevskii and Fourier serves more than one purpose. The debate about crime and the environment is a prologue to the deadly cat-and-mouse game between Porfirii Petrovich and Raskolnikov, of which Razumikhin is completely unaware. Porfirii professes interest in Raskolnikov's ideas about crime, which he has read about in an article that Raskolnikov has published. For Raskolnikov, crime is not merely a form of social protest, as it was for Lacenaire. As Porfirii tells us, Raskolnikov believes that society can be divided into two classes, the "ordinary" and the "extraordinary" (*PSS* 6: 199, *CP* 3.5). The extraordinary, the class of supermen, have the capacity "to utter their *new word*" and therefore have the right to commit crimes (*PSS* 6: 200, *CP* 3.5). Porfirii Petrovich playfully suggests that Raskolnikov counts himself as such a superman.

By the time Dostoevsky completed *Crime and Punishment*, the study of the social environment had gone beyond Fourier. We have spoken of the way statistics provided a new basis for evaluating behavior. N. Nekliudov's *Criminal Statistical Studies* (1865), for example, examined the physiological significance of the age of the "human organism" in relation to crime. The name for this new theory was "moral statistics," or, alternatively, "social physics." In *Crime and Punishment*, Dostoevsky reflects on the implications of "moral statistics" indirectly, relying, as we will see, on Raskolnikov's "word."

The Language of Moral Statistics

The "science of moral statistics" was developed by the Belgian mathematician A. Quêtelet.[5] His theories were promulgated in Russia for the most part by the publicist V. A. Zaitsev,[6] the author of such articles as "Natural Science and Justice," which appeared in the journal *The Russian Word* in 1863, and by A. Wagner, a German economist whose article on the predictability of human behavior had appeared in a collection entitled *The General Conclusion of the Positive Method*, which is mentioned in *Crime and Punishment*.

Wagner, drawing upon Quêtelet, argued that the regularity of human behavior could be seen only with the introduction of the statistical method. When very large numbers of cases are observed, regularities begin to be noticed, even in the instance of a departure from the rule, since the same "accidental or chance causes" always lead to the same results. Given the law of large numbers, the individual is replaced by a construct, "the average person," who is the by-product of all the observations made. Wagner's general conclusion was that any particular piece of human behavior was the end result of such various determining factors as climate, time of year, sex, age, and social and economic relations. Far from being freely willed, the individual's actions were to be seen as his unconscious obedience to the laws of nature (Wagner, "Zakonoobraznost'").

Similarly, Zaitsev argued that the study of criminality should ignore the problem of individual motivation—which is the central locus of *Crime and Punishment*, and about which the novel reaches no fixed conclusion—and concentrate instead on the influence of the "fatal numbers, which cheerfully laugh at mankind's certainty in its own freedom" (Zaitsev, "Estestvoznanie i iustitsiia," p. 76). Relying on a statistical table that Quêtelet had drawn up, Zaitsev pointed out that if, in France, "in the course of one year one person out of six hundred must commit a crime, is it possible to say that he did it voluntarily?" (Zaitsev, p. 78).

The science of moral statistics reduced every social phenomenon, from marriage to suicide, to some definite property of the social environment. In *Crime and Punishment*, Dostoevsky does not attack this theory head on. He is uninterested in the soundness of its scientific details. Instead, through Raskolnikov, he focuses our attention on what might seem to be the least likely problem, namely, language. In so doing, he displays his skill not only as a social historian but also as a dramatic artist. The deconstruction of the science of moral statistics coincides, as we will see, with a turning point in

Raskolnikov's intention to commit murder. The whole notion of the predictability of human behavior, upon which the theory of moral statistics rests, is thereby called into question.

In Part I, Raskolnikov receives a letter from his mother, who writes that all their troubles are over: Dunia, his sister, is to marry a certain Petr Petrovich Luzhin, a "seemingly good" man, and while there can be no question of love, Luzhin will be a benefit to them all. Luzhin's grasp of the new ideas of the time is evidenced in his statement to Raskolnikov that "science teaches us we must love ourselves best of all."[7] Upon finishing the letter, Raskolnikov falls into a reverie and then into a rage; he takes his cap and goes into the street, where he begins muttering to himself. He decides that while he is alive, no marriage will take place, that he will refuse the sacrifice. It occurs to him, however, that there is nothing he can do for his mother and sister. He begins torturing himself with the thought that he cannot provide for them, and suddenly a certain thought that only yesterday had been a dream—the idea of murdering the old pawnbroker—acquires a terrible reality. Everything grows dark before his eyes, and when he recovers he starts looking for a place to sit down. He spots a bench not far off, but on the way to it, a "little adventure" took place that "captured all his attention" (*PSS* 6: 39, *CP* 1.3).

Raskolnikov notices a young woman walking along. There is something so strange about her that little by little his attention begins to be "riveted to her." He observes that she is extremely young, that she has no parasol or gloves, that her dress has been put on very strangely, and that her scarf is crooked. Her walk is uneven, and she staggers all over the street. Here Raskolnikov's attention is finally and completely fixed. He follows her to the bench, and having a good close look at her, he realizes that she is drunk. He further observes that the girl has sat down in a slightly indecent position, probably unaware, he concludes, that she is on the street.

Raskolnikov also observes a gentleman, very well dressed, who is drawn to the girl, but for the purpose of seducing her. Raskolnikov tries to chase the man away; they quarrel and attract the attention of a policeman. Raskolnikov, quickly realizing that his opponent's word will he given far greater consideration than his own, grabs the policeman by the arm and takes him to where the girl is sitting. There he begins to re-create, in novelistic fashion, what has happened to her. He remarks that it is unlikely that she is a professional; it is more probable, he says, that she was made drunk and then deceived, and for the first time, he adds. As if he were a detective, Raskolnikov asks the policeman to take note of her torn clothing and the fact that she has been dressed "by incompetent male hands" (*PSS* 6: 41, *CP* 1.4). Then Raskolnikov invites the policeman to take another look at the dandy.

The policeman "understands" everything and sets about the business of getting the girl home. In the next instant, however, Raskolnikov experiences a sudden change of feeling. He shouts at the policeman, "Let the man enjoy himself," and goes off. Although he wants to forget everything, Raskolnikov's thoughts return to the "poor girl." He begins to imagine her future: her mother's reproaches, the inevitable hospitalization and then drunkenness, and how finally she will become a cripple. He concludes:

> Haven't I seen cases like this? But how does it happen? Like everything else happens.... And let it! They say it ought to happen. A certain percent, they say, has to go every year.... Percent! It's true, they have such wonderful little words; they're so soothing, so scientific. Once you say percent, there's nothing to worry about. If there were another word, well then ... perhaps it would be more upsetting.... And what if Dunechka somehow ended up in the percent! ... Not in this one, but in another? [*PSS* 6: 43, *CP* 1.4]

For Raskolnikov, what is particularly noteworthy about this new social science is its language. Raskolnikov is struck by the seeming neutrality of scientific language—a neutrality, he implies, that belies a series of emotional and moral repositionings. Raskolnikov is obsessed with words, with what he calls the "new word." His obsession makes him a particularly sensitive reader of another's language, enabling him to see that scientific language is not value-free. Once the word "percent" is uttered, the poor girl disappears from view, replaced by a statistic. But for Raskolnikov, the word "percent" is far from soothing. It is particularly bitter to him at this moment. He and the old pawnbroker, in a scene that comes before the episode of the poor girl, have just been quarreling about percentages—not statistical but financial—the interest that Raskolnikov still owes. Distracted by his efforts to save the girl, he puts aside, if only for the moment, his "new word." His eyes, before which "everything had grown dark," become sighted once again.

Raskolnikov's tirade about moral statistics is an example of the way the novel as a whole calls into question the new scientific ideology of the period, challenging its models of human behavior. There are other examples of this questioning in the novel.[8] At the end, during his trial, Raskolnikov refuses the "new fashionable" defense strategy of "temporary insanity" (*PSS* 6: 411). during the time when *Crime and Punishment* was written (1865–66) the concept of legal competence, upon which the insanity defense rests, was of recent vintage. A. Liubavskii's study of the legal aspects of mental illness offered, for example, the following criterion for the determination of competence. If it could be shown that the crime was committed in an "unconscious or abnormal state of mental capacities," then the criminal was not to be subject to punishment but to the appropriate medical care (Liubavskii, *Russkie ugolovnye protsessy*, p. 1). *Crime and Punishment* as a whole resists the notion that crime is the result of disease.[9]

In the episode about the poor girl, Dostoevsky suggests that scientific observation impedes the human capacity for sympathy, the recognition of the suffering of another.[10] Raskolnikov's story about the poor girl expresses what is best and most hidden in himself: his need to be rejoined with society, from which he has severed himself. "Scientific" discourse results in alienation and depersonalization for both those who utter it and those who are its object. Raskolnikov's critique of the language of "percentages" stands opposed to the new authority of science. Raskolnikov is not the only figure who embodies this critical stance. Some of the peripheral characters also speak in this register, in what can be called "countercultural," or holy-foolish voices. It is to these that we now turn.

A Drunkard's Vision

In the first part of the novel, after he has rehearsed the pawnbroker's murder, Raskolnikov enters a tavern, where he finds himself unaccountably drawn to the figure of Marmeladov, a drunkard, who tells him his life's story, culminating in what amounts to a vision of the Last Judgment. L. M. Lotman has convincingly argued that Marmeladov is based in part on the hero of a folk tale known as the "Story of a Drunkard."[11] The story originates in the seventeenth century but became a subject of ethnographic interest in Dostoevsky's time. It forms, as Lotman shows, an important part of the subtext of *Crime and Punishment*.

The "Story of a Drunkard" concerns, as its title indicates, "a man who drank exceedingly much during God's holidays and from early on in the day." But with every drink, "he sings praises to God" ("Povest' o brazhnike," p. 85). When he dies, God sends two angels to take his soul, which they deposit at the heavenly gates. The drunkard demands entrance into paradise, but each of the saints whom he meets refuses him. Each of the saints sings his own praises. Peter, for example, says that God entrusted him with the keys to the heavenly kingdom, Paul, that he baptized the Ethiopian church. The drunkard turns the tables on the saints, accusing each of some failure: he reminds Peter that he denied Christ, and Paul, that he threw stones at the martyr Stephen. Finally, the drunkard confronts John, whom he reminds of his words in the Gospel about love. He accuses John of loving only himself and demands that he either excise his words or recant them. Defeated, John lets the drunkard enter paradise.

In the tale, the separation between the damned and the saved is overcome. The final balance sheet is tempered with love and mercy. Similar themes emerge in Marmeladov's vision of the Last Judgment. In his vision, Jesus first judges all of mankind and then comes to the drunkards. He tells them to rise and come before him, and the drunkards are "not ashamed." Jesus tells the drunkards that even though they are "stamped in the image of the beast and with his seal," they may approach him. The reference here is to the beast in Revelation 13, who, prior to God's final triumph, is given power over all the peoples of the earth, whose image is worshiped by all, and without whose seal no one could act. In Marmeladov's vision, Jesus' invitation to those stamped with the image of the beast meets with great protest from "the wise men." Jesus responds by saying that he accepts these lowest of the low "because not one of them thought himself worthy."

In the Revelation of John, those marked with the seal of the beast are subject to eternal torment (Rev. 14: 9). In contrast, in Marmeladov's version, divine judgment gives way to divine mercy. In Marmeladov's vision and in the "Story of a Drunkard," we can identify a carnivalesque overturning of hierarchy. Judgment is suspended; the barrier between the saved and the damned collapses; and the last are made first. The stamp of the beast counts as nothing. In the notebooks to *Crime and Punishment*, Dostoevsky suggests that Jesus's mercy toward the drunkards is associated with holy foolishness. Marmeladov says that Jesus "pitied everyone, for which they laughed at him, and still laugh, and abuse him" (*PSS* 7: 87).

The carnivalesque motifs introduced in this episode are developed later in the novel at the scene of Marmeladov's funeral feast. Marmeladov is run over by a carriage, and his wife, despite their miserable circumstances, insists on honoring him for the sake of social proprieties. The feast, however, becomes the occasion for disgrace and scandal. The guests are the least desirable inhabitants of the lodging house. One arrives drunk; another in his dressing gown; another has a repulsive smell, and so forth. Marmeladov's wife and the landlady exchange invective and very nearly come to blows. Sonia, Marmeladov's daughter, creates a scandal by her mere presence—she has taken up prostitution as a way of supporting the family—and the more respectable tenants have stayed away. Someone sends her a plate upon which have been placed two hearts made of black bread, pierced by an arrow. When Katarina Ivanovna, Marmeladov's wife, describes Sonia's future role in the pension for "well-born girls" that she intends to establish, the guests burst into laughter. The grotesque feast culminates in a trial. Luzhin, whom Raskolnikov's sister has rejected, accuses Sonia of stealing one hundred rubles from him. Raskolnikov, playing the role of defense attorney (*advokat*), proves her innocence. It is revealed that Luzhin has planted the money on Sonia.

Marmeladov's vision of the Last Judgment and Sonia's mock trial reflect the central trial of *Crime and Punishment*, a trial that unfolds on several levels: Raskolnikov's self-imposed trial to determine whether he belongs to the class of supermen, and the more down-to-earth judicial proceedings that he faces for his crime, depending on the outcome of his struggle with Porfirii Petrovich, the court investigator. Dostoevsky builds on the theme of trial, adding, especially with Marmeladov, an eschatological dimension. The problem of confession receives a similar multiperspectival treatment, in which criminal and judicial elements are intertwined with religious motifs. The problem of confession is refracted through a peripheral character, Mikolka, who falsely confesses to the murder of the old pawnbroker and her sister. This false confession is, as we will see, a kind of holy foolishness.

Flight from Justice

Mikolka figures significantly in the complicated psychological trap that Porfirii Petrovich has set for Raskolnikov. Porfirii has let it be known, through Razumikhin, that Mikolka has confessed to the crime. This takes place near the end of the novel. The news disconcerts Raskolnikov, who decides to go see Porfirii himself. He sets off just as Porfirii arrives, announcing that he will finally explain himself. As Porfirii talks, Raskolnikov is thrown into a state of confusion. He cannot convince himself that Porfirii believes Mikolka, and yet he desperately wants to believe that Porfirii no longer suspects him. When Raskolnikov finally realizes that Porfirii is about to charge him with the murders, he interrupts to protest that Mikolka is now the suspect. Here Porfirii gives his account of Mikolka's confession.

Mikolka is innocent and a complete child, Porfirii says. He describes Mikolka as something of an "artist" (*PSS* 6: 347, *CP* 6.2). He attracts a crowd with his singing, dancing, and storytelling. Mikolka is an Old Believer, in Russian a *raskol'nik*. While he lived in the country, he was under the supervision of an elder. At night, he would pray and read the holy books. Petersburg acted on him too strongly. He forgot his elder, and he confessed to the murders, Porfirii explains, as a kind of penance, a form of self-imposed suffering. Porfirii asks Raskolnikov if he knows what is meant by "suffering"—not for the sake of gain, or even on behalf of someone else, but simply because "it is necessary." If the suffering can come from the authorities, so much the better (*PSS* 6: 348, *CP* 6.2). Porfirii suggests that it was in order to take on suffering that Mikolka made his false confession, and he recommends the same path to Raskolnikov.

As Philip Rahv has suggested, Raskolnikov is "a dissenter and a rebel, in essence, the type of revolutionary terrorist of that period, whose act of terror is somehow displaced onto a private object" ("Dostoevsky in *Crime and Punishment*," p. 555). His name indicates his participation in a schism of his own devising. Mikolka and Raskolnikov can be seen as doubles of each other, Mikolka as the true sectarian and Raskolnikov as the false one. It is significant that in the newspaper item that may have inspired *Crime and Punishment*, which described a double murder committed with an ax between seven and nine in the evening, the criminal was a *raskol'nik*, an Old Believer, whom Dostoevsky then transforms into the theorist Raskolnikov and the penitent Mikolka.[12]

It is possible to understand the dichotomy between these two opposing figures in terms of a clash between traditional Russian culture, with its emphasis on humility, and modernity with its emphasis on the self. This dichotomy has to be qualified somewhat. As we will see, it is not adequate to understand Mikolka's suffering as a passive form of self-emptying. His suffering, when seen in its specific historical context, can also be understood as a form of resistance directed against official authority.

Porfirii Petrovich says that in Mikolka's family there were members of the sect known is the *beguny* (literally, "those who flee"), one of the schismatic groups that arose in the eighteenth century in whom the tenets of Old Belief appear in a very extreme form. The *beguny* were closely associated with another schismatic group, called *stranniki* (literally "wanderers"'). According to a study by Bishop Makarii (1855), the *stranniki* believe that the Antichrist has already appeared and "visibly rules on earth" (Makarii, *Istoriia russkogo raskola*, pp. 280–81). Therefore, obedience to any form of earthly power, be it secular or clerical, is stamped with his seal. Since struggle against the earthly powers is impossible, the only remaining opportunity for salvation is flight (*begstvo*) and wandering (*stranstvovanie*)—from which the *beguny* and *stranniki* get their respective names.

Flight from all forms of official culture is one response to the Antichrist; other responses include lying and deception. L. Trefalev, in a study of the *stranniki* (published in the journal *The Russian Archive* in 1866), wrote that lying and deception during periods of official investigation were considered obligatory by the schismatics and were "openly sanctioned by the example taken from the life of the great Barbara, where it is said that someone spoke the truth and perished, another lied, and was made a saint." Trefalev goes on to say that among the *stranniki* lying is especially important because it is a way of abusing the "Antichrist and his servants" (Trefalev, "Stranniki," p. 615).

Mikolka's lie, as it is quoted by Porfirii Petrovich, has at least double meaning. It is a way of taking on suffering and also a judgment against those who would judge him. In this respect, Mikolka's lie can be seen as a piece of holy foolishness in which self-abasement and deliberate provocation are both part of the performance. The historical holy fool abused those who mocked him, as we have seen.[13]

The reference to the *beguny*, those who flee from the Antichrist, and to Marmeladov's vision lend an apocalyptic coloring to the themes of crime and punishment, trial and confession. The apocalypticism of *Crime and Punishment* emerges most clearly in the epilogue to the novel. Raskolnikov, lying sick in a prison hospital in Siberia, has a dream about a "new trichina" that infects Europe from Asia. The dream is replete with apocalyptic motifs, invasion from the east being one of them. Characteristically, Dostoevsky gives Raskolnikov's apocalyptic dream a contemporary flavor. Russian newspapers in 1865 and 1866 made frequent reference to a microbe previously unknown to medicine, which, it was feared, could be responsible for a new epidemic. In Raskolnikov's dream, the trichinae infect the world with an insanity that masquerades as wisdom. Those infected went mad but believed themselves to be sane, and became even more convinced as to the rightness of their moral convictions and their "scientific conclusions." No one could agree, and a period of war, famine, and fire ensued. Those chosen to save the world could not deliver their message; "no one heard their voices" (*PSS* 6: 420, *CP* Epilogue). Raskolnikov's dream is a kind of holy-foolish denunciation of what for Raskolnikov was the "wisdom of the world," as Paul says, that is, the new *scientific* wisdom.

In his *Diary of a Writer* for 1877, responding to the charge that he himself was abnormal, Dostoevsky wrote that in his novels he had, on occasion, succeeded in "exposing people who considered themselves healthy, and showing them that they were sick" (*PSS* 26: 107). We have traced in *Crime and Punishment* a similar kind of holy-foolish unmasking, which unfolds not simply in exchanges between characters but is dispersed throughout the novel as a whole in its complex orchestration of discourse. Among these, the most important is Raskolnikov's own "new word," his theory of the two classes of humanity, which he seeks to put into practice with the murder of the old pawnbroker. Raskolnikov's theory is the most essential feature of his identity; it is the test of who he is. His emphasis on the "word" is evidenced in a rather trivial, comical way in the novel's opening. As he cautiously makes his way out of his apartment building, terrified of encountering his landlady, Raskolnikov proclaims to himself that what people fear most is uttering their own "new word" (*PSS* 6: 6, *CP* 1.1). It is only at the very end of the novel that he attains inarticulateness. When Raskolnikov finally confesses to the police, all that comes out of his mouth, at first, are incoherent sounds. His wisdom is made foolish. In order to trace the process by means of which this change takes place, we must turn our attention to Sonia Marmeladova.

The Wisdom of Iurodivaia

Raskolnikov's first visit to Sonia occurs about halfway through the novel. His attention is drawn to her room, the angles of which are all wrong. It had the appearance of an "oddly angled square, and this gave it a deformed (*urodlivoe*) quality" (*PSS* 6: 241, *CP* 4.4). The word *urodlivoe* here is important; it is related to the word *iurodivaia* (the feminine for "holy fool"), which Raskolnikov is shortly to apply to Sonia. Her face, like her room, is also crookedly angled, and Raskolnikov suggests that there is something deformed about her as well.

To Raskolnikov, the sacrifice that Sonia has made of herself is futile. Suicide, madness, or complete depravity are the only paths open to her, he concludes. He wonders whether she has not already gone out of her mind. Is it possible for one in his right mind to contemplate destruction and still ignore the warnings of others? Raskolnikov sees in Sonia "the signs of madness" (*PSS* 6: 248, *CP* 4.4). He asks Sonia whether she prays to God and whether God does anything for her. Outraged, she answers by saying that God "does everything." It strikes Raskolnikov, looking at Sonia's thin face, that it is "very strange, almost impossible" that this sickly girl with her "mild blue eyes" should be capable of such righteous anger. At this moment he tells himself that she is a *iurodivaia*. A few lines later, when he learns that Sonia knew the sister of the pawnbroker, Lizaveta, whom he also murdered, and when he hears Sonia's "bookish words" that Lizaveta was "righteous" and that she will "see God," Raskolnikov decides that both Sonia and Lizaveta are *iurodivye* (holy fools) and that he is going to become a *iurodivyi* himself: "It's infectious!" (*PSS* 6: 249, *CP* 4.4).

In this passage, Raskolnikov's characterization of Sonia as *iurodivaia* has clearly negative connotations. The term occurs in a context in which other terms for madness and insanity are used, and Raskolnikov fears for his own sanity. The Coulson translation captures this sense by rendering *iurodivaia* as "She has religious mania."[14] At the same time, Dostoevsky emphasizes that the use of the word *iurodivaia* as a term of abuse is part of Raskolnikov's speech. Shortly thereafter, the tables are turned. Sonia thinks to herself that Raskolnikov is "mad" (*poloumnyi*). A deadlock of sorts results as to who is mad and who is sane. The boundary between sanity and insanity is for the moment suspended. This state of affairs is typical of the hagiography of the holy fools, who mock and abuse the "world" and are in turn the target of mockery and abuse—as Sonia was at her father's funeral feast.

Dostoevsky helps us out of the dilemma. The word *iurodivaia*, although given a negative meaning by Raskolnikov, also suggests a link between Sonia and the hagiographic ideal of the holy fool. The translation "religious maniac" is too one-sided. Sonia's name, Sophia, means "wisdom," not of this world, in the New Testament sense. Raskolnikov thought that his "new word" would make him into a new man. He fetishizes his word, his theory. Sonia, in contrast, is identified with the redemptive "word" of John's Gospel, which is the word made flesh and which, in the passage she reads to Raskolnikov, brings Lazarus back to life.

As Sonia comes closer and closer to the actual miracle, everything else recedes into the background: the fact of her prostitution, her room, her stepmother, Lizaveta, and even Raskolnikov. Her eyes grow dim, but she knows the words by heart, and her voice rings out, triumphant. For the reader, nothing remains on the page but John's words. Then Sonia can read no longer, and she and Raskolnikov sit in silence: "the murderer and the prostitute, strangely united by the reading of the eternal book" (*PSS* 6: 251-52, *CP* 4.4). In this scene, Dostoevsky emphasizes the process of reading: we know Sonia is reading from the eleventh chapter of the Gospel of John; we follow her from the nineteenth verse to the thirty-second; we are told that she accentuates the phrase "the fourth day."

The central fact of reading the text, the contrast between this "word" and Raskolnikov's, is emphasized in that Dostoevsky's narrative is, in a sense, suspended, and we read instead the words of the Gospel. The embedding of the Gospel text has another significance as well. Aside from this scene, Sonia, unlike Raskolnikov and Porfirii, is by and large inarticulate. Dostoevsky accentuates this feature by displacing it. The family from whom she rents her room suffer from speech defects. The children are "tongue-tied" (*kosnoiazychnye*), and the landlord stutters. Without the rest of the Gospel before her, Sonia has trouble speaking. We read that it was evident from her face that she "wanted terribly to express something, to say something, to intercede—an insatiable compassion ... was portrayed in all her features" (*PSS* 6: 243, *CP* 4.4).

Sonia Marmeladova appears as an icon, on which only suffering is expressed.[15] Raskolnikov's cure, if it may be said to take place at all, begins without words. Raskolnikov, above all, *looks* at Sonia. From their first meeting to the end of the novel, and in the complex of associations between Sonia and Raskolnikov's dead bride, Dostoevsky emphasizes Sonia's iconic function. In their first meeting, when Sonia reads the story of Lazarus to him, Raskolnikov takes Sonia by the arms and looks into her "weeping" face. He kisses her feet, explaining that he is "bowing before all of suffering humanity." In Part VI, Raskolnikov, alone with his sister Dunia, takes out a portrait of his dead bride, the landlady's daughter, "that strange girl who wanted to enter a convent." In the notebooks to the novel, this scene takes place with Sonia. Raskolnikov removes the portrait, kisses it and gives it to Sonia, saying, "She prophesied you to me" (*PSS* 7: 176). Raskolnikov's betrothed, who anticipates Sonia, appears in the novel only as a portrait or icon. Sonia's role as *iurodivaia* and her iconic function come together in Svidrigailov's reference to an icon of sorts, the Sistine Madonna, whom he says has a fantastical face, the face of a sorrowing *iurodivaia*.

It is to Sonia as to an icon that Raskolnikov first confesses and to whom he finally turns at the end of the novel. As he goes to visit her for the last time, Raskolnikov explains to himself that he feels the need to see her face, to "look at her suffering," to "look" at a person.[16] In the very last moment, just as Raskolnikov is about to leave the police station without having confessed, he sees Sonia waiting for him; he stops in front of her and sees that "something sickly, tormented, was expressed in her face, something full of despair." After looking at Sonia's face, Raskolnikov decides to go back and turn himself in. It is at this moment that he attains Sonia's inarticulateness. He wrenches out the first sounds of confession: "He wanted to say something, but could not, only incoherent sounds were heard" (*PSS* 6: 409, *CP* 6.8). Sonia's mute iconic authority triumphs, if only temporarily.

Sonia's success at winning a confession from Raskolnikov contrasts with the efforts of Porfirii Petrovich, the court investigator. Dostoevsky structures his narrative in such a way as to underscore the differences between Sonia and Porfirii. Raskolnikov's three meetings with Porfirii Petrovich occur in tandem with his visits to Sonia. In Part III, Chapter 4, Sonia comes to invite Raskolnikov to her father's funeral. From this meeting he goes to Porfirii, who asks him if he literally believes in the raising of Lazarus. In Part IV, Chapter 4, Raskolnikov goes to see Sonia in her room, and in the very next chapter, he meets Porfirii Petrovich for the second time. In the notebooks to the novel, the words "court investigator" and "Sonia" often appear together.

Porfirii's authority and that of Sonia are in sharp contrast. Porfirii's is from "on high," as Raskolnikov says. Porfirii urges Raskolnikov to confess by telling him that he will find peace thereby. Raskolnikov challenges him, asking what sort of prophet he is and whether he utters this prophecy of "peace" from "on high" (*PSS* 6: 352, *CP* 6.2). Sonia makes no such claim to superior vision. She cannot offer Raskolnikov knowledge about his future. She can provide, however, a model for imitation.

The relationship between the court investigator and the holy-foolish Sonia can be seen in terms of a set of oppositions: that between official and unofficial culture, between Porfirii's famous "double-edged" psychology, which functions, as Raskolnikov says, as a "trap" (*lovushka*), and Sonia's quotation from sacred discourse. However, Porfirii, like Sonia, is also involved in the Lazarus theme as well as in the theme of resurrection through suffering. Furthermore, Porfirii, like Sonia, is linked to the theme of foolishness. He takes on the role of a comic figure, calling himself, at one point, a "buffoon" (*PSS* 6: 263, *CP* 4.5); in the same scene, he races around the room, making gestures that do not correspond to his words; his facial expressions are mocking, mirthful, and also threatening.[17]

The question remains as to whether Porfirii is interested in Raskolnikov's salvation or in merely discharging his duty as an agent of the law.[18] Porfirii's account of Raskolnikov's crime as a "gloomy contemporary affair," the product of "bookish dreams and a theoretically irritated heart" (*PSS* 6: 348, *CP* 6.2), serves to re-create Raskolnikov as a criminal. The story of his resurrection is, as the narrator says, outside the scope of the novel, which raises a question about whether the novel can provide an account of resurrection, notwithstanding language in the notebooks to the novel indicating that "Orthodox resurrection" was its main "idea" (*PSS* 7: 154).

Indeed, it is not certain that Sonia has managed to resurrect Raskolnikov. Earlier in the novel, Raskolnikov had identified himself as Lazarus—not the Lazarus who is resurrected but the beggar Lazarus. Raskolnikov says that he would have to "sing Lazarus" (*pet' Lazaria*) by pretending to be mad. The source for this expression is Luke's parable of Lazarus and the rich man. The Gospel story was incorporated into the so-called spiritual songs of Russia's itinerant beggars, who thereby claimed a model in Luke's Lazarus.[19] The expression "to sing Lazarus" came to have a negative connotation, meaning to complain about one's fate, to be a false beggar. M. S. Al'tman suggests that Raskolnikov's profession to Porfirii Petrovich of his belief in the literal resurrection of Lazarus is a false front, a way of "singing Lazarus" (Al'tman, "Izpol'zovanie mnogoznachnosti," pp. 30–32). Raskolnikov's confession to the police has similar overtones.

The story of Raskolnikov's resurrection, the epilogue tells us, is outside the scope of this novel. But it is pointed to by the silences and inarticulateness within the novel. *Crime and Punishment* moves from speech to silence, from quoting the ideas and opinions of its time to pointing beyond itself. This gesture is made in the apocalyptic motifs introduced by Marmeladov, in the character of Mikolka the house painter, who falsely confesses to the murders, in Raskolnikov's dream of the "trichinae," which infect the world with madness, and, finally, in Sonia's iconic presence.

NOTES

1. Psychologists, psychiatrists, and literary critics have discovered an array of psychological disorders not only in Raskolnikov but in his creator as well. These include patricidal and matricidal impulses, latent homosexuality, and schizophrenia. For a survey of psychological approaches to Dostoevsky, see Kravchenko, *Dostoevsky and the Psychologists*. The literature on Dostoevsky and psychology is enormous. Sigmund Freud's

"Dostoevsky and Patricide" is perhaps the most well known example of the psychological approach. Freud sees in *The Brothers Karamazov* a masterful depiction of the Oedipus complex, in which the theme of sexual rivalry between fathers and sons is made explicit, as well as the son's wish for their father's death. Freud's essay can be found in the *Collected Papers*, vol. 5, and in many anthologies. For a recent psychoanalytic reading of *The Double*, see Rosenthal's "Dostoevsky's Experiment with Projective Mechanisms and the Theft of Identity in *The Double*," pp. 59–89. Part of the purpose of my study is to put the question of Dostoevsky and psychology into some historical perspective. I will discuss the specific problem of Dostoevsky's epilepsy in the next chapter.

2. For a discussion of *Crime and Punishment* as an ideological novel, see Frank, "The World of Raskolnikov."

3. For a discussion of Dostoevsky's participation in the Petrashevskii and Palm-Durov circles, see Frank, *Dostoevsky: The Seeds of Revolt*, pp. 239–91.

4. See Beshkin, *Idei Fur'e i l'etrashevskogo i Petrashevtsev*, p. 27.

5. Quêtelet's work appeared in Russian under the title *Chelovek i razvitie ego sposolmostei. Opyt obshchestvennoi fiziki* and was published in St. Petersburg in 1865.

6. For a discussion of Zaitsev, see Friedlender, *Realizm Dostoevskogo*, pp. 153–56.

7. Luzhin's "scientific" ethics are the product of Chernyshevskii's "rational egoism" and the utilitarianism of Bentham and John Stuart Mill. See Belov, *Romany Dostoevskogo Prestuplenie i Nakazamie: Kommentarii*, pp. 131–33.

8. As Bakhtin points out, Dostoevsky "ridicules" the physiologistic notion that "tubercles on the brain" cause mental illness. Bakhtin writes that "Dostoevsky constantly and severely criticized mechanistic psychology, both its pragmatic lines based on the concepts of *natural law* and *utility*, and even more its physiological line, which reduced psychology to physiology." (*Problems of Dostoevsky's Poetics*, p. 61).

9. *The Brothers Karamazov* contains a lengthy tirade against the concept of temporary insanity (*PSS* 15: 17-19). According to Mrs. Khokhlakova, "temporary insanity" is "that for which everything is forgiven" (*PSS* 15: 17). For more on Dostoevsky and the insanity defense, see Chapter 6 of the present study.

10. Readers of Dostoevsky's journal *The Epoch* in 1864 would have seen a similar argument made by the young philosopher M. I. Vladislavev, who raised questions about whether the positive methods of physiology, namely, observation and experiment, were adequate for the study of human psychology. The doctors tell us, Vladislavev writes, that "sorrow is a disturbance of the normal condition of the brain." But he argues that we cannot know from this explanation that another person is suffering. That knowledge comes only from our own experience and self-observation, by which we come to connect physical action and facial expression with specific psychological states ("Reformatorskie popytki v psikhologii").

11. See L. M. Lotman, "Romany v Dostoevskogo i Russkaia legenda."

12. See Catteau, *Dostoevsky and the Process of Literary Creation*, pp. 189–90.

13. See Panchenko's "Holy Foolishness as Social Protest," in Likhachev and Panchenko, *"Smekhovoi mir" drevnei rusi*, pp. 139–83, especially Panchenko's discussion of the holy-foolish behavior of Avvakum during his interrogation by the church authorities (pp. 157–58). Avvakum, the leader of the resistance to the reforms introduced by Patriarch Nikon in the seventeenth century, was the first Old Believer.

14. Translation of *Crime and Punishment* by Jessie Coulson (1953), reprinted in Feodor Dostoevsky, *Crime and Punishment*, ed. George Gibian (New York: W. W. Norton, 1975), p. 274.

15. Leslie Johnson identifies an iconic presence in Lizaveta, the sister of the pawnbroker, who, she writes, "functions both for Sonya and Raskolnikov as an icon or image of eternal life." Johnson uses the term "icon" somewhat more metaphorically than

I do, pointing to Lizaveta's kenoticism, for example, in her characterization of Lizaveta as one whose "human image was so transparent to the will of God that Sonya is convinced she will countenance eternal Being" (*The Experience of Time in Crime and Punishment*, p. 113). I will have more to say about icons and their theology in Chapter 6.

16. Peter Brown describes an episode from the *Life* of St. Anthony in which one hermit simply came to sit next to the saint, while the others came to talk to him. The hermit explains his silence in this way: "It is sufficient for me, Father, just to look at you" ("A Dark Age Crisis," pp. 280–81).

17. R. Ia. Kleiman also discusses Porfirii Petrovich's buffoonish qualities in *Skvoznye motivy*, p. 58.

18. For two opposing views of Porfirii, see Bakhtin, *Problems*, pp. 61–62, and Rozenblium, *Trovcheskie dvevniki Dostoevskogo*, pp. 104–5. Bakhtin sees in Porfirii's meetings with Raskolnikov "authentic and remarkable polyphonic dialogues" (p. 62). Bakhtin finds a distinction between Porfirii's use of psychology and its false "legal investigative" use in such characters as Fetinkovich in *The Brothers Karamazov*. Rozenblium, in contrast, finds that there is much of importance that Porfirii does not know about Raskolnikov, and points more to a monologic role for Porfirii.

19. The "spiritual songs" were compiled and published in the early 1860's by P. A. Bessonov under the title *Kaliki perekhozhnie: sbornik stikhov i issledovanie*. For a discussion of Dostoevsky's use of the spiritual songs in *The Brothers Karamazov*, see Chapter 6 of the present study.

DAVID MATUAL

In Defense of the Epilogue of Crime and Punishment

For many years the question of the relevance of the epilogue to the main body of *Crime and Punishment* has been heatedly debated. Some critics have condemned it as all undesirable addition, accusing Dostoevsky of concocting a *deus ex machina* in order to save his hero from a permanent state of alienation and moral corruption. Others, especially those of more recent times, have established a genetic link between the events of the novel proper and the dramatic transformation that begins to take place in Raskolnikov on the last few pages. Though there is still no consensus of opinion, the trend today is decidedly in favor of a more moderate, i.e., more positive judgment.[1] As part of this trend the present article seeks to refute some of the more hostile remarks made against the epilogue by summarizing the principal arguments in its favor and by exploring several approaches to the novel that have until now received rather scant attention.

Some of the most acerbic criticisms of the epilogue seem at times to be inspired by philosophical biases and literary preconceptions that have little to do with the actual text of *Crime and Punishment*. In fact they would hardly deserve any mention at all if they were not found in the writings of such notable figures in the field of Dostoevsky scholarship as Lev Shestov, Mikhail Bakhtin, and Viktor Shklovsky. In his comparative study of Dostoevsky and Nietzsche, for example, Shestov expounds the very Nitzschean thesis that

---

From *Studies in the Novel* 24, no. 1 (Spring 1992). © 1992 by the University of North Texas.

only the most crassly superstitious could accuse Raskolnikov of having committed a crime. According to this argument the hero's only "crime" is that he imagined he was incapable of breaking the law, and his tragedy is the "impossibility of beginning a new and different life."[2] Shestov cannot accept the epilogue because he cannot believe in the moral regeneration it promises. The fact that many details in the novel tend toward a "conversion" either fails to move him or escapes his attention entirely. M. M. Bakhtin, who has written one of the most insightful and widely read and discussed monographs on Dostoevsky's poetics, also rejects the epilogue out of hand. The apparent reason for his disapproval is that it does not support the central contention of his study, viz., that Dostoevsky's imaginative world is "polyphonic," peopled by autonomous beings who speak their own thoughts in their own voices. If his theory is correct, then the epilogue can be seen only as a "monophonic" addendum, an irritating authorial intrusion, and hence a violation of the novel's aesthetic integrity.[3] Bakhtin appears to be operating with certain *a priori* assumptions which give the novel a coloration that is peculiarly his. Any detail that appears to conflict with these assumptions is simply rejected. Such is the fate of the epilogue. Viktor Shklovsky's position is even more dubious. In his view, *all* epilogues, not only that of *Crime and Punishment*, are unnecessary and irrelevant. The characters in them, he claims, are dead as far as the author is concerned, for "epilogues are to novels what life in the other world is to our life."[4] Precisely why he thinks the characters in an epilogue no longer mean anything to the author is never fully clarified. Moreover, he seems not to notice the inappropriateness of his comparison between epilogues and the afterlife in view of the fact that Dostoevsky, like any other Orthodox Christian, believed in a direct and intimate link between life on earth and life hereafter.

More serious strictures against the epilogue are made by Ernest J. Simmons, who argues that it is "neither artistically palatable nor psychologically sound."[5] His objections are thus founded on aesthetic and psychological considerations—the only valid criteria for a sound judgment in this matter. Other critics have followed much the same line. Julius Meier-Graefe, author of one of the earliest and best studies of Dostoevsky, is similarly critical of the psychological preparation, denigrating and dismissing all the events in Raskolnikov's life which might make his spiritual rebirth seem plausible.[6] Jean Drouilly is less categorical but arrives at essentially the same conclusion. In his view Raskolnikov cannot rise up to new life without "denying his intelligence the power to judge."[7] Once again psychology is the decisive factor. Edward Wasiolek also argues against the epilogue, and like the others he too thinks that Dostoevsky has failed to give his readers any compelling evidence that Raskolnikov has the spiritual prerequisites to repudiate his theories (much less his pride) and to direct his life along the path that Sonia is showing him.[8]

A close examination of the epilogue and the rest of the novel, however, reveals that the connections between the two are numerous and pervasive both in a psychological and in an aesthetic sense. There is no reason to believe that in the end Raskolnikov rises to new life spontaneously and without warning. Meier-Graefe's argument to the contrary notwithstanding, there is a wealth of biographical data indicating that the hero is psychologically capable of the extraordinary events that begin in the epilogue. In fact, the possibility of his conversion should be obvious to those who read carefully and without prejudice, allowing themselves to be persuaded by the tendency of Dostoevsky's thought and by the numerous clues that point to the inevitability of a happy conclusion. While it is true that some of the positive events and actions in the hero's life can be interpreted in more than one way (as is so often the case with Dostoevsky), it is also true that much of this material does not admit of ambiguity at all and contributes mightily to the plausibility of the ending.

Raskolnikov's relationships with other people provide the principal psychological evidence that despite his conceit and his exaggerated self-consciousness he is nevertheless able to accept Sonia's love and guidance and thus begin the long spiritual journey she exhorts him to make. Robert Louis Jackson has emphasized the fact that in his dealings with others Raskolnikov's behavior passes through two distinct and seemingly contradictory phases, the one quickly succeeding the other: first, he shows a profound sympathy toward those in need and takes immediate steps to alleviate their suffering; afterwards he feels disgust with himself for having betrayed his intellectual principles.[9] Though strongly opposed to each other, these two aspects of his behavior are nevertheless equally genuine and worthy of any critic's serious consideration. Until recently far too much attention has been given to the second aspect while the first has been largely ignored. Yet Razumikhin, Raskolnikov's only friend and the one who knows him as well as anyone can, speaks of "two opposite personalities" in his friend." On the one hand, he is "generous and kind;" on the other, "cold and unfeeling.[10] We see the more human Raskolnikov in the second chapter of Part One, when he experiences an inexplicable urge to mingle with people after a long period of self-imposed isolation. This pattern is repeated several times in the novel. Often enough his attempts to reestablish contact with the world around him end with a concrete act of charity. Thus he gives twenty copecks to a policeman for the care of a young girl who is harassed by a lecherous middle-aged man. He gives five copecks to a street singer and an organ-grinder. He is very solicitous of Marmeladov and later helps defray the cost of his funeral. He defends Sonia from Luzhin's machinations during the funeral repast and exposes him as a contemptible liar. After confessing his crime, he embraces Sonia and weeps. During his trial we discover that he once supported a sick and impoverished fellow student for six months and that after his friend's death he showed himself equally generous toward the bereaved father. When the father also died, he paid the burial expenses. In addition to all this, he once risked his own life to save two children from a burning building. His sense of compassion, which has been an integral part of his personality since childhood and which is manifested from time to time throughout the novel, is undeniable. It endows his actions with a magnanimity that runs counter to the malevolence of his scheme and the cruelty of his crime.

Before he commits the murder, Raskolnikov's thoughts reflect a curious ambivalence that suggests a certain disenchantment with his plan and even a desire to be delivered from it. After making a trial visit to the pawnbroker in the very first chapter, he feels a profound repugnance. At that moment and at various other times as well he is horrified by the thought of what he intends to do. In his first dream he sees a horse flogged to death by its drunken owner and is appalled by the realization that he will kill the old woman in the same way. As the time of the murder approaches, he begs God to show him how to renounce his plan forever. Still, the plan is carried out and the pawnbroker is brutally killed. She is not the only victim, however. Her childlike half sister Lizaveta returns to the apartment unexpectedly, and Raskolnikov is forced to kill her, too. After this unexpected turn in his fortunes he feels a compelling need to run to the police station and confess his crime. This he does not do, of course, until the end of the novel. Nevertheless, the fact that he leaves so many incriminating traces of his guilt and behaves in a way that arouses suspicion suggests not only that he is willing to turn himself in to the authorities but that he positively wants to be caught. Several critics have explained this desire in terms of Raskolnikov's scheme, claiming that by accepting the punishment for his crime he shows that he is truly one of the "great men" of history, whose suffering is often commensurate with their greatness. Yet it is also possible that in drawing the attention of the police to himself he is seeking a kind of spiritual purgation and renewal much like his thematic double, the peasant Mikolka, who confesses to a crime he has not committed in order to assume the burden of expiation. Maurice Beebe has even suggested that "the ending [of the novel] is artistically and psychologically inevitable because the basic motive of regeneration is the same as the underlying motive for the crime," and that motive, in his view, is the desire to suffer.[11]

Raskolnikov is emphatically not bereft of lofty sentiments, nor does he lack the capacity to change. The most impressive and perhaps least often adduced evidence for this is the abundance of references to his childhood. The theme of childhood is vitally important in the mature Dostoevsky, and *Crime and Punishment* is, among many other things, a novel about children— their degradation, the profanation of their innocence, and the saving power of their presence. We find them throughout the book: in the grimy streets, in the crowded little apartments, and even in the dreams of the principal characters. Raskolnikov's recollections of his own childhood highlight the noble but long suppressed elements of his personality which come to full fruition only in the epilogue. Mention is first made of them at the end of the long letter he receives from his mother, who implores him to recall how he used to pray when his father was still alive. Further reference is made to Raskolnikov's early piety in his first dream. There we see him as a seven-year old boy walking to the cemetery with his father. In a prefatory remark the narrator observes that the boy loved the cemetery church and the old priest who served there. As the events of the dream unfold the child is moved to pity at the sight of the horse dying under the blows of its master and his friends. His pity is mixed with anger as he rushes to strike at those who have committed this barbarous act, which symbolically parallels the act that he himself will commit as an adult. Even after he murders the pawnbroker and her sister, he is haunted by reminiscences of his boyhood piety. In a series of apparently disconnected dreams and musings he recalls a church and the ringing of bells on a Sunday morning. It may well be the very church of which he was so fond as a child.

All the factors mentioned above—Raskolnikov's compassion for the oppressed, his feeling of revulsion toward the crime, and the haunting memories of an early innocence—provide a solid psychological foundation for the changes that begin to stir in him in the epilogue. The evidence indicates that he is and always has been ready for conversion. Indeed, it would be arbitrary to assert that his proud resistance to the lofty impulses within him is the true bedrock of his personality and that everything else is a superstructure imposed on the reader by a tendentious author. The goodness of Raskolnikov's childhood is the core of his being, and his dalliance with social theories is precisely what his mother calls it—"fashionable disbelief" (p. 34).

Yet Raskolnikov is a fallen angel, and his estrangement from God and from all that is good in him is profound and apparently insuperable. The periodic manifestations of kindness in his behavior represent only the *potential* for rebirth. Something more powerful is required to arouse him from his spiritual lethargy and lead him toward the events of the epilogue. The immediate stimulus, of course, is the crime itself, but there is also an external power in the background, variously described as "fate" or "God." In

Parts One and Six especially Raskolnikov seems driven by a supernatural force to which he must ultimately yield. When, for example, he visits the pawnbroker in order to probe the venue of the crime, he manages to slip by several janitors unnoticed. The same sort of luck characterizes the actual commission of the murder as well. Moreover, the hero is not unaware of this strange power guiding him along his way. One day, on the outskirts of the city, he falls asleep in a clump of bushes and has his first dream—the dream that is simultaneously a salubrious reminiscence of childhood and a dire omen of his fate. When he wakes up, he exclaims with relief: "Thank God, it's just a dream" (p. 49). Only seconds later he addresses God once more, now in a tone of despair and entreaty: "God! Can it really be, can it really be that I will actually take an axe, hit her [i.e., the pawnbroker] on the head and shatter her skull? That I will slip in her sticky, warm blood, force the lock, steal, and tremble and hide all covered with blood? With an axe? Lord, can it really be?" (p. 50). He gets up and begins his walk back to the city, now feeling refreshed and free from "the spell, the sorcery, the charm, the obsession" (p. 50). It is not long, however, before he succumbs once more to the power of the mysterious force. Instead of returning directly to his apartment building, he unaccountably takes a circuitous route which leads him through Haymarket Square. There, by chance, he overhears a conversation and learns that the pawnbroker will be alone in her apartment that evening. This news does not encourage him but instead makes him feel "like a condemned man" (p. 52). To this the narrator adds the following comment: "Suddenly with all his being he felt that neither his reason nor his will were free any more and that everything had been settled for good" (p. 52). Raskolnikov now attributes everything to a "predetermination of fate" (p. 50). The information that Lizaveta will leave her sister in the apartment alone in the "seventh hour" (in Russian, "v semom chasu") is later echoed when the hero, rising from sleep, is goaded to action by a cry from the street: "It's long past six!" ("Semoi chas davno," literally: "It's been the seventh hour for a long time," p. 57). The use of the substandard Russian word for "seventh" (*semoi* instead of the usual *sed'moi*) in both cases appears to be more than coincidental: in fact, it tends to fortify the impression that an indefinable force is impelling Raskolnikov to carry out his scheme. The events leading up to and following the murder further confirm this supposition: the axe he is looking for shines at him as if it were trying to catch his eye; a haycart hides him from view as he enters the courtyard of the pawnbroker's apartment building; an apartment on the second floor in which painters had been working only minutes before happens to be vacant when the hero needs a temporary refuge; the axe is returned to its place, and no one notices a thing.

All these coincidences and happenstances can be and often have been explained away as Raskolnikov's rationalizations. According to this point of view, he is merely projecting his own guilt on his surroundings and attributing everything to blind chance. In Part Six, however, the police inspector Porfiry Petrovich lends weight to the hero's assertions that fate has had a hand in his undoing. The only difference in their positions is that Porfiry Petrovich puts everything in a Christian context, preferring to speak of God rather than fate. In their last conversation he tells Raskolnikov: "So, I've been waiting and watching, and God is giving you over to me. You are coming to me" (p. 346). After formally accusing him of murder, he remarks that God has been "waiting" for the crime and has perhaps been saving Raskolnikov for some future feat of spiritual fortitude (p. 351). In other words the inspector believes that God has both permitted the crime and beckoned the criminal to the purgatory of Siberian exile. It is in Siberia that Raskolnikov after months of muted defiance responds to Sonia's love, accepts his ordeal as a necessary catharsis, and proceeds to a new life and a "new story" (p. 422).

If the latent goodness in Raskolnikov's character or the motivating power of the divinity are insufficient to prove that the epilogue is a crucial and even indispensable part of *Crime and Punishment*, the evidence of a purely aesthetic nature is overwhelming. The logic of art is in fact so forceful that the novel seems virtually unthinkable without its concluding chapters. Recurrent numbers, themes, images, symbols, and character traits all point the way to the hero's conversion. Even the chronology of the novel is ordered to this end. Although the events leading up to the crime are often presented out of sequence, there are enough allusions and hints to reconstruct the history of the origin, development, and execution of the hero's plan. We learn, for example, that one year before the murder, Raskolnikov's fiancée, his landlady's daughter, dies of typhus. Three months later, i.e., nine months before the crime, he gives his landlady an IOU for 115 rubles. These early financial difficulties of his are the first clear reference to a condition that steadily worsens and eventually produces in him a state of mind that conceives and justifies a violent crime. In the epilogue we are told that one and a half years have passed since the events of the novel proper and that Raskolnikov has served nine months of his prison sentence in Siberia. In short, the novel encompasses three nine-month periods: 1) from the genesis of the crime to its perpetration, 2) from the confession to the trial and the journey to Siberia, and 3) from the beginning of Raskolnikov's exile to the moment when he embraces Sonia and a new life begins for him. Why does Dostoevsky insist on nine months? The obvious answer is that he is thinking of the period of gestation: it takes nine months for the crime to be "hatched,"

nine months for the punishment to begin, and another nine months for
Raskolnikov to be reborn in the epilogue.

Still another number runs through the fabric of *Crime and Punishment*
and leads inexorably to the concluding scene. That number is four. The
pawnbroker and her half sister, the Marmeladov family, and Raskolnikov's
landlady all live on the fourth floor of their respective buildings. The police
clerk's office is in the fourth room on the fourth floor. There are four children
in the Marmeladov family, and Sonia takes care of the four Kapernaumov
children. The number appears so often that its frequency cannot be
considered fortuitous. On the contrary, it can only be associated with
something of extraordinary significance. Just what that may be becomes more
evident in Part IV, Chapter 4, when Raskolnikov pays his first visit to Sonia.
He is eager to read the biblical story of Lazarus, a story that has weighed
heavily on his mind since his first interview with Porfiry Petrovich. When he
cannot find it, she tells him it is in the "fourth gospel" (i.e., the gospel
according to John) and reads it herself: "Martha, the sister of the dead man,
said to him: Lord, there is a stench already, for he has been in the grave *four*
days [author's italics]" (p. 251). It is in the emphasis Sonia gives to the word
"four" that we must look for the answer to the riddle of the number. But the
first thing to be noted is that in the Russian version of the gospel text the word
corresponding to "grave" is *grob*. In spoken Russian *grob* normally means
"coffin," an object with which Sonia has already compared Raskolnikov's tiny
room. In reading the biblical story she plainly regards Raskolnikov as a
contemporary Lazarus who has been lying in his grave for four days
(approximately four days have passed since the murder) and who is destined
to be raised from the dead and called forth to new life. In short, Dostoevsky
uses the number four to underscore the importance of this episode and to
pave the way for the long delayed revival of his hero in the epilogue.

In addition to the numerical patterns there is still another motif which
argues cogently in favor of the epilogue. In his highly instructive article on
recurrent traditional imagery in *Crime and Punishment* George Gibian singles
out water and vegetation and their obvious connection with life itself as
central motifs in the novel.[12] In Raskolnikov's ambience water and greenery
are resuscitating and curative. When he goes to the islands on the outskirts
of the arid, stifling city, he admires the flowers and shrubs and watches
children playing in a garden. He falls asleep in the bushes and there has the
first dream of the novel. Later, on his way to the pawnbroker's apartment, he
thinks not about the murder he will soon commit but about the beauty of the
fountains and parks he sees all around him. His thoughts are only an echo of
a dream he had had before leaving his room. The description of that dream,

which foreshadows the dramatic finale of the epilogue, is worth quoting in
its entirety:

> He kept daydreaming, and what strange daydreams [*grezy*] they
> were. Most often he imagined that he was somewhere in Africa,
> in Egypt, at some oasis. A caravan was resting. Camels were lying
> peacefully. Round about grew a solid circle of palm trees.
> Everybody was having dinner. But he kept drinking water,
> directly from a brook which flowed and gurgled there beside him.
> And it was so cool, and the wonderful, wonderful cold blue water
> coursed over the multi-colored rocks and the clean sand speckled
> with gold. (p. 56)

This is only one of several dreams, semi-conscious imaginings, or desultory
reveries reported in the novel. As one of the shortest it would seem to be
relatively unimportant. But taken in conjunction with the scene that
immediately precedes Raskolnikov's embrace of Sonia in the epilogue, it
becomes one of the major passages in the novel since its imagery clearly
foreshadows the hero's conversion. Before he is joined by Sonia, Raskolnikov
is sitting on the bank of a "broad and desolate river" (p. 421). The word
"desolate" is especially significant because its Russian equivalent (*pustvnnyi*)
is directly derived from the noun meaning "desert" or "wilderness"
(*pustynia*). Once again, as in the imaginary oasis, Raskolnikov finds himself
next to a body of water in the midst of a wilderness. From the other shore he
hears the singing of nomads who live in a world where "time itself had stood
still just as if the age of Abraham and his flocks had not yet passed" (p. 421).
The nomads correspond to the caravan and the camels of the oasis. As
Raskolnikov views the scene, his thoughts dissolve into daydreams (*grezy*),
and a vague longing torments him. At that moment Sonia sits down beside
him, and the miraculous moment toward which the entire novel is directed
finally arrives.

Although the epilogue has struck many excellent critics as contrived
and extraneous, it emerges from a thorough examination as an essential
component of *Crime and Punishment*. Raskolnikov is psychologically capable
of the metamorphosis he is destined to undergo. He is impelled by a
preternatural force to conceive, commit, and confess the crime.
Furthermore, the numerical motifs, the Lazarus theme, and the nature
imagery of the novel all prepare the reader for the concluding scene. The
epilogue is the inevitable result of all that precedes it and is, in Robert Louis
Jackson's felicitous phrase, the "transformation of ends into beginnings."[13]

NOTES

1. See, for example, Donald Fiene, "Raskolnikov and Abraham: A Further Contribution to a Defense of the Epilogue of *Crime and Punishment*," *Bulletin of the International Dostoevsky Society* 9 (1979): 32–35: George A. Panichas, *The Burden of Vision: Dostoevsky's Spiritual Art* (Chicago: Gateway Editions, 1985): David Palumbo, "Coincidence, Irony, and the Theme of the Fortunate Fall in *Crime and Punishment*," *University of Dayton Review* 18, (1987): 27–35.

2. Lev Shestov, *Dostoevsky i Nitshe* (Berlin: Skify, 1923), pp. 71–72.

3. M.M. Bakhtin, *Problemy poetiki Dostoevskogo*, 3rd ed. (Moscow: Khudozhestvennaia literatura, 1972), p. 155.

4. Viktor Shklovsky, *Za i protiv: zametki o Dostoevskom* (Moscow: Sovetskii pisatel', 1957), p. 185.

5. Ernest J. Simmons, *Dostoevsky: The Making of a Novelist* (New York: Vintage, 1962), p. 153.

6. Julius Meier-Graefe. *Dostojewski der Dichter* (Berlin: Ernst Rowahlt Verlag, 1926), p. 153.

7. Jean Drouilly, *La Pensée politique et religieuse de F. M. Dostoïevski* (Paris: Librairie des Cinq Continents, 1971), p. 293.

8. Edward Wasiolek, "On the Structure of *Crime and Punishment*," *PMLA* 74 (1959): 135.

9. Robert Louis Jackson, "Philosophical Pro and Contra in Part One of *Crime and Punishment*," *Twentieth Century Interpretations of Crime and Punishment* (Englewood Cliffs: Prentice-Hall, 1974), p. 27.

10. F. M. Dostoevsky, *Polnoe sobranie sochinenii*, 30 vols., ed. V. G. Bazanov et al (Leningrad: Nauka, 1972–90), 4:165. All subsequent references to *Crime and Punishment* pertain to this edition and will be given parenthetically in the text. All translations are mine.

11. Maurice Beebe, "The Three Motives of Raskolnikov: A Reinterpretation of *Crime and Punishment*," *College English* 17 (1955): 151.

12. George Gibian. "Traditional Symbolism in *Crime and Punishment*," *PMLA* 70 (1955): 991–92.

13. Robert Louis Jackson, "Introduction: The Clumsy White Flower," *Twentieth Century Interpretations of Crime and Punishment*, pp. 6–7.

LIZA KNAPP

The Resurrection from Inertia in Crime and Punishment

MECHANICS, MATHEMATICS, MURDER

In *Crime and Punishment*, Dostoevsky dramatizes the conviction voiced in the diary entry written at the time of his first wife's death—that "inertia" and "the mechanics of matter" result in death (20:175): Raskolnikov, acting under the influence of mechanistic principles, commits murder. The link between deterministic natural law and death, which appeared theoretical or metaphorical in the diary entry, becomes actual and violent. In *Crime and Punishment* Dostoevsky also seeks to illustrate the conviction (voiced in the diary entry) that the "annihilation of inertia" results in eternal life: the murderer, Raskolnikov, is liberated from mechanical determinism and begins a new life. In *Crime and Punishment*, the earthly reversal of the laws of nature and the annihilation of inertia are brought about by faith and love, the salvific forces alluded to in Dostoevsky's diary entry and most of his fictional works but emerging triumphant in few of them. The novel thus depicts a dramatic opposition between mechanical laws and resurrection, an opposition which becomes more explicit as the novel progresses.

Dostoevsky insists on the connection between mechanics and death by using mechanical imagery to describe Raskolnikov's behavior prior to and during the murder. Dostoevsky writes, for example, that Raskolnikov performed the act "barely sentient and almost without effort, almost

From *The Annihilation of Inertia: Dostoevsky and Metaphysics.* © 1996 by Northwestern University Press.

mechanically [*mashinal'no*]" (6:63). While such details communicate the calculating, cold-blooded nature of Raskolnikov's act, they also serve to imply that Raskolnikov had lost what in the physics of the time was termed "vital force": he had become inertial matter, whose behavior is determined by mechanical law. In describing Raskolnikov's state of mind in the period leading up to the murder, Dostoevsky depicts him as passive and devoid of will.[1] Once Raskolnikov's original plan was conceived, the rest followed mechanically, according to logic.[2] Necessity and mechanics seem to determine Raskolnikov's behavior; he acts "as if someone compelled him and drew him toward it" (6:58). Dostoevsky expands on this notion by developing the following simile: "The last day, having dawned so accidentally, deciding everything at once, had an almost totally mechanical effect on him: it was as though someone had taken him by the hand and was dragging him behind, irresistibly, blindly, with unnatural strength, without objections. It was as if part of his clothing had fallen into the wheel of a machine and [the wheel] was starting to pull him into [the machine]"[3] (6:58). This image of a machine suggests that the circumstances that "compelled" Raskolnikov to murder are related to the realm of mechanics, at least metaphorically. Dostoevsky's strategy in using this mechanical imagery conditions the reader to accept the important connection between death and mechanics—which Dostoevsky spelled out for himself in his diary entry of 16 April 1864 and which he spends much of the rest of *Crime and Punishment* developing.

The association of violent death and machines can also be seen in the works of Victor Hugo. In *Notre Dame de Paris*, the evil priest who murders Phoebus (the man Esmeralda loves) and ultimately destroys Esmeralda's life speaks of fate having taken Esmeralda and "delivered her into the terrible wheelworks [*rouage*] of the machine that [he] had constructed in darkness."[4] In *The Last Day of a Condemned Man*, the hero, having commented to himself on the mechanical (or, more literally, machinelike: he speaks of his eyes fixing *machinalement*) nature of his perceptions as he approaches death, carries the metaphor even further, concluding that he "had become a machine like the carriage [carrying him from one place of imprisonment to another as he awaits his death]."[5] Dostoevsky incorporated, along with other aspects of Hugo's depiction of death, the image of the machine into his own visions of death.[6]

The significance of Dostoevsky's machine imagery was appreciated by Tolstoy, who was to refer to Raskolnikov's acting "like a machine" in his 1890 essay "Why People Stupefy Themselves," a fact that has been discussed by Robert Louis Jackson.[7] According to Tolstoy, man consists of two beings, one sensual, the other spiritual. The sensual being "moves as a wound-up machine moves," whereas the spiritual being judges the activity of the sensual being. Tolstoy sees Raskolnikov's mechanical murder as the result of his spiritual side having been stifled—a process that came about not through dramatic decisions but as a result of a series of "inchmeal" inner changes. He writes:

> Raskolnikov's true life transpired not when he killed the old woman or her sister. Killing the old woman and especially her sister, he was not living true life, but rather *was acting like a machine*, he did what he could not help but do: he let out the energy he had already been charged with. One old lady was dead, the other was there in front of him and the ax was there in his hand.
>
> Raskolnikov's true life took place not when he saw the sister of the old woman but rather when he hadn't yet killed a single old lady, hadn't intruded into an apartment for the sake of murder, didn't have the ax in his hands, didn't have the loop in his coat on which he hung it—[it took place] when he wasn't even thinking about the old woman but was lying home on his couch and not pondering the old woman at all or even whether or not it's allowed for the will of one man to erase from the face of the earth a useless and harmful other person, but rather was pondering whether or not he ought to live in Petersburg, whether or not he ought to take money from his mother and still other questions having nothing whatsoever to do with the old lady. And was it not then, in this sphere totally separate from animalistic activity, that the questions about whether or not to kill the old woman were decided? These questions were decided not when he, having killed one old lady, stood with an ax before the other but rather when he was not acting but only thinking, when nothing but his consciousness was working and when inchmeal changes were taking place in his consciousness. And it's at such a point that absolute clarity of thought is most crucial to making a correct decision on any question that arises, it's at such a point that one glass of beer, one cigarette smoked can impede making a decision on some question, can put off a decision, can stifle the voice of conscience, influence the decision in favor of the lower, animalistic nature, as was the case with Raskolnikov.[8] (my emphasis)

Tolstoy's basic understanding of Raskolnikov's mechanical behavior resembles Dostoevsky's in the sense that both writers believe such machinelike behavior to result from a "stifling" of "the voice of conscience." Both Tolstoy and Dostoevsky regard the murder of the pawnbroker as the mechanically determined outcome of a series of mental operations that began long before the murder was conceived and that allowed Raskolnikov to "stifle the voice of conscience."

Another evaluation of Raskolnikov's murderous behavior is offered in the novel by Porfiry Petrovich, who attributes it to Raskolnikov's excessive reliance on the mind, which he sees partly as a function of youth. He tells Raskolnikov: "you will have to forgive me, an old man, for this, but you, Rodion Romanovich, are still young, that is, in your first youth, and consequently you value the human mind above all else, following the example of all youth. The playful keenness of the mind and the abstract conclusions of reason seduce you" (6:263). In the notebooks, Porfiry went further in pointing out why Raskolnikov's rationalism falls short: "Your ideas are most clever but that's the trouble: all this would have been fine if man were like a machine or if, say, he operated solely on reason" (7:183). Excessive reliance on the mind reduces human existence to a science and man to a machine.

In having Raskolnikov murder "in a machinelike way" and under the influence of the conviction that man is "like a machine," Dostoevsky challenges the legacy of Descartes. Descartes's assertion that animals are machines prompted a discussion by Strakhov in his "Letters about Organic Life."[9] As Strakhov notes, Descartes stopped short of calling man a machine, but his desire to see animals as machines results, like the materialists' denial of the human soul, "from a striving to transform nature into naked mechanics."[10] The French materialists of the eighteenth century carried Descartes's vision to the ultimate limit, most notably, La Mettrie in his *Man-Machine* [*L'Homme-machine*].[11] In a discussion of Descartes, whom he admires for his logical consistency, if disapproving of his conclusions, Strakhov writes:

> Stories are told of how Descartes had two beloved dogs and he would often amuse himself by beating them since he assumed them to have no real sensations and consequently [*sledovatel'no*] he considered their plaintive yelping to be just as innocent a sound as those sounds extracted from some musical instrument.
>
> Whether this story is true or not, the point is that it is completely in accordance with the teaching of Descartes.[12]

Strakhov then goes on to compare and contrast the materialists to Descartes, noting that Descartes's view that animals are machines is "of course ... an insignificant matter in comparison to the denial of the spirituality of man [by the materialists]."[13] Strakhov, concerned as he is with logical consistency (both his own and that of others), seems dismissive of the logical consequences for Descartes's dogs.

The beating of animals figures in the dream Raskolnikov has in which, as a child, he witnessed a drunken peasant beating a horse to death (6:4650). The young Raskolnikov was filled with horror at what the peasant was doing to the horse and pity for the horse, which he embraced and kissed. Here again Dostoevsky depicts someone face-to-face with a cadaver, albeit that of an animal. Although it has been suggested that this dream reflects Dostoevsky's own experience of witnessing a horse being beaten, as well as treatments of this theme in the poetry of Nekrasov and periodicals of the day (7:368–69), the dream may also be a response to the story of Descartes beating his dogs, highlighted by Strakhov in his "Letters on Organic Life." The drunken peasant may seem an unlikely double for Descartes; yet, like Descartes, he justifies his act on the grounds that the horse is his "property."

Raskolnikov emerges from the dream horrified that he too could beat a living being:

> "My God!" he exclaimed, "can it be, can it be that I will really take an ax and start to beat her on the head.... Good Lord, is it possible? ... No, I will not be able to bear it, no! Even if there are no uncertainties in all my calculations [regarding his murder plan], even if all has been reckoned in the past month so that it is as clear as day, as correct as arithmetic. Good Lord! Why even so I cannot make myself do it!" (6:50)

Raskolnikov here expresses his horror at the act he has been contemplating or, more accurately, calculating. This passage clearly shows the dichotomy in Raskolnikov between his spiritual side (expressed in his appeals to God, in his horror at the notion of spilling blood) and his intellectual side (expressed in terms of calculations and indirect appeals to Descartes.) The references to the mathematics of the murder again evoke the Cartesian aspect of the act he contemplates. Not only will he be imitating Descartes in beating another living being, but his rationale for beating is arrived at through Cartesian methods.[14]

Descartes, in the view Herzen expresses of him in his "Letters on the Study of Nature," was "a completely mathematical and abstract mind."[15] All of the mental qualities that figure negatively in *Crime and Punishment* are those Descartes was thought to embody. (Herzen, noting Bacon's understanding of "the importance mathematics in the study of natural sciences," credits him with an awareness of the "danger of mathematics overwhelming other aspects [of science]." Even Strakhov argues in his "Letters about Organic Life" that a mathematical "means of understanding" is not right because "nothing in the world unfolds according to arithmetic; nothing represents a simple sum."[16]

In the novel and particularly in its notebooks, Dostoevsky terms Raskolnikov's rationale for the murder "arithmetic" and "mathematics," suggesting the decision to murder to be the result of a mental calculus that does not take "life" into account.[17] For example, at one point in the notebooks, an interlocutor tells Raskolnikov (in reference to his published article, which presents a theory to justify certain crimes): "Once you've lived a bit, you'll see that there's more to a crime than arithmetic. Here you have arithmetic, and there is life" (7:93). Contributing to make Raskolnikov a murderer were his Cartesian reliance on the mind, abstract reason and mathematics, and his application of mathematics to other realms.

The mathematicization of human existence makes life a living death, as is documented by several of the notebook entries, which present "arithmetic" as antithetical to life. (The underground man arrives at a similar insight when he declares twice two is four to be "the beginning of death" [5:118–19].) When Dostoevsky writes that "arithmetic destroys," he speaks metaphorically, but when he has Raskolnikov, under the influence of mathematical reasoning, destroy another life, the metaphor is realized (7:134). Similarly, Raskolnikov's "machinelike" behavior during the murder is more than a descriptive metaphor; it implies that Raskolnikov's abstract reason has succeeded in reducing him to a machine lacking "vital force."

When Dostoevsky presents the machine as a sinister, life-destroying force, his protest against mechanics stems from his religious views of human freedom. But also contributing to Dostoevsky's negative use of the image of the machine were its eighteenth-century associations with deism and a vision of the universe as a machine created by a god who had then turned his back on it. The subsequent industrialization of Europe made the machine a symbol, and agent, of material progress and of the promise of increased economic welfare. Dostoevsky vilifies the machine because it operates on a mechanical (deterministic) principle, but also because it symbolized philosophical outlooks and instrumented Western social developments he mistrusted.

In Dostoevsky's conception, Raskolnikov's mental operations were influenced by new social theories, with which he had become acquainted since moving to Petersburg. It was under their spell that he developed his murderous plan. These new social theories, associated with positivism and materialism, arose when physics, mechanics and mathematics were applied to the social sciences in the attempt to order human life in terms of laws analogous to those discovered by Newton.[18] In an unsigned review of the Russian translation of George Henry Lewes's *Physiology of the Common Life*, published in Dostoevsky's *Time*, Lewes is praised for militating against the practice of applying the ideas and methods of one branch of learning to another.[19] The reviewer quotes the following passage from Lewes:

> There is one basic law the violation of which cannot go unpunished and which, nevertheless, is constantly violated in our attempts to reach the truth. This law consists of the following: *one should never try to solve the problems of one science by means of a set of concepts that are exclusively characteristic of another.*
>
> There is one set of concepts characteristic only of physics, another belonging to chemistry, a third to physiology, a fourth to psychology, and a fifth is appropriate to the social sciences. Although all these sciences are closely linked, nevertheless each has its own independent domain and that independence must be.[20]

In the passage cited in the review, Lewes goes on to note that the laws of physics and chemistry, while they may be used to explain some aspects of life, leave much unexplained; "in addition to these laws, and above them, stand the particular laws of life, which can be deduced neither from the laws of physics, nor from the laws of chemistry." Lewes comes across as a champion of "vital life." Perhaps more than coincidentally, Marmeladov mentions to Raskolnikov that Sonya read with great interest Lewes's *Physiology of the Common Life*, thanks to Lebeziatnikov, the fervent socialist who is the Marmeladovs' neighbor and Luzhin's ward (6:16). More broadly, *Crime and Punishment* illustrates the very notion suggested by Lewes in the passage quoted above: that attempts to apply the principles and methods of one form of learning to another (or to life itself) "never remain unpunished."

Many of the new social and psychological theories amounted to attempts to create a new "social physics" and a new "mechanics of passions."[21] In his "Letter about Organic Life," Strakhov comments on this desire "to apply, regardless of the consequences, the methods used by Newton for strictly mechanical phenomena to the phenomena of life."[22] For example, Charles Fourier, whose teachings became known to Dostoevsky while he was associated with the Petrashevsky group, believed that he had discovered the social and behavioral corollaries of Newton's physical laws.[23] Fourier believed in a "unity of system of movement for the material world and the spiritual world," arguing the human passions were governed by gravitational attraction such as that discovered by Newton for the physical world.[24] Fourier believed that "it is necessary for God to act in accordance with mathematics in moving and modifying matter. Otherwise he would be arbitrary in his own eyes as well as in ours. But if God submits to mathematical rules that he cannot change, he finds in doing so both his glory and his interest."[25] Various other social thinkers more or less self-consciously applied the methods of physics and mathematics to human psychology and society.

In using metaphorical references to mechanics to describe behavior inspired by these new theories, Dostoevsky hints at the mechanical models on which these theories were based. Dostoevsky was more direct in his notebooks, which include statements such as "the main idea of socialism is *mechanism*" and "[the socialists] are wild about the notion that man himself is nothing more than mechanics" (7:161). Lumped together with "socialism" in Dostoevsky's mind were laissez-faire capitalism, Malthusian attitudes toward population control, and in general any theory invoking intellectual constructs such as the good of the many, progress, and so forth, to stifle innate moral precepts such as love of one's neighbor and the commandment not to kill.

Dostoevsky shows Raskolnikov alternating between, on the one hand, spontaneous behavior inspired by compassion and, on the other, acts stemming from the calculated and rational application of new social scientific theory to life. For example, in one of the early scenes of the novel, when he chances on a young woman who is drunk and being pursued by a man intent on harming her, Raskolnikov impulsively attempts to help her. (He is moved to help partly because in his mind he identifies her with Sonya, whose fate he has just heard from Marmeladov. Similarly, he identifies the man stalking her with Svidrigailov, who had taken advantage of his sister Dunya, as he has recently learned in a letter.) Pondering the incident afterwards, Raskolnikov has second thoughts about his attempts to help (which included giving money for her ride home), and reverts to a fatalistic determinism about her life. Imagining that the young girl will inevitably become a prostitute, he rationalizes this, appealing to social science:

> So be it! This is the way things are meant to be, or so it is said. A certain percentage, it is said, is supposed to fall by the wayside every year ... somewhere ... let them go to the devil, in order to keep things fresh for the rest and not bother them. A percentage! What truly splendid wording they use: they make it so comforting, so scientific. They say: "a percentage" and that means there's nothing to worry about. And if it were worded differently, well then ... it would perhaps be more worrisome ... (6:43)

In speculating about a "percentage" of the population becoming prostitutes, Raskolnikov refers to the theories of Adolphe Quetelet, as presented in his *Treatise on Man and the Development of his Faculties, or Essay on Social Physics* [*Sur l'homme et le développement de ses facultés, ou essai de physique sociale*] (1835), which was translated into Russian in 1865 and debated in the press of the time.[26] As the second part of the title implies, this work attempts to reduce human existence to physics. Following Quetelet's statistical methods, one could predict the percentage of the population that would murder, turn to prostitution, marry, divorce, commit suicide, and so on. In the context of Quetelet's "social physics," crime is regarded as an unavoidable fact of life. When Raskolnikov applies this social theory to the young woman he met on the street, he reasons that there is no point in helping her, since her fate had already been determined statistically by the laws of social physics. Dostoevsky thus demonstrates how the laws of social physics conflict with Christ's commandment to love one's neighbor.

Raskolnikov's murder of the pawnbroker is likewise based on a kind of social physics or mathematics. As Raskolnikov is first contemplating this crime, he overhears a conversation between two students who happen to be considering the very same application of mathematical logic to human lives, as they argue that the murder of the pawnbroker would be justified on the grounds of the good of the many that could result from the distribution of the money she has been selfishly hoarding: "Kill her and take her money in order to use it to dedicate oneself to the service of humanity and the common weal: what do you think, can't a thousand good deeds make up for one tiny little crime? For one life, a thousand lives saved from corruption and decay. One death and a hundred lives in exchange, why it's a matter of arithmetic!" (6:54). The murder of the pawnbroker is thus reduced to a mathematical formula: $1 < 100$ (or $1 < 1000$). Social physics inverts the lessons of the Gospels, which are not ruled by arithmetic logic: in Dostoevsky's beloved parable of the lost sheep, "What man of you, having a hundred sheep, if he has lost one of them, does not leave the ninety-nine in the wilderness, and go after the one which is lost, until he finds it?" (Luke 15:4).

Raskolnikov develops his own social physics in his article "About Crime," which is discussed by Raskolnikov, Porfiry Petrovich, and Razumikhin at the end of the third part of the novel. In his article, Raskolnikov argues that humanity is divided into two categories, ordinary men and extraordinary men; the latter have the right to commit crimes, including murder. This division follows from a "law of nature" that is as yet unknown but may still be discovered (6:202). As historical examples of "extraordinary men" who would have had the right, and would even have been duty-bound, to commit whatever crimes were necessary in order to

make their ideas known to the world, Raskolnikov cites Kepler and Newton.
He then goes on to note that the great law-givers, such as Lycurgus, Solon,
Mohammed, and Napoleon, were all criminal, spilling great amounts of
blood in order to ensure that their "new law" replaced, and destroyed, the
old. Dostoevsky's association of Newton with obvious "bloodspillers" (6:200)
such as Napoleon is striking; in *Crime and Punishment*, Dostoevsky seems
bent on showing that the indiscriminate application of Newton's "new
covenant" could lead to the spilling of blood.[27]

Raskolnikov's "extraordinary man" theory formalizes the Napoleonic
complex in the Russian context. What it means to be a Napoleon was defined
for Russians by Pushkin in *Eugene Onegin* when he wrote:[28]

Мы почитаем всех нулями
А единицами—себя.
Мы все глядим в Наполеоны;
Двуногих тварей миллионы
Для нас орудие одно;

[We deem all people zeroes
And ourselves units.
We all expect to be Napoleons;
The millions of two-legged creatures
For us are only tools;]

Although the theories of social physics directly and indirectly referred to
within *Crime and Punishment* involve more complex mathematical operations
(percentages, calculations about the welfare of a hundred being worth one
life), they are but variations on Pushkin's definition of Napoleonic behavior.
Crime and Punishment explores the tragic consequences of the Napoleonic
tendency to regard other people as zeroes.

Crime and Punishment also dramatizes the protest against the rule of
"social" laws voiced in Odoevsky's *Russian Nights*. In discussing advances in
various realms (mathematics, physics, chemistry, astronomy), one of
Odoevsky's characters protests, asking "Why are crime and misfortune
considered a necessary element of the mathematical formula of society?"[29]
At another point, the new view that "the happiness of all is impossible; all
that is possible is the happiness of the greatest number" is bemoaned:
"people are taken for mathematical ciphers; equations and computations are
worked through, everything is predicted, everything is reckoned; but one
thing is forgotten—forgotten is the profound idea, which has miraculously
survived only in the expressions of our ancestors: the happiness of *one* and

all."[30] *Crime and Punishment* dramatizes this same conflict between utilitarian social physics and traditional Christian values and thus carries on the tradition of Odoevsky (whom Dostoevsky knew and admired before his exile).

In *Crime and Punishment*, Raskolnikov's friend Razumikhin opposes the new social physics. If Razumikhin stands for any ideology, it is one that holds that one never knows what human beings will do. He rejects all social theory on the grounds that it tends to mechanize human existence, ignoring intractable human nature and the "living soul":

> Nature is not taken into account, nature is banished, nature doesn't figure in! What they have is not humanity, having developed by a historical, living means to the end, finally transforming on its own into a normal society; on the contrary what they have is a social system, coming out of somebody's mathematical brain, and it will immediately put all humanity in order and make it righteous and sinless in a flash, sooner than any living process and without any historical or living means! This is why they so instinctively dislike history: "it contains nothing but disorder and stupidity"—and everything is attributed simply to stupidity! But what they have, although it stinks of corpses, you can make it out of rubber—and, what's more, it's not living, it's without a will, it's servile, it won't revolt. (6:197)

In this outburst, made in front of Raskolnikov and Porfiry Petrovich, Razumikhin outlines the basic opposition between mechanics and life. (This dichotomy had previously been delineated by the underground man.) Razumikhin champions the "living soul" and rejects social physics. He does so not simply on the grounds that it denies free will, but also on the grounds that it is simplistic. He declares: "With logic alone you can't skip over nature! Logic foresees three cases whereas a million exist! Cut out the whole million and reduce everything to a question of comfort!" (6:197). What Razumikhin also objects to in contemporary social theory is its assumption that the supreme goal of human existence lies in obtaining material comfort. Dostoevsky presents Razumikhin as someone who looks after other people, but lives in near poverty. We are told, for example, that he goes without heat for whole winters, claiming that he sleeps better that way. Material comfort is of little concern to Razumikhin, who seems to embody what Dostoevsky referred to as the "idea of the novel" and the essence of Orthodoxy—the notion that "there's no happiness in comfort" (7:154).[31]

If Razumikhin stands as the ideological opponent of socialism and its concern with material comfort, then Pyotr Pyotrovich Luzhin stands as the major exponent of these principles. Luzhin adheres to socialist ideals insofar as they advance his own cause and promote his own material well-being and his own egotistical self-assertion. (His views are more akin to "rational egoism" and "laissez-faire capitalism" than socialism; within the novel, however, Dostoevsky does not distinguish between such theories, since all of them ultimately mechanize and mathematicize human life and deny the "living soul.") In explaining his stance to Raskolnikov, Luzhin touts what he refers to as "new ideas" that have replaced the "dreamy and romantic ones of the past" (6:115). These new ideas will lead to progress—"progress, if only in the name of science and economic truth" (6:116). But, as his behavior reveals, Luzhin's adherence to these new social ideas has allowed him to "stifle the voice of conscience," to use Tolstoy's phrase; or to ignore "the living soul," to use Razumikhin's. He appeals to the new social physics to justify having replaced love of neighbor with love of self:

> If, for example, I have been told up until now: "Love [your neighbor]," and I have loved, well what has come of it? ... What's come of it is that I tore my cloak in two, shared it with my neighbor and both of us have been left half naked, in accordance with the Russian proverb: "If you run after several hares at once, you won't catch any." Science, on the other hand, says: love yourself before all others, for everything on earth is founded on personal interest. If you love yourself alone, then you manage your affairs properly and profitably and your cloak will remain whole. Economic truth indeed adds that the more private enterprises prospering in society, the more, so to speak, whole cloaks there are, the more firm bases society will have and the better off the public's affairs will be. Consequently, acquiring solely and exclusively for myself, I am in fact at the same time as if acquiring for all and leading towards my neighbors' receiving something more than a torn cloak. And not merely from private individual munificence but as a result of a general increase in prosperity. (6:116)

Claiming Christ's covenant to have been deficient, Luzhin embraces the new covenant of Adam Smith, Jeremy Bentham, Auguste Comte, and Nikolai Chernyshevsky,[32] which promotes self-assertive, inertial behavior.

When he hears Luzhin's speech, Raskolnikov is outraged, partly because he recognizes points of similarity between Luzhin's rationale for egoism and his own theorizing. Thus he tells Luzhin: "If you follow through on the consequences of what you were just preaching, the result will be that it is permissible to murder people" (6:118). In this polemical, perhaps hyperbolic, verbal gesture, Raskolnikov calls attention to the fact that the new social covenant, in condoning Napoleonic behavior, results in other people being treated as zeroes. As the plot develops, Luzhin proves that he will trample on others to further his own interests. In a calculated attempt to reinstate his broken engagement to Raskolnikov's sister Dunya, he wrongs Sonya by making her look like a thief. The shame inflicted on Sonya precipitates the death of Katerina Ivanovna, thus making Luzhin indirectly responsible for her death.

SVIDRIGAILOV, SONYA, AND THE GOSPELS

Two characters in the novel, Svidrigailov and Sonya, appear, for opposite reasons, to transcend the new social physics. It is to them that Raskolnikov is ultimately drawn in his attempt to escape from social physics. Although Sonya is treated as a "zero" by most people, and although she is a statistic for Quetelet's percentages, and although she has had some limited exposure to the new science, having read and enjoyed Lewes's *Physiology of the Common Life* (6:16), Sonya embodies Christ's covenant. Svidrigailov, in contrast, adheres to no covenant. Although, in the final version of the novel, Svidrigailov does not explicitly state his views on socialism, Dostoevsky made implicit in his behavior the ideas of the following passage from the notebooks for the novel, in which Svidrigailov declares:

> If I were a socialist, then, of course, I would remain alive. I would remain alive because I'd have something to do—there's no group with stronger conviction than the socialists. And in life the most important thing is conviction. Just go and try to dissuade one of them. For indeed he senses that he's losing all his vital material. For him the most important thing is conviction. What conviction? the main idea of socialism is *mechanization*. There man becomes man by means of mechanics. There are rules for everything. The man himself is eliminated. They've taken away the living soul. Of course, people say, they're progressives! Good Lord! If that's progress, then what is *kitaishchina*![33]
>
> Socialism is the despair of ever putting human existence in order. They ordered it by means of despotism and say that that's freedom!
>
> And lest man start to get notions of grandeur, they're terribly fond of the notion that man himself is nothing more than mechanics. (7:161)

Whereas the socialists' lives are ruled by mechanical law—they have "rules for everything"—for Svidrigailov there appear to be no rules. He appears to embody the principle of "everything is allowed." But although he may reject all social, ethical, and temporal laws, he still remains subject to one type of law: natural law. Svidrigailov's whole existence is a struggle against the laws of nature. Like the socialists, he "senses that he's losing all his vital material," but, lacking any conviction, he does not console himself with the notion that humanity is progressing while he personally is perishing. Aware that he can neither escape their jurisdiction nor transcend them, Svidrigailov tries to beat the laws of nature at their own game.

In the course of the novel, Svidrigailov evinces an interest in two ventures: an expedition to the North Pole and going up with Berg in a balloon over Petersburg's parade grounds. He does not believe in the spiritual progress of mankind, but the technological advances that make such ventures possible hold a fascination for him. What both trips represent, aside from their upward direction, is a desire to triumph over the laws of nature. Going up in a hot-air balloon defies the law of gravity; going to the North Pole implies mastery of the planet. Yet the two means contemplated by Svidrigailov of rising above earthly existence depend on the same laws of nature that govern and restrict earthly existence to begin with. Both means are mechanical; there is nothing supernatural, miraculous, or law-of-nature-defying about them.

The trips to the North Pole and over Petersburg are passing fancies; Svidrigailov's main activity is *razvrat*: debauchery and corruption. When Raskolnikov asks him, in their last interview, "So the only thing you have left to live for is debauchery?" Svidrigailov explains that "in this debauchery, at least, there's something constant, founded on nature and not subject to fantasy, something abiding like an eternally glowing coal in the blood" (6:359). Debauchery and corruption are for Svidrigailov what money is to Luzhin: a perverted means of transcendence. Both men seek something eternal that is exempt from the natural law of the transience of existence. The "sensualist" Svidrigailov is aware of the limitations inherent in his flesh—of the fact that all flesh is subject to the natural law of decay, to the φθορά referred to by Saint Paul in Romans 8:21. His willing surrender to debauchery implies an element of triumph. By enacting his own corruption, he attempts to preempt the laws of nature, whose eventual effect would be death, the ultimate form of decay. His attempt to achieve some form of transcendence through his surrender to sensualism and consequently to the laws of nature resembles his attempt to rise above earthly existence by means of physics and technology.

According to Orthodox theology, man became subject to the laws of nature, implying death and decay, with his fall into sin.[34] The spiritual corruption spread by Svidrigailov (he is reputed to have caused several deaths) is so vile that it causes the physical decay of others as well as of himself; his final dream about the child-seductress also substantiates this notion (6:392–93). From this viewpoint, Svidrigailov's sinful behavior amounts to a spiritual surrender to the law of decay and death that governs his body as a result of the Fall.

In contrast to Svidrigailov, Sonya Marmeladov embodies the notion that the laws of nature can be reversed, that resurrection of the flesh is possible. She does so most overtly by reading with Raskolnikov the Gospel story of the raising of Lazarus from the dead. Moreover, by sacrificing herself to others in love, she fulfills the commandment Christ issued at the Last Supper: to love others as he loved mankind. According to John, Christians prepare themselves for resurrection through Christlike love and through anamnesis of Christ in the Eucharist. Sonya's love associates her with the promise of bodily resurrection. For Dostoevsky, selfless love like Sonya's implies triumph over the laws of nature and even the annihilation of inertia.

Fittingly, Sonya and Svidrigailov are presented in the novel as antithetical forces between whom Raskolnikov is torn. Raskolnikov is fascinated by the two of them partly because of the otherworldly dimension of their existences. Both appear to be concerned with matters that are not ruled by the laws that bind existence on this earth. Both characters at some point convey to Raskolnikov a vision of the afterlife, a concept that by definition implies some form of triumph over the natural law of this life. Svidrigailov, to Raskolnikov's horror, depicts eternal life as a bathhouse filled with spiders—a perpetuation of this (decayed) earthly existence into infinity, a transplanting of the corruption of earth to paradise.[35] Sonya, in contrast, believes in the Christian afterlife, but more than that, she is concerned with the institution of the Kingdom of God on earth. Her vision is the antithesis of that of Svidrigailov: it is that of paradise transplanted onto the earth.

Their opposing stances on the natural law of decay—Svidrigailov's submission to it and Sonya's reversal of it—are revealed in other details. The two lodge in the same building, but in very different households, each of which in some way reflects its tenant's relationship to the laws of nature. Sonya rents a room from the Kapernaumov family, whose last name evokes the biblical town of Capernaum, seat of Christ's ministry and hence the locale of many or the miracles he performed.[36] The fact that several members of this family are handicapped and have a speech impediment enhances this association with Jesus as a miracle-worker—as someone who reverses the laws of nature; within the Gospel context, the infirmities healed by miracle were seen as manifestations of the general imperfection of the flesh and of the law of decay. In this possible allusion, Dostoevsky reveals his understanding of Christ's miracles to be close to that of the early Christians, who saw miracles not as a sign of Christ's divinity or as individual instances of healing or "wonder-working," but as evidence that "the general fatalities and impasses of our human nature" could be overcome.[37] The Kapernaumovs have not experienced a miracle; they suggest rather the possibility (and the need) of one. This aura enhances the association between Sonya and the hope of a miraculous reversal of natural law.

Their neighbor, Svidrigailov's landlady Gertruda Karlovna Resslich, creates an antithetical atmosphere. In her case, the symbolism does not necessarily stem from her last name,[38] except insofar as its Germanic origins portend sinister dealings, particularly since the other three German women in the novel (Luisa Ivanovna, Mme. Lippewechsel, and Darya Franzovna) are all connected to the institution of prostitution. Mme. Resslich promotes the corruption of flesh literally and symbolically opposes the Kapernaumovs. Mme. Resslich is rumored to have allowed Svidrigailov to violate her deaf niece, who killed herself as a result. The fact that the child was deaf adds to the symbolism: she was in need of a miracle, not corruption.

Svidrigailov's Gospel prototype might be seen as the man Jesus warns against, saying: "whosoever shall offend one of these little ones which believe in me, it were better for him that a millstone were hanged about his neck and that he were drowned in the depth of the sea" (Matt. 18:5–6).[39] Yet Svidrigailov's fondness for children (he tells Raskolnikov that he "like[s] children") combines erotic and philanthropic elements. He tells of saving a young girl at a dance from being seduced; at the end of the novel, he contributes to the upkeep of Katerina Ivanovna's children.

Sonya, in contrast, is full of agapic love for children. At a certain point she is discovered giving tea to the Kapernaumov children. She has become a prostitute in order to provide for Katerina Ivanovna's children. When Raskolnikov wishes to torment her, he suggests, to Sonya's horror, that Polechka will follow in her path. At this point, Raskolnikov realizes the depth of her love for these children and the fact that her concern for their well-being is what keeps her alive. "What on earth, what on earth could, he thought, have kept her up until then from ending it all? And then he understood fully what those poor, small orphans and that pitiful, half-crazed Katerina Ivanovna meant to her" (6:247). In loving children, Sonya shows her innately Christian spirit. Raskolnikov reminds Sonya that "indeed children are the image of Christ: 'of such are the kingdom of God.' He ordered them to be revered and loved; they're the future of humanity" (6:252), an obvious reference to Christ's statements about children (Matt. 19:14). Russian Orthodoxy in fact holds that children, although they have inherited mortality from Adam, are not guilty of original sin.

Sonya and Svidrigailov, both concerned with children (albeit in different ways), share the additional trait of debauchery [*razvrat*]. As noted, Svidrigailov is both debauched himself and attempts to debauch children. On the other hand, Sonya's debauchery, her prostitution, appears not to have corrupted her, a fact that Raskolnikov recognizes but cannot fully fathom: "All this shame apparently touched her only mechanically; real debauchery had not yet penetrated her heart even the slightest bit; he saw this" (6:247). Raskolnikov insists on lumping together the three fates—his own, Sonya's, and Svidrigailov's—so that the prospects he sees for her future are the same as those facing Svidrigailov (and perhaps himself).

> "There are three paths open to her," he thought, "—throwing herself into the canal, landing in an insane asylum, or ... or, finally, throwing herself into debauchery, which stupefies the mind and petrifies the heart." This last thought was the most repugnant of all to him; but he was already a skeptic, he was young, he was abstract and, consequently, cruel and for this reason he couldn't not believe that this final outlet—that is, debauchery—was the most likely. (6:247)

Whereas Svidrigailov fulfills Christ's prophecy for the seducer of children (who is better off with a millstone around his neck, drowned in the depths of the sea), Sonya's evangelical prototype (Luke 7:47), with whom she is associated from the time in the tavern when her father first tells Raskolnikov about her, is the harlot who is forgiven and regenerated for "having loved much" (6:21). As the novel progresses, she also becomes identified with Mary Magdalene (Luke 8:2; John 20:1–18) and Mary, the sister of Lazarus (John 11:1–53). Although the church fathers and biblical scholars have insisted on separate identities for these three figures, popular belief has fused them into a single figure who took on great significance. Sonya thus partakes of the triple symbolism of this one figure, who embodies the notion that the laws of nature can be reversed, corruption can be overcome, and that the flesh can be regenerated.[40]

The fact that Mary Magdalene is traditionally credited with the discovery of Christ's resurrection is significant because she herself has been regenerated through Christ's love. Her experience of his "miracle" makes her the natural witness to an even greater miracle, the resurrection of Christ. The concept of spiritual regeneration begun in this life is linked to Christ's resurrection, and to the eventual resurrection of the dead, in reversal of the necessity that ordinarily governs earthly life. All of these associations figure in the Russian Orthodox understanding of Mary Magdalene.

Mary Magdalene also figures in Ernest Renan's *Life of Jesus* [*Vie de*

Jésus] (1863), a book Dostoevsky knew,[41] as the mastermind (or, on his interpretation, "masterheart") of the resurrection:

> Let us say, however, that the vivid imagination of Mary Magdalene played a crucial role in this matter [the establishment of the notion of Christ's resurrection]. Divine power of love! Sacred moments when the passion of a hallucinating woman gives to the world a resurrected God!
>
> The glory of the Resurrection belongs thus to Mary Magdalene. After Jesus, it is Mary who has done the most for the foundation of Christianity. The shadow created by the delicate senses of Magdalene still glides over the earth. The queen and patroness of idealists, Magdalene knew better than anyone how to enforce her dream, how to impose on everyone the blessed vision of her passionate soul. Her great woman's affirmation "He is resurrected!" was the basis of the faith of mankind. Far from here, impotent reason! Do not go applying cold analysis to this masterpiece of idealism and love. If wisdom fails to console this poor human race, betrayed by fate, then let folly give it a try. Where is the wise man who has given as much joy to the world as the possessed woman, Mary Magdalene?[42]

Renan's impulse was, to borrow his term, "to apply cold analysis." Dostoevsky, on the contrary, embraced the folly of Mary Magdalene and imparted to Sonya Marmeladov the very qualities scorned by Renan.

Renan: would "apply cold analysis" not only to Mary Magdalene but to his whole subject, the life of Jesus. In keeping with his mission, Renan reminds his reader of the naive and unsophisticated minds not only of Jesus' followers but of Jesus himself. "We must remind ourselves that no conception of the laws of nature entered either his [Jesus'] mind or that of his audience to delineate the limit of the impossible."[43] Renan implies that early Christians were more ready and able to accept Jesus and his ministry because they lacked any scientific understanding of the physical world and its laws. And what Renan sees as backwardness, Dostoevsky sees as grace.

Sonya Marmeladov thus embodies not the spirit of her own times, heavily under the influence of the new positivistic science, but the spirit of Jesus', pre-Newtonian, time.

RASKOLNIKOV AND RESURRECTION

In the novel Sonya Marmeladov makes good on the promise implied by her association with Mary Magdalene. Sonya "resurrects" Raskolnikov and frees him from the determinism of social physics, from the mechanical behavior of the criminal, and from the decay of spiritual corruption. She does this most explicitly when she reads the story of the resurrection of Lazarus to him (at this point, the "hypostasis" of Mary Magdalene she embodies is that of Mary, the sister of Lazarus). The passage she reads from the Gospel of John in which Christ says "I am the resurrection and the life; he that believeth in me, though he be dead, yet shall he live: And whosoever liveth and believeth in me shall never die" (John 11:25–26) was familiar to the faithful as part of the liturgy.

The Russian religious tradition cherishes the notion that the laws of nature can be overcome by God's will. For example, the Archpriest Avvakum, in his seventeenth-century, thoroughly pre-Newtonian autobiography, reminds his reader that "God whensoever he chooses triumphs over Nature's laws. Read the Life of Theodor of Edessa; there you will find that a harlot raised a man from the dead."[44] Avvakum did not believe that the universe was governed by an inviolable system of laws; nor did he hold that God had any obligation to keep the universe functioning in a fashion scientifically intelligible to man.[45] The episode Avvakum describes serves as proof that human existence is not subject to determinism. It demonstrates not only God's triumph over nature's laws but also that he can grant individuals the power to do so. Here again, a "harlot" serves as the instrument for this reversal of the laws of nature, the symbolic effect being the same as in John's version of Christ's resurrection where Mary Magdalene, while not the actual instrument of resurrection, is still its first witness. Dostoevsky, in having the "harlot" Sonya "resurrect" Raskolnikov (who is spiritually dead as a result of his crime), follows a Russian religious tradition.

Throughout his writings, Dostoevsky stresses the essentially miraculous power of Christian love. Just as Renan suggests that the resurrection was the result of the "divine power" of Mary Magdalenes love, so too does Dostoevsky present Sonya's love for Raskolnikov as the regenerating force. In the notebooks Dostoevsky also returns over and over to Sonya's regenerating effect on Raskolnikov:

> An argument of his with Marmeladova. She says: repent. She shows him the perspectives of love and a new life. (7:138)

> On the one hand, burial and damnation, on the other— resurrection. (7:138)

> A meeting with Marmeladova: he explains to her everything, the bullet in his head. She restores [*vosstanovliaet*] him. He goes to bid her farewell—she restores [*vosstanovliaet*] him. (7:139)

"Undo them in another way. Repent and begin another life."
From the midst of despair, a new perspective. (7:139)

Such notebook entries indicate that when Dostoevsky refers to resurrection
in the novel he uses it largely as a metaphor for spiritual restoration. In this
fashion, *Crime and Punishment* is thematically linked with other Dostoevskian
works that treat the theme of regeneration, restoration, resurrection, that
imply a triumph over inertia.[46]

Through this depiction of the regeneration of Sonya and Raskolnikov,
Dostoevsky places his novel within what he himself had earlier identified as
the tradition of nineteenth-century European literature. In 1862,
Dostoevsky had named Victor Hugo as the founding father of this tradition
when he wrote:

> His idea is the fundamental idea of all of the art of the nineteenth
> century and Victor Hugo as an artist was all but the first herald.
> This idea is Christian and highly moral; its formula is the
> restoration of a ruined man unjustly crushed by the oppression of
> circumstances, of the stagnation of centuries and of societal
> prejudices. This idea is the justification of the pariahs of society,
> humiliated and rejected by all....
>
> Victor Hugo is all but the main herald of this idea of
> *"restoration"* in the literature of our century. At least he was the
> first to announce this idea with such creative skill in art. Of
> course, it is not the invention of Victor Hugo alone; on the
> contrary, according to our conviction, it is the inalienable
> property and, perhaps, the historical necessity of the nineteenth
> century, although, in fact, it has become the fashion to find fault
> with our century for not having introduced anything new in
> literature or art after the great examples of the past. (20:28–29)

The "fundamental idea of all nineteenth-century art" is also embodied in
Dostoevsky's own works. Like Victor Hugo, Dostoevsky wrote about the
"humiliated" and the "pariahs of society." (He used "pariah" in reference to
Raskolnikov and Sonya.) In this passage he goes further to suggest that the
inertia, so often depicted in his works as a force threatening an individual life,
is a historical trend.

Whereas Dostoevsky in the forties had seemed to believe that
institutional changes (such as the abolition of serfdom) might bring
deliverance from the force of inertia, as time went on, he grew increasingly
mistrustful of attempts at a large-scale cure for society. Just as he rejected

Peter's reforms on the grounds that they were despotically inflicted on the people from above, so too did he reject socialist attempts to rehabilitate mankind. He wrote in his notebook in 1864: "The socialists want to regenerate man, *to liberate* him, to present him without God and without family. They conclude that, having once change his economic situation by force, the goal will have been achieved. But man changes himself not because of *external* causes, but by no other means than a moral transformation" (20:171). This passage sheds light on Dostoevsky's views of socialism and advocates of new social theory, such as Luzhin, in *Crime and Punishment*. Here Dostoevsky recognizes that the socialists seek to regenerate man,[47] but he objects because they attempt to do it externally, just as in the notebooks to *Crime and Punishment* he recognizes their belief in progress but objects because they attempt to achieve it by mechanizing human existence (7:161).

Although Dostoevsky may have believed inertia to be a sociohistorical phenomenon, the realm in which he sought solutions to this inertia was the individual human soul. In *Crime and Punishment*, Dostoevsky does not advocate political and social reform but moral transformation through love. Love becomes the means to annihilate inertia. But without the active participation of Raskolnikov, no regeneration can occur. Until the last possible moment, he remains torn between Svidrigailov and Sonya. In the notebooks for the novel, Dostoevsky explicitly outlines the two alternatives that are implicitly illustrated in the novel itself. In an entry entitled "Finale of the Novel," he writes:

> Svidrigailov:—despair, the most cynical.
> Sonya:—hope, the most unrealizable. (7:204)

The despair embodied by Svidrigailov proves that this man, for whom all seemed to be "allowed," is ruled by necessity; in contrast, Sonya embodies hope but a hope that appears to contradict the laws of nature and the necessity they imply. As solutions to Raskolnikov's dilemma, Sonya represents confession, repentance, regeneration, and the start of a new life, while Svidrigailov represents suicide. Sonya's solution is clear from the start, but Svidrigailov's becomes fully real for Raskolnikov only when (ready to confess in the police station) he hears that Svidrigailov took his own life. This suicide, hinted at more than once in the novel, is the logical consequence of Svidrigailov's debauchery: in the context both of this novel and of patristic thought, suicide amounts to an absolute surrender to the law of corruption and decay.

If suicide marks the triumph of the laws of nature over man, resurrection marks man's triumph over the laws of nature. Up until the last moment, Raskolnikov, in typical fashion, is undecided about which of these stances to take in regard to the laws of nature. He starts out of the police station but returns. He was propelled back not so much by *esprit d'escalier* (which he demonstrated so many times before) as by Sonya's dogged devotion, evidence of which is given him when he finds that she has followed him there. At this point, suicide is out of the question.

The laws of nature are not fully reversed until the end of the epilogue when Raskolnikov, inwardly transformed, realizes his love for Sonya (because there is a synergy between the two, the change that takes place is not externally inflicted): "They would have liked to talk but they could not. Tears were in their eyes. They were both pale and thin; but in these sick and pale faces there already shone the dawn of a renewed future, full of resurrection into new life. They were resurrected by love, the heart of one contained infinite sources of life for the heart of the other" (6:421). By referring to the "dawn of their renewed future," to their "resurrection into a new life," and to "the infinite sources of life" they provide each other, Dostoevsky indicates that physical necessity has been reversed, the laws of nature have been vanquished and that vital force will keep Raskolnikov and Sonya immune from further threat from these laws. When Dostoevsky then notes that in Raskolnikov "life had taken the place of dialectic," he makes it clear that Raskolnikov's behavior is no longer threatened by the mechanization of social physics (6:422). Raskolnikov and Sonya are clearly experiencing "vital life" [*zhivaia zhizn'*], as opposed to the mechanical, inertia-ridden existence to which so many of Dostoevsky's heroes fall victim.

Implicit in this epilogue is Dostoevsky's rejection of social physics as well as his embrace of Orthodoxy. He suggests that in their triumph over the laws of nature, Raskolnikov and Sonya return to a state of innocence and freedom. Even the Siberian setting evokes such a state:

> Raskolnikov went out of the shed onto the shore, sat on the logs by the shed and started to stare at the wide, empty river. From the high shore a wide panorama opened up. From the distant opposite shore a song was dimly heard. There, in the boundless steppe washed in sun, nomad yurts could be seen as barely noticeable dots. There there was freedom, another kind of people lived, not at all like those here, as if time itself had stopped there, just as if the age of Abraham and his tribes was not yet over. (6:421)

Through this reference to Abraham's tribe, Dostoevsky evokes the Gospel notion that human beings can, through faith, achieve freedom from the sin to which all are enslaved as a result of mortality.[48] This notion of a return to a pre-Fall state of freedom from sin resonates with the notion that the laws of nature have been reversed, for Dostoevsky held that man's subjection to necessity, to inertia, and to a mechanistic existence, was directly related to his sinfulness. In this sense, he echoes the patristic notion that God's image—in which man was originally created, which he forfeited through sin, and which he may regain through faith—was "a state of not being bound by any law of nature."[49] Accordingly, subjection to necessity of any sort (and not simply to the laws of nature) implied that this divine image has been dissolved.[50] In the epilogue to *Crime and Punishment*, Raskolnikov and Sonya, when they are "resurrected into a new life," renew their divine likeness.

They are delivered not simply from the laws of nature but also from another manifestation of physical necessity of paramount importance to the novel: economic necessity. In the epilogue, through Svidrigailov's largesse, through Razumikhin's acumen and through apparent good luck, the families of both Raskolnikov and Sonya, the support of which had formerly caused such anguish and hardship, are provided for. In addition, Sonya—who had been forced to turn to prostitution because she was not able to make money as a seamstress (whether because, as her employer claimed, she sewed on the collars crookedly or because her employer was dishonest)—has become a successful seamstress in Siberia (6:416). Indeed, all of this economic good fortune visited upon the remaining characters of the novel might seem bewildering, since money had been obtained primarily through self-sacrifice and/or crime.

Yet perhaps Dostoevsky was not simply creating a happy ending but demonstrating a theological point, that freedom from necessity follows from the "resurrection" that occurs. In this sense, Raskolnikov (and perhaps Sonya as well) resembles the poor man Lazarus, who is refused crumbs from the table of the rich man, but who eventually ends up in the bosom of Abraham (Luke 16:19–25). Since popular religious tradition lumps together this Lazarus and Lazarus the resurrected brother of Mary and Martha (much as it associates the various Marys) and since, according to Georgii Fedotov, "of all of the Lord's parables, of all of the gospel stories, only the tale about Lazarus penetrates the soul of the people, as a clear expression of the social injustice reigning in the world,"[51] Dostoevsky quite possibly meant for Raskolnikov to be identified with Lazarus the poor man who ends up in the bosom of Abraham as well as with Lazarus the man resurrected from the dead.[52] Both Lazaruses experience a certain "restoration." Hence both serve as perfect prototypes for nineteenth-century literature, whose main idea, according to Dostoevsky, was restoration of the ruined man. In the process, both Lazaruses gain freedom from necessity—the one transcends the laws of nature and the other, economic determinism.[53]

In Orthodoxy, the Resurrection implies freedom from economic necessity. John Meyendorff explains this as follows: "The Resurrection delivers men from the fear of death, and, therefore, also from the necessity of struggling for existence. Only in the light of the risen Lord does the Sermon on the Mount acquire its full realism: 'Do not be anxious about your life, what you shall eat or what you shall drink, nor about your body, what you shall put on. Is not life more than food, and the body more than clothing?'" (Matt. 6:25).[54] Of course, Dostoevsky does not explain exactly how the law of economic necessity is reversed, just as he does not explain exactly how Raskolnikov is "resurrected": both events are miraculous. Dostoevsky thus simply suspends the sway of the laws of nature over the novelistic universe of *Crime and Punishment*.

NOTES

1. This aspect of Raskolnikov's behavior is discussed by Robert Louis Jackson in *The Art of Dostoevsky* (Princeton: Princeton University Press, 1981), 203.

2. Raskolnikov thus illustrates the theory whereby once a violent act is contemplated, its execution follows as if by mechanics. The husband who narrates "The Meek One" explains the dynamic: "They say that people standing on an altitude somehow gravitate of their own accord downwards, into the abyss. I think that many suicides and murders have been committed simply because the revolver had already been taken in hand. That is also an abyss, it's a forty-five degree inclined plane which one has no choice but to slide down, and something invincibly causes you to pull the trigger" (24:21). In drafts of the story, the husband refers to the "downhill inertia of weakening of feeling" as the cause of his wife's attempt to murder him (24:318-19).

3. In this passage Dostoevsky repeatedly uses words based on the root *tiag*– [to pull]. He thus conveys the notion that Raskolnikov felt that fate was "dragging" him; this root also evokes the concept of gravitational attraction, one of the basic principles of Newtonian mechanics.

4. Victor Hugo, *Notre Dame de Paris* (Paris: Flammarion, 1967), 345. Hugo uses other references to mathematical calculation and machinelike behavior that prefigure Dostoevsky's use of these images in *Crime and Punishment*. Hugo and Dostoevsky both use these images to suggest the destructive effects of a scientistic, mathematical approach to human life.

5. Victor Hugo, *Le dernier jour d'un condamné* (Paris: Gallimard, 1970), 312–13.

6. Dostoevsky's appropriation of Hugo's depiction of death culminates in *The Idiot*, where, fittingly, the machine also figures prominently. For more on this subject, see Chapter 4.

7. Robert Louis Jackson interprets Tolstoy's idea in "Why People Stupefy Themselves" that Raskolnikov's "real life" does not occur when he acts "like a machine" as follows (*Art of Dostoevsky*, 205): "What is crucial in Raskolnikov's situation is not so much the factor of chance as *his disposition to be guided by chance*, his readiness, as it were, to gamble, to seek out and acknowledge in chance his so-called fate. What is crucial to his action is the general state of consciousness that he brings to the moment of critical

accident; and consciousness here is not only his nervous, overwrought state but the way he conceives of his relationship to the world. Such is the background of Tolstoy's keen perception that Raskolnikov's true existence and true moment of decision occurred not when he met the sister of the old lady, not when he was 'acting like a machine,' but when he was 'only thinking, when his consciousness alone was working and when in that consciousness barely perceptible changes were taking place'—in realms affecting the total scope of his existence."

8. L. N. Tolstoi, "Dlia chego liudi odurmanivaiutsia," *Polnoe sobranie sochinenii*, ed. V. G. Chertkov (Moscow: Khudozhestvennaia literatura, 1933), 27, 280.

9. See also A. I. Gertsen, "Pis'ma ob izuchenii prirody," *Sobranie sochinenii v tridtsati tontakh*, ed. V. P. Volgin (Moscow: AN SSSR, 1954), 3:249. Whether, strictly speaking, it was Descartes or his followers who asserted that man was a machine is immaterial.

10. N. N. Strakhov, "Pis'ma ob organicheskoi zhizni," *Mir kak tseloe. Cherty iz nauki o prirode* (Saint Petersburg: [K. Zamyslovskii], 1872), 61–64.

11. E. V. Spektorskii, *Problema sotsial'noi fiziki v XVII stoletii* (Warsaw: Varshavskii uchebnyi okrug, 1910–17), 2:408.

12. Strakhov, *Mir kak tseloe*, 63.

13. Strakhov, *Mir kak tseloe*, 63.

14. As Robin Feuer Miller observed, Raskolnikov's plan harks back not just to Balzac's *Père Goriot* (an oft-discussed source) but also—via Balzac—to Rousseau's *Confessions*: the idea of acquiescing to a murder of a Mandarin in China in order to make one's fortune is attributed by Rastignac to Rousseau; see *The Brothers Karamazov: Worlds of the Novel*, Twayne's Masterwork Studies 83 (New York: Twayne 1992), 62–63. To the list of literary sources for Raskolnikov's murder of the pawnbroker should be added the name of Descartes. Thus both Descartes and Rousseau become, in Dostoevsky's view, proponents of murder.

15. Gertsen, "Pis'ma," 247.

16. Strakhov, *Mir kak tseloe*, 61–64.

17. For references to mathematics and arithmetic, see, for example: 7:134, 138, 146, 151, 188. The references to mathematics and arithmetics are also noted by V. N. Belopol'skii (*Dostoevskii i pozitivizm* [Rostov: Rostovskii universitet, 1985], 22).

18. On this subject, Alexandre Koyré writes (*Newtonian Studies* [Cambridge: Harvard University Press, 1965], 23): "so strong was the belief in 'nature,' so overwhelming the prestige of the Newtonian (or pseudo-Newtonian) pattern of order arising automatically from interaction of isolated and self-contained atoms, that nobody dared to doubt that order and harmony would in some way be produced by human atoms acting according to nature, whatever this might be—instinct for play and pleasure (Diderot) or pursuit of selfish gain (A. Smith)." Koyré cautions: "Newton, of course, is by no means responsible for these, and other, *monstra* engendered by the overextension—or aping—of his method. Nor is he responsible for the more general, and not less disastrous, consequence of the widespread adoption of the atomic pattern of analysis of global events and actions according to which these latter appeared to be not *real*, but only *mathematical* results and summings up of the underlying elementary factors."

19. "'Fiziologiia obydennoi zhizni.' Soch. F. F. L'iusa. Perev, S. A. Rachinskogo i Ia. A. Borzenkova, vol. 1, 1861," *Vremia* 11 (1861): 50–63. V. S. Nechaeva, author of monographs on the journals of the Dostoevsky brothers, has not been able to determine the author of this unsigned review (*Zhurnal M.M.iF.M. Dostoevskikh "Vremia" (1861–1863)* [Moscow: Nauka, 1972], 180–81).

20. *Vremia*, 55.

21. I. Zil'berfarb, *Sotsial'naia filosofiia Sharlia Four'e i ee mesto v istorii sotsialisticheskoi mysli pervoi poloviny XIX veka* (Moscow: Nauka, 1964), 21. E. V. Spektorskii explores the development of this "social physics" in *Problema sotsial'noi fiziki v XVII stoletii*.

22. Strakhov, *Mir kak tseloe*, 46.

23. Jonathan Beecher, *Charles Fourier: The Visionary and His World* (Berkeley and Los Angeles: University of California Press, 1986), 67, 225. Although Beecher questions the precise nature of borrowings from Newton, he stresses that Fourier consciously used Newton as a model.

24. I. Zil'berfarb, *Sotsial'naia filosofiia Four'e*, 110.

25. Fourier's formulation, quoted in Beecher, *Charles Fourier*, 335.

26. The commentary (7:368, 339) calls attention to the fact that later in the novel (6:307) one of Quetelet's popularizers, A. Wagner, is referred to directly. The theme of "social statistics" is treated by Harriet Murav in *Holy Foolishness: Dostoevsky's Novels and the Poetics of Cultural Critique* (Stanford: Stanford University Press, 1992), 55–59, and by Irina Paperno in her forthcoming *Suicide as a Cultural Institution*.

27. Kjetsaa catalogues and analyzes the radical response to *Crime and Punishment* and notes that Pisarev in particular objected to Dostoevsky's (or Raskolnikov's) discussion of Newton and Kepler as potential bloodletters; at the least, Pisarev's response shows that Dostoevsky struck a nerve; Geir Kjetsaa, *Fyodor Dostoyevsky: A Writer's Life*, trans. Siri Hustvedt and David McDuff (New York: Viking [Elisabeth Sifton], 1987], 182-89, esp. 188).

28. A. S. Pushkin, *Evgenii Onegin. Pushkin. Polnoe sobranie sochinenii*, ed. B. V. Tomashevskii (Moscow: AN SSSR, 1937), 6:37 (2.14), accompanied here by Nabokov's translation, slightly modified (Aleksandr Pushkin, *Eugene Onegin. A Novel in Verse*, trans. Vladimir Nabokov, Bollingen Series 72 [Princeton: Princeton University Press, 1964]). The last three lines are quoted at 7:343 in the discussion of the Pushkinian influence on *Crime and Punishment*. The commentary suggests that Porfiry Petrovich's question to Raskolnikov "who in Russia nowadays does not consider himself a Napoleon?" (6:204) may echo these lines from Pushkin (7:381).

29. V. K. Odoevskii, "Russkie nochi," *Sochineniia v dvukh tomakh* (Moscow: Khudozhestvennaia literatura, 1981), 1:35. Later in *Russian Nights*, Odoevsky refers directly to Quetelet, citing his statistics showing that crime is more widespread in industrial areas (1:209). That there is some similarity between Odoevsky and Dostoevsky in their attitudes toward utilitarianism has been suggested by Simon Karlinsky in "A Hollow Shape: The Philosophical Tales of Prince Vladimir Odoevsky," *Studies in Romanticism* 5, no. 3 (1966): 181. Some direct parallels are discussed by R. G. Nazirov, "Vladimir Odoevskii i Dostoevskii," *Russkaia literatura* 3 (1974): 203–6. He suggests echoes of Odoevsky's views on Bentham expressed in *Russian Nights* in the depiction of Luzhin's utilitarianism and also parallels between Raskolnikov's dream in the epilogue and parts of *Russian Nights*.

Neil Cornwell also discusses the influence of Odoevsky on Dostoevsky in: *V. E. Odoyevsky: His Life, Times and Milieu* (Athens: Ohio University Press, 1986), 260–63. He suggests that the relations between Odoevsky and Dostoevsky "were somewhat closer than a purely literary acquaintance" (261). He notes that the epigraph from *Poor Folk* is from Odoevsky, whom Dostoevsky met shortly after its publication. Dostoevsky wrote to Odoevsky while he was in exile and reestablished contact on his return to Saint Petersburg. The works of Odoevsky in the context of the nineteenth-century Russian response to science deserve further study.

30. Odoevskii, "Russkie nochi," 48.

31. Dostoevsky continues: "Happiness is bought with suffering. Such is the law of our planet, but this immediate consciousness, felt in the vital process, is such a great joy for which it's worth paying with years of suffering" (7:154).

32. The notes at 7:375 mention the latter three as possible sources of Luzhin's speech.

33. This word, a substantive made from the proper name *Kitai* [China], might be translated as "Chinesitis." Belinsky had used the term *kitaitsy* [Chinamen] to refer to "the

enemies of progress" in his "Glance at the Russian Literature of 1847." Having introduced this term, Belinsky declares: "Such a name decides the issue better than any investigation and debate"; V. G. Belinskii, "Vzgliad na russkuiu literaturu 1847 goda," *Sobranie sochinenii v trekh tomakh* (Moscow: Khudozhestvennaia literatura, 1948), 3:768. The commentary (902) notes that "the term *kitaizm* is used by Belinsky in the sense of backwardness, despotism, absence of culture." Here Dostoevsky throws the term *kitaishchina* back at the radicals, in effect declaring their socialism to be more backward and despotic than the status quo that, in the name of "progress," it sought to change.

34. John Meyendorff (*Byzantine Theology: Historical Trends and Doctrinal Themes* [New York: Fordham University Press, 1979], 144–45) describes this phenomenon as follows: "Mortality, or 'corruption,' or simply death (understood in a personalized sense), has indeed been viewed, since Christian antiquity, as a cosmic disease which holds humanity under its sway, both spiritually and physically and is controlled by the one who is 'the murderer from the beginning' (John 8:44). It is this death that makes sin inevitable:, and in this sense 'corrupts' nature."

35. V. Ia. Kirpotin (*Razocharovanie i krushenie Rodiona Raskolnikova* [Moscow: Khudozhestvennaia literatura, 1978], 231) writes of Svidrigailov's conception of paradise: "Svidrigailov has in mind a transfer from one physical world to another physical world with a different structure, with different laws but in its own way just as subject to determinism as ours and hence just as much outside the laws of justice and truth. If the other world is also just a physical world, then according to the logic of the faithless and despairing Svidrigailov, it can turn out to be a world of other physical beings, not people but spiders. A mechanical, vile and soulless world, its ideal-less and meaningless life can be equated to the life of spiders."

36. The notes at 6:365–66 discuss the possible association between this name and the nineteenth-century Russian word *kapernaum* [tavern], with references given to discussions by V. Ia. Kirpotin (*Razocharovanie i krushenie Rodiona Raskol'nikova*, 167–69) and M. S. Al'tman ("Iz arsenala imen i prototipov literaturnykh geroev Dostoevskogo," *Dostoevskii i ego vremia*, ed. V. G. Bazanov and G. M. Fridlender [Leningrad: Nauka, 1971], 209–11). The former notes the general association of Sonya with early (noninstitutional) Christianity, that of the poor and downtrodden—or, in other words, of the "anawim." Al'tman associates the Kapernaumov family's infirmity with that of those who were brought to Christ for healing. He quotes two pronouncements made in the Gospels about Capernaum: "And thou, Capernaum, which art exalted unto heaven, shalt be brought down to hell: for if the mighty works, which have been done in thee, had been done in Sodom, it would have remained until this day. But I say unto you, that is shall be more tolerable for the land of Sodom in the day of judgment, than for thee" (Matt. 11:23–24) and "The people which sat in darkness saw great light" (Matt. 4:16). Al'tman notes the apparent contradiction and asks: "Was it not also from such frightful and contradictory gospel prophecies as those about Capernaum that Kapernaumov, although he didn't grow dumb from fright, developed a speech impediment?" It does not, however, seem that Dostoevsky was interested in the cause of Kapernaumov's infirmity (or that this would have been it). Rather, he seems interested simply in evoking the Gospel setting and the notion that the laws of nature can miraculously be reversed.

37. Amos N. Wilder, *Early Christian Rhetoric: The Language of the Gospel* (Cambridge: Harvard University Press, 1971), 64–65.

38. In the drafts for the novel, her name was Ressler, the name of one of Dostoevsky's actual creditors at the time (7:385).

39. The Russian *soblaznit* is quite strong, suggesting seduction.

40. Although others identify her with Mary Magdalene, Sonya tells Raskolnikov, on reading the gospel story to him, that she herself is Lazarus.

41. Dostoevsky mentions Renan in notes for "Socialism and Christianity" in 1864

(20:192). The connection between Dostoevsky and Renan is discussed in E. I. Kiiko, "Dostoevskii i Renan," *Dostoevskii: Materialy i issledovaniia*, ed. G. M. Fridlender (Leningrad: Nauka, 1978), 3:106–22. Kiiko discusses the evidence of Dostoevsky's familiarity with Renan, the points of similarity and divergence in their views of resurrection, and the possible influence of Renan's portrait of Jesus on Dostoevsky's creation of Myshkin. She does not mention influence of Renan on *Crime and Punishment*.

42. Ernest Renan, *Vie de Jésus, Oeuvres complètes*, ed. Henriette Psichari (Paris: Calman-Lévy, 1947), 4:237.

43. Renan, *Vie*, 356, 478.

44. Avvakum, "The Life of Archpriest Avvakum by Himself," *Medieval Russia's Epics, Chronicles and Tales*, ed. Serge Zenkovsky (New York: Dutton, 1974), 418.

45. That "nature is governed by an inviolable system of physical laws intelligible to rational men" and that God "would never arbitrarily change the rules by which [the universe] functions and thus make His handiwork inexplicable in scientific terms" are two requirements introduced by Newton, according to Gale Christianson (*In the Presence of the Creator: Isaac Newton and His Times* [New York: Free Press; London: Collier Macmillan, 1984], 235.

46. The concept of a "new life" figures in virtually all of Dostoevsky's works, but with particular prominence in his confessions, where the heroes often desire some change, or conversion, and dream of beginning a "new life." These other works of Dostoevsky might employ the term "resurrection" but they do not necessarily make heavy use of the Gospel symbolism. For example, the following passage from *Notes from Underground* deals with corruption, love, resurrection, and rebirth, but with less emphasis on the symbolism than in *Crime and Punishment*. (Perhaps the inclusion of the sections censored from part 1, containing references to Christ and faith, would have given greater emphasis to the religious symbolism of this passage from part 2.) The underground man declares: "And what was most unbelievable about it all was that I had managed to corrupt myself morally to such a degree, I had grown alien to vital life [*zhivaia zhizn'*] to such a degree, that I got the notion to reproach and shame her for coming to me to hear 'words of pity'; it didn't even enter my head that she hadn't come to me to hear words of pity but to love me, because, for a woman, in love lies complete resurrection, complete salvation from whatever ruin and complete rebirth, and it can't even manifest itself in any other way than this," (5:176). The underground man thus attributes to all women the trait Renan identified in Mary Magdalene, that of belief in the resurrecting power of love.

47. In 1873, Dostoevsky noted that the utopian socialists, with whom he was associated in the forties, had prepared "darkness and horror" for humanity—"under the guise of renewal and resurrection" (21:131). Indeed, these socialists used the same salvific terminology as the church. Dostoevsky implies that the socialists were guilty of catachresis of the most inexcusable sort: their false uses of words such as "resurrection" and "renewal" had led Dostoevsky and others like him into temptation.

48. A reference to John 8:33, according to George Gibian (Feodor Dostoevsky, *Crime and Punishment*, ed. George Gibian [New York: Norton, 1975], 463, n): "Then said Jesus to those Jews which believed on him, If ye continue in my word, then are ye my disciples indeed; And ye shall know the truth, and the truth shall make you free. They answered him, We be Abraham's seed, and were never in bondage to any man: how sayest thout, Ye shall be made free? Jesus answered them, Verily, verily, I say unto you, Whosoever comitteth sin is the servant of sin. And the servant abideth not in the house for ever: but the son abideth ever. If the Son therefore shall make you free, ye shall be free indeed" (John 8:31–36).

49. Gregory of Nyssa, as quoted in G. V. Florovskii, *Vostochnye ottsy IV-go veka. Iz chtenii v Pravoslavnom Bogoslovskom Institute v Parizhe* (Paris, 1931; reprint, Westmead, Eng.: Gregg International Publishers, 1972), 158.

50. Florovskii, *Vostochnye ottsy*, 158.

51. Georgii Fedotov, *Stikhi dukhovnye* (Paris: YMCA Press, 1935), 86. As a result, Lazarus became the subject of many folk poems of a spiritual nature.

52. The mention of Abraham and his tribe in the epilogue (6:431) might contain an allusion to the bosom of Abraham (where Lazarus ends up) as well as to John 8:31ff.

53. By reintroducing this economic issue in the epilogue, Dostoevsky provides a refutation of Luzhin, for whom money is the only lasting thing, and of the socialists, with their belief in economic improvements.

54. Meyendorff, *Byzantine Theology*, 146.

NAOMI ROOD

Mediating the Distance: Prophecy and Alterity in Greek Tragedy and Dostoevsky's Crime and Punishment

> We have corrected Thy work and have founded it upon *miracle, mystery* and *authority*.
>
> The Grand Inquisitor in *The Brothers Karamazov*
> (Dostoevsky 1976, 237)

All literary art presupposes conventions, and Athenian tragedy is surely one of the most conventionalized genres. Some conventions arise out of the demand upon a fictional work to provide motivations for the events of its plot; as Aristotle deemed, the best kind of plot is that in which things happen by probability or necessity.[1]

One way of supplying causation to a plot, of course, is simply to involve or to invoke the divine. If the phrase, "and the will of Zeus was accomplished," as in *Iliad* 1.5, prefaces all the actions to come, no further explanation of motive is needed.[2] Furthermore, when the divine becomes expressed in language, the resulting divine word takes on the supplementary authority of a performative utterance, i.e. speech identical with action.[3] Divine speech which is not differentiated from its actualization encloses necessity within itself. For an author, then, it can provide necessary and sufficient causation.

As Oedipus acknowledges at the beginning of *Oedipus Tyrannus* (278–86), however, the gods do not necessarily speak just at those times when

---

From *Russian Literature and the Classics*. © 1996 by Overseas Publishers Association.

we might wish them to. In the second best case, mortals can learn their will and words from prophecy, the speech of the oracle who speaks forth for another (*prophemi*).[4] For the majority of mortals, that is, for those not continually graced with divine epiphanies, prophecy supplies the primary vehicle of the divine word. This article considers the use of prophecy within two different but associated genres, Athenian tragedy and the novels of Dostoevsky.

I.

The questions behind this comparison concern the attitude of these two genres to the use of prophecy: under what conditions is prophecy the awesome expression of the divine word to humanity which contains causality within it? And when might this capacity of divine speech to create causality be exploited for literary demands, thus utilizing prophecy as a convention? I have chosen to focus on prophecy for the wider view to which I believe it provides access: to the text's conception of the divine, and subsequently, to the ways in which language signifies. For it seems that when prophecy in a text is of the monologic, "singularly-signifying" sort, it is thus determined by a close proximity to the divine. But when prophecy becomes wider, not quite dialogic, but with some room for choice, it is caused by a more distant relation to the divine. For dialogue presupposes the presence of a complete other:[5] in tragedy, the word of the divine cannot yet be dialogic because the divine is not yet sufficiently other. In tragedy, the gods often speak and act on stage, or second best, become heard through oracles. As another and supreme actor and interlocutor, their speech-acts are effected directly. In the world of Dostoevsky's novels, by contrast, the divine word has grown more distant both in space and time. The imagined (and singular) epiphany of Christ in the Grand Inquisitor, for example, in which Christ remains perfectly silent, affords only an opportunity to remind him that having spoken, he can add nothing to what he has spoken of old. But this completion of the divine speech itself comprises the freedom of humans: as the alterity of the divine other becomes more complete, the possibility for dialogue increases. The following discussion of prophecy, then, ultimately refers to the particular relationship to the divine expressed in these two versions of the genres of tragedy and novel. I will seek to show that, while both tragedy and the Dostoevskian novel centrally include prophecy in their plots, tragedy reaffirms the inevitable dynamic of the divine word, whereas, in the construction of his novels, Dostoevsky rejects this kind of divine causality. Prophecy in tragedy provides, at least in part, a genuine motivation for the events of the plot; this type of prophecy is laid bare in Dostoevsky as a conventionalized device for *falsely* creating necessity. In other words, to invoke the familiar Bakhtinian categories, tragedy operates according to the monologic word, whereas Dostoevsky's rejection of prophecy constitutes one aspect of his dialogic word. But in the end, as I hope to demonstrate (*contra* Bakhtin), Dostoevsky is still not free from the dynamics of prophecy. Instead, he only slightly complicates the matter when he gives humans more of an initial choice; after this point things grow generally more inevitable. Thus, while Dostoevsky does not absolutely import Greek antiquity's conception of prophecy into his novels, he nevertheless underscores its continuing importance as he raises it to a new and more complex level of significance.

The debate over the "tragic" reading of Dostoevsky began with two of his earliest and most influential posthumous critics, both of them Classicists. These were the Symbolist poet and philosopher Vyacheslav Ivanov (1866–1949), and the quasi-Formalist/Symbolist member of the Bakhtin circle, Lev Pumpyansky (1894–1940). Ivanov, following the cues of Dmitry Merezhkovsky, promoted the notion of Dostoevsky's works as tragedy. Starting in 1917, he published in *Russkaya mysl'* [*Russian Thought*] a series of revisions of earlier lectures which interpreted Dostoevsky's major works as "novel-tragedies." Ivanov's view of Dostoevsky's writings as tragedies forms one part of a larger concept of tradition as cultural agglutination which was common to the Symbolists. Part of their philosophy included the incorporation of past texts into a mystical synthesis which would culminate in their own writings. Such a philosophy of history and literature, in its eagerness to detect syntheses, often led to an exaggerated perception of likenesses between literary works and genres. In this instance, Ivanov claimed to perceive both the form and content of Classical tragedy in Dostoevsky's prose.

Formally, Ivanov understands all the episodes in Dostoevsky's plots as mini-tragedies, each leading to an inevitable catastrophe. He explains that the tragic episodes are interrupted by digressions characteristic of the storytelling of his times, as seen in Balzac or Dickens. Yet every particular action participates in the unity of the successive episodes.

> These episodes, in turn, are worked into the shape of acts, so to speak, in a continually unfolding drama; and these acts, finally, represent in their sequence the iron links of a chain of logic—on which, like a planetary body, hangs the main event which was from the beginning the theme and purpose of the whole work, with all the weight of its contentual and solemn significance. (Ivanov 1952, 10–11)

Such a catastrophic end hung on the fatal decision of the hero: whether to be with God or without God. Once such a choice has been made, all else inevitably follows. Ivanov frequently refers to Dmitry Karamazov's famous

statement that life is a struggle between God and the Devil and the
battlefield is the heart of man.[6] Thus, like a drama which demands the
expression of every spiritual development portrayed in action, the one who
chooses against God becomes the transgressor of the cosmic and social
orders. Crime then becomes the center of Dostoevsky's tragic world, much
like the content of ancient tragedies. Ivanov discusses at length Dostoevsky's
exposition of solitude, which always threatens to collapse into solipsism. The
sole relief from such solitude comes through *proniknovenie*, the penetration
into the Other as another subject. This kind of penetration, more suggestive
and powerful than the "I–Thou" relationship, approaches another I and
happens only through God. Essentially, then, Ivanov's argument is this:
Dostoevsky's writings consider man's position in relation to the divine, just
as tragedy continuously explores man's tense connection with the gods.[7]

Soon after Ivanov's syncretic reading of Dostoevsky's novels had
captured the imagination of the Russian public, a voice arose in objection. In
1922, Lev Pumpyansky published his argument against Ivanov in an article
entitled "Dostoevsky and Antiquity." Pumpyansky had been a close friend
and "partner in dialogue" of Bakhtin since their undergraduate years in the
Department of Classics at Petersburg University under the direction of the
evangelical and charismatic scholar, Faddei Zelinsky. Unlike Ivanov, who
received a traditional Classical training under Mommsen in Germany,
Pumpyansky, studied Classics in Russia during the frenetic pre-revolutionary
years, when antiquity was enjoying an oddly active revival. Perhaps in
connection with the idealization of the war of independence in Greece,
Hellenism became a movement espousing the eventual resurrection of an
ancient model of society in Russia, a projection they referred to as the "Third
Renaissance." The circle which formed around Bakhtin—who was somewhat
reminiscent of Zelinsky—valued independence of thought, unconventionality,
and eccentricity.[8] Thus Pumpyansky approached Dostoevsky with the aim of
debunking any dogmatic approach to literary canons and texts, and so sought
in him the new and the different. In response to Ivanov's invocation of
ancient genres, Pumpyansky remarked almost sarcastically:

дошло ли эстетически непоколебимым трагическое
искусство за столь долгое странствие от Афин до
Петербурга? осталось ли тем же дионисическое
божество на всем протяжении страстного путешествия?[9]

Like most members of the Bakhtin circle, Pumpyansky insisted on the
effects of historical time. He concluded that the changes of the Renaissance
had necessarily transformed the genre of tragedy in an essential way. In a

nonconformist spirit, he wrested Dostoevsky's writings out of the grasp of their Classical, and even Russian genre associations, and wedged them into a typology alongside other more modern—although not modernist— European works, such as Shakespeare's *Hamlet* and Hugo's *Les Miserables*. What was Pumpyansky's thesis against Ivanov? In brief, he objected to the understanding of Dostoevsky as tragic on the grounds that neo-Classicism and Romanticism in Europe had corrupted the idea of the "truly Classical." In consequence, Russia received a somewhat damaged Muse, already self-conscious and anxiety-ridden. While Classical poetry could be marked by a definite distinction between author and hero, the modern hero rebels against the author and eventually assumes the authorial function and position. Thus Pumpyansky conceived of the shift from antiquity to modernity as the change from the author's dream about the hero, to the hero dreaming his own dream, or nightmare, about himself. This has its parallel in Bakhtin's view of the Dostoevskian hero, published in 1929, whose dominant feature will be self consciousness. Because the hero is without an external author, he wanders through life, hallucinating his own reality. Ultimately, dream space becomes the hero's—and specifically Raskolnikov's—"aesthetic homeland, that is, his Classicism." For herein the hero assumes authorship of himself as an "envisioned hero." Finally, Pumpyansky conclusively dismantles Dostoevsky as tragic poet through the orientation of the dream. In Dostoevsky, the coincidental dreaming of the poet and hero is always prophetic, a "son prorochesky [prophetic dream]." This evaluation of the dream informs Dostoevsky's whole perspective, and his difference from tragedy: "Трагедия есть всегда *память* о событии никогда *пророчество* о нем" [Tragedy is always a *memory* about an event, never a *prophecy* about it] (italics in original). Tragedy, Pumpyansky elaborates, is the last wave of an event already fictive and no longer real; the poetry of Dostoevsky, on the other hand, is the wave of an event still to be. In other words, tragedy moves out of reality into fiction, while Dostoevsky's poetry moves from fiction into reality. From this it follows, Pumpyansky concludes, that Dostoevsky is not a tragic poet: "ego slovo ni vspominaet, a predvaryaet [his word does not remember, but anticipates]" (Pumpyansky 1922, 8–25). Pumpyansky's commitment to Dostoevsky's "anticipatory word" reminds us of Bakhtin's famous gloss on the Dostoevskian opposition to Aristotelian catharsis:

> Certain, scholars (Vyacheslav Ivanov, Komarovich) apply to Dostoevsky's works the ancient (Aristotelian) term "catharsis" (purification). If this term is understood in a very broad sense, then one can agree with it (without catharsis in the broad sense there is no art at all). But tragic catharsis (in the Aristotelian

sense) is not applicable to Dostoevsky. The catharsis that finalizes Dostoevsky's novels might be—of course inadequately and somewhat rationalistically—expressed in this way: *nothing conclusive has yet taken place in the world, the ultimate word of the world and about the world has not yet been spoken, the world is open and free, everything is still in the future and will always be in the future.* (italics in original) (Bakhtin 1984, 165–66)

Thus, we can see that both Ivanov and Pumpyansky discern the central role of fate in Dostoevsky's novels, although they define this role differently. For Ivanov, fate consists in the direction of events once man has chosen for or against God. Prophecy, we can thus deduce, would occur at the moment of this human choice, with God or Devil marking the events to come. Pumpyansky, on the other hand, calls the totality of a Dostoevskian novel prophecy. Tragedy portrays events already completed in the past; Dostoevsky describes events yet to occur. In either case, both Ivanov and Pumpyansky foreground the human construction of the prophetic word, with its relation to the divine being perceived as secondary; rather than the divine word coming through the oracle to man, prophecy appears as the human word which aims at approximating to a more distant relationship to the divine. Prophecy has thus lost its intrinsic causality. It will be the task of the second half of this essay to demonstrate that Raskolnikov in *Crime and Punishment* suffers from this transformation of prophetic speech.

In antiquity, as we have noted, prophecy comprised the most traditional means of divine communication to man. If man communicated to the gods through hymn and sacrifice, the gods communicated to man, equally obliquely, but equally reliably, through the riddling words of the oracle. The most obvious example of this in tragedy is the *Oedipus Tyrannus*. Prophecy, or prophecy configured as curse, functions to some degree in almost all the tragedies. The traditional hermeneutics of prophecy entails a kind of "bindingness", of word and deed; because the prophetic word originates in the divine will, speech and action contain their consequences within themselves. In such a divinely bound cosmos, there is no arbitrarily signifying word, even if that signification cannot be understood until later, the time of the tragically "too late." Prophecy then, traditionally, describes a single path of action, the effect of which makes necessary every step upon that path.

Prophecy denotes an ordered and meaningful universe, albeit inexplicably so. For example, Oedipus had to become upset by the offhand remark of the drunken guest that Polybus was not his true father, in order to set out to question the oracle. Eteocles had to arrange his men so that he would fight last, and thus against his brother. It makes little sense to keep asking ourselves: "Why didn't Ajax just stay in his tent?" In a universe which plays by the rules of prophetic speech, that is, speech which signifies its realization because of its divine referent, things simply *have* to happen. Yet the first dream in *Crime and Punishment* and Raskolnikov's response to it suggest the breakdown of these traditional assumptions. When Raskolnikov tries to read it like an ancient prophecy, the surrounding narrative opposes his misreading. Already in the *Oedipus Tyrannus* the materialized "path" of prophecy is depicted as treacherous: both Oedipus and his father left home to consult the oracle (868–70; 130–31), and both arrived at disaster. In this way, Sophocles suggests that the road to the oracle is a dangerous one, which can even lead to murder. As Creon says of Laius' death: "He went to consult an oracle, Apollo said, and he set out and never came home again" (130–31; Sophocles 1977, 165). Raskolnikov demonstrates this danger again, with greater insistence, in his own search for the prophetic.

For Raskolnikov, born into the post-Hamlet world of doubt and self-consciousness (Pumpyansky 1922, 13), necessity has grown elusive. There are no more prophecies, even for heroic men. There are no more assured definitions. As Ivan Karamazov envisioned in his story of the Grand Inquisitor, Christ chose not to enslave man with miracles, mystery and authority. Instead he gave the respectful, but difficult gift of freedom.[10] In a sense, Christ widened the possibilities of signification, removing the necessity of a single referent; by introducing choice into destiny, he thereby dismantled the dynamic of prophecy.

But Raskolnikov is not yet ready for this freedom. Rather than the great freedom of acting in a dialogically signifying world, Raskolnikov desires the lesser, monologic freedom from doubt. He wants the certainty of extreme definition and classification: Am I a Napoleon? Or am I a louse? With prophecy erased from the universe, Raskolnikov endeavors to reestablish such a constricted universe for the sake even of a constructed, illusory necessity.[11] So Raskolnikov explains his idea of the "ordinary" and the "extraordinary," which he published in an article:

> As for dividing people into ordinary and extraordinary, it's a bit arbitrary, I agree, but I don't insist on exact figures. I believe only in the basic conception. Merely that people *in general* are divided by a law of nature. The lower part, ordinary people I mean, just stuff, so to speak, good only to reproduce their own kind. The other part consists of people in the true sense. I mean those who are gifted, those who have the talent to shape a *new word* in the context of their environment. The subdivisions, of course, are

endless. Yet the distinguishing features of both parts are clear
enough. (italics in original) (Dostoevsky 1968a, 258)

As the novel uncovers Raskolnikov's self-construction of divine speech,
we perceive the deceit inherent in his progression; we see Raskolnikov as
though we were witnessing one who, although he is in the process of carving
a false idol, tries to convince himself that he is engendering God in his own
creation. Raskolnikov searches for an authoritative and absolute prophetic
word vis-à-vis himself, not the universe. He wants God's voice, in response
to his problem of self-consciousness, to answer his question: who am I? But
this desperate search unravels only to reveal the impossibility of such a singly
referential word's existence in the world of the polyphonic novel. We meet
Raskolnikov as a seeker after the new, determinedly forgetful of the old and
the past. The problem with Raskolnikov's conception of prophecy is that he
has forgotten, along with much else, the ancient prowess of the prophet: not
just one who foretells, the prophet knows the things having been, the things
being, and the things yet to be.[12] The prophecy desired early on by
Raskolnikov is a naive and partial one, which looks only toward the future
and speaks solely in signs particular to the individual.

Raskolnikov's failure, and concomitantly the novel's success in exposing
it, is rooted in his obstinate desire for a regressive, obsolete prophetic word
which plots a singular monologic path. Raskolnikov's yearning for prophecy
becomes indistinguishable from his mission for the new: the new step, the
new word, the new man. Having embarked on this crusade for the new, the
forward, the authoritative-prophetic, Raskolnikov continuously "forgets" (as
Freud would have it) to see the old and past, yet without these the new
becomes meaningless. Raskolnikov clumsily stumbles "singularly" forward,
necessarily half-asleep or in delirium in order to ignore the other half of the
new, the old and past. The following reading seeks to show the way in which
the text, in a crosscurrent to Raskolnikov, consistently and explicitly presents
the new in combination with the old. In other words, the archaic type of
prophecy, as the singularity of forward-moving plot and action, is
consistently coupled with its opposite—past and memory. The very
presentation of this duality or plurality of signification inherently defies the
false conception of the traditionally prophetic word. Raskolnikov always has
a choice throughout the novel; the text again and again presents a plurality
of options. But as Raskolnikov repeatedly chooses from only one set of
options, consciously refusing to acknowledge the other of the old and past,
the blindness of his vision becomes apparent. Not until the road of the new
leads him right back to the old does he come to see his own self-deception.
The final destination of Raskolnikov's story of murder reminds us of Ivan

Karamazov's tale of the Grand Inquisitor; when Ivan has finished his narration, his brother Alyosha declares: "Your poem is in praise of Jesus, not in blame of Him—as you meant it to be" (Dostoevsky 1976, 241). So also the gradual dismantling of Raskolnikov's authoring of divine speech turns into praise of Christ; the deconstruction of Raskolnikov's false prophecy praises a universe ruled not by monologic miracle, mystery, and authority, but by the freedom of people to speak and act dialogically as agents in the world.

The rest of this article, then, will trace the definitive dismantling of the authoritative prophetic word primarily through a consideration of Raskolnikov's first dream, which he finds to be a major source of his prophecy. This analysis concentrates on two areas. First, it attempts to show how the dream, which blends past and future, remembering and forgetting, becomes "monologized" by Raskolnikov, who reduces it solely to a sign of the future and its correlative, forgetting. Secondly, in an effort to show the inadequacy of Raskolnikov's interpretation of the dream, it will also focus on the dream's commentary on Raskolnikov's relation to the divine. Raskolnikov's discomfort in the state of separation from the divine both explicates his yearning for the monologic word in the way he seeks to destroy the old woman, and further illustrates the more distant position of the divine in a dialogic universe. The discussion of the divine, then, reverts to the discussion of prophecy.

II.

The first description of Raskolnikov names his general condition in terms reminiscent of not-remembering: "He soon plunged into deep thought, or rather, into a kind of oblivion [zabyt'e]" (Dostoevsky 1968a, 14).[13] Indeed, variations of "zabyvat' [to forget]" and "zabyvat'sya [to forget oneself, to doze off]" figure prominently in the narrative. The first dream, a sojourn into memory and densely surrounded by a haze of forgetting, thoroughly examines the coexisting relationships of these juxtaposed forces. Raskolnikov's second and third dreams are introduced simply yet significantly: "He lost consciousness [On zabylsya]" (Dostoevsky 1968a, 120, 272; 1989, 111, 261). Forgetting, and subsequently, remembering, intersect directly with dreaming. Thus the preface to Raskolnikov's first dream says:

> Such dreams, pathological dreams, make a powerful impression
> on man's disordered, already aroused organism, and are always
> remembered for a long time [vsegda dolgo pomnyatsya].
> (Dostoevsky 1968a, 62; 1989, 54)

A vivid dream comprises that which is long remembered; a dream creates, or triggers memory. Raskolnikov's forgetting himself causes his dream visions, sites in which, as the first dream shows, memory returns.

A series of "forgettings," while Raskolnikov is walking across Vasilevsky Island, precedes the first dream. "When he raised his head again with a start, he immediately forgot [zabyval] what he had been thinking about and where he had gone" (Dostoevsky 1968a, 61; 1989, 54). After noting several summer houses and flower beds, he comes across carriages and riders on horseback: "He followed them with curious eyes and forgot [zabyval] about them even before they disappeared from sight" (Dostoevsky 1968a, 61; 1989, 54). Finally, he pauses to count his money, accounting for his recent expenditures, "but soon forgetting [zabyl] why he had taken his money out" (Dostoevsky 1968a, 61; 1989, 54). The series of things forgotten, which leads up to his dream, occurs not by coincidence but clearly shows Raskolnikov's need or desire—yet ultimately his inability—to forget. For while he almost succeeds in forgetting while conscious, he can no longer do so while dreaming.

Raskolnikov's dream takes him back to childhood. The time, the day, and the place are just as they are preserved in his memory, but they are even sharper in his dream: "The neighborhood was very much as he remembered it, though he did not remember it as clearly as he saw it in his dream" (Dostoevsky 1968a, 62). Thus, dream not only presents a memory, but a memory more vivid and accurately detailed than one held in mind and subject to conscious recall. Dream then goes back beyond memory, to something beyond recall, to something *forgotten*. What is it that dream recalls and memory has forgotten? It must be that, like Raskolnikov's sudden recollection that he is planning to commit murder, memory usually forgets the thing buried and unlawful. And so what does Raskolnikov's first dream recall?

First the dream reveals Raskolnikov's innocence; he is a little child, afraid of the unruly crowd around the tavern, attached to his father, innately reverent towards the rites and symbols of the Church. When he sees the beating of the old mare, encouraged by the jeering crowd, he tears himself away from his father in passionate empathy. Indeed, Raskolnikov identifies with the poor innocent beast: upon waking up: "His whole body felt as if it had been beaten" (Dostoevsky 1968a, 67). But Dostoevsky's later extrapolations of this theme suggest that, in his universe, the very conception of innocence necessarily signifies a knowledge of guilt.[14] The dream, in fact, portrays the very conjunction of Raskolnikov's innocence and guilt; the moment he understands that he is, or was, innocent signifies the loss of innocence. Raskolnikov, because of his hyper-consciousness, perhaps more extremely than the rest, becomes part of the despicable crowd; his horror and his fascination draw him deeper and deeper into their midst. He, too—he especially—cannot stop looking. Thus, Raskolnikov dreams of the time when he was still innocent and yet already guilty; his dream presents to him the drama of his loss of innocence. Yet the beating of the mare does not recall the source of his guilt as much as the scenes with his father do.

Raskolnikov's father is absent from the novel. Having died many years earlier, he exists once in the closing words of his mother's letter and then again in this dream. The beginning of the dream recalls Raskolnikov's activity of walking with his father past the tavern, whose drunken and brawling crowd frightens him. He responds to his fear of encountering the terrifying crowd by drawing closer to his father: "He would pull himself close [tesno] to his father and tremble" (Dostoevsky 1968a, 62; 1989, 55). But by the end of the dream, the closeness to his father becomes a tightness in his chest: "He throws his arms around his father, but his chest feels very tight [tesnit, tesnit]" (Dostoevsky 1968a, 67; 1989, 59). What has occurred to create this subtle, yet significant, change?

Raskolnikov first responds to the beating of the mare with an appeal to his father: "'... Daddy, Daddy,' he shouts to his father, 'Daddy, what are they doing!'" (Dostoevsky 1968a, 64). The father responds by urging Raskolnikov away from the horrible "sight": "You mustn't look, let's go!" (Dostoevsky 1968a, 64). And, though his father endeavors to lead him away, Raskolnikov "tears himself loose from his father's hands" (Dostoevsky 1968a, 64). The father returns only at the end of the dream after the mare has finally been beaten to death. Having long chased after Raskolnikov, he seizes him and carries him out of the crowd. Again he responds to Raskolnikov's imploring query with an imperative "let's go," adding the explanation, "it's not our business" (Dostoevsky 1968a, 67). Although less conspicuous, if perhaps more consequential than the beating of the mare, Raskolnikov witnesses in his dream the crime of betrayal by his father. Here Raskolnikov experiences the limitations of his father's moral and physical power. The father, omniscient and omnipotent in the world of the child, falls into the realm of the weak and merely human in his willingness not to see the suffering of the mare and of his son. In this dream the father betrays the son when he urges him to come away and not to look. And just as the father betrays the son, the son then betrays the father, tearing himself away from the father's hand. And in the same way that the conception of innocence simultaneously comes to exist and ceases to be through the acknowledgement of guilt, the moment of the betrayal of the father marks the recognition of the self through the not-self; or, in terms of that other Father, Raskolnikov learns here of God through himself as not-God. The road that leads to the Sacred, to the church with the green cupola, winds past the tavern, the temple of earthly sin and vice. Raskolnikov never reaches the destination of the Sacred in this dream;

instead of the Sacred, he discovers, through the rebellion against the father, the not-Sacred, himself.

One could read this dream, then, as Raskolnikov reexperiencing his first conception of the other and of himself as separate from it. But more than the trauma of the experience of separation, the dream portrays the problem of the incompleteness of the division; the very connectedness between the self and the other becomes the source of Raskolnikov's mad sense of necessity to act. In this dream, Raskolnikov is too much like too many of its characters; both as Mikolka and the mare, both as innocent child and part of the guilty crowd, Raskolnikov stands in clear distinction only from his father. Only the act of breaking away from the father, only the uncoverable and unrecoverable distance from the tavern to the Church, seems an irremediable break. And yet, the very violence of this severing and the absence of overt signs characterizing the similarity (as with the mare and Mikolka) between f/Father and son, mark the extreme and unbearable character of this closeness and separation. Two possibilities arise from this position of bound separation: one may, emphasizing either the connection or the division, strive to bridge the distance and thereby to minimize it, or conversely, to complete the division and render it absolute. Raskolnikov chooses the second option, only to discover that the attempt to divide absolutely produces the opposite result; Raskolnikov identifies both with Mikolka and the mare. The attempt to separate by violence yields only to a deeper degree of non-separability. In the dream, Raskolnikov is both murderer and murdered, as he will be in his dream-filled life after the murder.

Appropriate to the motifs with which the dream is concerned, Raskolnikov's connection to the old pawnbroker is figured in terms of memory and forgetfulness. When Raskolnikov goes to the old woman's apartment for a trial run, he presses her doorbell which rings with a tinny and weak sound:

> In the cramped little apartments of such houses, there are always
> bells that sound like that. Its tone had slipped his mind [on uzhe
> zabyl]. Now this peculiar tone reminded [emu chto-to naponmil]
> him suddenly of something. (Dostoevsky 1968a, 16; 1989, 8)

Already on the doorstep of the old woman's apartment, Raskolnikov experiences a progression of forgetting and then recollecting (a process similar to that of a dream and the language associated with the dream, "predstavil"). What does imminent contact with the old woman call to mind? When Raskolnikov first addresses the old woman, he bows slightly, "recalling [vspomniv] that he had to be more polite" (Dostoevsky 1968a, 17; 1989, 9). Her very proximity produces remembering. And Raskolnikov, introducing himself as having visited a month earlier, prompts the old woman's first speech: "Oh, I remember [pomnyu],[15] my good man, I remember quite well [ochen' khorosho pomnyu] that you were here" (Dostoevsky 1968a, 17; 1989, 9). The old woman, in contrast to Raskolnikov's continual forgetting, defines herself here by absolute memory. Clearly, the old woman presents in her remembering a difference from Raskolnikov. The otherness of the old woman stems from her association with memory; she represents the past, the old and faded in all the yellowness that surrounds her. Raskolnikov, on the other hand, is the new, striving towards a fearlessness of the "new step, an authentic new word" (Dostoevsky 1968a, 14). Their difference is encapsulated in their very appellations: "young man [molodoi chelovek]"/"old woman [starushka]." But also, as in the dream, the otherness never exists as a distinct separation, but signifies a connection. Thus, while Raskolnikov so drastically opposes the old woman, as new versus old, future versus past, their difference turns into likeness. When Raskolnikov stands on her threshold prepared for murder, he bends his ear to her door and hears her movements behind it:

> Someone was standing silently at the threshold, and exactly as he
> was doing on the outside, was lurking and listening within; also,
> it would seem, with an ear to the door. (Dostoevsky 1968a, 81)

Raskolnikov imagines the old woman as mirroring his every movement, enacting his actions simultaneously with him. Thus, while she stands opposite to him, she also becomes like him in this stance, reflecting him like a mirror. Just behind the very penetrable divider of a door, she performs the same actions as he does. Can there now be an answer to the question of what the old woman causes Raskolnikov so discomfortingly to recollect?

It was argued earlier that the dream presented the horror not simply of a brutal murder, but also of the recognition of guilt which comes from the rebellion of separating from the f/Father and the recognition of one's individuality. But while the act of separation constituted a division, it also revealed a connectedness, compromising the division into incompleteness. On the one hand, the lingering bond can be a source of continued nurture and sustenance; on the other hand, the attenuation of the previous whole can be unbearable. For Raskolnikov, the desire for completion then arose as a relief from the tension of being both bound and apart; he mistakenly believes that murder will overcome the division by fully severing the remaining bonds, yet the violent act only tightens the inextricability between murderer and victim, thus casting him as both Mikolka and the beaten mare.

Raskolnikov stands in just such a tense relation to the old woman. When we think about the role of prophecy as indicative of the position of the divine, his relationship to her takes on significance when she becomes an attainable substitute for God. A beacon of memory, she causes him to recognize her as different, but also to remember uneasily the significance of that difference. The otherness of the old woman recalls the initial pain of separation from the father when the wholeness becomes irremediably divided but still bound; she recalls the original conception of the self in view of the other, a self eternally divided. She reminds him of the separation from God on a journey that arrives not at the Church, but at the understanding of the self as not-God. Raskolnikov cannot "kill" God in his effort to obliterate the object from which he is separated, and thus relieve his pain. Instead, he can destroy a different other, the old woman; ironically, the "louse" becomes a stand-in for God. The distinction of the self demands the sacrifice of the whole; the knowledge of the self demands the distance of the other. Raskolnikov, "the split one," tries to forget the pain of the loss of the whole but cannot endure the tension of the distance. He murders the old woman in an effort to obliterate the other, to relieve the tension of the distance by destroying that from which one is separated. Raskolnikov's act is tragic because of the futility of his effort; the desire to obliterate the tension by completing the division through the destruction of the other unavoidably becomes the destruction of the self. I suggest that Raskolnikov here occupies the exact position of the tragic hero as described by Vernant, situated in the not-divided-enough division out of which tragedy arises:

> For there to be tragic action it is necessary that a concept of human nature with its own characteristics should have already emerged and that the human and divine spheres should have become sufficiently distinct from each other for them to stand in opposition; yet at the same time they must continue to appear as inseparable. (Vernant 1990b, 46)

There is too much likeness between the self and the other to destroy successfully the distanced object of desire, and therefore the source of pain, without also destroying the self. Thus Raskolnikov cries to Sonya: "Did I kill the old hag? No, not the old hag—I killed myself! I went there, and all at once I did away with myself forever!" (Dostoevsky 1968a, 407). And thus the road to the church also leads to the cemetery, where the grave of the little brother lies alongside the grave of the grandmother.

At this point, we can see how Raskolnikov interprets his dream as prophetic. Raskolnikov, the dreamer of the new word, the "forgettor" of the old and the past, reads his dream exclusively with an eye to the future. Upon awakening, he responds to his dream:

> "God!" he exclaimed. "Will I really? ... Will I really take the ax, will I really hit her on the head, split open her skull ... will I really slip in the sticky warm blood, break open the lock, steal, and shiver ... and hide, all bloody ... with the ax ... Good Lord, will I really?" (Dostoevsky 1968a, 67)

Raskolnikov reads his dream strictly "forwardly," as a prophetic warning dream. Although it recalls to him the past and the road to God, Raskolnikov forgets this fact again. He "forgets" the past when he sees the dream as a picture of the possible future, just as he "forgets" God when he kills the old woman.

Raskolnikov has already shown himself as a forward-looking reader in areas other than his reaction to his dream. Throughout the first part of the novel, Raskolnikov several times admits that he knows something is going to happen, that he has a presentiment. Early on, his response to the drunken man's ridicule of his hat introduces his general stance toward events: "'... So I knew!' he muttered in confusion. 'I thought so!'" (Dostoevsky 1968a, 15). Raskolnikov's first look at Marmeladov has special significance for him: "Later, Raskolnikov would recall that first impression and think of it as an omen [predchuvstviyu]" (Dostoevsky 1968a, 21; 1989, 13). Walking through the park the next day, the horrible thought comes into Raskolnikov's mind: "For he had known, he had *felt* [*predchuvstoval*] that inevitably it would 'flash,' and he had been waiting for it" (italics in original) (Dostoevsky 1968a, 53; 1999, 46). This sensation of presentiment recurs to Raskolnikov when he later considers how he unnecessarily detoured through the Haymarket on the way home after his dream:

> Subsequently, when he recalled everything that happened to him in those days, moment by moment, point by point, bit by bit, he was always struck, almost superstitiously by that one circumstance, not in itself unusual, but which afterward constantly seemed to him a kind of predestined turning point of his fate.... Yet why, he always asked, why did such an important meeting, for him so decisive and yet so extraordinarily accidental, take place in the Haymarket (where he had no reason to be going) just then at just that hour at just that moment of his life when he happened to be in just the mood and under just those circumstances when that meeting alone could have exerted the

most decisive and the most conclusive influence on his entire
destiny? It was as though it had purposely been lying in wait for
him! (Dostoevsky 1968a, 68)

Circumstances have grown fateful in Raskolnikov's mind; the very accidental
nature of this encounter in the Haymarket engenders its contrary sense of
necessity. As a further explanation of Raskolnikov's developing feeling of
being "dragged along by a wheel in which his coat became entangled," he
provides a second anecdote similar to his learning the fateful piece of news
in the Haymarket. That other encounter involves overhearing a student tell
a soldier in the tavern Raskolnikov's exact thoughts about killing the old
pawnbroker. Intellectually, they debate the morality of killing the shrewish
old pawnbroker for the improvement of the general welfare: "For one life,
thousands of lives saved from ruin and collapse. One death and a hundred
lives—there's arithmetic for you!" (Dostoevsky 1968a, 73). The student
concludes that the only justice consists in murdering her oneself.
Raskolnikov's reaction to this as a sign of his destiny is symptomatic of his
general tendency towards searching after oracles and omens:

> Recently, however, Raskolnikov had grown superstitious. Traces
> of superstition remained in him for a long time afterward, too.
> And he was always inclined to see a certain strangeness, a
> mystery, in the whole affair; he assumed the working of special
> influences and coincidences. (Dostoevsky 1968a, 70)

Raskolnikov becomes superstitious; particular events assume special
significance, as prophetic of the future or as logical steps in the progression
of his unfolding destiny. In his interest in the prophecy of a straight and
single forward path, Raskolnikov forgets the other, backward-looking half of
the dream.

For readers of the novel, more aware of what has been and then what
will be, the dream does not appear disconnected from the earlier events.
Rather, just as we sometimes anticipate "bad dreams" from watching a horror
movie late at night, themes and images from Raskolnikov's waking life cross
over into his dream. Thus, the imagery of Raskolnikov's dream finds
correspondences in where he has been and in what he has experienced prior
to it. His trip to the old woman with the "offering" of his father's watch
recalls the visit to his grandmother's grave accompanied by his father and the
gift of the rice dish. The drunken peasant who "rode past him on the street,
in an enormous cart drawn by an enormous dray horse" (Dostoevsky 1968a,
15), prefigures Mikolka in his large cart (usually drawn by a large horse)

tormenting the mare. Raskolnikov's first visit to a tavern presumably marks taverns as significant places, towards which he is drawn and wherein he encounters the crowd. Marmeladov conveys himself to Raskolnikov as both the sacrificer (of Sonya, his wife and her children) and also as the sacrifice in his bestial form: "I am the shape [obraz] of a beast" (Dostoevsky 1968a, 24; 1989, 17), the victimized end of his wife's physical aggression, that is. The letter from home links his mother and sister with Sonya in the ranks of women who sacrifice themselves, and who, like the mare, live on with determination. The closing words of his mother's letter further remind Raskolnikov of his childhood and the time of happiness when his father was alive, that is, the time of the dream: "Remember, my dear, how when you were still a child, when your father was still alive, you used to babble your prayers on my knee and how happy we all were then!" (Dostoevsky 1968a, 47). Lastly, the maternal letter arouses his indignation at her willingness *not to see*, to accept the way things "seem," rather than are, particularly in Luzhin, the despicable fiance (Dostoevsky 1968a, 49). The final event before the dream, the encounter in the park with the abused girl, cements the motif of the beaten women—Sonya, Dunya, his mother. In this last situation, Raskolnikov behaves both like the child and father in the dream. First he does intervene to help the suffering girl, but then he shifts to speak his father's words ("it's not our business"), but with even greater malice when he advises the policeman to stop his efforts at helping the girl: "'... Stop! Why bother? Let it go! Let him have his fun.' He pointed to the dandy. 'What's it to you?'" (Dostoevsky 1968a, 57). Also the very last images on Vasilevsky Island play a role in his dream: the interrupted journey (to Razumikhin), the tavern again, the carriages and horses, and the general sensation of the countryside. Clearly, the events of the chapters preceding it become recast in the images and events of the dream.

The dream, then, provides a pre-telling and a retelling, yet Raskolnikov chooses to see only the former. The very irony of his prophetic reading, however, is that it reverses linearity—he has to read backwards, to remember, in order to see how the dream reads forwards. For the text explains Raskolnikov's consideration of his walk home via Haymarket as fatefully laden upon his *later* contemplation of events.

It is worth making several observations about the nature of dreaming itself as Dostoevsky understood it and aesthetically presented it. First, although dream must be told in narrative, one of its marvels is the way it functions in absolute disregard of the laws of narrative.[16] The dream, not subject to space and time, poses a challenge to the causality and linearity which narrative imposes. When Raskolnikov reads his dream as strictly prophetic, he loses sight of it as dream, and sees it only in narrative terms.

He forgets that the law of causality intrinsic to narrative need not extend beyond it, into, for example, the non-narrative of dream.

Thus the contents of the first dream, and Raskolnikov's partial response to it, reveal the complexity of time and motivation. Raskolnikov endeavors to draw a sharp line between past and future, turning exclusively towards the latter, in his murder of the old woman; yet any such violent division only binds the two sides together more tightly. Raskolnikov's "loss of memory" initiates his return to it: in his dream, in his attraction to the old woman, even in the murder. Raskolnikov acts from a deep immersion in memory and demonstrates in his action the inextricability of past and future, of memory and novelty. And when he ceases to dream in the second half of the novel, turning over his position of dreamer to Svidrigailov, it seems that he has seen what his dreams made visible: the past, the time of his childhood. Raskolnikov comes to see that there is no obliteration of the past in light of the future. Raskolnikov's act of murder reestablishes the totality of the dialogic word. His reading of the exclusively new implies, even if violently, another signification, that of the old. Thus the demon of Raskolnikov's monologic self-appointed prophecy is exposed.

III.

An application of this reading to Athenian tragedy seems more radical. Vernant's analysis, building upon Lesky's, of the shared, albeit tense, responsibility of both man and god in the enacting of destiny in ancient tragedy seems to me persuasive and satisfying. To make it work, we must to a certain extent approach the question of agency differently, without the modern requirements of the term; for tragedy occurred at the crossroads between old and new. On the one hand, tragic guilt arises from the ancient religious conception of an inherited familial or tribal defilement, an *ate* or madness sent by the gods; on the other hand, the rule of law has begun to define a person as an individual acting independently and unconstrainedly, and so deliberately committing crime. Thus, tragic man is always divided, between *aitios*, his character, and *daimon*, the urging of the gods. The earmark of tragedy consists in the tension between the two areas of decision and guilt: the categories remain open and inseparable (Vernant 1990a, 49–84). But what happens if we entertain for a moment the possibility of taking a less moderate viewpoint, and stand together with Peradotto and his "Sophist Other" to see tragedy from a very rational and scientific glance? For in a recent article, having nothing to do with Dostoevsky, Peradotto seeks a reconsideration of *Oedipus Tyrannus* without the concession to the convention of prophecy. Peradotto deplores what he sees as the degradation of the standards and goals of literary interpretation and in assigning blame for this, he has a bone to pick with Aristotle. Seeking the reinstatement of reason as the primary hermeneutic tool, which naturally discounts chance as a force of causation, Peradotto wonders how Aristotle, the greatest scientist of antiquity, could esteem the *Oedipus Tyrannus*, "a play so riddled with chance, so crippled by coincidences" (1992, 4), most highly. It is as though we have all been coerced into reading like Raskolnikov, making inferences and connections where none necessarily exists. Despite the fact that Sophocles admittedly wrote an "anti-Sophist" (1992, 1) play, Peradotto encourages us to free ourselves from the shackles of authoritative ideology and reinstate our disbelief, like full Sophists, not the "half-baked Sophist" Oedipus (1992, 13). Then we will be free to rewrite Sophocles' play into one of "emancipation" rather than "enslavement" (1992, 2). While Peradotto acknowledges at the outset the "particular contemporary perspective" (1992, 1) of his reading, I suggest that he would be a happier reader of Dostoevsky than of Sophocles. In my opinion, Peradotto reads either anachronistically, aiming to reroute the ancient text into a modern one, or non-poetically as a scientist, rather than a literary critic. Peradotto raises the question of the moral and social implications of a literary work (1992, 6). He wonders why Aristotle's *Poetics* aligns itself more closely with his *Rhetoric* than with the *Physics* or *Metaphysics* (1992, 5–6). While Peradotto attributes this to some fault in Aristotle's thinking, or to his falling to the degraded logic of the general public, it seems important to keep in mind the consistency of Aristotle's categories and his brilliance; Poetics *is* like Rhetoric and different from Physics, as Aristotle clearly demonstrates. Literary narrative is not science: *chance in the "real" world ceases to be chance once it is plotted.* While Peradotto understands this capacity of language to turn the "merely *accidental* into the *necessary*" (1992, 6), he rejects precisely this poetic and narrative function of language. Peradotto longs for the dialogic, for the prophecy of Dostoevsky's novel. Yet I fear that this is premature for a reading of the *Oedipus Tyrannus*, and I think this may be seen based on Perladotto's own insights on the narrative and performative nature of ancient prophecy:

> Prophecy is not conceivable apart from narrative. It *derives from* narrative, from the representation of causal continuity in time. It is, I believe, less accurate to say that a narrative represents a prophecy than to say that prophecy represents that narrative, and does so by *pre-presenting* it, the frame paradoxically embedded in what it frames. Prophecy derives from the narrator's foreknowledge (in reality, his afterknowledge) of his own products, from a process of retrogressive composition—from end

to beginning (the end coming first and justifying the means),
disguised in performance as a progression from beginning to end.
(italics in text) (1992, 10–11)

Peradotto here summarizes the workings of prophecy in ancient
drama, which he sees as the most suspicious genre; drama masks the author
as the source of discourse and does not allow for rereading, thereby creating
an audience disabled from producing meaning (1992, 9). But herein lies the
crux of Peradotto's insight and blindness: to reject the monologic prophecy
of ancient drama is to reject ancient drama itself. For, essentially, there is no
difference between prophecy and narrative performance. Prophecy was a
verbal genre, and, like tragedy, a performative one. The delivery of a
prophecy took place through an "oracular performance." I agree with
Peradotto: "Prophecy is not conceivable apart from narrative" (1992, 10).
And this is so because prophecy is narrative. Thus Vernant's categorization
of the *Oedipus Tyrannus* as a riddle has been extended to liken the structure
of the play to an oracle: "Since riddles and oracles are often
indistinguishable, we may also say that the *Oedipus Tyrannus* is constructed
like an oracle" (Maurizio 1993, 139). The play is essentially an oracular
performance, whence, its context and power. I think we could claim that
monologic prophecy denotes the genre of tragic drama, and it is not until the
change to the genre of the polyphonic novel, which blurs the distinction
between author and hero and allows for rereading, that the construction of
prophecy can be exposed and dethroned. Thus, unwittingly, Peradotto—in
his desire in contrast to his material—has demonstrated for us the difference
between the genres of ancient tragedy and the modern polyphonic novel.
Had Peradotto sat amongst the 5th century sophists at a performance of the
Oedipus Tyrannus, he alone would have been uncomfortable. It seems to me,
that like Aristotle, the sophists recognized the difference between poetics
and physics. And if the power of poetics to make the accidental necessary
upsets one's civic order, ban it from your city, but let it remain itself, poetry,
not science.

As suggested earlier, Dostoevsky in part escapes the interdependence of
prophecy and narrative by displacing false prophecy into the non-narrative
of dreams. But he does not escape it entirely. We recall that Pumpyansky
called the whole of the Dostoevsky novel "prophecy." Why? Perhaps
ironically, it is his rival, Vyacheslav Ivanov, who clarifies Pumpyansky's
pronouncement. Dostoevsky portrays a universe significantly changed from
that of antiquity. His perception of the Divine as unwilling to enslave with
miracle and mystery opens up the word, allowing for true dialogicity.
Raskolnikov's search for the prophetic led to the past: he no longer inhabits

a universe permissive of simple prophetic speech which describes a single path of action. Rather, his is a universe of choice, of agency, of freedom and respect for man. Yet within this freedom, Dostoevsky's heroes face a choice, to be with or without God. Once the choice is made, there remain two directions with innumerable permutations of events within them. In the beginning, Raskolnikov chooses against God and in favor of the Grand Inquisitor when he tries to set up the idol of the prophetic speech of his own making. But once its false mechanics have become exposed, he chooses God, and moves along that other general path. In a sense we can conceive of this as another form of prophecy, but a kind which allows for two described paths rather than one. We may go as far as to say that Dostoevsky exposes one kind of prophecy almost as a foil in order to elevate another kind. Prophecy in the Dostoevskian novel becomes wider, more complete and inclusive. This greater prophecy offers the more complete vision of past, present and future which views the overall direction for humankind. This is not a one-to-one type of prophecy, either between signified and signifier or between divinity and individual. Rather it outlines a direction within which man as agent speaks and acts with a large margin of choice and reference. In a sense it is also a more enclosed prophecy as the universe itself has become teleological.

In conclusion, we can spatially reformulate some of the discussion above. If we conceive of both the *Oedipus Tyrannus* and *Crime and Punishment* as stories of self-discovery in relation to the divine, we could picture the moment of Oedipus' separation from his father on the road to Apollo's oracle as not unlike Raskolnikov's on the road to the Church. A difference, however, consists in the trajectory of those paths. Oedipus kills his father because the path does not allow for two to pass: this road to the word of God is straight and narrow. In *Crime and Punishment*, the road to the Church, "the word of God," bends around in a circle: this road never leads directly to the divine, yet makes room for both father and son. Both Oedipus and Raskolnikov stand in a tensely bound and discreetly separate relation to the divine. Yet there is a difference of emphasis: tragedy underscores the closeness, while the novel highlights the distance. From this we have our two kinds of prophecy, indicative, it seems, along with Pumpyansky, of two distinct genres separated by the great waves of literary evolution.

NOTES

1. *Poetics* (1752a). Unless otherwise indicated, all translations refer to the editions cited in the bibliography.

2. This is not to say that Homer wrote epics of fate: Achilles's wrath was his own and his *choice* to kill Hektor and thus himself be killed was completely commensurate with his own character, while simultaneously fulfilling the plan of Zeus. See Vernant 1990a, 49–84.

Vernant shows tragic decision rooted in two types of reality: *ethos* and *daimon*, character and divine power (77). He summarizes: "The nature of tragic action appears to us to be defined by the simultaneous presence of a 'self' and something greater that is divine at work at the core of the decision and creating a constant tension between the two opposed poles" (75).

3. Two matched lines of Achilles and Athena in Book I of the *Iliad* demonstrate this capacity of divine speech, in contrast to human:

> all'ek toi ereo, to de kai teleesthai oio (204) (Achilles)
> ode gar exereo, to de kai tetelesmenon estai (212) (Athena)

> [Yet I will tell you this and I think it will be accomplished;
> For I will tell you this and it will be a thing accomplished]

The change of verbs at the end of the line summarizes the matter: while Achilles *thinks* that what he says will be accomplished, for Athena it *will be*. See Parry 1981, 24. Vernant paraphrases this weakness of human speech: "What it lacked was the power of realization, the efficacy that was the exclusive privilege of the divine" (1990a, 83).

4. Nagy provides an etymology for *prophetes*: a *nomen agentis* of the verbal stem **pha–* "to say," "to speak," and the prefix *pro–*, which means "forth," rather than "in advance," where the dependent object has no relation to the future. Thus the word means most often "one who proclaims publicly." *Prophetes* = declarer (1990, 162–64).

5. This model of dialogue comes, of course, from Bakhtin. Morson and Emerson summarize thus: "Bakhtin argued, without a finalizing other, 'I' cannot achieve an image of myself, just as I cannot be aware of how my mind works when I am unself-conscious, and cannot know how I really appear to the world by looking in a mirror. An integral self, a tentative self-definition, requires an *other*. To know oneself, to know one's image in the world, one needs another's finalizing outsideness" (italics in original) (1990, 91).

6. It is probably worth noting that the significance of Ivanov's aesthetics is based on Dmitry, the most iconic, revelation-oriented, and dramatic of the four brothers. Bakhtin summarizes Dmitry's binary character in his comments on the picture of false psychology portrayed in the scenes of his preliminary investigation and trial. "The investigator, judges, prosecutor, defense attorney, and commission of experts are all equally incapable of approaching the unfinalized and undecided core of Dmitry's personality, for he is a man who stands, in essence throughout his entire life, on the threshold of great internal decisions and crises" (1984, 62). Such a threshold position characterizes Ivanov's conception of the hero in Dostoevsky's universe.

7. See Vernant 1990b, 43–48. For the collected essays of Ivanov in English translation, see Ivanov 1952, esp. 3–47.

8. See Clark and Holquist 1984, 30–42. See also Emerson 1993, 125–26.

9. "Did aesthetically unshakable tragic art arrive, after such lengthy wandering, from Athens to Petersburg? Did the Dionysian divinity remain the same during the whole period of the passionate journey?" (Pumpyansky 1922, 9; my translation).

10. Dostoevsky elaborates on the state of this new, prophecy-seeking world, in *The Brothers Karamazov*. In the chapter of the same name, The Grand Inquisitor makes clear to Christ that he can now add nothing to what he has said and done. He could have converted the people by miracle, but instead gave them freedom: "Thou [Christ] did not come down [from the cross], for again Thou wouldst not enslave man by a miracle, and didst crave faith given freely, not based on miracle" (1976, 236). Christ left man in a state of too much freedom, without miracles and mysteries, which were binding upon the world

of prophecies. As Ivan Karamazov formulates, in his great respect for humankind, Christ refused to enslave man with miracles.

11. So the Grand Inquisitor understood: "Is the nature of men such, that they can reject miracle, and at the great moments of their life, the moments of their deepest, most agonizing spiritual difficulties, cling only to the free verdict of the heart? ... But Thou didst not know that when man rejects miracle he rejects God too; for man seeks not so much God as the miraculous. *And as man cannot bear to be without the miraculous, he will create new miracles of his own for himself*" (my italics) (Dostoevsky 1976, 236).

12. For example, the following is said of Calchas in *Iliad* 1.70: "os ede ta t'eonta ta t'essomena, pro t'eonta [he knew the things being, the things yet to be, and the things having been]."

13. I am using Sidney Monas' translation of *Crime and Punishment*, with several slight alterations. I include words of special significance from the original in transliteration in brackets. The first citation refers to the English translation, the second to the Russian in Dostoevsky 1989.

14. Cf. *The Dream of a Ridiculous Man*: "When they [the inhabitants of the star] became wicked, they began talking of brotherhood and humanity and understood the meaning of those ideas. When they became guilty of crimes, they invented justice!' (Dostoevsky 1968b, 734).

15. "Pomnyu" actually comprises her first word.

16. Cf. *The Dream of a Ridiculous Man*: "Dreams as we all know, are very curious things: certain incidents in them are presented with quite uncanny vividness, each detail executed with the finishing touch of a jeweller, while others you leap across as though entirely unaware of, for instance, space and time!" (1968b, 724).

Works Cited

Bakhtin, Mikhail M. 1984. *Problems of Dostoevsky's Poetics*. Tr. Caryl Emerson. Minneapolis: University of Minnesota Press.

Clark, Katerina and Holquist, Michael. 1984. *Mikhail Bakhtin*. Cambridge: Harvard University Press.

Dostoevsky, Fyodor M. 1968a. *Crime and Punishment*. Tr. Sidney Monas. New York: Penguin Books.

———. 1968b. "The Dream of a Ridiculous Man." Tr. David Magarshack. *Great Short Works of Fyodor Dostoevsky*. New York: Harper & Row, 715–38.

———. 1976. *The Brothers Karamazov*. Tr. Constance Garnett. New York: W.W. Norton & Company, Inc.

———. 1989. *Prestuplenie i nakazanie. Sobranie sochinenii v pyatnadtsati tomakh*. Tom 5. Leningrad: Nauka.

Emerson, Caryl. 1993. "Irreverent Bakhtin and the Imperturbable Classics." *Arethusa* 26: 123–40.

Ivanov, Vyacheslav. 1952. *Freedom and the Tragic Life*. Tr. Norman Cameron. New York: The Noonday Press.

Maurizio, Lisa. 1993. "Delphic Narratives: Recontextualizing the Pythia and Her Prophecies." Diss.: Princeton University.

Nagy, Gregory. 1990. *Pindar's Homer*. Baltimore: Johns Hopkins University Press.

Parry, Adam. 1981. *Logos and Ergon in Thucydides*. New York: Arno Press.

Peradotto, John. 1992. "Disauthorizing Prophecy: The Ideological Mapping of *Oedipus Tyrannus*." *Transactions of the American Philological Association* 122: 1–15.

Pumpyansky, Lev V. 1922. *Dostoevskii i antichnost'*. Petrograd: n.p. (Pumpyansky first delivered the thesis as a paper on 2 October 1921.)

Sophocles. 1977. *Oedipus the King*. Tr. Robert Fagles. New York: Penguin Books, 158–251.

Vernant, Jean-Pierre. 1990a. "Intimations of the Will in Greek Tragedy." *Myth and Tragedy in Ancient Greece*. Tr. Janet Lloyd. New York: Zone Books, 49–84.

———. 1990b. "Tensions and Ambiguities in Greek Drama." *Myth and Tragedy in Ancient Greece*, Tr. Janet Lloyd. New York: Zone Books, 29-48.

OLGA MEERSON

How Dostoevsky Inscribes
"Thou Shalt Not Kill" in a Killer's Heart.
The Decalogue Taboo Internalized: The It of "It"

"How, then, do you know about it?" [...] she asked after [...] almost a
whole minute of silence.

"Might it not have been some future Napoleon who bumped off our
Alyona Ivanovna with an axe last week?" Zamyotov suddenly blurted out
from his corner. [...] A moment of gloomy silence passed.

Crime and Punishment (VI. 315, 204)

Raskolnikov's Victory

The plot of *Crime and Punishment* can be summarized in terms of
tabooing. Raskolnikov violates the taboo on murder in thought and in deed:
first he develops an ideology which justifies murder and then he becomes a
murderer. When, however, he is not engaged in "thought" or in "deed," and
gets a chance to come into contact with his own conscience, he finds this
taboo still inviolable: he cannot refer to the murder directly in his own mind
or in talking to Sonia. His violation of social taboo becomes his own *personal*
taboo: deep down, he regards as unmentionable that which he himself
proclaimed and did. Since Raskolnikov always observes this personal taboo
unconsciously, it is only in the epilogue that he comes to *recognize* it or its
implications for his ability to speak or act. But as a seed, as Raskolnikov's

From *Dostoevsky's Taboos*. © 1998 by Dresden University Press.

personal mental idiosyncrasy, or his "sore spot" unmentionable in private rather than in public, this taboo has always been present in the plot.

Raskolnikov's interactions with other characters make this "seed" grow by challenging it, for the other characters in the novel have their own idiosyncratic taboos, or personal "sore spots," symptomatic of their systems of values. As Raskolnikov interacts with other characters, his system of values thus clashes with theirs. The system of values in *Crime and Punishment*, therefore, emerges *not* from an interaction among characters' utterances or intellectual speculations (as Bakhtin believed), and not from the interplay of different reactions to a central taboo (as in *Demons*) but rather from the collision among the value systems underlying different characters' idiosyncratic taboos. Although Raskolnikov's *ideas* "lose" (to those of both Porfiry and Svidrigajlov), the values underlying his personal taboo "win," and he emerges as the victor in his own personal moral battle.

Besides the battle with other characters' taboos, Raskolnikov's absolute moral voice is engaged in another battle, with his own rationalizing voice. In this battle Raskolnikov's absolute moral voice also emerges as the victor. Raskolnikov himself feels defeated for as long as he identifies with his rationalizing voice, rather than this absolute moral voice within him. As L. D. Opul'skaia writes, "the dramatic [component] of the conflict is strengthened by the fact that outwardly, rationally [*logicheski*], Raskolnikov will turn out to be the victor, but morally [he will be] defeated."[1] By "morally" Opul'skaia means Raskolnikov's own inviolable standards.

Who Taboos What in *Crime and Punishment*?

Although no conspicuous word or notion in *Crime and Punishment* is consistently omitted, the tone of avoiding the mention of what is important permeates the novel. Different characters have different "sore spots" which they taboo in their discourse or behavior. Besides Raskolnikov, the most important tabooer's are Katerina Ivanovna, Raskolnikov's mother, his sister Dunia and Svidrigajlov.

Katerina Ivanovna's sore spot is Sonia's profession. This sore spot motivates her suicidally aggressive behavior at Marmeladov's wake, and yet she is ready to kill anyone who would dare to refer or allude to it (VI:298–9).

Raskolnikov's mother stubbornly "blocks" her awareness of her son's crime and punishment (VI:412–13, 415), even though she is interested in his article which provides, through its ideology, an indirect and yet insistent reference to the tabooed subject of his crime. At the end of the novel, in her delirium, she reveals that "she knew much more than anyone ever suspected" (VI:415), thereby confirming that she had from the beginning blocked this awareness.

One of Dunia's sore spots, at a certain moment, is that she has sold herself to Luzhin. Speculating on this sore spot, Raskolnikov lays out, almost programmatically, the significance of the issue of taboos in the novel:

> It would be rather interesting to clarify one more issue: to what extent were they open with each other that day and that night, and throughout the whole period that followed? Were all *the words* [Dostoevsky's emphasis] between them enunciated or did both of them understand that both one and the other had the same thing in their hearts and thoughts—so there was no point in putting everything into words and letting things slip out in vain [*tak uzh nechego vslukh-to vsego vygovarivat' da naprasno progovarivat'sia*] [...] the naive maman started bothering Dunia with her comments. And [Dunia], of course, was enraged and "responded with annoyance." Sure! Who would not be enraged when everything is clear even without naive questions and when all's decided upon and there's nothing, to talk about (VI:35–36).

Svidrigajlov dismisses Raskolnikov's questions about his reason for coming to Saint-Petersburg because this reason is his secret sore spot: he wants to make one last attempt to win Dunia's love. Yet when Raskolnikov raises this issue, Svidrigajlov feigns disinterest, "not answering the main point of the question" (*ne otvechaia na glavnyj punkt*—VI:217). Of course, Svidrigajlov might be trying to put him off the scent because Raskolnikov is Dunia's brother. But Svidrigajlov acts the same way regarding another issue that has no personal significance for Raskolnikov—the issue of Svidrigajlov's own suicide. In this case, the form of the dismissal signals the importance of the dismissed issue: asking Raskolnikov not to mention suicide, Svidrigajlov lays aside "all the buffoonery which characterized all of his previous words," and it even seems that "his countenance underwent a great change." (VI:362). In a conversation with Sonia (VI:384) and just before his suicide (VI:394), Svidrigajlov refers to this suicide as "going to America." Earlier, in his first conversation with Raskolnikov, he refers to his suicide as "a certain... voyage" (VI:223, 224). He also tempts Raskolnikov himself with "going to America" (VI:373). Svidrigajlov's euphemisms are as perfect for the suicide taboo as, for example, the traditional totemic euphemism "honey connoisseur/ eater" (*medvied'*) of some Slavic cultures is for "bear."[2]

Svidrigajlov impatiently dismisses Raskolnikov's mention of his deceased wife's (and apparent victim's) "apparitions" (VI:362) and refers to what most likely is his upcoming meeting with Dunia as "just a woman, a certain random occurrence" (*Da, zhenshchina, tak, nechaiannyj odin sluchaj ... idem*), adding after three significant dots: "... no, that's not what I was referring to" (*... net, ia ne pro to.—idem*). Then he adds, rather apophatically:

"There is another circumstance which has really perked me up (*montirovalo*) but concerning which I ... [Dostoevsky's ellipsis] will remain silent" (*idem*). Throughout this conversation Svidrigajlov insistently and conspicuously dismisses what matters to him.

In this respect Svidrigajlov's tabooing behavior mirrors Raskolnikov's, apparently because the non-ideological aspects of their crimes (which also are their sore spots) are comparable. Raskolnikov's concern about Lizaveta, his non-ideological victim, parallels Svidrigajlov's concern about Martha Petrovna. When Nastas'ia "blurts out" [*briaknula*] that Lizaveta was also murdered, Raskolnikov loses his voice (VI:104). When Sonia mentions Lizaveta to him, Raskolnikov's reaction resembles Svidrigajlov's even more: Raskolnikov changes the subject "after a moment of silence and dismissing the question" [*pomolchav i ne otvetiv na vopros* VI:245].

Raskolnikov dismisses references to Lizaveta in a Svidrigajlovan manner because her murder disturbs him irrationally. He remains as "armless" against this sore spot of his as Svidrigajlov is against his own. Lizaveta's murder cannot be justified by Raskolnikov's theory. It was so unplanned that it became the beginning of his punishment, rather than the completion of his ideological crime. Unlike her sister, Lizaveta could in no way fit the rationalizing category of "a louse" whose slaughter may benefit the rest of humanity. In Raskolnikov's personal combat between his rationalizing voice and his absolute moral voice, Lizaveta's murder cannot be "defended," even temporarily, by the rationalizing voice. Since in Lizaveta's case, Raskolnikov's absolute inner voice does not have to compete with any other voice within him, Lizaveta's murder, unlike the other, "ideological" murder, becomes Raskolnikov's totally irrational unmentionable sore spot immediately after it is committed.

Important as it is, however, the taboo on Lizaveta's murder cannot become the central taboo in the novel precisely because it "wins" immediately, bypassing the stage of the ideological combat. The polyphonic interaction of taboos in *Crime and Punishment* requires that the central taboo in this novel must be agonistic; it must withstand and overcome an opposition, and only Raskolnikov's *ideological* murder entails such an agonistic taboo. Just as Bakhtin believes that in Dostoevsky there is "a dialogue of antagonistic truths,"[3] I believe that in *Crime and Punishment*, there is a dialogue of antagonistic taboos.[4]

Raskolnikov's Main Taboo and its Formal Makings

Though Lizaveta's murder acts as a sore spot for him, Raskolnikov has an even sorer spot—his ideological crime. This crime, in turn, becomes the focus of the narrative attention. Although the crime and its scene are obviously mentioned and described extensively in the novel, Dostoevsky finds ways to signal that *within himself,* Raskolnikov treats his crime as taboo. Of these ways, the most consistent is the device of referring to the place, time, victims or trophies of the crime and the crime itself with italicized (originally underlined) pronouns—primarily, but not exclusively, demonstrative: *that* house (VI:133, 272); *that* evening (VI:133); *that* money (VI:317). Occasionally the italicized word is not a pronoun but still fulfills the pronominal function of pointing to the crime without naming it: "*The thought* did not enter her mind" (meaning that Sonia did not think that Raskolnikov was the murderer of Lizaveta VI:253). This particular use of deictics—similar to what we will see in Stavrogin's final conversation with Liza in *Demons*—signals the taboo on their referent and therefore the significance of both the referent and the taboo.

Italicized pronouns creating the sememe of the murder-taboo appear as early in the novel as page 6. While still planning the murder, Raskolnikov already calls it "*it*" (*eto*—VI:6, 45) and "*that* [thing]" (posle *togo, to*—each expression occurs twice in the same five lines—VI:45), and he refers to the time which he sets aside for his crime as "*then:*" "*Then* the sun will be shining just as it does right now" (VI:8). After the murder Raskolnikov continues to refer to it as "*that* [thing]" (*to* VI:87).

Dostoevsky makes the taboo-signaling function of italics very clear to his reader. When Raskolnikov actually makes his confession at the district police office, Dostoevsky italicizes the whole confession, thereby linking all of the tabooing references to the murder with its actual confession: *It was I who killed the official's old widow and her sister Lizaveta with an axe and robbed them* (VI:410).[5] By italicizing first the pronominal euphemisms and then the overt confession, Dostoevsky the author encourages his readers to perceive the latter as the *dispelling* annulment of the taboo signaled by the former. Dostoevsky thereby reveals that while intact this taboo was as inviolable as a magic spell. Only Raskolnikov's confession could break this spell. That it succeeds is obvious: following the confession, there are no more italicized deictic pronouns. It can no longer haunt Raskolnikov.[6]

The tabooing function of italicized deictics/pronouns is most obvious in the scene of Raskolnikov's confession to Sonia. This scene is especially important since Sonia embodies Raskolnikov's conscience, i.e., the way he speaks of things to himself rather than to others. Despite his numerous promises to himself and to Sonia to "tell her who killed Lizaveta" (VI:253, 311, 312, 314), in this conversation he never actually says that he murdered the old woman and Lizaveta. Nonetheless, he refers to the murder through

italicized demonstrative pronouns which point to the message more
conspicuously than if he had verbalized it directly:

> Suddenly a strange unexpected feeling of some vitriolic hatred
> toward Sonia crossed his heart [...] That was not it [...] It only
> meant that *that* minute came (VI:314). [...] "How do you know
> who killed Lizaveta?" [...] "I know." ["Did they find *him* or what?"
> [...] "No [...]" "So how do you know about *it*?" [...] "Guess. [...]
> That means I am great friends with *him* [...] So you can't guess,
> can you?" [...] "N-no—" whispered Sonia. [...] "Have you
> guessed?—" he whispered finally. "Oh, Lord—" a horrible cry
> came forth from her bosom. [...] She wanted to find and seize the
> last hope for herself [*sic: pojmat' sebe posledniuiu nadezhdu*]. But
> there was no hope; no doubt was left; everything was *so/thus*. [...]
> "You're strange, Sonia: you hug and kiss me when I've just told *you*
> about *this/it* (*pro eto*). [...] And *that* money ... I actually don't even
> know if there was any money." (VI:315–317).

Here Raskolnikov's repeated injunction "guess!" strengthens the tabooing
effect of the italicized pronouns referring to the murder and its various
circumstances. The italicized pronouns convey the emphasis on their
tabooed referent.

The Circumstances of Observing or Violating Raskolnikov's Taboo

Raskolnikov's inability to speak of the murder is a very private matter. He can
mention it to Zametov or Razumikhin but not to his Sophia, or even to
himself when he is alone. In real life people tend to observe taboos more
when they are with others than when they are alone, but this murder is not
a *conventional* taboo of the kind that Dostoevsky's scandal scenes violate so
strongly and so frequently in *Crime and Punishment* and *The Idiot*. Rather
than annulling the conventional taboos by violating them, Dostoevsky moves
the observation of conventional taboos to the realm of unconventional
circumstances; he thereby defamiliarizes them and focuses his reader's
attention on their importance. In *The Idiot*, Dostoevsky transforms the social
and accepted ways of observing taboos to idiosyncratic and seemingly
unmotivated ones. In *Crime and Punishment*, he removes taboos from the
social realm to the intimate, i.e., he internalizes them.[7] Entering
Raskolnikov's mind, the narrator thus describes his innermost thoughts:

> But about *that* thing—about *that* thing (*no ob tom, ob tom* ...) he
> forgot completely; and yet, he remembered every minute that he

forgot about something which one should not forget; he tormented himself, suffered, tried to recall [it]... (VI:92).

What Values Underlie Raskolnikov's Taboo

Raskolnikov taboos most when he is most honest with himself about the tabooed issue—i.e., when he has no one else to cheat. He is not honest when he addresses others, and then he uses the word "murder" or even calls himself a murderer relatively easily—as he does in his conversation with Zametov. When the taboo on "murder" is moved from the social realm to the personal, or "internalized," its observation, on the literary level, no longer signifies the observer's adherence to social norms, since the observation cannot possibly be conditioned by any social conventions: no one (except God) sees the murderer when he is alone. The only plausible literary motivation for such non-social observation of the taboo is one's inability to violate it. Such an inability presupposes—and signals to the reader—the absolute sincerity of the one who observes the taboo. Raskolnikov's non-mention of the important is not his device but Dostoevsky's; it is not a device to deceive a Zametov but the way to talk sincerely to himself or to his Sophia. Disappearing as a social regulation, the taboo on mentioning the murder emerges as a factor in Raskolnikov's inner, non-social system of values. The fact that Raskolnikov obeys this taboo unconsciously makes it all the more inviolable.

The distinction between public circumstances where the taboo on mentioning murder is neglected and private circumstances where it is observed structures the novel by creating two realms, or energy fields in its plot. In the first, public realm Raskolnikov actually violates the taboo on murder by committing it. But in the second, private realm of Raskolnikov's thoughts, this taboo remains inviolable, no matter what Raskolnikov does.[8] In this second realm—the realm of his conscience—he cannot utter what he himself did. When he actually does utter what he did—as in his conversation with Zametov or with Porfiry (about his article)—he does not violate the taboo in his private realm in which the deed is unutterable; he merely shifts himself into the public realm where language functions as a form of communicative manipulation. The realm of his conscience itself remains inviolable and invincible. Raskolnikov believes that if he "transgresses the border" (*prestupit chertu*) by committing the murder, he will violate this realm. But the more he "transgresses the border" with the old woman and Lizaveta (in deed) and with Zametov or Porfiry (in words), the less he is capable of violating this realm within himself. Significantly, he cannot violate the taboo in this internal realm when he is with Sonia who, etymologically and theologically, embodies Sophia, the Wisdom of God within his heart. In

Crime and Punishment, Dostoevsky defines the realm and nature of human conscience apophatically: in terms of the inviolable unmentionable.

Dostoevsky's notebooks reveal that the tabooing function of the italicized pronouns in Raskolnikov's external or internal discourse developed over time. At first the italics designated merely an intonational stress. An example of this intonational stress from the preliminary notes to the novel provides an illustrating contrast to the *mental*, tabooing stress on demonstrative pronouns, which predominates in the final version. Describing his first visit to the district police office (still in the first person), Raskolnikov says about his own bravura: "I myself am amazed how I could even then exercise such bravura" [*I sam udivliaius', kak ia mog togda eshche v ambitsiiu vojti*] (VII:18, n. 12). This use of the italicized pronoun is clearly intonational: the "then" here stresses the idea of the particular danger of exercising bravura at the police office—and refers to the time of being in the office, rather than of the murder. Dostoevsky subsequently removed this comment, even from the same variant of the text (VII: *idem*), apparently because Raskolnikov's own intonational stress on the *togda* obscured the motif of the murder and its circumstances, which this italicized pronoun eventually came to signify whenever it pertained to Raskolnikov's inner self-analysis. Thus as Dostoevsky internalized Raskolnikov's taboo by making him commit the murder in deed but unable to refer to it in thought, the writer also inevitably internalized the tabooing element itself: the stressed pronouns moved from the realm of Raskolnikov's speech intonation to the realm of his innermost thoughts.

Who Does the Tabooing for Raskolnikov's Conscience?

Although in the passage which labels murder as "*that* thing" (VI:92, cf. above) it is the narrator—rather than Raskolnikov—who refers to the murder as *that* [thing], he clearly conveys Raskolnikov's own state of mind, using Raskolnikov's terminology and observing those taboos which are important specifically to Raskolnikov. The narrator talks "from inside" Raskolnikov, using the type of discourse known as *erlebte Rede*, or "double/free indirect discourse," i.e., what Bakhtin called "the double-voiced word," or "another's speech" (*chuzhaia rech'*).[9] The reasons for the *erlebte Rede* obtain here as they do throughout the novel. Dostoevsky originally conceived the novel as a first-person narrative and then changed it to third-person[10] for a reason: describing one's subconscious in the first person presumes the identity of the described and its describer. First-person narration blurs the boundary between the narrator's conscious and subconscious, for any description is filtered through the describer's conscious mind, thereby obscuring from view any elements of the subconscious that distinguish it from the conscious. The use of third-person narration allows the narrator to describe Raskolnikov's stream of consciousness. By creating a distance between the describer and the described the narrator can demonstrate that Raskolnikov taboos the notion of his crime most when he is least aware of so doing.

The function of the narrator's *erlebte Rede* as a specific designator of Raskolnikov's inner realm emerges especially clearly in the argument presented by M. L. Kovsan, since Kovsan discusses the correlation between marked pronouns and Raskolnikov's self-consciousness.[11] Kovsan notes that when alone or absorbed in his theory, Raskolnikov is called, "he," rather than Raskolnikov. This is partially understandable because there are no other possible referents for this pronoun under the circumstances. Raskolnikov, however, is called by his name even when he talks to a "she," unless this "she" is Sophia. Kovsan explains this usage by claiming that the referent is alienated from the signified: "His "I" is replaced with the generalized/abstracted "he" (*ibid.*, 79), and "'he' is a step toward creating a double for Raskolnikov" (*ibid.*, 81). I assess this usage differently: I believe that the pronoun "he," like the italicized pronouns in *Crime and Punishment*, refers to an aspect of Raskolnikov's true *inner* self, not a false, external double. When the narrator refers to Raskolnikov as "Raskolnikov," he does so only to technically differentiate him from other individuals. When, however, the same narrator refers to Raskolnikov as "he," he thereby translates the "I" of Raskolnikov's innermost voice into *erlebte Rede*—as if introducing himself as an empathizing character who contemplates Raskolnikov's person from within.

In *Crime and Punishment*, however, the frequent use of *erlebte Rede* by characters other than the omniscient narrator creates a special problem which makes it harder for the reader to determine the borders of the realm of Raskolnikov's inviolable unmentionable. On the one hand, this type of discourse externalizes Raskolnikov's conscience or state of mind, however idiosyncratic and introverted, by voicing it through other dramatic personae. On the other hand, other characters' speeches intrude into the voice of Raskolnikov's conscience—or rather are involuntarily dragged into it—and use italicized pronouns as Raskolnikov does. Instead of the principal authorial narrator, *they* begin to cite Raskolnikov through the *erlebte Rede*, being (unlike the author) totally or partially unaware of it themselves. (Their intrusion into Raskolnikov's inner voice is what Bakhtin describes in Chapter 5 of *The Problems of Dostoevsky's Poetics*.[12]) These characters include "the man from under the earth" (*chelovek iz-pod zemli*, the *meshchanin*), Porfiry, Razumikhin, Dunia, and Sonia. All except "the man from under the earth" break into Raskolnikov's inner voice in order to make it one with his social voice: Porfiry and Sonia, who believe he is guilty, want him to confess and Razumikhin and Dunia, who believe that he is psychologically ill, want to heal him (although I will show below that Razumikhin has yet another purpose in mind).

"The man from under the earth" who says "thou art the murderer" (VI: 209) does not have any such special purpose or mission concerning Raskolnikov. His function turns out to be more mechanical than what Raskolnikov expected it to be. The man stresses the "thou" intonationally, with an air of omniscience. But he is not all-knowing as a plot character: he prophesies a truth of which he himself is unaware. (The man's eventual apology to Raskolnikov reveals his objective lack of omniscience.) Nonetheless, the man's lack of awareness does not actually relieve Raskolnikov of his worry, since Raskolnikov perceives him as an extension of his own stream of consciousness. This isolation of the man's symbolic function from all his human and social features scares Raskolnikov: he encounters a person with whom he has nothing in common socially, and yet this person speaks Raskolnikov's own idiosyncratic language, italicizing "*his*" pronouns. The man uses *erlebte Rede* to express not Raskolnikov's word (the italicized *thou*) but Raskolnikov's *attitude* to this word (the italicizing itself). The man's lack of awareness regarding his own function as the summoner of Raskolnikov's conscience reveals a particular feature of *erlebte Rede* in the novel: when characters other than the authorial narrator use this discourse, they are often not aware of Raskolnikov's "reading" of their own speech. Their motivation for stressing "his" pronouns might greatly differ from Raskolnikov's; they may even use "his" pronouns to refer to another thing, thus creating the effect of dramatic irony.

This use of *erlebte Rede* or the "double-voiced word" for dramatic irony allows Dostoevsky to express the idea that one cannot judge one's neighbor: unlike the judged, God, or the writer, the one who judges cannot be fully aware of what his own words actually mean and to what degree they are valid. Raskolnikov—rather than the man himself—regards the man's words as absolutely and unconditionally valid. Since the man later confesses that he was wrong, Raskolnikov alone knows that the man actually was *not* wrong. Raskolnikov, therefore, endows the man's words with a validity and significance that have nothing to do with the man's intentions. For this reason, it is possible that in the sentence below the italicized *that* does not convey the man's own intonational stress on the word but rather Raskolnikov's attitude to the word which he recognizes as "his own." The man says: "Why did he come down [here to find out] about *that*; what does he have in mind, ah?" (*Zachem ob tom dokhodil, chto u nego na ume, a?*—

VI:135). The stressed "about that" suggests Raskolnikov's subjective and idiosyncratic perception of the man as an extension of his own stream of consciousness.[13] This case exemplifies the ways in which, according to Bakhtin, Raskolnikov "suffuses his inner speech with others' words, complicating them by his own stresses or directly reaccentuating them."[14]

The next example demonstrates that Raskolnikov notices threats *only* insofar as they resemble the voice of his own conscience. Porfiry says to Raskolnikov: "*She* had your things wrapped all in one paper" [*Vashi veshchi byli u nej pod odnu bumazhku zavernuty*] (VI:194). Here, the italicized *she* (*u nej*) most likely does not convey any rise in the pitch or dynamics of Porfiry's voice; instead, it signals Porfiry's launching an attack on Raskolnikov's inner, unproclaimed system of values by using idiomatically "Raskolnikovian" terms, or, in Bakhtin's words, by "addressing Raskolnikov's inner voice."[15] Raskolnikov immediately notices the attack-launching in Porfiry's *u nej*: "Why did he say directly (*priamo*) 'she had?' ... [*u nej*]" (VI:195). Saying directly is not stressing. By "directly" Raskolnikov means the opposite of what one might expect: not "without euphemisms," but rather "in my own, 'Raskolnikovian' terms." He is concerned with this understanding of his own terms—conveyed through the italicized pronoun—rather than with the actual intonational stress. In Porfiry's speech, should there be a stress.

Numerous confusions as to who italicizes the "loaded" pronouns occur in Raskolnikov's conversations with Razumikhin, where Raskolnikov's personal taboo actually clashes with Razumikhin's (who has his own). This clash of two or more tabooed issues or taboo interests, will become the main motif of *The Adolescent*, where the protagonist's maturing can be described entirely in terms of both his growing sensitivity to others' sore spots, and his growing ability *not* to mention the important. In *Crime and Punishment* this clash of two idiosyncratic taboos comes out especially strongly in the conversation which Razumikhin himself considers crucial (VI:207):

> "Just think of it: if you were the one who did *it*, how could you possibly let things slip out? [...]" "If I did *that deed*, I would definitely say I saw the workers and the apartment," Raskolnikov replied reluctantly and with apparent disgust (VI:207).

Here Razumikhin's *it* could be stressed by Razumikhin himself or just by Raskolnikov's imagination. At the beginning of the episode, however, the narrator defines Razumikhin's state of mind, using italics to convey his perception of the crime: "Razumikhin [...] [was] excited if only just because it was the first time they spoke about it openly" (VI:206). But Razumikhin has his own "taboo-agenda" here. To Razumikhin the "*it*" taboos not the notion of the actual murder but rather his suspicion that Raskolnikov is the murderer. Elsewhere he condemns himself for suspecting Raskolnikov as if this suspicion were his own secret vice: "What a disgusting, crass, base thought it was on my part!" (VI:341). Later, in *The Idiot*, Myshkin will echo this self-condemnation, being ashamed of his (justified) suspicion that Rogozhin attempted to kill him. Similarly in *The Adolescent*, Versilov, Akhmakova, the old Prince Sokol'sky, and eventually Arkady will actively refuse to learn others', or each other's, shameful secrets, sensing that learning these secrets will somehow bring shame upon them, the listeners. In *Demons*, Liza refuses to listen to Stavrogin's confession for the same reason. In Razumikhin's *it*, Raskolnikov and Razumikhin himself perceive two different and seemingly mutually exclusive taboos. For Raskolnikov the taboo is the mention of his actual crime, and for Razumikhin it is the suspicion that his friend has committed this crime. Both of these taboos are important in Dostoevsky's system of values. Raskolnikov's taboo reveals what is important for the murderer. (In *The Idiot*, Dostoevsky will reintroduce this motif as Rogozhin's conspicuous silence or tongue-tiedness concerning the issues of murder and death.) Razumikhin's taboo, on the other hand, suggests the overarching taboo of Dostoevsky's poetics everywhere: it is forbidden to condemn even the one who is "objectively" guilty.

The difference in the meaning which two interlocutors may ascribe to the same italicized pronoun comes out especially strongly, and with a twist of irony, when Dunia tells Raskolnikov: "Brother, I know *everything* [...] They persecute and torment you because of a stupid suspicion ... [...] I won't tell Mother anything about *it* [...]" (VI:326). For Raskolnikov the *it* (*eto*) and the *everything* (*vsë*) still refer to the tabooed motif of the murder, while for Dunia they do not. Like "the man from under the earth," Dunia does not know the *everything* she is talking about. Only Raskolnikov himself does. The fact that Dunia and the man are not omniscient adds irony to the situation, but it still does not deprive their inadvertent reference to Raskolnikov's own taboo of the meaning Raskolnikov perceives in it.

Raskolnikov, therefore, does "italicize" the pronouns referring to the murder when he addresses others, and even others themselves "italicize" these pronouns. But instead of depriving these pronouns of their function of tabooing what is important to Raskolnikov, these two facts actually "drag" the dramatic personae involved in the italicizing into the realm where the values of Raskolnikov's conscience are unmentionable and therefore hold true: Sonia, Razumikhin and Dunia, "the man from under the earth" and— to some extent—Porfiry acquire some access to the field of Raskolnikov's conscience where the taboo on "murder" remains inviolable, whereas Zametov or Il'ia Petrovich will never "make it" to that realm. The realm, therefore, is not superscribed dramatically: others may enter it occasionally (although for Raskolnikov's purposes, not their own—as the cases of "the man from under the earth" and Dunia clearly show), and Raskolnikov himself may leave or betray (but not violate) it occasionally through the demagoguery which he uses to deceive himself or Zametov. Most interestingly, Sophia, not Raskolnikov, can never escape this realm, and Raskolnikov senses that being with her will determine him to stay in it. ("Sonia presented a sentence without appeal." [*Sonia predstavliala soboiu neumolimyj prigovor*] VI:354).

In addition to italicized pronouns Dostoevsky uses puns on roots as signalers of the violation of Raskolnikov's personal taboo—just as he will use them in *Demons* to provide euphemistic, or rather pseudo-euphemistic substitutes for the root *–bes–*, which signal the taboo on the literal meaning of this root. Like pronouns italicized "in Raskolnikov's sense" by his unwary non-omniscient interlocutors, these puns also involve dramatic irony, or "a double-voiced word," i.e., a discrepancy between the ways the speaker and the listener understand the same expression. After Raskolnikov murders the old woman and Lizaveta, he gets out to the street, and people outside say, taking him for a drunk: "*Ish', narezalsia!*" ("Look, here's one who has had a drop too many taken!"—VI:70). The literal, etymological meaning of this rather common expression is "had his full share of butchering." That Dostoevsky deliberately used this expression, is clear: the pun appears, in the same context, in the very first paragraph of the first draft to *Crime and Punishment*, still narrated in the first person (VII:5).

Certain other accentuating episodes turn the pun on this root (*–rez–*) into a motif: when Dunia says, "I haven't butchered anyone yet" [*Ia eshche nikogo ne zarezala* VI:179]—Raskolnikov almost faints. Like Petrov in conversation with Gorianchikov, or later Stavrogin with Liza, and unlike Dunia herself, Raskolnikov reacts to the literal rather than the metaphoric meaning of this expression; he takes it as a violation of his personal sore spot. Svidrigajlov uses two verbs of the same root *–rez–* when telling Raskolnikov of his love for Dunia: "In short, I fell for her so hard (*tak vrezalsia*) that if only she said 'butcher [*zarezh'*] Martha Petrovna,' it would have been done right then" (VI:367). Although Svidrigajlov is to blame for Martha Petrovna's death, he did not butcher her. He uses the *–rez–* root here metaphorically, whereas Raskolnikov, his listener, takes it literally, at least to some extent. As in *Demons*, or *The Notes from the House of the Dead*, the discrepancy between the tabooed and the "innocent," taboo-violating use of the same expression, amounts to the discrepancy between the literal and the metaphorical realization of its meaning or root (in this case, *–rez–*). By metaphorizing the meaning of some roots, Dostoevsky's characters may inadvertently violate an actual taboo on these roots' *literal* meaning. In *Crime and Punishment*, "the blame" for violating the taboo by metaphorizing the tabooed expression is not on the violators (as it was with the unwary Gorianchikov and will be in *Demons*) but on Raskolnikov, the only one sensitive to the taboo which is caused by his unclean conscience. This notion of "blame," however, is relative. As we saw with Petrov or Svidrigajlov and will see with other Dostoevskian crooks sensitive to taboos, their sensitivity has a redeeming merit of its own. Having sore spots maintains a certain level of humanity even in villains and criminals.

Paradoxically, Raskolnikov's amazingly private taboo on killing is sometimes signaled (to us and him) by other characters' invasions of his private realm, and occasionally even through means other than italicized pronouns (e.g., the root *–rez–*). The italicized pronouns are also sometimes used in other ways in the novel, or for the purposes of other people's unmentionables—as when Sonia calls her family *they* [*oni, te*].[16] But Raskolnikov's motifs—and therefore the taboo he observes—predominate in the novel. Consequently, italicized pronouns are also used predominantly (although not exclusively) to signal this taboo. Tracing how italicized pronouns or puns taboo the notion of the already committed murder in the murderer's own mind (without having the same meaning for the others) helps one understand the way in which Dostoevsky subliminally yet insistently imposes on the reader his own system of values—in which conscience (even the conscience of a murderer) is absolute, inviolable, uncompromising and invincible.

Raskolnikov's Idiosyncratic Taboo Translated into Philosophical Terms

Viacheslav Ivanov, a poet and a religious thinker, maintains that the distinction between the inner, absolute realm of consciousness and the outer, relative realm of empirical behavior, characterizes all Dostoevsky's post-prison work. In his *Dostoevsky: Tragedy—Myth—Mysticism*, Viacheslav Ivanov observes that after the mock execution, Dostoevsky started not only to define the borders between the internal ("immanent") and the external ("transcendent") aspects of human personality and of crime—but to redefine these borders in a uniquely Dostoevskian way:

> The entire work of the insightful writer became the [further] internalization of the inner man born from the Spirit—[of the man] in whose world-perception **that which we consider transcendent often became the immanent in some sense, and our immediate internal givenness, on the other hand,**

was partially transferred to an [external] sphere. For the personality was split into [two:] the empirical or external on the one hand, and the higher and freer, the metaphysically significant, on the other.[17] [...] Dostoevsky's inner experience taught him the distinction between the empirical and the metaphysical aspects of man, [...] which was philosophically defined by Schopenhauer following in the footsteps of Kant. The same distinction is implied in Dostoevsky's utterances about the nature of crime.[18]

Ivanov's philosophical categories correspond to the elements of Raskolnikov's taboo. Raskolnikov's metaphysical, inner man is the one who cannot mention the murder when alone (or with his Sophia) and thus substitutes italicized pronouns for this mention. His empirical, outer man is the one who violates the taboo "thou shalt not kill" in practice, by rationalizing this murder, committing it, and then teasing Zametov and trying to escape from Porfiry. The same distinction between the transcendent (outer) and the immanent (inner) realms applies to the crime itself. Dostoevsky taboos only the immanent, inner aspect of this crime. On the outer, empirical level Raskolnikov succeeds in violating the taboo against this crime. But on the metaphysical level, within himself he still experiences this taboo as inviolable and absolute. By establishing Raskolnikov's taboo only on an unexpectedly *non*-social level, Dostoevsky manages to defamiliarize the distinction between the social, "transcendent," and the meta-social, "immanent" aspects of this taboo.

Dostoevsky not only established or defamiliarized but indeed *shifted* the border between the outer and the inner realms of both the crime and the criminal's personality. In *Crime and Punishment*, Dostoevsky achieved this shift by introducing unexpected interference and/or overlapping of Raskolnikov's taboo with others' taboos or sore spots. The instances of *erlebte Rede* in *Crime and Punishment* suggest that the realm of Raskolnikov's inner life may at times encompass others and yet exclude Raskolnikov himself. Dunia, Razumikhin, Sonia, Porfiry, and even "the man from under the earth" occasionally speak in Raskolnikov's inner voice whenever they observe or signal "his" taboo." "The external" Raskolnikov himself does not speak in his own voice when, teasing Zametov or any of his interlocutors, he violates his own taboo on mentioning the murder. Thus, in order to redefine and defamiliarize that which Ivanov considers the distinction between the outer and the inner realms of the human being, Dostoevsky (a) unexpectedly limits the applicability of Raskolnikov's taboo to his inner realm, and (b) reshapes this realm itself by shifting the borders between Raskolnikov's inner voice and the voices of others. This border-reshaping can be defined in Bakhtinian terms as "the double-voiced word," the characters' ability to speak in each other's inner voices.[20] In the specific case discussed here, it is important that the characters penetrate into that aspect of Raskolnikov's inner voice which concerns his personal taboo.

Ivanov does not apply his distinction between the immanent and the transcendent realms to tabooing in *Crime and Punishment*, but this distinction can and should be correlated with the system of tabooed values in the novel. Taboos are the best signalers of the distinction between the outer and the inner realms in both a human being and a crime. In *Crime and Punishment*, it is not "Dostoevsky's utterances about crime" (Ivanov) that imply the distinction between the empirical/transcendent/outer realm and the metaphysical/immanent/inner one—but rather his character's peculiarly conspicuous non-utterances about the crime, his inability to mention this crime under particular circumstances.

In *Crime and Punishment*, Dostoevsky explores the relation between these inner and outer realms by pursuing the effects of conscience and law in Raskolnikov's mind. Like Mary Douglas, I believe that taboos can regulate those aspects of human conscience which formal social law cannot regulate or even approach. In the societies Mary Douglas studied, the "jurisdiction" of taboos is considered complementary to that of the law because their violation does not subject the violator to any legal punishment, and yet it seems to bring about an immanent, mystical punishment, such as paralysis, possession or illness.[21] I correlate Douglas' distinction between taboos and social regulations with the split between the inner and outer minds and crimes of Raskolnikov, Stavrogin, and Ivan Karamazov. Of these three, Raskolnikov best exemplifies the distinction between the inner and the outer crime, because in his case, not only is this distinction a motif but it is also marked as central to "his" novel by his idiosyncratic taboo which, in Douglas's terms, marks this distinction better than any pronouncements, legal or literary.

The Correlation Between Raskolnikov's Napoleonic Idea and his Main Sore Spot

In the introduction I speculated on the ways in which Dostoevsky may have transformed the sore spots of two public figures, tsars Paul I and Nicholas I, into the idiosyncratic taboos of private people (Raskolnikov, for one) in his fiction. In this chapter, I have described how Dostoevsky transformed a universal taboo, expressed in the Decalogue as "thou shalt not kill," into Raskolnikov's private sore spot. Raskolnikov failed to recognize the universality of this commandment in the first place because he had caught the disturbing idea that the violation of this commandment never seemed to cause any sore spots for a truly great public figure like Napoleon, or even for a merely extraordinary person (VI:199–200). The theory that the truly great are allowed to behave immorally and are immune to the pangs of conscience, was originally formulated by Napoleon III, a great apologist of Napoleon I. Since Napoleon III rationalized and theorized this idea in a book (*The Life of Julius Caesar*), rather than merely naturally living by it the way his great model Napoleon I did, it is likely that while Napoleon III tried to practice this idea, it was not self-evident for him, but rather a sore spot which *required* a theoretical apology. This monarchial sore spot, although it consists of the monarch's vehement argument that great monarchs should have no sore spots, nevertheless typologically resembles the sore spots of the Emperors Paul and Nicholas, which I have linked to parricide. Dostoevsky manages to internalize yet another monarch's sore spot by tabooing the product of Raskolnikov's realization of Napoleon III's theory in a very idiosyncratic way. The product of Napoleon III's theory is the murder that Raskolnikov has committed, and the taboo on it operates only in non-social circumstances.

At first Raskolnikov fully adheres to Napoleon III's theory. He actually theorizes this sore spot in his own article, as Napoleon III theorized it in a book.[22] Even after committing the murder he continues to believe that his murder of the old "louse" has become his privately unmentionable taboo only because he is no Napoleon (VI:211).

Porfiry also seems to agree with Raskolnikov (and with Napoleon III) that Raskolnikov's problem is that he is no Napoleon. He likens Raskolnikov's ideological defeat to General Mack's strategic defeat by Napoleon. According to Porfiry, both Raskolnikov and the general were "seduced by mental games"—to which the blissfully non-reflective Napoleon himself was apparently immune:

> A playful sharpness of wit and the abstract arguments of reason are what seduce you, sir. Which is exactly like the former Austrian *Hofskriegsrat* [...] on paper, [to be sure], they had Napoleon crushed and taken prisoner, it was all worked out and arranged in the cleverest manner in their study, and then, lo and behold, General Mack [there] [*general-to Mak*] surrenders with his entire army, heh, heh, heh!" (VI:263).[23]

Thus for Porfiry, just as for Raskolnikov himself, Napoleon's main strategic advantage over Raskolnikov (or over Mack) was the emperor's lack of excessive reflection, a peculiar virtue which Raskolnikov describes in the following terms:

> [T]he true master [*vlastelin*], to whom everything is permitted, sacks Toulon, makes a slaughterhouse of Paris, forgets an army in Egypt, expends half a million men in a Moscow campaign, and gets off with a pun in Vilno; and when he dies they set up monuments [idols: *kumiry*] to him—and thus everything is permitted. No, obviously such men are made not of flesh but of bronze! (VI:211/P&V 274)

This theory of the problem of excessive reflection still cannot cure Raskolnikov of his Napoleonic idea, because it allows him to elevate himself over Napoleon intellectually. Only when he realizes that his Napoleonic "idea" is actually a sore spot that possesses him, can he exorcise it. (The epilogue vision of ideas infecting people's minds as bacteria marks the arrival of this exorcism). Only Sonia, being suspicious of ideas that poison one's mind, can help Raskolnikov to begin exorcising this sore spot. Paradoxically, she does it by regarding his Napoleonic idea as something purely mental, and therefore dismissable. By the time Raskolnikov describes his Napoleonic theory to Sonia, she lets him feel that the Napoleonic rationalization for his crime is somewhat faulty. She regards Napoleon not as Raskolnikov's philosophical role model, but as a mere allegory that actually prevents her from perceiving his real reasons for committing the crime: "You'd better tell me straight out ... without examples [*bez*; *primerov*]" (VI:319/P&V 415). Until Sonia makes this request, Raskolnikov believes that Napoleon's (or any great man's) lack of a sore spot concerning his conscience serves him, Raskolnikov, as the basis of his *ideology*. The eventual development of his idiosyncratic taboo on mentioning murder to himself or to Sonia, however, reveals that the emperor's lack of scruple actually affects Raskolnikov's "gut-feeling," becoming his sore spot rather than a rational idea. Consequently, only Sonia, who instinctively realizes this distinction, can cause Raskolnikov to overcome the distorting rationalization of his sore spot, i.e., to overcome reasoning as a form of possession—and thus, eventually, to repent.

A temporary *taboo* on mentioning the parallel between Raskolnikov and Napoleon proves the validity of Sonia's intuition that for Raskolnikov, the Napoleonic "idea" was indeed a sore spot rather than merely an idea. In the following conversation, all the classical elements of a signaled taboo violation obtain: the unwary violator (Zametov) and his interlocutors, who react to his violation by remaining silent, pretending to ignore it as a *faux-pas*:

> "Allow me to observe", he answered dryly, "that I do not consider myself a Muhammad or a Napoleon ..." [Dostoevsky's three dots]

[...]

"But, my goodness, who in our Russia nowadays doesn't consider himself a Napoleon?" Porfiry suddenly pronounced **with horrible familiarity. There was something particularly clear this time even in the tone of his voice**.

"Might it not have been some future Napoleon who bumped off our Alyona Ivanovna with an axe last week?" Zamyotov suddenly **blurted out** [*briaknid vdrug*] from his corner.

Raskolnikov was silent, looking firmly and fixedly at Porfiry. Razumikhin frowned gloomily. He seemed to have begun noticing **something** even earlier [*Emu uzh i prezhde stalo kak budto chto-to kazat'sia*]. He looked wrathfully about him. **A moment of a gloomy silence passed** (VI:204/P&V 265–266).[24]

The general silence marks Zametov's violation of the "local sore spot." Yet each character also has his own way of reacting to it. Razumikhin, who has his own taboo on *suspecting* Raskolnikov, reacts to the imminent possibility of *his* taboo being violated. Furthermore, Razumikhin's taboo is signalled in the way traditionally reserved for Raskolnikov's (or for the interaction between his *and* Raskolnikov's taboos, which I discussed above)—namely, the accumulation of loaded indefinite pronouns [*kak budto chto-to*].

Raskolnikov reacts to the violation of his sore spot with silence. Porfiry's silence, on the other hand, turns this sore spot into "something" [*nechto*] shared by everybody present. He reacts to Zametov's *faux-pas* the way Petrov in *The Notes from the House of the Dead* reacts to Gorianchikov's. Of course, Gorianchikov violates Petrov's personal taboo, but he also mentions something very important and truly valid that is *in the air*, and *therefore* should not be mentioned. Porfiry uses his silence to "chastize" the unwary Zametov for a similar *faux-pas*. Although Porfiry provokes Raskolnikov to talk about his sore spot here—"there was something particularly clear this time even in the tone of his voice" [*dazhe v intonatsii ego golosa bylo na etot raz nechto uzh osobenno iasnoe*] (VI: 204; the cluster of emphatic words, pronouns and adverbs, in the Russian text is particularly conspicuous)—he himself never mentions Raskolnikov's sore spot. As I will demonstrate in the chapters on *The Eternal Husband* and *The Brothers Karamazov*, taboo signalers may use "horrible familiarity" to provoke others to violate a taboo, but they do not violate it themselves. Unlike Zametov, Porfiry understands that Raskolnikov's Napoleonic "idea" is not merely an idea but a sore spot, and that consequently, it can be exorcised only as a sore spot, i.e., from within, by *internalizing* the taboo on it. He also understands that in the act of internalizing it, he cannot compete with Raskolnikov's conscience (which uses the language of italicized pronouns throughout the novel). Only Sonia can, because she loves Raskolnikov and intuitively regards his ideas as sore spots subject to exorcism.

It takes Raskolnikov himself a while to realize that his Napoleonic "idea" haunts him as a sore spot. Developing his Napoleonic theory rationally, Raskolnikov tells Porfiry that if an extraordinary person "needs, for the sake of his idea, to step even over a dead body, over blood, then within himself, in his conscience, he can [*mozhet*] [...] allow himself to step over blood (VI:200/P&V 261)." The word *mozhet* in Russian may designate either "can" or "may." Although when Raskolnikov uses it in this passage, he believes that he means "can," the italicized pronouns which I have interpreted as the signalers of his *internal*, socially unimposed taboo on the murder scene, reveal that the only *viable* meaning of his *mozhet* here is "may:" Raskolnikov himself is *not able* to violate inwardly what he allows himself to violate in practice.

Thus the Napoleonic motif, the myth of the moral distinction between great and ordinary people, being Raskolnikov's personal sore spot rather than merely his abstract idea, determines the particular nature of tabooing in *Crime and Punishment*. The chief taboo in the novel ("thou shalt not kill") was to be transformed from universal to idiosyncratic, and to be signalled by italicized demonstrative pronouns only in non-social circumstances.

Tabooing in *Crime and Punishment* vs.
Other Dostoevskian Taboos

In *Crime and Punishment* the eventual destiny of the taboo is to be abolished. The moment Raskolnikov confesses, he no longer needs to load any of the pronouns with a special meaning, although in the epilogue, after he repents, he italicizes, for the last time, the word "everything" which signifies his now passed moral and ideological torments. This final use of italics marks the overcoming of the gap that existed in Raskolnikov's mind between formal confession and repentance. The taboo on mentioning murder to himself, which persisted even after the law was violated, originally *marked* this gap between the realms of Raskolnikov's absolute conscience and his very relative sense of social duty or obedience. The italicized "everything" (*vsè*) signifies and lexically symbolizes his overcoming of this gap through repentance.

The function of the taboo in *Crime and Punishment*, which is to be abolished when the two elements of the protagonist's consciousness are reconciled, is similar to the function of psychological suppression. The main *difference between* the two functions, however, lies in the presence of a moral and didactic aspect to Raskolnikov's tabooing. The nagging fact that he cannot mention the murder scene to himself teaches him a lesson: despite all his rationalizations to the contrary, murder is *always* forbidden.

One may ask: If the taboo on murder is a personal one for Raskolnikov, how can it signal a universal moral law? If the taboo is personal, does this mean that all is permitted for Napoleons, who do not have this personal taboo? *Crime and Punishment* suggests that others do not share Raskolnikov's personal taboo because and only as long as they are not murderers (i.e., not Napoleons). In this novel, as in *The Notes from the House of the Dead*, the absolutely inviolable aspect of the taboo on murder is revealed only as the immanent *punishment* for the crime: the criminal discovers that he is *not able to talk* about the very crime he *has* committed in deed; the mention or non-mention of the crime is no longer "up to him." For a murderer, this verbal taboo is actually much more viable and inviolable as a personal one than is the social interdiction against the criminal deed itself. Unless the commandment "thou shalt not kill" *becomes* a personal taboo, i.e., part of the punishment, rather than the interdiction on the crime, it remains a purely technical legal regulation which holds only for non-Napoleons, who do not know how to get around it. Dostoevsky does not say that there are no Napoleons in this world, rather he suggests that the Napoleons are those who cannot personalize the taboo on murder, or simply put, have their conscience atrophied.

In other novels taboos are not abolished but discovered, or at least constantly observed. In *Demons* the non-mentioning of the word *besy* (demons/devils) is indispensable for correctly functioning in, or understanding the system of values in that novel, and this taboo is not to be abolished. But the taboo on mentioning devils, although implying and designating a system of values, does not *operate* on values: devils are not a moral value. In *The Idiot* and *The Adolescent*, the protagonists learn about taboos as they learn about values, and any violation of these taboos leads to a catastrophe, rather than to a beneficially dispelling effect as it does in *Crime and Punishment*. In his last novel, *The Brothers Karamazov*, Dostoevsky returns to what he developed in his first, namely a taboo which implicates those who generate it by suppressing their guilt. In the last novel, however, the dispelling of the taboo *never occurs* within the story, and the taboo is not intended to be abolished. The guilt of those implicated in *The Brothers Karamazov* consists of suppression; there the chief taboo and its suppression—or possibly repression as it is unclear to what extent these implicated are conscious of the taboo—are *identical*, whereas in *Crime and Punishment*, the suppression is the cause of the taboo. If so, once the guilt is gone the taboo should be abolished as a sign of redemption. This last function of taboo is unique to *Crime and Punishment*.

NOTES

1. Cf. VII:321.

2. Cf., for instance, Max Vasmer, *Etmologicheskij slovar' russkogo iazyka*, Moscow: Progress, 1986, vol. 2, 589.

3. In Russian, *dialog protivoborstvuiushchikh pravd*, cf. Bakhtin (1979), 88: "No important act, no essential thought of any leading character is realized outside of this dialogue of "antagonistic truths."

4. Beside this dialogue of taboos in *Crime and Punishment*, as well as the Bakhtinian dialogue of ideas and personal discourses, Dostoevsky's novels exemplify other types of dialogues. Thus, as Diane Thompson maintains, the characters in *The Brothers Karamazov*, as well as its narrator, engage in an ongoing dialogue of personal memories (Thompson, 19 ff., *passim*). The reader is also engaged in this dialogue, as Belknap suggests and R. F. Miller maintains in her book on *The Brothers Karamazov*. Cf. Belknap (both 1967 and 1990), *passim*; R. F. Miller (1992), esp. 131, also 23, 74, 79, 107–8, also 4, 19–21, 127, 133.

5. Cf. the Pevear-Volokhonsky translation, *Crime and Punishment*, New York: Alfred Knopf, 1992, 531. Henceforth I refer to this translation of *Crime and Punishment* as P&V and the page number.

6. Dostoevsky italicizes one more pronoun referring to the murder in the epilogue, but in a non-mysterious way. Actually, this pronoun refers not to the murder itself but to the mysterious and oppressively haunting effect it once had had upon Raskolnikov, and to the subsequent dispelling of this effect: "Besides, after all, what worth are they all—all the torments of the past! *Everything*, including even his crime itself, even his sentence and exile—now seemed to him [... something] that even happened to another person" (VI:422).

7. L. D. Opul'skaia and G. M. Fridlender suggest that in *Crime and Punishment* Dostoevsky internalized several other motifs related to Raskolnikov's taboo, such as the "internal aspect of crime" and Raskolnikov's conflicting interactions with other characters. Cf. VII:320–321, 334.

8. My conviction that in *Crime and Punishment* what one does matters less than what one cannot utter somewhat challenges the proposition of Robert Belknap and Robin Miller, both of whom contend that Dostoevsky's characters' deeds—as opposed to their words—signal their "true worth" to the reader. (Cf. the introduction.) Deeds matter more than uttered words, but unutterable words matter even more than committed deeds.

9. Cf., for instance:. Wolfgang Kayser, *Das sprachliche Kunstwerk*, Bern & Munich: Francke (first edition 1948), 1967, 146–147, 412. Kayser considers *erlebte Rede* to be a way in which the 19th century rebelled "against the supreme rule of grammar." (He calls this rebellion "den Kampf gegen die Regeln der Grammatik," ibid., 147). I believe, however, that Dostoevsky uses this type of discourse to subjugate all of grammar's power to his own expressive needs. Cf. also Marguerite Lips, *Le style indirect libre*, Paris, 1926; Melvin J. Friedman, *Stream of Consciousness*, New Haven: Yale University Press, 1955; R. Langbaum, *The Poetry of Experience*, London: Chatto & Windus, New York: Random House, 1957. Langbaum's title explains why I prefer to use the German term: the idea that a narrator has a momentary empathy with his character's experience is more concrete than the notion of a discourse somewhere between the direct and the indirect.

For empathy as a grammatical shifter and, potentially a dialogizer of a monologic discourse, cf. also Olga Yokoyama, "Shifters and Non-verbal Categories of Russian" in *New Vistas in Grammar: Invariance and Variation*. ed. Linda R. Waugh and Stephen Rudy, Amsterdam-Philadelphia: J. Benjamins, 1991.

For *erlebte Rede* specifically in Dostoevsky, although with examples only from *The Brothers Karamazov*, cf. Terras, 90, 135 n. 108, 463, and many more. Cf. also Bakhtin (1979), 214 ff., 252–3, 277. Also, Voloshinov, 3. Also Morson and Emerson, 161–170, esp. 169.

10. VII:399–401 gives a detailed history of the evolution from the first-person narrative to the third. (Cf. esp. 400).

11. M. L. Kovsan, "Prestuplenie i nakazanie": "vse" i "on," in Bazanov, vol. 8, 74, 76, 79.

12. Cf. Bakhtin (1979), 252–53 and, specifically about Raskolnikov, 277.

13. *Erlebte Rede* characterizes even those instances of italicized pronouns which do not refer to Raskolnikov's idiosyncratic taboo. Raskolnikov himself uses erlebte Rede, assuming Sonia's point of view: "'No! That cannot be'—he exclaimed as Sonia did earlier (!OM)—'no, she was saved from the pit by the thought about sin, and by them, those ... (*oni, te*)'." (VI:248). Earlier Sonia herself says: "What will happen to them?—" meaning Katerina Ivanovna and the children (VI:147). She does not italicize the pronoun, even though she probably stresses it intonationally. But since she herself is speaking, there is no possibility for *erlebte Rede*—and therefore no place for italicizing. This example—especially because it does not pertain to Raskolnikov's taboo—brings into relief the function of *erlebte Rede* as the alternative to the common and expected function of italicizing pronouns— which is conveying intonational stress.

The same happens when Sonia reads the Gospel to Raskolnikov, and the narrator doubles the *erlebte Rede*: he italicizes "her" pronouns, assuming Raskolnikov's point of view: "Raskolnikov partially understood [...] how hard it was for her to disclose and expose all that was her own (*svoe*) [...] but that [...] she badly needed/wanted to read [it] [...] to him, and now (*teper'*) [...]" (VI:250). In this "triple" indirect speech, Sonia's or Raskolnikov's "now" (*teper'*) does not become "then" (togda zhe), and "he" is neither the projection of Raskolnikov's "I" (which would be normal for the *erlebte Rede* of the first degree), nor that of Sonia's "thou" (which would be normal if only the narrator—rather than Raskolnikov too—exercized the *erlebte Rede* on Sonia's point of view. Rather, Sonia's "he" is an exact citation, for within herself she calls Raskolnikov he, inwardly "italicizing" the word [cf. also VI:251, 252]).

14. Bakhtin (1979), 277.

15. *Ibid.*, 306.

16. Cf. earlier in this chapter, the reference to VI:248–252.

17. Viacheslav Ivanov, *Esse, stat'i, perevody*, Brussels: D. Ivanov and Foyer Oriental Chrétien, published as *Logos* 45, 1985 (the chapter "Roman-tragediia, II. Tragicheskij printsip mirosozertsaniia," the end of section 4, in "Dostoevskij. Tragediia—mif— mistika"), 27.

18. *Ibid.*, 28 (the beginning of section 5 of the same chapter).

19. In his theology of the antinomy of God's mercy and just punishment, Pavel Florensky interprets one's subjective hell as the loss of one's true personality to others. Cf. Florensky (1914), the chapter "On the Judgment" ("*O sude*").

20. Cf. Bakhtin (1979), Ch. 5.

21. Cf. Douglas, Chapter 8.

22. On the influence of *The Life of Julius Caesar* by Napoleon III on Raskolnikov's theory, cf. VII:338–339; also F. I. Evnin, "Roman 'Prestuplenie i nakazanie,'" in *Tvorchestvo Dostoevskogo*, Moscow: AN SSSR–Nauka, 1959, 153–157.

23. P&V, 341 (cf. above 58, n. 5).

24. In this passage, I retain the transliteration of names used by Pevear and Volokhonsky.

VICTOR TERRAS

The Art of Crime and Punishment

> A literary creation can appeal to us in all sorts of ways—by its theme,
> subject, structure, characters. But above all it appeals to us by the
> presence in it of art. It is the presence of art in *Crime and Punishment*
> that moves us deeply rather than the story of Raskolnikov's crime.
>   Boris Pasternak, *Doctor Zhivago*

Dostoevsky was a master of montage. He skillfully covers the seams that
join the several distinct themes, genres, and styles of which the novel is
composed. The duel between Raskolnikov's godless Nietzschean humanism
and Sonia's Orthodox faith is high (if you want) religious drama. The sad
story of the Marmeladov family is vintage naturalism.[1] The story of
Svidrigailov is melodrama, with a touch of Gothic horrors. What else could
one call this passage: "Never had he seen her so beautiful. The fire that was
blazing from her eyes at the moment when she raised the revolver virtually
burnt him as his heart winced in pain" (*PSS* 6: 301–2).[2]

Svidrigailov's story is integrated with that of Mrs. Raskolnikov and her
daughter Dunia, though rather carelessly (where are the children Miss
Raskolnikov is supposed to teach?). In that story we recognize the British
novel about the virtuous but indigent governess and her rakish and/or
mysterious employer. The Pecksniffian solicitor Luzhin, to whom Dunia is

From *Reading Dostoevsky.* © 1998 by the Board of Regents of the University of Wisconsin
System.

engaged as the novel starts, adds a Dickensian flavor to the governess's story. The detective novel enters the plot through the presence of Porfiry Petrovich, a master investigator. The detective is not really needed in the plot, since the perpetrator of the crime is known to begin with and eventually surrenders of his own free will, induced more by Sonia's pleas than by Porfiry's promise of a lighter sentence.

Throughout the novel, scraps of Platonic philosophical dialogues, sophisms, and aphorisms appear, almost always topically related to the ideological struggles of the 1860s. Elements of satire appear throughout the text, some with a point (the socialist Lebeziatnikov is presented as a ridiculous character), some quite gratuitous: the all too familiar "Poles of Dostoevsky," the Jewish fireman, unsavory German (of course!) landladies, madams, and procuresses.

Like most of Dostoevsky's novels, *Crime and Punishment* is a psychological and an ideological novel. The action develops on three levels: that of physical action and spoken discourse, that of the workings of the characters' minds, and that of the philosophical argument, developed in part explicitly, in part as a subtext.

In spite of various spurious insertions, *Crime and Punishment* is a *roman à thèse* of the dramatic type with a dominant central theme.[3] The theme is an age-old one: "What is the greatest good?" The question is asked in terms of a confrontation, on an existential plane, between Sonia Marmeladov's unshakable Christian faith and self-effacing humility and the carnal hedonism of Svidrigailov, the Benthamite utilitarian ethics of Luzhin, the socialist positivism of Lebeziatnikov, and, of course, Raskolnikov's notion that power is the greatest good. At one point the question is reduced simply to Svidrigailov's amoralism versus Sonia's submission to God's law: "Here I must go either her way or his" (p. 354). Inasmuch as the ideological plane is synchronized with the character traits of its bearer, the confrontation is apparently arranged so as to present the Christian answer in an attractive light while discrediting all opposing views. It must be observed that Dostoevsky has managed to introduce at least one significant encounter between Sonia and all four characters whose views oppose hers.

Sonia has all the Christian virtues. Though she has suffered much injustice, she never claims to be a victim but, on the contrary, calls herself "a great sinner," reminding herself of an act of unkindness to her stepmother. Her whole being is penetrated by Christian *agape*. The impression that she is really a saint is supported by the wealth of New Testament symbolism associated with her.[4] It is made explicit in the Epilogue when we learn that the convicts "even went to her to be healed." Sonia, like other characters in the novel, has literary antecedents of which Dostoevsky was well aware, particularly a saintly prostitute called Fleur-de-Marie in Eugène Sue's novel *Les mystères de Paris*. Even her name is symbolic: Sophia is Divine Wisdom, in both the Orthodox and the romantic tradition.

Svidrigailov, a former guardsman, is literate and has the air of a gentleman. He is a more subtle version of Valkovsky in *The Insulted and Injured* and, as it were, a study for Stavrogin of *The Possessed* (down to the theme of an abused child in his past). All these characters are versions of the supercilious dandy (or "libertine") of the English novel, with a hint of Byronic ennui and satanism. Utterly amoral, Svidrigailov follows his appetites and impulses, which lead him to heinous crimes but also to acts of kindness. He can be cynical and overbearing, but also tolerant and understanding, depending on his mood of the moment. Svidrigailov kills himself, apparently because he can no longer stand the nightmares that well up from his subconscious. In a way, he admits defeat by becoming a benefactor and savior of Sonia and the Marmeladov children.

Luzhin, a self-made man of humble origins (his education was paid for "in small change," he admits), prides himself on his hard-earned fortune and middling rank in the civil service. He lacks Svidrigailov's gentlemanly scruples. Where the former guardsman is ruthless, Luzhin is mean in a self-righteous way. Foiled in his clumsy attempt to frame Sonia, he disappears from the novel, a loser.

Lebeziatnikov is a more attractive figure. He naively parrots the socialist line, but in a pinch acts like the silly but harmless little man he is. He betrays his socialist principles ("free love," in this case) when put to the test of applying them in real life (when Sonia is forced into prostitution), but also shows he is an honest man with a kind heart when he foils Luzhin's plot and later tries to help the crazed Katerina Ivanovna.

Raskolnikov, aside from being a murderer, has much going against him. He is intolerant of the foibles of others and sounds downright priggish in his encounters with Svidrigailov. He is naively conceited:

> "A thought then occurred to me, for the first time in my life, which no one before me had ever thought of! No one! It became suddenly clear to me, like the sun, that nobody had ever dared, or dares, to walk past all this absurdity, to grab it all simply by the tail and send it to the devil." (p. 321)

After a few condescending gestures, Raskolnikov is, inexplicably and without self-awareness, drawn to Sonia. He is much the weaker party in all of their encounters, right to the end of the novel. His mental imbalance, his uncontrollable swings from momentary bravado to animal fear, from spontaneous generosity to cold heartlessness, cannot stand up to Sonia's moral strength and integrity.

The argument is complicated, however, by deep ambiguities that emerge if one views the novel as a whole. Like Sonia, her father, a drunken derelict, is a believer. He dies in a state of grace, confident that God will forgive him. Meanwhile, his virtuous and hardworking wife dies in a state of acedia, a mortal sin, rejecting the sacraments: "I have no sins to confess! ... God must forgive me even without [the sacrament of Penance]. He knows how I have suffered! ... And if He will not forgive me, I have no need of it!" (p. 333).

The crux of the argument appears more clearly and more poignantly in the case of Marmeladov. Sonia's faith is accompanied by every conceivable human virtue. Her father's faith did not prevent him from taking his daughter's last thirty kopecks to keep his binge going. Pleading the case for faith with Sonia is playing with loaded dice. Her father presents the argument on a razor's edge.

Crime and Punishment is a novel with a less than elegant and streamlined plot and a less than clear and convincing argument. What gives it unity and sustains the reader's interest is not to be sought in a linear dimension, but rather in the drama of each successive scene and the variety of particular effects that energize the text.

Dramatic qualities prevail. A series of dramatic scenes follow one another: "duels" (Raskolnikov's duel with Zametov at the "Crystal Palace," his two duels with Porfiry Petrovich, his two duels with Sonia, Dunia's duel with Svidrigailov); mass scenes (the scene at the police station, the wake, Katerina Ivanovna's death); "conclaves"[5] (in Raskolnikov's room, in Porfiry's, at the rooming house); a series of dreams (Raskolnikov's and Svidrigailov's); some great silent scenes (the scene where Razumikhin suddenly, without a word's being said, realizes the truth about his friend). Narrative passages are filled with action: the "rehearsal" and the murder, Raskolnikov's aimless but eventful wanderings, Svidrigailov's last hours.

Dialogue is the dominant form of the text, particularly if one considers the inner dialogue Raskolnikov and some of the other characters (Razumikhin, Luzhin) conduct in their own minds. The narrator often engages in a dialogue with the words or actions he reports. His observations on tone of voice, mimicry, and gestures, which accompany dialogue and action with great consistency, often amount to stage directions. The dialogue between Raskolnikov and Sonia that finally states the opposing positions of hero and heroine (pp. 311–14), essentially a dialogue of the deaf, since each speaker ignores the position of the other, comes alive precisely through the narrator's comments on the emotions that animate the speakers.

Time and space are treated dramatically and figure in the action directly and explicitly. The locales of several scenes are symbolic of the action: the sleazy tavern in which Marmeladov meets Raskolnikov, Sonia's monstrously misshapen room (symbolic of the perverseness of her condition), Raskolnikov's room, which resembles a coffin. The circumstance that Svidrigailov rents a room adjoining Sonia's, and is thus able to overhear Raskolnikov's confession to her, is of course a purely theatrical device.

Clock time is crucial to the commission of the murder. We are told that Raskolnikov took exactly 730 steps going from his lodging to the pawnbroker's residence. The plot hinges on a series of coincidences in time, such as the summons delivered to Raskolnikov the morning after the murder.

A pattern of playacting dominates many of the scenes of the novel. Several of the principal characters are presented playing a role other than their natural selves, for various reasons. It is made explicit that Marmeladov is in fact putting on a show at the tavern, and that it is a repeat performance (pp. 9–10). The novel actually begins with Raskolnikov's rehearsal of his planned crime. Subsequently he is forced to put on a show at the police station. He then stages a dramatic scene with Zametov at the Crystal Palace and stages his entry to Porfiry Petrovich's flat. He affects a pose throughout, even with Sonia. His attempt at a public confession in the square turns into grotesque comedy.

Luzhin, as he appears at Raskolnikov's room, tries to present himself as a liberal in step with the times. He puts on a show of righteous indignation when trying to frame Sonia. He is a bad actor throughout.

Katerina Ivanovna tries to play the role of a lady even in the sordid ambience of a slum tenement. She ends up staging a heart-rending street scene with her children and even dies dramatically. Sonia's first scene shows her, too, playing a role: she appears at her father's deathbed dressed up in her streetwalker's finery, carrying a parasol (it is night).

Svidrigailov plays the role of a suitor and bridegroom, knowing full well that it is a farce. Further examples of roleplaying may be readily adduced. They all add dramatic tension to the action.

Individualization of his characters, even minor ones, is characteristic of Dostoevsky's art. The concreteness that it gives them is one of his main assets. A *dramatis personae* has a specific function in the plot and, in most instances, also a function in the development of the ideological argument. In any case, a Dostoevskian character has a personality and a story of his or her own. Another tendency of Dostoevsky's art is to give his characters more idiosyncratic traits, more eloquence, wit, and imagination, than might be expected of average individuals. A favorite device is marking a character by polarized contradictory traits.

Porfiry Petrovich, the detective, is a case in point. To begin with, he does not look like a master detective: he is a rolypoly little man with a round face, a snub nose, and an unhealthy dark-yellow complexion. His face

> might have even appeared goodnatured, but for the expression of his eyes, which had a kind of watery luster and were covered by almost white eyelashes, continually blinking, as if winking at somebody. The gaze of these eyes clashed strangely with his whole figure, which actually had something womanish about it, and made him look much more serious than might have been expected at first glance. (p. 192).

The contradictions in this description are typical of Dostoevsky's manner of characterization.

Porfiry Petrovich's speech and mannerisms are highly idiosyncratic and, again, hardly typical of a successful detective. Who ever thought of a garrulous detective? Porfiry is in perpetual motion and appears nervous and self-conscious, yet is in full control of the situation. He suspects from the very first moment of their first meeting that Raskolnikov is his man. Raskolnikov has staged his entry to Porfiry's flat so as to appear casual and carefree, needling his friend Razumikhin about the latter's incipient infatuation with the beautiful Dunia. The embarrassed Razumikhin looks very funny, and Raskolnikov joins the rest of the company in a good laugh. This is the first instance of what Porfiry calls "double-edged psychology." No guilty man would enter a detective's place laughing—unless he is a truly formidable fighter, reasons Porfiry, realizing that it will take patience to get his man. So he enters into the spirit of goodnatured camaraderie and light banter, then springs his first surprise on Raskolnikov: the latter's article "On Crime." He soon steers the discussion to the question of those extraordinary individuals who have a right to break established laws. In the ensuing discussion (a Platonic dialogue, really), Raskolnikov parries Porfiry's probing questions well enough. They are slyly aimed, as it were by a narrow-minded philistine, at the practical consequences of Raskolnikov's subtle (Hegelian!) theory. The discussion ends when Zametov overplays his hand by blurting out: "Wasn't it perhaps some future Napoleon who last week did in our Aliona Ivanovna?" Porfiry tactfully changes the subject, only to spring another surprise. He asks Raskolnikov a question that he could have answered only if he was at the pawnbroker's the day of the murder. Double-edged psychology enters the picture once more: Raskolnikov sees the trap and answers "correctly," in the negative. But the fact is that an innocent but flustered man might have given an incriminating answer, and Raskolnikov's correct answer merely proves that he is on his guard. Porfiry profusely apologizes for his "mistake."

Eye to eye with Raskolnikov at their next meeting, Porfiry welcomes him warmly, and with the greatest solicitude, calling him "sir" and even "my dear sir" (*batiushka*, literally "little father"). Raskolnikov observes, however, that Porfiry stretches out both hands to greet him, yet does not shake hands. Porfiry agrees with everything Raskolnikov has to say (not much) and even with what he has not said: "Just as you, my dear sir, deigned to observe justly and wittily" (p. 258). The detective assumes a self-deprecating stance, complains about his health (he ought to quit smoking, his doctor told him), ruefully admits his weakness for military history (though himself a civilian, he might have made it to major, though not to Napoleon). This follows a long tirade on the fiasco of the Austrian *Hofkriegsrath*, who planned the capture of Napoleon in minute detail, only to see its own General von Mack surrender to him instead.

There are moments when Porfiry seems to be in a dither, mouthing strings of empty phrases, developing his ideas on investigative and interrogation strategy. Of course he is playacting, trying to provoke Raskolnikov into an angry outburst that would be tantamount to an admission of his guilt. He comes close, but Raskolnikov is saved when the interview is interrupted by the young painter's sudden confession to a crime he did not commit. At this point both antagonists quit playacting for a moment, as Porfiry observes: "Why, my dear, you didn't expect it either. Look how your hands [*ruchki*, "little hands"—Porfiry is very fond of diminutives!] are shaking! He-he!" Raskolnikov responds: "Why, you are shaking, too, Porfiry Petrovich!" And Porfiry: "Yes, I am shaking, sir, I did not expect it, sir!" (p. 272).

When they meet for the last time, Porfiry puts his cards on the table. He quits playacting and coolly assesses the situation. He is convinced that Raskolnikov is guilty, but admits that he has no hard evidence (he had his room searched, but *umsonst!*—the German word emphasizes his frustration). He offers Raskolnikov a few more days of freedom to confess his crime, which would mean a reduced sentence, but warns him that he will have to arrest him if he does not take advantage of the offer. Here, finally, Porfiry abandons his self-deprecating bantering manner. He speaks with precision and authority, though not without a note of sympathy for the young man. He is aware of his duty as a magistrate and asks Raskolnikov to leave a brief note in case he chose "to resolve the matter in a different, fantastic manner, to

raise your hands [*ruchki*, again!] against yourself." After all, Nikolai the
painter, a wholly innocent man, is still in prison.

Altogether, Porfiry Petrovich remains psychologically ambiguous. We
learn little about his personal life, except that he is thirty-five, a bachelor, and
very sociable. We know also that he likes to play pranks on his friends: at one
time he made them believe that he planned to become a monk, and recently,
inspired by the acquisition of a new suit of clothes, he had intimated that he
was about to get married—all in jest. Is Porfiry Petrovich a believer? He asks
Raskolnikov if he believes in God, in a new Jerusalem, and in the raising of
Lazarus. Raskolnikov, an unbeliever, answers in the affirmative. Porfiry gives
no indication of his own position. His argument in favor of a confession is
purely utilitarian: no mention is made of moral or religious reasons. One
may suspect that behind Porfiry's cheerful and playful façade is hidden a
rather sad character, a "finished man," as he says at one point. But perhaps
he is only joking,

A pattern of inner contradictions prevails in other characters of the
novel. Marmeladov is in some ways close to Porfiry. Like the latter, he is a
middle-aged civil servant of some education. But he is older, and he is from
the provinces, so his literate Russian sounds old-fashioned and smacks of the
seminary. Like Porfiry, he is playing a role. Like Porfiry, he keeps qualifying,
retracting, and conceding points. For example, as he talks about his efforts to
impart to his growing daughter some knowledge of history and geography,
he concedes that they did not get very far, for "whatever books we had ...
well, we no longer have those books [note the "doubletake," a favorite
mannerism of his!] ... so that was the end of it. We got as far as Cyrus of
Persia" (p. 16). That is, they stopped after the second lesson.

Marmeladov's performance at the tavern is deeply ambiguous. It is, of
course, a *cri de coeur*, but it is also, after all, a repeat performance before drunken
strangers in a lowly tavern. The following passage may serve as an example:

> Marmeladov knocked himself on the forehead with his fist,
> clenched his teeth, closed his eyes, and firmly dug his elbow into
> the table. But in a moment his face suddenly changed, and he
> looked at Raskolnikov with a feigned show of roguishness and
> simulated insolence, laughed and said: "And today I went to
> Sonia and asked her for some money for a drink to cure me of my
> hangover!" (p. 6)

Thus, Marmeladov's version of the Last Judgment may be understood as an
expression of true faith, but also as a carnivalesque—and, to some,
blasphemous—travesty of scripture.

Marmeladov's performance, like Porfiry's, is clearly far too brilliant and imaginative to be taken for honest realism. Besides the spirited, metaphysical Judgment Day passage, he comes up with several other memorable aphorisms—about the difference between poverty and beggarliness; about the condition of no longer having a place to go; about begging without the faintest hope of being heard—each more poignant than the other. There are some marvellous clashes of pathos and bathos, as when a pompous Slavonic word clashes with a sordid vulgarism: "When my firstborn and only daughter [the adjective is *edinorodnaia*, usually applied to Jesus Christ in relation to God the Father] was certified a prostitute" (*po zheltomu biletu poshla*, "got her yellow ticket," which she would have to renew by submitting to medical examination). Marmeladov's monologue also establishes a list of *realia* that will keep returning in the course of the novel and acquire symbolic status, such as the "family" shawl and Katerina Ivanovna's finishing school diploma. All around, a sense of the marked detail prevails: Marmeladov actually sold his wife's stockings for drink—"not her shoes, for that would have been still in the order of things, but her stockings" (p. 16).

The whole story is marked by contradictions. Marmeladov lost his first job through no fault of his own but lost his second for drunkenness; he was given a second chance and blew it. He knows that his long-suffering wife will pull his hair and beat him when he comes home drunk, but "such beating, sir, causes me not only pain, but enjoyment" (p. 22). Katerina Ivanovna has cruelly forced her stepdaughter into prostitution, yet when Sonia comes home after surrendering her virginity for thirty silver rubles, she "knelt down before Sonia's bed and kissed her feet" (p. 17).

Katerina Ivanovna's character is as full of contradictions as her husband's. "She was by nature of cheerful and peaceloving disposition, and much inclined to laugh easily" (p. 296). But the misfortunes of her life have made her shrewish and quarrelsome. She beats her children when they cry because they are hungry. She is in the last stages of consumption and is beginning to lose her mind. Her fantasies invade reality. She introduces Raskolnikov to her guests as a young scholar who "is getting ready to take over a professor's chair at the local university" (pp. 293–94). Katerina Ivanovna's fantasizing and roleplaying lack the imagination and wit of her husband's, being confined within the narrow experience of the daughter of a minor provincial official. The highlight of her life was the graduation ceremony of her finishing school, at which she "danced a *pas de châle*" before the Governor and other personages of high rank.

Pulkheria Aleksandrovna Raskolnikov is another figure associated with deep ambiguities. Her long letter to her son is heavily stylized to create the effect of a painful and at times comical contrast between the scandalous and sinister happenings at the Svidrigailov estate and the writer's naive efforts to downplay their impact and her own reaction to them. This contrast grows even sharper when Mrs. Raskolnikov faces Luzhin's sordid actions and, finally, the perplexing predicament of her only son, which she cannot fathom. Dostoevsky mercifully avoids the climax of a mother learning that her son is a murderer by letting Mrs. Raskolnikov fall ill and die without being told the terrible truth. But he cannot resist adding yet another ambiguity by suggesting that in the final stages of her illness, "in her feverish ravings, some words escaped her from which it could be gathered that she suspected much more about her son's terrible fate than had been assumed" (p. 415).

Svidrigailov is of all the characters in the novel the most literary. Dostoevsky in a way apologizes for this by letting Svidrigailov say: "What the devil? I see that I may in fact appear to some people like a person from a novel" (*litsom romanicheskim*, p. 315).[6] Svidrigailov, too, is a deeply contradictory figure:

> This was a strange face, rather resembling a mask: white, red-cheeked, with bright red lips, a light-blond beard, and still rather thick blond hair. His eyes were somehow too blue; their gaze was somehow too heavy and too immobile. There was something terribly unpleasant about this handsome and extraordinarily youthful face, considering his age. (p. 357)

The demonic and evil is lurking behind Svidrigailov's gentlemanly façade: "Svidrigailov took an attentive look at Raskolnikov, and it appeared to the latter that in this glance there flashed momentarily, like a bolt of lightning, a malevolent sneer." Svidrigailov is very literate and, his mind is sharp. He can be civil, tolerant, and capable of self-criticism, but he can also be cynical and overbearing:

> "Considering that Avdot'ia Romanovna is essentially a pauper (oh, excuse me, I did not want to be ... but isn't it all the same, if the same concept is expressed?), in a word, she lives by the labor of her hands and has to support her mother and you (oh, the devil, you are frowning again ...)." (p. 367)

Svidrigailov, like Porfiry and Marmeladov, delivers himself of occasional aphorisms and words of wit. An expert at seduction, he declares that flattery is the surest way to even a virtuous woman's heart: "If a straight approach contain even a hundredth part of a tiny note of falsehood, the result is an immediate dissonance, and thereafter a scandal. But if flattery is utterly false to the last tiny note, it still pleases" (p. 366).

The ultimate function of Svidrigailov in the novel's argument may be sealed by the good deeds that he does before killing himself. He undoes the evil done to Sonia and Katerina Ivanovna's children. Paradoxically, Marmeladov dies in a state of grace, while Svidrigailov is damned. The point of this can only be that the subject's salvation depends solely on his emotional state, not on his deeds. This notion will be pursued further, and more explicitly, in *The Idiot*.

Razumikhin, to whom Svidrigailov superciliously refers as "a seminarian, most likely," is also marked by contradictions, but in a wholly different way: "This was an extraordinarily cheerful and sociable lad, goodnatured to the point of being considered a simpleton by some. However, beneath this simplicity there were hidden both depth and dignity" (p. 43). Razumikhin is the very last to realize that his friend Raskolnikov is a murderer. But he sticks with him all the way and is rewarded by winning the hand of Raskolnikov's beautiful sister. Razumikhin is always his own honest self. But he is never dull. His views are in accord with his character. Speaking of his socialist friends, he observes:

> "They demand complete loss of individuality and find it very much to their taste! How not to be themselves, how to resemble yourself as little as possible! This they consider the highest progress. If they would at least talk rubbish in their own way ..." (p. 155)

Razumikhin's speech is laced with students' jargon: "Let us now proceed to the United States of America, as they used to be called at our school," he says as he presents a pair of trousers to Raskolnikov. But he can argue a point with logic and eloquence, though without subtlety. Razumikhin, too, has his moments: the wonderfully carnivalesque paean to talking rubbish (*vran'e*, a word that means "telling lies, fibbing, talking nonsense, make-believe"), delivered in a state of advanced intoxication on a sidewalk in the middle of the night before two mildly frightened ladies, and followed by a spontaneous declaration of love uttered while kneeling on the sidewalk.

The hero and heroine of the novel are less challenging, Raskolnikov because we are allowed to follow the workings of his mind all along, and Sonia because her character and mind lack psychological complexity. In contrast to the characters already discussed, the speech of neither has any idiosyncratic traits.

Raskolnikov is a bundle of contradictions. Razumikhin says of him: "Really, it is as though two contradictory characters were taking turns in him" (p. 165). The contradictions in Raskolnikov's mind prior to the crime may be reduced to a conflict between the normal emotions of an intellectually alert but emotionally immature young man (his normal, healthy self is released by the dream that returns him to his childhood) and a paranoid obsession with an idea that leads to a compulsive crime. After he commits the crime, the struggle is between the criminal's natural desire to evade detection and the growing sense of isolation and alienation that results in a subconscious desire to rejoin the human race by accepting the punishment for his crime. Raskolnikov's efforts to escape detection are subverted, time and again, by compulsive actions that put him in jeopardy: virtually admitting his guilt to Zametov, returning to the scene of his crime, challenging Porfiry needlessly. All along he puts himself into a position that forces him to playact, something that is in crass conflict with his proud and self-assured nature. At Porfiry's, he is tricked into declaring not only that he believes in God, a new Jerusalem, and the raising of Lazarus, but also, implicitly, that he is a failed pseudo-Napoleon who ought to and will rightly suffer the full severity of the law.

With Sonia, Raskolnikov can be himself. He develops his gloomy view of life, his denial of God's existence, and his idea that power is the only good worth pursuing—not as well as he had developed his idea of the exceptional individual and his right to transgress at Porfiry's, but in a rambling, staccato monologue. He believes that he can overpower Sonia with the force of the "facts of life" that are destroying her and will similarly destroy Polechka, her ten-year-old stepsister. He is foundering in a sea of bitterness, self-pity, and hurt pride. When he confesses his crime to Sonia in their second meeting, he shows no remorse, only self-hatred and despair.

Sonia is, of course, the winner all the way, even if Raskolnikov refuses to admit defeat until the last page of the Epilogue. Her second dialogue with Raskolnikov is a masterful composition of dissonant tonalities. Raskolnikov is trying to analyze the motive of his crime and passes judgment on himself in terms of a Darwinist anthropology and anticipated Nietzschean ethics. Sonia responds, point after point, in terms of New Testament ethics and the movements of her heart:

"But I only killed a louse, Sonia, a useless, repulsive, noxious louse!"—"So a human being is a louse?" (p. 320)

"I had to find out, find out precisely, if I am a louse, like all, or a man? Find out if I can cross the boundary or not? Find out if I dare reach for it and take it, or not? Find out if I am a trembling creature or have the right..."—"To kill? You have the right to kill?" (p. 322)

The point is that neither can convince the other, because Raskolnikov's heart is not ready to accept Sonia's truth, and because she loves him and will not give up on him until he is saved.

Sonia, too, has her great moment:

> "What to do?"—she exclaimed, suddenly leaping up from her seat, and her eyes, filled with tears up to this moment, flashed: "Get up" (she grabbed his shoulder; he arose, looking at her almost in amazement). "Go right away, this very minute, stop at the crossroads, bow down, first kiss the earth, whom you have desecrated, and then bow down to the whole world, in all four heavenly directions, and say to all, aloud: 'I have killed!' Then God will return you to life, Will you go? Will you go?" she asked him, all trembling, as in a seizure, clasping him firmly by both hands and fixing a fiery gaze at him. (p. 322)

The narrator of *Crime and Punishment* is different from Dostoevsky's other narrators, in part because some of the initial first-person narrative mode was left in the text. The narrator's frequent remarks pointing to a future when Raskolnikov will look back at the events related are one trace of this circumstance.[7] As is, *Crime and Punishment* has a narrator without a distinct voice. The narrative mode of this novel is uneven and takes different forms. Basically, we have a selectively omniscient narrator who follows action and dialogue rather as a careful director would follow the performance of his ensemble. But the narrator enters the text in other ways as well.

Occasionally, the narrator's observations stand apart from the drama; for example:

> There are some encounters, even with people entirely unknown to us, in whom we begin to take an interest at first sight, suddenly, without a word having been said. (p. 12)

The passage introducing Raskolnikov's first dream (pp. 45–46) provides another example:

> In a diseased condition, dreams are distinguished by an unusual plasticity, expressiveness, and extraordinary resemblance to

reality. Sometimes a monstrous image develops, but the setting and the entire process of the representation are so plausible nevertheless, and have details so subtle, unexpected, yet artistically perfect, that no person awake, including the dreamer himself, even if he were an artist like Pushkin or Turgenev, could imagine them.

In a few instances the narrator makes his presence felt by referring to the text itself. "We shall omit the whole process by way of which he reached his final decision" (p. 59); or: "I shall not describe what took place at Pulkheria Aleksandrovna's that night" (p. 240). But these instances are hardly characteristic of the whole text.

Sometimes the narrator will let his own emotions come to the fore: "And this unfortunate Elizaveta was so simpleminded, downtrodden, and frightened that she did not even raise her hand to defend herself" (p. 65). Here, "unfortunate" belongs to the narrator, for the murderer cannot have had this reaction as he was striking her with his axe. (He may have said this later, when recalling the scene in a confession.)

When we read: "Sonia understood that this somber catechism had become his creed and his law" (p. 328), these are clearly the narrator's words, not Sonia's. Then there is this famous passage: "The candle was barely flickering in the crooked candlestick, dimly illuminating in this beggarly room the murderer and the harlot, who had so strangely come together reading the eternal book" (pp. 251–52). Here "harlot" is *bludnitsa*, a biblical word not used in ordinary speech. The pathos is the narrator's. By the way, this solemn scene has a counterpoint. We learn, a page or so later, that the whole scene was witnessed by Svidrigailov, whose reaction was not at all like the narrator's.

Throughout the text, in narrative as well as dialogue, many comments that amount to inner hermeneutic or semiotic analysis occur with some regularity. Raskolnikov interprets his mother's letter (p. 35); Raskolnikov's analysis of a criminal's state of mind (pp. 58–59) fully applies to him, as he will soon learn; Zosimov's observations on mental disease describe Raskolnikov's condition (p. 174); Porfiry and Raskolnikov discuss interrogation techniques (pp. 256–62); Porfiry reviews Raskolnikov's article (pp. 345–46). Other examples are readily found.

The narrator sometimes assumes the role of a chorus responding to the hero's condition at that moment:

If only he could have grasped all the difficulties of his situation, its whole desperation, its hideousness and absurdity, and understood how many obstacles and, perhaps, crimes he might have to overcome and commit in order to get out of there and get back home, it is quite possible that he would have left it all and turned himself in, and this not even out of fear for himself, but solely out of horror and revulsion for what he had done. (p. 65)

In fact, none of these thoughts occurred to Raskolnikov, for the drama has only just started. An important choral passage introduces the leitmotif[8] of the murderer's profound sense of alienation and isolation from the whole human race:

> A somber sense of excruciating, infinite isolation and alienation suddenly took hold of his soul. It was not the baseness of his heartfelt effusion before Il'ia Petrovich, not the baseness of the lieutenant's triumph over him that was suddenly turning his heart. Oh, what did he care about his own baseness, all those egos, lieutenants, German women, liens, offices, and so on and so forth? If he had been condemned to be burnt at the stake this very moment, he would not have made a move, in fact, he would hardly have listened to the verdict. (p. 82)

Obviously, Raskolnikov was not thinking of being burnt at the stake at this moment, So the image belongs to the narrator, as does the whole tirade, a response to an as yet dim and indistinct feeling that is taking hold of Raskolnikov's soul. There is a similar passage in response to the experience that sends Sonia on her way to her part in the drama:

> She was awfully glad that she could finally leave. She walked along, hunched and hurried [...] to be at last alone and thus, walking along hurriedly and looking at no one, taking note of nothing, to think, to remember, to take in every word that had been said, every detail. Never, never had she experienced anything like this. A whole new world had entered her soul, dimly and unawares. (p. 187)

The narrator's comments differ in their mode and intensity, depending upon the character in question. When Luzhin first comes to Raskolnikov's room, his appearance and behavior are described in detail and commented upon (pp. 113–14). The narrator proceeds to follow this character's every move and explains his motives as if he were reading his mind. His dislike of Luzhin is obvious. On the other hand, the workings of Porfiry Petrovich's mind are never revealed, while his appearance and behavior are described in meticulous detail. Svidrigailov's treatment is somewhere in the middle between these: up to a point, he is viewed from the outside, though very carefully. But then we are allowed to follow his every thought and emotion, to a degree, we are never given access to the innermost recesses of his psyche. Glimpses of it are provided by Svidrigailov himself (the ghosts he sees and his vision of Hell as a place with spiders) and by a description of his last nightmare.

The narrator comments on the characters' language, behavior, mimicry and gestures, and, occasionally, their motives. For example, the narrator explains why Marmeladov would open his heart to a bunch of drunks in a lowly tavern:

> Obviously, Marmeladov had been known here for a long time. Also, his penchant for flowery language he had probably acquired as a result of a habit of engaging in bar-room conversations with assorted strangers. This habit turns into a need for some drunkards, particularly those who are dealt with sternly at home and hear frequent reproaches. This is why, in the company of other drunks, they try to obtain, after a fashion, some justification and if possible even some respect for themselves. (pp. 13–14)

This remark also draws attention to a stylistic trait: the flowery language of Marmeladov's monologue. Observations on the style or tone of the *dramatis personae* occur throughout the text; for example: "When Andrei Semionovich concluded his prolix disquisition with such a logical conclusion [...] Alas, he could not even express himself in decent Russian" (p. 307). Or this: "She was saying this as if she were reciting from memory" (p. 319). The characters of the novel occasionally engage in similar observations. Razumikhin and Raskolnikov discuss the style of Luzhin's letter (p. 180). Raskolnikov gives Razumikhin credit for a good synopsis of the scene at the police station (pp. 206–7). At one point Raskolnikov congratulates himself on having found the right word: "I became *angered* (this is a good word!)" (p. 320). The Russian text: *ozlilsia (eto slovo khoroshee!).*

Sonia's inner life is hardly shown or her words and actions analyzed, while every movement of Raskolnikov's mind and soul is reported and commented upon in a sympathetic manner. Throughout the text, we find hundreds of passages such as the following:

> Let us note one particular trait regarding all these definitive decisions which he had made earlier in this matter. They had one

strange quality: the more definitive they became, the more hideous, absurd, they also became immediately in his eyes. In spite of all the torturous inner struggle, he could never for a moment believe in a realization of his plans. (p. 57)

At times, the narrator will illustrate his description with a simile of his own: "It was as if he had gotten a strip of his clothes caught in the wheel of a machine, and it was beginning to pull him inside" (p. 58).

The whole murder scene is observed in minute detail by a narrator studiously producing specifics and avoiding commonplaces. Who would expect a narrator describing a murderer on his way to his victim's place to say: "Fortunately, everything went well at the gate," as Raskolnikov slips by unseen? And what narrator would have thought of a murderer being overcome by "a kind of absentmindedness, or a pensive mood, as it were"? Or this: when Raskolnikov finds a piece of red cloth in the victim's chest, looking for her money, he wipes his bloody hands, thinking, "It is red, and on red the blood will be less noticeable," then immediately: "My God, am I going out of my mind?" (p. 65).

After the murder, the narrator's observations deal mostly with Raskolnikov's enforced roleplaying and his growing sense of isolation. Mood swings from apathy to fierce determination are noted repeatedly:

He stood there, as it were lost in thought, and a strange, suppressed, half-senseless smile was playing on his lips. He finally took his hat and quietly left the room. His thoughts were getting confused. (p. 208)

But also this, after the threat of a surprise witness has evaporated:

"Now we shall yet put up a fight," he said with an angry smirk, as he walked down the stairs. His anger was directed at himself. He remembered his "faint-heartedness" with contempt and shame. (p. 276)

The key scene of Raskolnikov's second meeting with Sonia begins with this introspective passage. As so often, Raskolnikov's feelings are polarized:

He stopped at her door with a strange question: "Must I tell her who killed Lizaveta?" It was a strange question because suddenly, at the same time, he felt that it was quite impossible not only not to tell her, but even to postpone it, even for a short time. He did

not know as yet why this was impossible, he only *felt* it, and this
excruciating awareness of his own powerlessness before the
inevitable almost crushed him. (p. 312)

It is almost a foregone conclusion that the passage that first introduces
Raskolnikov's love for Sonia would start as it does: "And suddenly a strange,
unexpected sensation of a burning hatred for Sonia passed through his mind"
(p. 314).

The principle *les extrèmes se touchent* appears here in its crassest form.

The principal qualities of Dostoevsky's art in *Crime and Punishment* are a
wealth of factual, psychological, and intellectual detail, an insistence on
markedness in every aspect of the text, dialogue or narrative, at almost any
cost, and an equally uncompromising ambiguity of every position taken.

Markedness is achieved in various ways. The most pervasive is the
steady flow of concrete and meaningful facts, such as the "Zimmermann hat"
on the second page of the novel (it will recur a few pages before the end), or
this specific detail as we see the hero leave his room on page one: "as if he
were trying to make up his mind" (*kak by v nereshimosti*). Such concreteness
is often enhanced by presenting extreme facts and conditions. The novel
starts with the words: "Early in July, on an extraordinarily hot day a young
man was leaving his room"—not "on a warm summer day"! We are
immediately told that the young man is dressed in "rags" (*lokhmot'ia*),
objectively an overstatement, for we will soon learn that he has not been *that*
destitute very long.

The emotions that move the young man are also extreme: "A feeling of
the deepest revulsion flashed momentarily in the fine features of the young
man." (We already know that he is "remarkably handsome.")

The extremes in the text are often polarized, which marks them even
more effectively. After we have heard that "the young man, who was deeply
in debt to his landlady, was afraid to meet her," we are immediately told:
"Not that he was fearful and downtrodden, quite the contrary: but for some
time now he was in an irritable and tense condition, resembling
hypochondria." As early as page three, we find this example of psychological
polarization:

At the time he did not himself believe in his daydreams and
merely titillated himself with their hideous but alluring audacity.
But now, a month later, he was already beginning to take a
different view and, in spite of all his mocking monologues about
his own weakness and indecision, had willy-nilly gotten used to

considering the "hideous" daydream an undertaking, though still
not believing it himself. In fact, he was on his way to make a test
of his undertaking, and his excitement was growing stronger and
stronger with every step. (p. 7)

This example is also typical in that it presents, as it were, an inner dialogue
after the fashion of a pendulum swinging wide to both sides—in this case,
from disbelief in the possibility of a hideous idea awareness of its actual
happening. Many such inner dialogues appear throughout the text. Some
have been mentioned earlier. A similar polarization appears in other
characters as well. One more example from the Marmeladov episode:

But there was one very strange thing about him: in his gaze there
was a glimmer of, as it were, yes, rapture—perhaps, there was
sense and intelligence in it, too—but at the same time, also a
flicker of madness. (p. 12)

Extremes and their polarization may assume the form of paradox, such
as when Katerina Ivanovna is said to pull her husband's hair "from
compassion" (*ot zhalosti serdtsa*); outright overstatement (when Raskolnikov's
room is called a "closet," though a group of people meet there); or pathos
and bathos (when the story of Dunia's proven innocence becomes the talk of
the town).

Suspense, such as when we are not immediately told what
Raskolnikov's "undertaking" (*delo, predpriiatie*) might be; surprise, such as
when Svidrigailov keeps showing up unexpectedly or even without
Raskolnikov and Sonia's being aware of his presence; and symbolic repetition
of leitmotifs[9] or "situation rhyme," such as when Katerina Ivanovna's last
words ("They have ridden the nag to her death") remind one of
Raskolnikov's dream, are some other ways to achieve markedness.

A constant source of markedness is the Sophoclean irony that
permeates almost the entire text. Time and again, we observe Raskolnikov
listening to conversations about the murder he has committed. At times he
almost gives himself away by appearing to know too much. The whole action
that unrolls independently of Raskolnikov's crime is marked by its presence.
Raskolnikov's strange behavior mystifies his mother and sister, who do not
know what the reader knows. This irony becomes particularly cruel toward
the end, when everybody except Raskolnikov's mother knows the truth.

Dostoevsky does not spurn any device to achieve markedness. Name
symbolism,[10] catachresis,[11] and occasional literary allusions[12] are employed.

Like markedness, ambiguity, itself a form of markedness, assumes various forms. The theme of double-edged psychology extends far beyond its relevance to detection of the perpetrator of a crime. In Dostoevsky's world, any attempt at understanding human nature elicits a dialectic, rather than an unequivocal answer. The "real" motive of Raskolnikov's crime remains unresolved. There is overwhelming evidence that it was an intentional, deliberate "thought crime." In fact, we learn that he had paid little attention to "the material difficulties of the matter" (p. 89). But there is also ample evidence that the crime was committed under irresistible compulsion. Was the murderer in a condition to tell right from wrong? Yes, of course, for Raskolnikov has a conscience (he often blames himself for his base and cowardly behavior, has noble impulses); but, also, no: he considers his undertaking "no crime" (p. 59), suffers no pangs of conscience after the double murder, and says, "I only killed a louse," forgetting that he also killed Lizaveta.

Sonia, a saint, humbly calls herself "a great sinner." Paradoxically, Raskolnikov agrees, showing the gulf between their respective worldviews: to him she is a sinner because she thinks only of others, never of herself, to herself she is a sinner because she once, only once, thought of herself.

Katerina Ivanovna, certainly not blameless, feels she has nothing to confess. Her husband, a serious sinner, is eager to confess. She does not want forgiveness; he hopes for it. The slimy Luzhin feels good about himself. The evil Svidrigailov seems secure in his amoral ways but is shown, after all, to have a "deep" conscience, which destroys him. The conclusion to be drawn from all this appears to be that guilt and innocence, and hence right and wrong, are existentially ambiguous.

A peculiar form of ambiguity is due to the presentation of themes and characters, particularly those that are central to the drama, in travesty. By "travesty" I mean an action, sentiment, or thought whose performance or expression falls drastically short of its intended or normal effect, or distorts it so badly that it is in danger of turning into its opposite. Marmeladov's travesty of Judgment Day on the first pages of the novel sets the tone for much of the rest of the text.

The whole story of the Marmeladov family is an exercise in travesty. Theirs is a marriage in travesty, for Katerina Ivanovna married a man twice her age only because she had "no place to go" with her three small children. The St. Petersburg of the slums, where they land, is a travesty of "that magnificent capital city, decorated by numerous monuments" (p. 16). Marmeladov's wake is an ill-conceived affair and ends in a scandal. Katerina Ivanovna's death in the streets of St. Petersburg is an ugly tragedy, a tragedy in travesty.

Raskolnikov's quest for the status of an extraordinary man (a Hegelian "world-historical personage"), who has the right to break the law and seize power, turns into a ludicrous travesty: a future Napoleon climbing under an old woman's bed to steal her few rubles. Worse yet: Raskolnikov is not even a passable common criminal. He must hear Razumikhin say: "He didn't even know how to rob, the only thing he knew how to do was kill! His first step, I'm telling you, his first step; he lost his nerve!" (p. 117). Later, in prison, Raskolnikov must hear from his fellow convicts that killing with an axe was none of his, a gentleman's, business. Only luck keeps him from being caught in the act. He has every chance to escape justice, but manages to compromise himself enough to attract suspicion. The travesty he makes of a clever criminal is compounded by the fact that he actually evokes Porfiry Petrovich's pity.

When Raskolnikov finally yields to Sonia's urging and stages a public confession, as she demands, even this act turns into a travesty. As he kneels down in the square and kisses the ground, he hears this:

> "Look at him, isn't he plastered!" And there was laughter. "He is headed for Jerusalem, my dear brothers, he's saying good-bye to his children, to his native land, and bows down to the whole world, kisses the capital city of St. Petersburg and its ground," some drunken tradesman commented. (p. 405)

Many other instances of travesty are found throughout the text. Luzhin and Svidrigailov (and even Porfiry, after a fashion) are bridegrooms in travesty. Lebeziatnikov makes a travesty of a socialist believer. Svidrigailov joins the long line of Byronic charactersin travesty who have populated Russian literature since *Eugene Onegin*. In fact, Svidrigailov's hell is a travesty.

Even Sonia is, after all, a saint in travesty. She is a "rather pretty blonde" when first presented in her streetwalker's finery at her father's deathbed, but we later learn that she has a "pale, thin face, with irregular and angular features" (p. 248), hardly the image of a traditional Mary Magdalene. She is a very ordinary, very cheap streetwalker, decidedly unglamorous. The Slavonic *bludnitsa*, applied to her in the scene described above, rings false. The point is that she is saintly and firm in her faith even while she walks the streets. In fact, Raskolnikov asks her if she had gone to work the night of the reading of the Gospel, and her answer is yes.

Where, then, is the art of *Crime and Punishment*? First of all, it rises from the vigor of Dostoevsky's imagination, which produces an abundance of wonderfully alive scenes, images, characters, and ideas. Second, it comes from the extraordinary power of his language, activated by a great variety of devices. Among these, the most important are a dramatic technique of scenic presentation, the presence of dialogic form even in narrative passages, the use of polarized extremes in every aspect of the text, and a playing down of the melodramatic effects of the action by travesty. The result is a virtual (or "poetic") reality that makes all but the most critical readers disregard the conventional literary quality of some of the characters and the rather makeshift plot. In *Crime and Punishment* Dostoevsky has not quite reached the consummate dramatic structure of *The Possessed*, nor the superb dialectic skill of *The Brothers Karamazov*. The devil's case is not presented nearly as well, but it is to Dostoevsky's credit that he lets his hero hold out, bloodied but unbowed, almost to the end, and that Sonia is, amazingly enough, almost a credible character.

Notes

1. We know that Dostoevsky was at one time working on apiece entitled "Dear Drunks" (*P'ianen'kie*). It became the nucleus of the Marmeladov episode.

2. Dunia is a rarity in Dostoevsky's work: an entirely one-dimensional and stereotypical character.

3. A fairly accurate description of the central theme is found in Dostoevsky's notebooks. See *PSS* 7:154–55.

4. See George Gibian, "Traditional Symbolism in *Crime and Punishment*," *PMLA* 70 (1955): 979–96.

5. L. P. Grossman's term for a scene in which the key characters meet to reach some momentous decision.

6. In the notebooks, Svidrigailov emerges more clearly as a murderer, sadist, and child-abuser, a Gothic character, In the definitive text, his nature is covered by a veil of ambiguity. For some excellent observations on Svidrigailov, see Joseph Frank, *Dostoevsky: The Miraculous Years, 1865–1871* (Princeton: Princeton University Press, 1995), pp. 94–95.

7. "He later remembered that he was actually very attentive, cautious" (p. 63). Other examples: pp. 92, 270, 316, 422. For an excellent analysis of the narrator in *Crime and Punishment*, see Gary Rosenshield, *Crime and Punishment: The Techniques of the Omniscient Narrator* (Lisse: Peter de Ridder, 1978).

8. Other instances in which this leitmotif appears: pp. 90, 150, 176, 201, 324. Another leitmotif involves the raising of Lazarus and the New Jerusalem, about which Porfiry asks Raskolnikov: see pp. 201, 250, 405, 422.

9. See n. 8 above.

10. Raskolnikov, Luzhin, Svidrigailov, Zametov, and Razumikhin have symbolic names: *raskol'nik*, "schismatic"; *luzha*, "puddle"; Svidrigailov has a foreign ring (a Lithuanian prince of that name figured in medieval Russian history); Razumikhin, *razum*, "(good) sense"; Zametov, *zametit'*, "to notice." Further observations may be readily added.

11. For example, when Marmeladov relates that Lebeziatnikov beat up Katerina Ivanovna "with his very own hands" (*sobstvennoruchno izbil*), using a pompous literary word for a minor domestic squabble.

12. It has been noted that Raskolnikov uses the very same examples as Hegel when he develops his theory of "extraordinary men" (Hegel's "world-historical personages, who trample on many an innocent flower"). But there are also minor details worth noticing. The State Councilor who refuses to pay Sonia for her sewing because the shirt collars were crooked, and stamps his feet at her, is called Klopstock—a German, of course, but also the namesake of a famous German poet with a ludicrous name derived from *kloppen*, "to give a beating," and *Stock*, "stick."

JANET TUCKER

The Religious Symbolism of Clothing in *Dostoevsky's* Crime and Punishment[1]

In *Crime and Punishment*, the religious theme that would dominate all of Dostoevsky's subsequent fiction emerges as a central element for the first time. Dostoevsky embedded this theme not only in the behavior of his characters, but also in their clothing references and the clothing itself. He redirected the inherited focus of the physiological sketch, in which a character's apparel was principally a socio-economic indicator, to invest clothing with intense spiritual power. Clothing now symbolized a character's spiritual state, specifically, his/her acceptance or rejection of Christ.[2]

The symbolic use of cloth/clothing has traditionally been an accepted practice in the Western tradition. We encounter it in works as wide-ranging as the Bible (Joseph's coat), Greek myth (the fates who spin and sever man's fate), and Homer's *Odyssey* (Penelope's "web" or shroud, with its "unraveling" of fate). Lear's storm-soaked clothing is a mark of impending tragedy and a generalized symbol of the human condition (Champion 1:38, 49–50, 56–57, 82; Spurgeon 325–26). Clothing acquires a socio-economic dimension in Thomas Hood's "Song of the Shirt"[3] and Eugène Sue's *The Mysteries of Paris*, as well as poignant overtones in Dickens (Miss Havisham's wedding finery).[4] Of course, Dostoevsky read these Western models with an enormous appetite (Belknap 17, 37). But he clearly broke new ground in *Crime and Punishment* by using cloth and clothing as a specifically Christian symbol. No

From *Slavic and East European Journal* 44, no. 2 (Summer 2000). © 2000 by the American Association of Teachers of Slavic and East European Languages of the U.S., Inc.

longer the passive toy of fate that we associate with the Greek model, or merely the victim of social injustice central to Sue, Hood, Hugo or Dickens, man now chooses his destiny by following or disavowing the Gospels and Christ. His attitude toward clothing mirrors that choice.

It is the purpose of the present essay to discuss the symbolic role of clothing in *Crime and Punishment* and to analyze the relationship between the central characters in the novel and their attire. A character's attitude toward clothing in *Crime and Punishment* is variously a marker for charity or hoarding.[5] Charity is expressed by donating or repairing clothing, trading in used clothing, and sometimes even making do with poor-quality clothing. These all denote *caritas* (love, esteem, affection) and *agape* (love of mankind).[6] But hoarding it signifies a denial of that love and, ultimately, a rejection of the Gospels and Christ.

References to clothing—denoting material wealth, as opposed to spiritual riches—are infrequent yet momentous in the New Testament, a crucial backdrop for *Crime and Punishment*. The "coat" in the English translation becomes a "shirt" (*rubaška*) in the Russian, echoed in Lizaveta's links with shirts. Had Luzhin read the Bible more carefully, he would surely have recalled the message in Matthew 5:40, where we are exhorted to give away our outer garments to the man who successfully sues for our shirt.[7] Luke 6:29 echoes this sentiment: "And unto him that smiteth thee on the one cheek offer also the other: and him that taketh away thy outer garment forbid not to take thy shirt also." This message is especially cogent for Sonya and Lizaveta. Matthew 25:43 reminds us of the need for charity—symbolized by clothing: "I was a stranger, and ye took me not in: naked, and ye clothed me not...." Charity joins faith and hope as one of the three virtues in the New Testament (I Corinthians, I Thessalonians, Colossians, Romans, I Peter, Hebrews). It is "[t]he greatest of the 'theological virtues'.... It is directed primarily towards God; but it is also owed to ourselves and our neighbours as the objects of God's love. Its natural opposite is hatred, which may also take the negative form of indifference" (Cross 321).[8]

Since, charity is linked with humility and Christ's love, it is often connected with the wearing of unfashionable or rough clothing. Revelling in his luxurious attire, Svidrigailov has forgotten this crucial point. Not so Lizaveta, clad in goatskin shoes. In Matthew 6:28, Jesus reminds us: "And why take ye thought for raiment? [Revised Standard Version: And why are you anxious about clothing?] Look at the lilies of the field, how they grow; they toil not, neither do they spin." Garments purified with the blood of Christ appear in Revelation 7:14: "And I said unto him, Sir, thou knowest. And he said to me, These are they which came out of the great tribulation, and have washed their clothing, and made it white with the blood of the

Lamb."[9] Dostoevsky fuses clothing, blood and sacrifice in Lizaveta's rough, bloody garments (*PSS* 6:51–54). They symbolize kenotic humility, which echoes Christ's incarnation and functions as an important and related principle of Russian Orthodoxy. It is "the most ambiguous among Christian virtues ... The consciousness of one's sins ... is enhanced by the feeling of the abysmal distance between God and man ... [and is] an expression of nearness to the incarnate God" (Fedotov 210).

Hoarding or taking clothing denotes rejection of the Gospels and functions as a negative marker. Characters who dress too well have failed to heed the message of Christ's Sermon on the Mount (Matthew 5:40). So has the pawnbroker, who conceals bits of hoarded cloth among her pledges. Expensive, ostentatious clothing is a distinctly negative image in Revelation 17:4-5: "And the woman was arrayed in purple and scarlet colour, and decked with gold and precious stones and pearls, and held a golden cup in her hand full of abominations and filthiness of her fornication: And upon her forehead was a name written, Mystery, Babylon the Great. The Mother of Harlots and Abominations of the Earth." Babylon and St. Petersburg—linked as two corrupt capitals—are personified by Svidrigailov and Luzhin. That this accusation does not also refer to the humble, self-sacrificing prostitute Sonya Marmeladova and the ever-pregnant Lizaveta follows from their association with Christian charity.

Raskolnikov's clothing points to revolt and murder right from the start, an immediate marker of his rejection of Christ. In spite of the heat, Raskolnikov wears a foreign-looking hat in addition to his usual rags:[10]

> He was badly dressed, such that someone else, even a man used to it, would have been ashamed to go out into the street in such rags.... And meanwhile, ... one drunk, who—for some unknown reason and to some unknown destination—was being hauled off down the street in an enormous cart pulled by an enormous dray horse, shouted to him all of a sudden while he was going past: "Hey you there, you German hat-wearer!" ... (6:6–7)

His foreign hat—a special marker of revolt—and his rags do not really bother him because of his *zlobn[oe] prezreni[e]* ("malicious contempt," "defiance," 6:6) for the world, the opposite of charity. He could be better dressed: At the beginning of Part One, Chapter Five, Raskolnikov muses that he could have approached Razumikhin, who would have readily shared his meager funds with his friend for shoes and clothing. But Raskolnikov has chosen not to do so, having dismissed the whole thing as *sme?no* ("ridiculous," 6:44). He is concerned only that his obviously foreign hat will make him look conspicuous on the day of the actual murder, missing entirely the more important point that his German "Zimmermann" hat (meaning "carpenter" and tied in, perhaps, with the axe, the murder weapon) cuts him off still further from Russian traditions and mores. As Ewa Thompson has noted (116), "the Christian custom [is to wear] garments that are as plain and ordinary as possible, so as not to stand out in the crowd and not to attract attention."

Suspecting Raskolnikov from the start, the police inspector Porfiry associates the cardinal idea of Raskolnikov's essay, that everyone is divided into the extraordinary and the ordinary, with distinctive clothing that could distinguish them from each other. Wondering how to tell these two groups apart, Porfiry muses that there must be some kind of external sign: "[W]ouldn't it be possible, for example, for them to acquire some special clothing...." (6:198–201). Lurching toward murder in his distinctive hat, Raskolnikov has anticipated him.

His student overcoat, a frequent symbol of rebellion, merges with the Zimmermann hat to engulf Raskolnikov in garments linked with Western ideas and the Western-oriented city of Petersburg.[11] This rebellion is enacted as murder. A sartorial accomplice, his overcoat even abets his crime. Raskolnikov's preparations for committing the murder entail altering his coat by sewing a sling inside to hold his murder weapon, an axe. He tears the cloth for the sling from an unwashed shirt (6:56), having transformed a "seamless" garment (cf. John 19:23) into bits of cloth. Now linked with Lizaveta, the shirt will come back to haunt him. Clothing has been transformed from a Christian symbol into part of the murder weapon:

> 'Lizaveta was killed too!' Nastasya suddenly blurted out, turning toward Raskolnikov... 'Lizaveta?' muttered Raskolnikov in a barely audible voice. 'You really don't know Lizaveta, the second-hand clothes dealer? She used to come here. Fixed a shirt for you once.' Raskolnikov turned toward the wall.... (6:105)[12]

Following the murders, he wipes the axe on some laundry, once again connecting crime, guilt, blood and clothing. Then he worries about his blood-soaked clothing, particularly a sock and pocket (6:65–66; 6:72). That Raskolnikov carries this bloody clothing around with him underscores the fact that the murders are always with him now. One of Dostoevsky's masterful touches lies in placing these bloody pieces of cloth—a sock and pocket—inside Raskolnikov's clothing. Hidden from view to outsiders, they are lodged in his memory forever. The pawnbroker's hidden scraps of cloth form a counterpoint to Raskolnikov's.[13] He committed murder to elevate himself above others and attain man-Godhood, but the blood that adheres to his clothes is the obverse of the blood that Christ (God-manhood) shed as a sacrifice for the sake of others, the blood of the Lamb from Revelation 7:14. Murder born of intellect undermines charity born of Christian faith.

Luzhin's expensive attire echoes the New Testament twice. In his initial appearance in the novel when he drops in on Raskolnikov's miserable garret, Luzhin shows off his finery, designed to appeal to and conquer his fiancée Dunya, Raskolnikov's sister. Dostoevsky's irony knocks the props out from under Luzhin:

> In the first place, it was evident and even too noticeable that Pyotr Petrovich had earnestly rushed to make use of his several days in the capital to make time to outfit himself and adorn himself in anticipation of his bride, this, however, being highly innocent and proper. Even his perhaps too self-satisfied consciousness of his pleasant change for the better could have been forgiven, since Pyotr Petrovich was on the verge of being a bridegroom. All his clothes had just come from the tailor and everything was good, even though it was perhaps too new and too evident in its obvious purpose. (6:113)

Dostoevsky next alludes to Luzhin's top hat, lilac-colored Jouvenet gloves, the light and youthful color of his clothing, with each item listed in a detailed description. Luzhin appears younger than forty-five. "If there was anything in this quite handsome and solid-appearing physiognomy that was really unpleasant and repulsive," the narrator informs us, "then it came from other causes" (6:113–14). Which other causes? We know that Luzhin is planning to marry a much younger woman whose poverty puts her into a weak position (see 6:165). And pride in his new clothing is the opposite of humility. In a deliberate and stunning misreading not only of Matthew 5:40 and Luke 6:29, cited above, but also a parody of Raskolnikov's own philosophy underlying the murders, which itself reverses the message of the Gospels, Luzhin informs Razumikhin, Zosimov and Raskolnikov that "if I were to rip my coat in half and share it with my neighbor, we'd each be left half-naked" (6:116). The larger point he overlooks is the essence of the Gospel message: not to render clothing unusable by transforming it into bits of cloth, but to give of one's intact "seamless" garment.[14] Luzhin leaves his fiancée and her mother in want while spending money on himself. As Raskolnikov bitterly observes, "[y]ou cut your coat according to your cloth" (6:36). Within the world of material possessions, Luzhin acts out Raskolnikov's own philosophical premise of taking power and life.[15]

Dunya's relatively weak position as Luzhin's and Svidrigailov's potential victim is also denoted by clothing. She was "dressed in some sort of dark dress of flimsy material, and with a white sheer scarf tied around her neck. Razumikhin immediately noticed that ... [her] situation was extremely poor" (6:165). His reaction places him in the camp of the charitable. Even her clothes are "insulted" upon her abrupt expulsion from the Svidrigailovs': Her possessions are carried to her mother's in a "simple peasant cart, into which all her things—linen, dresses, everything ... unpacked and messed up—had been tossed" (6:29).

If Dunya and her mother are poor, Katerina Ivanovna and her family are destitute, the clothing representing their former status literally in tatters. The narrator muses that "[e]verything at the Marmeladovs' was scattered about and in disorder, especially children's rags" (6:22). Katerina Ivanovna still tries to keep up appearances, as evidenced by desperate laundering and sewing. She washes her little boy's only shirt at night. Any rips must be fixed immediately, perhaps opposing the negative symbolism of bits of cloth. But her most precious garment is the one lost to her, the shawl she wore before the governor that at once conflates clothing, status, and pride (6:138–139). We can see this same link between urban decay and poverty symbolized by clothing—in Dickens' character Little Nell from *The Old Curiosity Shop*.[16]

Yet poverty in and of itself is not destructive in Dostoevsky. In spite of Lizaveta's murder, she re-emerges within the context of memory, initially Sonya's, eventually even Raskolnikov's. Katerina Ivanovna's suffering, which she could have lessened had she only heeded the lessons of the Gospels, results in part from her injured pride, one of the seven deadly sins. What of Marmeladov himself, the cause of so much distress? Even before the murders, he regales Raskolnikov with a spirited monologue about the domestic wreckage his drinking has precipitated. He finally obtains a bureaucratic position, symbolized by his uniform. A salary would enable him to support his family. But he soon drinks away his new post, with his official uniform lying on a saloon floor (6:13–22). Marmeladov plays out Raskolnikov's rebellion on a sociological level. Marmeladov undermines clothing as a symbol of self-sacrifice and destroys the larger connection between clothing and charity.

It would be instructive to consider Luzhin in the light of Svidrigailov's analogous combination of sartorial splendor and moral repulsiveness. Interestingly, these characters are presented at neighboring points in the novel:

He [Svidrigailov] was a man of about fifty, taller than average....
He was elegantly and comfortably dressed and looked like a
portly gentleman [*barin*]. In his hands was a red walking-stick

[suggesting his aggressive sexual behavior] which he tapped, at each step, on the pavement, and on his hands were a pair of brand-new gloves.... Generally, he was a superbly preserved man who seemed much younger than his years. (6:188)[17]

We encounter Svidrigailov later, when Raskolnikov runs into him in a tavern, in a scene that eerily anticipates Ivan Karamazov's encounter with his brother Alyosha in *The Brothers Karamazov* (*PSS* 14:208–41). Raskolnikov finds Svidrigailov being entertained by a boy-accordionist and a girl with a tucked-up striped skirt and Tyrolean hat with ribbons—once again linking Western attire with prostitution, as well as with Raskolnikov's hat. Svidrigailov's clothing was "foppish [dandified], summery, light; his linen was especially foppish. On his finger was an enormous ring with a precious stone" (6:355–358). Expensive, ostentatious jewelry denotes hoarding as well as sexual predation, and tailor-made summer clothing in Russia suggests ostentatious expenditure. Blatant materialism suggests rampant sexuality.

Svidrigailov's sexual stalking extends beyond young women to include children, dressed in a way that hints at once at their sexual vulnerability and, in the case of his fiancée and the child in his nightmare, at their resemblance to prostitutes. His fiancée is still young enough to be in a short little dress (*v koroten'kom plat'ice*, 6:369), a garment recalling the singer's dress in the tavern. The figure of the child-bride or child-prostitute will evolve during Svidrigailov's macabre last night. She will take the initial form of the child-victim dressed all in white satin, an image of desecrated purity. The girl of Svidrigailov's first nightmare is a suicide lying in her coffin and surrounded by flowers, symbols of spring and the Resurrection.[18] Her white garment parodies raiment washed with the blood of the Lamb:

> The floors were strewn with freshly-mowed, fragrant grass, the windows were open, fresh, light, cool air penetrated into the room, little birds chirped under the windows, but in the middle of the chamber, on some tables covered with white satin shrouds, stood a coffin.... Garlands of flowers entwined it on all sides. A young girl, all in flowers, lay in it, in a white tulle dress ... her hair... was wet; a wreath of roses encircled her head. (6:391)

This image degenerates in Svidrigailov's final nightmare about the wet little girl in the hallway. Because of his past history, the repetition of wetness is a negative reversal of baptism, suggesting damnation instead of salvation. Svidrigailov has already been "assaulted" by legendary Petersburg wetness and "never liked water" (6:389), "symbol of rebirth and regeneration [for

Dostoevsky]" (Gibian 529).[19] Undressing the girl exposes her, undermines his charitable act, and associates wetness with sexual predation:

> Her scarlet lips seemed to burn and seethe.... It suddenly seemed to him that her long black lashes appeared to quiver and wink, as though they were going to lift, and from under them there peered out a sly, sharp little eye, which gave a wink that was somehow not childlike, as if the little girl weren't sleeping but pretending. Yes, that's how it was, her little lips parted in a smile.... now this was laughter ... There was something infinitely hideous and outrageous in that laughter. (6:393)[20]

Embodied in a corrupted child, the corruption of baptism confirms Svidrigailov's fate.

While Dostoevsky frequently couples clothing with sexual predation, greed and acquisitiveness, and even murder, it also symbolizes and reinforces positive qualities in Sonya Marmeladov, Lizaveta, and Razumikhin. Clothing denotes the charitable impulse that symbolizes Christ and salvation for all, even the pawnbroker and Raskolnikov. Both Lizaveta and Razumikhin are associated with charity, in contrast to Luzhin's and Svidrigailov's hoarding, symbolized by a new and stylish wardrobe.[21] Although acting on the mistaken assumption that his friend's troubles are principally economic in nature, Razumikhin extends charity to start Raskolnikov back on the road to redemption. This scene contrasts ironically to our introduction to Luzhin:

> [H]e spread out before Raskolnikov a pair of gray trousers made of light-weight woolen material.... [saying, 'here's] a waistcoat to match, just as fashion demands.... I made a summer purchase, because toward autumn you'll need warmer material.... But what's this?' And he pulled from his pocket Raskolnikov's old shoe, cracked, all caked with dry mud, full of holes. 'I went out with this in reserve and managed to reconstruct some actual measurement on the basis of this monster... Here ... are three shirts, unbleached linen, but with stylish fronts...' (6:101–102)

Acceptance of clothing anticipates Raskolnikov's acceptance of Christ in the epilogue.

Work with clothing seems to be the only type of legitimate employment available to women except prostitution. Just before she became a streetwalker, Sonya made a half-dozen Holland shirts for State Councillor

Klopstock, who never paid her for her work (6:17). He is just another predator linked with the West, as is reflected in his name. After reading about Dunya's projected marriage to Luzhin, Raskolnikov conjectures (surely correctly) that his mother would have to live on her own, supporting herself by knitting winter kerchiefs and "embroidering cuffs," a detail echoed in a later scene between Sonya and Katerina Ivanovna (6:36). His mother's sacrifice is underscored by her probable loss of vision: "in ten years, mother will have managed to go blind from these kerchiefs ..." (6:38). Raskolnikov's bitter irony recalls Hood's "Song of the Shirt":

> A woman sat in unwomanly rags, / Plying her needle and thread / Stitch! stitch! stitch! / In poverty, hunger and dirt.... Work— work—work—/ Till the brain begins to swim! / Work—work— work / Till the eyes are heavy and dim!" (Hood 123–25)

The theme of women depersonalized as part of a cloth-making mechanism recalls the negative machine imagery running through nineteenth-century Russian literature (Baehr 86–87, 97–98). Dostoevsky has transformed an economic symbol into an Orthodox one.

Where a mother's loss is visual, a daughter's is moral. Daughters turn to streetwalking. Sonya sacrifices herself (kenotic humility, *agape*) for her stepmother, step-siblings, and father Marmeladov, who drinks up her earnings: "Well, here I, her own blood father, took those thirty kopecks and filched them for myself, to get drunk" (6:20). Linked with prostitution, her degradation is far lower than Katerina Ivanovna's destitution and embittered, injured pride at her ruined nobility (6:22–25). Humility and innate purity protect Sonya and recall the redemption of prostitutes in the New Testament, most notably Mary Magdalene's. Her parents' impoverishment highlights the economic suffering of an oppressed urban bureaucratic class composed principally of fallen members of the aristocracy, the embedded plot of *The Drunks* (Mochulsky 271–74). In *Crime and Punishment*, Dostoevsky associates this theme with the larger religious issues of the novel, linking poverty specifically with *agape* and *caritas*. He realizes this goal through Lizaveta and Sonya, their *caritas* showing Raskolnikov the way to redemption.

More to the point, both women are poor at least in part because of acts of charity. The opposite of Raskolnikov, Lizaveta anticipates Stinking Lizaveta from *The Brothers Karamazov*. Three different observers—the narrator, Raskolnikov, and the student Raskolnikov overhears in the tavern— concur in their description that she is a tall, awkward, shy and meek wench [*devka*] somewhat retarded, about thirty-five, a complete slave to her sister... Lizaveta dealt in [second-hand clothes], took a commission .... and had a large clientele, because she was very honest and always gave a fair price .... She generally spoke little and, as I've [the narrator] already said, was very humble and timid.... Lizaveta was a petty-bourgeois, not of the civil-servant class, an old maid, and terribly clumsy, incredibly tall, with long, splayed feet, always in goatskin shoes.... the main thing was that Lizaveta was always pregnant (6:51–54).[22]

She pays with her life for her devotion (*caritas*) to her sister, their bond symbolized by the crosses around the pawnbroker's neck.

Why is Lizaveta always pregnant? Corresponding to used clothes, her body functions as a literal marker for charity and echoes the kenosis and Passion of Christ (6:57). She somehow remains pure in the Russian Babylon. Perhaps her pregnancies are a literal, physical manifestation of charity, extending eventually to her ultimate sacrifice as an innocent. Imbued with humility, Lizaveta has transformed *eros* into *agape*. Symbolized especially by the goatskin shoes, she is typical among Dostoevsky's prostitutes and/or childlike or even retarded women—Liza in *Notes from Underground*, Sonya, Stinking Lizaveta—for practicing *agape* stripped of all sexual coloration. Her trade in second-hand clothing parallels and is in contrast to the pawnbroker's trade in used objects. Raskolnikov's realization of her *caritas* engenders his anguished reaction noted above.

While Sonya sacrifices the physical purity by which society judges her, she retains her innocence throughout:

At this moment the door quietly opened and a young girl [*devuška*, not *devka*] entered the room..... This was Sophia Semenovna Marmeladova.... she was a modestly and even poorly dressed girl, still very young, almost resembling a little girl, with a modest and attractive manner, with a clear but somehow frightened face. She was wearing a very simple house dress.... only in her hands, like yesterday, she had a parasol. (6:181)[23]

Sonya's clothing basically confirms her purity. Yet even Sonya has a moment when selfishness gets in the way of her usual charitable impulse, and she refuses to give something away. Significantly, that "something" takes the form of clothing. Quite naturally, Lizaveta figures in this small but significant episode which encapsulates the central issues of the novel:

Lizaveta the peddler brought me some cheap collars and cuffs, pretty ones, almost new and with embroidery. And Katerina Ivanovna liked them a lot, she put them on and looked at herself in the mirror, and she really liked them very much. She said '[G]ive them to me, Sonya, please.' She asked *please*, she liked them so much! And where could she wear them? ... But I regretted giving them away and said, 'What do you need them for, Katerina Ivanovna?' That's how I said it: 'what for?' I never needed to say that to her! The way she looked at me, and she became so terribly, terribly pained because I'd refused.... If I could take it all back, do the whole thing over, all those former words.... (6:244-45, emphasis in the original)[24]

Why did Sonya act in so uncharacteristically selfish a way, even though her joy at having something pretty to wear almost seems to have justified her actions? Katerina Ivanovna, the stepmother who in desperation forced Sonya into prostitution, is the very person who wants the clothing earned at such enormous cost. Sonya's negative, even selfish, reaction to Katerina Ivanovna's appeal (for charity in the larger sense of love?) and her later recollection, tinged with guilt and sorrow, are played out in this seemingly minor scene. At this very point Raskolnikov's own vanity and selfishness slowly begin to yield, through the unswerving support of Sonya herself, who also carries a burden of guilt.[25] Her acknowledgment of her own guilt engenders a sense of *shared* guilt that leads to Raskolnikov's redemption. It enfolds him once again within the larger community. She recounts this central episode to him alone, a parallel of his confession to her. Clothing and bits of cloth, the earlier accessories in two murders and in the sexually predatory (read anti-Christian) behavior of Svidrigailov and Luzhin, is now an instrument of redemption.

In the course of *Crime and Punishment*, indeed, throughout his *oeuvre*, Dostoevsky blurs the line between saint and sinner. The pawnbroker wears *two* crosses, perhaps to emphasize her need for redemption. Fyodor Karamazov, as repulsive a character as ever emerged from Dostoevsky's pen, bears the name "Theodore," "God-Given." For each of them, something worn or borne (here, a cross, a name) denotes God's love for man, even when that man would be deemed unlovable to our limited human perception. Sonya, the meekest and most selfless of pure souls, falls prey to the combination of pride and immersion in the material (non- or anti-spiritual) world of St. Petersburg that ensnares the most negative characters in the novel: Svidrigailov, Luzhin and, most significantly, Raskolnikov himself. The painful guilt she shares with Raskolnikov kindles his eventual attempt to come to terms with his own horrific crimes. The clothing that figures in this scene, as in the novel as a whole, symbolizes the great universal issues of pride, humility, forgiveness and redemption central to *Crime and Punishment* and, for that matter, to all of Dostoevsky's great novels.

NOTES

1. I wish to thank Stephen Baehr and the anonymous readers for their perceptive comments and suggestions. I am also grateful to Joseph Candido, Beth Juhl and Brian Wilkie for their generous assistance. Sandra Sherman's and William Tucker's insightful suggestions improved this essay immeasurably.

2. John Jones (237) has commented briefly on Katerina Ivanovna's green shawl, which Sonya takes with her to Siberia.

3. Hood's "Song of the Shirt" was translated into Russian by M.L. Mihajlov and D.D. Minaev in 1860, well before Dostoevsky wrote *Crime and Punishment* (Nikolyukin 535).

4. In Sue's *The Mysteries of Paris* (1:25), La Goualeuse learned to sew in prison.

5. Charity is central to Orthodoxy. John Chrysostom preached the necessity of charity to the poor, and charity is combined with *agape*, love for the poor being synonymous with alms giving (Fedotov 219, 222, 269).

6. I am grateful to Donald Engels for pointing out these distinctions to me.

7. Grinev's gift to Pugachëv in Pushkin's novel *The Captain's Daughter* recalls this passage from Matthew; it functions as an ironic subtext to Luzhin's miserly selfishness. I would like to thank Stephen Baehr for this observation.

8. The legend of St. Veronica, said to have wiped Christ's face with a cloth when He fell on his way to Calvary, comes to mind here (Farmer 477). I am grateful to Dennis Slattery of the Pacifica Graduate Institute for this suggestion.

9. The legend of St. Veronica is also part of *Orthodox* apocrypha, as attested to in the *Chronographia* of Johannes of Malala, X, 306–08 (cited in Jackson 166). I am grateful to Joseph Candido for reminding me of St. Veronica.

10. There is a possible link here between Raskolnikov and the *yurodivye*, who typically went around in rags (Thompson 1–2).

11. Baedeker informs us that "[n]early one-tenth of the male population of St. Petersburg wear some kind of uniform, including not only the numerous military officers, but civil officials, and even students, schoolboys, and others" (Baedeker 101; cited in Maguire and Malmstad 310). Like Raskolnikov, Ivan Karamazov was a former university student. See Dostoevsky, *PSS* 14:14.

12. This passage is almost identical in the earliest (short) redaction of the novel, demonstrating that Dostoevsky developed his shirt image early on. See *PSS* 7:64. On the whole, however, cloth figures much less prominently in Dostoevsky's earlier drafts. I am grateful to Brett Cooke of Texas A & M University for the suggestion to consult the early redactions.

13. Although Jones asserts (204) that these bits of odd cloth "belong with the extremely important disjunctive flotsam of the book: paintpots, old rope, the odd sock, boots ..., flayed blood-soaked strips torn from trouser bottoms and coat pockets, an axe-sling in ribbons ..." I maintain that cloth plays a unique role because of its overriding religious purpose.

14. Luzhin's philosophy of acting according to what *seem* to be his own best interests fits in with the materialism of one of Dostoevsky's favorite targets, Chernyshevsky. For a

discussion of the materialism that Chernyshevsky admired, Luzhin reflected, and Dostoevsky abhorred, see Anchor 9–10, 107, 109.

15. As Knapp observes (65), the message from "The Sermon on the Mount" is: "Do not be anxious about your life, what you shall eat or what you shall drink, nor about your body, what you shall put on. Is not life more than food, and the body more than clothing?" (Matt. 6:25).

16. I would like to thank Olga Cooke for her observations on Little Nell. For an examination of this theme in Dickens, see Schwarzbach. Fanger's *Dostoevsky* contains a fine treatment of Dickens' impact on Dostoevsky.

17. Shortly before the murders, Raskolnikov encounters this same combination of victimized, poorly-dressed girl-victim and dandyish, well-dressed sexual predator on the street. Significantly, he calls this man a "Svidrigailov" (6:40).

18. In his 12th-century "Sermon on the First Sunday After Easter" ("Slovo v novuju nedelju posle Paskhi"), Kirill of Turov links spring with the Resurrection of Christ (Stender-Petersen 119–20; Cizevskij 86–87). Dostoevsky's contemporary Russian reader familiar with Kirill of Turov would also have been familiar with Hilarion's "Sermon on Law and Grace." Dostoevsky recapitulates Hilarion's opposition of law—Raskolnikov, who has created his own—with grace, embodied in Lizaveta and Sonya (Stender-Peterson 109–13; Cizevskij 36–39).

19. Liza Knapp suggests that "the specific activity of washing is [normally] symbolic of purification" (77).

20. Svidrigailov is also responsible for the deaths of his wife Marfa Petrovna and servant Filip, his actions in counterpoint to Raskolnikov's (6:175, 219–20).

21. In *Crime and Punishment*, Dostoevsky savagely parodies Chernyshevsky's *What is to Be Done?* (Chernyshevsky 392–97; Knapp 19). Lizaveta's charity is juxtaposed to Chernyshevsky's secular sewing co-operative.

22. A merchant woman in goatskin shoes (like Lizaveta's) later gives the poorly-dressed Raskolnikov a coin (6:89).

23. If Lizaveta is always pregnant, why is Sonya never pregnant? Perhaps Dostoevsky wants the reader to view her as a figure totally divorced from *eros*.

24. We encounter Katerina Ivanovna's collars and cuffs still earlier, in Marmeladov's drunken confession to Raskolnikov (6:19); these small items are clearly her last vestiges of respectability.

25. Jones (233) points out that "the main and mystic burden of creative, regenerative suffering" falls on Sonya.

WORKS CITED

Alexander, A.B.D. "Seven Virtues (or Gifts of the Spirit)." *Encyclopaedia of Religion and Ethics*, ed. James Hastings, with John A. Selbie and Louis H. Gray. Edinburgh: T. & T. Clark, 1925.

Anchor, Robert. *The Enlightenment Tradition.* Berkeley: U of California P, 1967.

Baehr, Stephen. "The Troika and the Train: Dialogues Between Tradition and Technology in Nineteenth-Century Russian Literature." *Issues in Russian Literature Before 1917: Selected Papers of the Third World Congress for Soviet and East European Studies.* Ed. Douglas Clayton. Columbus: Slavica Publishers, 1989. 85–106.

Belknap, Robert. *The Genesis of* "The Brothers Karamazov." Evanston: Northwestern UP, 1990.

Champion, Larry S. "King Lear": *An Annotated Bibliography*, 2 vols. New York: MacMillan, 1980.

Chernyshevsky, Nikolai. *What is to Be Done?*. Trans. N. Dole and S.S. Skidelsky. Ann Arbor: Ardis, 1986.

Cizevskij, Dmitrij. *History of Russian Literature from the Eleventh Century to the End of the Baroque*. 'S-Gravenhage: Mouton, 1962.

The Compact Edition of the Oxford English Dictionary. Vol. I. Oxford: Oxford UP, 1971.

Cross, F.L. *The Oxford Dictionary of the Christian Church*, 3rd ed. Ed. E.A. Livingstone. Oxford: Oxford UP, 1997.

Discherl, Denis. *Dostoevsky and the Catholic Church*. Chicago: Loyola UP, 1986.

Dostoevsky, Fëdor. *Polnoe sobranie sochinenii v tridtsaii tomakh*. Leningrad: Nauka, 1972–90.

Emerson, Caryl. "Boris Godunov": *Transpositions of a Russian Theme*. Bloomington: Indiana UP, 1986.

Fanger, Donald. *Dostoevsky and Romantic Realism: A Study of Dostoevsky in Relation to Balzac, Dickens, and Gogol*. Cambridge: Harvard UP, 1965.

Farmer, David Hugh. *The Oxford Dictionary of Saints*. Oxford: Oxford UP, 1992.

Fedotov, G.P. *The Russian Religious Mind: Kievan Christianity: The 10th to the 12th Centuries*. New York: Harper and Brothers, 1960.

Frank, Joseph. *Dostoevsky: The Miraculous Years, 1865–1871*. Princeton: Princeton UP, 1995.

———. *Dostoevsky: The Seeds of Revolt, 1821–1849*. Princeton: Princeton UP, 1976.

George, Albert Joseph. *The Development of French Romanticism: The Impact of the Industrial Revolution on Literature*. Syracuse: Syracuse UP, 1955.

Gibian, George. "Traditional Symbolism in *Crime and Punishment*." In Feodor Dostoevsky, *Crime and Punishment*. New York: Norton Critical Editions, 1989. 526–543.

Grant, Richard B. *The Perilous Quest: Image, Myth, and Prophecy in the Narratives of Victor Hugo*. Durham: Duke UP, 1968.

Greenfield, Thelma. "The Clothing Motif in *King Lear*," *Shakespeare Quarterly* 5 (1954): 281–86.

Heilman, Robert B. "Poor Naked Wretches and Proud Array: The Cloth Pattern in *King Lear*." *Western Review* 12 (1947–1948): 5–15.

———. *This Great Stage: Image and Structure in King Lear*. Seattle: U of Washington P, 1963.

Heywood, Colin. *Childhood in Nineteenth-Century France: Work, Health, and Education among the 'Classes Populaires'*. Cambridge: Cambridge UP, 1988.

Holquist, Michael. *Dostoevsky and the Novel*. Princeton: Princeton UP, 1977.

Hood, Thomas. *The Poetic Works*. Enlarged and Revised Edition. New York: Hurst & Company, n.d.

Jackson, Samuel Macauley, ed. *The New Schaff-Herzog Encyclopedia of Religious Knowledge*. Vol. XII. New York: Funk and Wagnalls, 1912.

Jones, John. *Dostoevsky*. Oxford: Oxford UP, 1983.

Knapp, Liza. *The Annihilation of Inertia: Dostoevsky and Metaphysics*. Evanston: Northwestern UP, 1996.

Lixacëv, D.S. *Celovek v literature drevnej Rusi*. Moscow: Akademija nauk, 1970.

MacPike, Loralee. *Dostoevsky's Dickens: A Study of Literary Influence*. Totowa, New Jersey: Barnes and Noble, 1981.

Maguire, Robert A, and John E. Malmstad. "Notes." Andrei Bely, *Petersburg*. Bloomington: Indiana UP, 1978.

Mochulsky, Konstantin. *Dostoevsky: His Life and Work*. Trans. and with an Introduction by Michael A. Minihan. Princeton: Princeton UP, 1971.

Murav, Harriet. *Holy Foolishness: Dostoevsky's Novels and the Poetics of Cultural Critique*. Stanford: Stanford UP, 1992.

Nikoljukin, A.N. "Hood, Thomas." *Great Soviet Encyclopedia*. Ed. A.M. Prokhorov. 3rd ed.; English trans. Rachel Berthoff *et al*. New York: MacMillan, 1975. 7:535.

Paperno, Irina. *Chernyshevsky and the Age of Realism*. Stanford: Stanford UP, 1988.

Robertson, Noel. "Fate." *The Oxford Classical Dictionary*. Ed. N.G.L. Hammond and H.H. Scullard. 2nd ed. Oxford: Oxford UP, 1970. 430–32.

Schwarzbach, F.S. *Dickens and the City*. London: Athlone Press, 1979.

Shakespeare, William. *The Complete Works*. Roslyn, N.Y.: Walter J. Black, 1937.

Smith, Grahame. *Dickens, Money, and Society*. Berkeley: U of California P, 1968.

Spurgeon, Caroline. *Leading Motifs in the Imagery of Shakespeare's Tragedies*. New York: Haskell House, 1970.

Stauffer, Donald. "The Dark Tower." *Shakespeare's World of Images: The Development of His Moral Ideas*. New York: Norton, 1949. 163–220.

Stender-Petersen, A.D. *Anthology of Old Russian Literature*. New York: Columbia UP, 1954.

Sue, Eugène. *The Mysteries of Paris*. 2 vols. Philadelphia: Henry T. Coates & Co., n.d.

Thompson, Ewa M. *Understanding Russia: The Holy Fool in Russian Culture*. New York: UP of America, 1987.

Watson, Duane F. "Babylon." *The Anchor Bible Dictionary*. Ed. David Noel Freedman. Vol. 1. New York: Doubleday, 1992.

HENRY M.W. RUSSELL

Beyond the will: Humiliation as Christian necessity in 'Crime and Punishment'

T he most disturbing message of Dostoevsky's *Crime and Punishment* is its insistence that humiliation is the necessary precondition for Christian life. In a move that powerfully repels even the Catholic West, much more mainstream Protestantism or existentialism, Dostoevsky forces his characters far beyond a comfortable exercise in the virtue of humility to an abject state of humiliation. Only those individuals who admit the justice of being mocked and despised by all normal-minded people realise clearly enough the truth of human kind's fallen condition honestly to feel the necessity for grace. This theme binds into a remarkable unity characters as different as Marmeladov, Marmeladov's daughter Sonya, Raskolnikov and Svidrigailov. Each character must decide between an assertion of will and complete humiliated acknowledgment of his or her non-being without the creative power of God. The emphasis on true humiliation as true humility is a doctrinal commitment which should not be translated into any psychological category of masochism as a physical or psychic eros. Similarly the conception of humiliation pushes the reader beyond noble tragedy or transcendentalism. The doctrine of self-abnegation does not spring from a diseased psyche but from the Orthodox tradition of apophatic knowledge. It is within that tradition that Dostoevsky's meaning can best be grasped.

Apophatic knowledge, as Bishop Kallistos Ware explains, is a way of

From *Dostoevsky and the Christian Tradition*. © 2001 by the Cambridge University Press.

knowing that employs negative as well as affirmative statements, saying what God is not rather than what he is.[1] Through this method human beings can describe God's essence or their own only by a set of assertions and negations which admit the incomplete and distorting nature of the ideas asserted. In a tradition of theology best represented by Dionysius the Pseudo-Areopagite, St Gregory Palamas writes that 'The super-essential nature of God is not a subject for speech or thought < ... > There is no name whereby it can be named, neither in this age or in the world to come, nor word found in the soul and uttered by the tongue, nor contact whether sensible or intellectual.'[2] St Gregory of Nyassa's Answer to Eunomius's Second Book asserts that the intellect is most useful when it give names that 'furnish a sort of catalogue and muster of evil qualities from which God is separate. Yet these terms employed give no positive account of that to which they are applied.'[3] Certainly this mystic way of negation is a major part of the Western Catholic tradition as well (whether we look at St Augustine, St Francis of Assisi, St John of the Cross, Margery Kemp or William Langland, among others), but that tradition of beatific illumination has been much obscured by the achievements of rational, discursive theology.

Lest apophatic knowledge be misunderstood, however, for its mute step-brother deconstruction, it is important to note that human inability to refer with full truth to God is a result of God's perfection which we, as sinful creatures, cannot know. Language about God refers then to a plenitude which it cannot contain, not to an absence. Gregory of Nyssa writes that God 'is named, by those who call upon Him, not what He is essentially (for the nature of Him Who alone is unspeakable), but He receives his appellations from what are believed to be His operations in regard to our life.'[4] But the cataphatic or positive and constructive side of Orthodox theology allows St Gregory to assert that 'in applying such appellations to the Divine essence, "which passeth all understanding", we do not seek to glory in it by the names we employ, but to guide our own selves by the aid of such terms towards the comprehension of the things which are hidden.'[5] Insofar as our words are said with a thorough awareness of their partial apprehension, then language can speak truly. 'The way of "unknowing" brings us not to emptiness but fullness', Bishop Ware explains, 'Destructive in outward form, the apophatic approach is affirmative in its final effects: it helps us to reach out, beyond all statements < ... > towards an immediate experience of the living God.'[6] This experience, as for Gregory Palamas in The Triads, can become for the most holy a kind of 'durable vision of light, and the vision of things in the light, whereby < ... > the future is shown as already existing', a state of being which is 'incomparably higher than negative theology, for it belongs only to those who have attained impassability.'[7]

What becomes interesting when the apophatic insight is applied to the human condition is that negations of the words said about persons might lead close to an almost overwhelming emptiness of spirit. If any single word is used about human virtues, and if we then examine to what extent a single virtue is truly within us, we come swiftly to a realisation of how tiny is our share, in the plenitude of goodness, courage and gratitude. Here indeed a word may refer to a dwindling referent. The logical end of such examination is not a comfortable humility which retains a proud sense of our solid middle-class virtues or our pious religiosity.

In Dostoevsky, awareness of human insufficiency leads to an almost hysterical signalling of vice from characters who retain any vestige of social respectability, whether an old Karamazov, a Marmeladov or a Raskolnikov. These characters and many others intermittently seek exterior humiliation in the eyes of society while refusing to see the full contemptibility of their lives; thus they court punishment rather than mercy. They are honest enough to judge themselves harshly, but their pride in such self-condemnation—combined with an awareness that other people share their vileness without exercising a similar honesty of judgment—leads them to assume that they have seen the fullness of their debased condition. This is a false humiliation that, in the words of the old Russian proverb, is 'worse than pride'. This false humiliation, if maintained, will lead its bearer to seek extinction. Dostoevsky mercilessly pushes the reader onwards to see that anyone who fully understands the depths of his own sinful negations can have only the response of complete humiliation, one so profound that it cannot speak at all except to ask for grace or extinction. Filaret, Metropolitan of Moscow for much of Dostoevsky's lifetime, explains this vision: 'All creatures are balanced upon the creative word of God, as if upon a bridge of diamond; above them is the abyss of divine infinitude, below them that of their own nothingness.'[8]

This logic of personal abnegation propels R. P. Blackmur's eloquent and ignorant attack on Dostoevsky's vision of 'society with a drive toward collapse whether into the arms of God or the embrace of the devil', of which Blackmur writes further 'I cannot think of anything more repulsive; it is a fascist society in extremis' which reduces human life to 'the desperate virtue of idiots or of the damned'.[9] Here Blackmur ignores the fact that in Dostoevsky's world those who collapse in God's arms are then taught to stand anew; he obscures the fact that the great totalitarian societies have all been neo-pagan in their spirit; and finally he forgets that precisely such religious ideas as Dostoevsky's supported the High Middle Ages and a large portion of later Western society whether Renaissance or Puritan. Certainly Blackmur ignores the fact that such humiliated recognition is only a first step towards Father Zosima's famous declaration of Christian responsibility: 'There is only one means of salvation, then take yourself and make yourself responsible for all men's sins, that is the truth, you know, friends, for as soon as you sincerely make yourself responsible for everything and for all men, you will see at once that it is really so, and that you are to blame for everyone and for all things.'[10] Does anyone seriously believe this is fascism?

Crime and Punishment presents us with at least four characters who have explored deeply into humiliation, although they form unlikely groupings. Marmeladov is the first to assent to the depths of his own shame; his appearance in the second chapter establishes his role as an emblem for all characters in the novel. As he often mentions, he takes pains to keep his shame visible and to obtain suffering. Yet in the weakness of his physical and moral nature, he does not move towards any proper response to his emptiness. Instead he seeks only the punishment and pity of a wife who beats him, even as she has forgiven him. Stubbornly, however, he refuses to change his life and ends by throwing himself under the feet of an aristocrat's horses. This fate is remarkably prefigured by Raskolnikov who himself is almost run down by a carriage after burying his loot and visiting Razumikhin. He 'had almost fallen under the horses' hooves, in spite of the coachman's repeated cries' [since] 'for some unknown reason he had been walking in the middle of the roadway' (96). This unconscious suicidal urge, a twisted form of the natural urge for expiation, is part of a larger set of false options to human unworthiness that includes the conscious suicide that Raskolnikov and Svidrigailov contemplate, the denial of guilt, the blaming of others, or false humiliation. Because Marmeladov will not go beyond the false humiliation which he insists on parading, he can choose only death, symbolically putting the blame for his fate on an unknown member of a higher economic class. Yet even death does not spare him the final agonised glimpse of his daughter Sonya in her trumpery costume as a prostitute. In this moment he does not know, at first, who she is. As he slowly realises her identity:

> with unnatural strength he managed to prop himself on his arm. His wild unmoving gaze remained fixed for some time on his daughter, as though he did not recognize her. Indeed he had never before seen her in such a costume. Suddenly be did recognize her, humiliated, crushed, ashamed < ... > Infinite suffering showed in his face.
> —'Sonya! Daughter! Forgive me!'

he cries, as he falls in his death.[11] Only at this point do his pleas for forgiveness seem to pass beyond ritual into true realisation and repentance.

Marmeladov is most clearly paired by Dostoevsky with Svidrigailov; each chooses suicide over action based on a knowledge of his humiliated condition. These men also form the poles of a continuum between someone who almost cannot control his bestial desires to a man who will not control them as a matter of principle. Marmeladov refuses to act on his shame; Svidrigailov endures longer because he refuses to acknowledge that shame exists. The squire will calmly acknowledge that he has been a card-sharp, a bought husband, a seducer of children, and probably a murderer, several times over. His attraction to the sewer runs very deep and, unlike Raskolnikov, he has been able to maintain this crossing of moral boundaries for years. Indeed, he is the very Jacob of a false God. He labours for seven years to pay the price of his marriage to Leah (in the form of Marfa Petrovna), a bargain consummated in the best modern style by getting the goods first as a loan to be paid back. During that seven-year servitude he continues a life of debauching others by a cynical knowledge of their own hidden attractions to evil. Instead of seeing a community of suffering and wretchedness in this bondage to evil, he seizes it as an instrument of pure power, destroying any vestiges of innocence in his path.

His one great failure comes with Raskolnikov's sister Dunya. Totally smitten by her goodness he attempts to defile her in a lengthy philosophical seduction that suggests she should replace Christian humility with the will to power. So seriously does Dunya shatter his self-control that Svidrigailov, who hates overt violence, resorts to poisoning his wife and running like a spurned young lover to St Petersburg. Although he attempts to be subtle and Machiavellian, he ends up declaring: 'I love you so I love you infinitely. Let me kiss the hem of your dress, let me! Let me!' (474). Finally he even gives his will completely over to her in a way that is perfectly sincere, if frenzied and momentary: 'Say to me, "Do this!" and I will do it. I will do anything. I will do the impossible. Whatever you believe in, I believe will believe in too' (474).

When Dunya resists this total surrender of herself to his cynicism, Svidrigailov reveals that he has locked the room, saying prophetically, 'I have lost the key and I shall not be able to find it' (474). What he has actually lost is the key to his own illusory world where his mind suavely reigns. Once he has been rejected by the one love which he cannot soil he must face his complete lack of power in the situation. And if there is a power acting through Dunya that does not submit to the sewer then his dominion, even over those whom he has dragged downwards, is as nothing compared to the power that can control him without such evil. In desperation Svidrigailov threatens ravishment and forces Dunya to draw a pistol she has hidden to defend herself. He believes this to be the perfect trap: either she will submit and join him or she will shoot him and prove that her goodness must use an evil instrumentality, if only once, in killing him. Of course, if his plot works, there is no way out for him either; he is still trapped in the sewer.

When Dunya almost kills him but then puts down the pistol, Svidrigailov feels some relief from his own huge fear of death but 'The relief he felt was from another emotion, gloomier and more melancholy, which he could not have defined in all its force' (477).[12] This relief is at the knowledge—which he will not fully face—that he is glad Dunya cannot fall into his trap and do evil for the sake of good. When she implores him with her eyes not to hurt her it is the force of his love and her innocence that wins out and makes him give her the key to the room. In this moment Dostoevsky's classically evil character is possessed by a pure love that overwhelms his whole world of nihilism, a love that could save him if he assented wholly to it. Such assent demands, however, a complete change of all his values for Dunya's, not for the sake of possessing her, but for the sake of that by which she is ruled. Svidrigailov seems to see and reject what Zosima says in *The Brothers Karamazov*; 'Loving humility is a terrible force; it is the strongest of all things, and there is nothing else like it' (298).

Svidrigailov's suicide is not best understood as a final bored choice of nothingness. It is the choice of nothingness over an honest recognition of his own humiliation. Throughout a long career of negation he was able to look at his shameful actions, see their evil, understand the obloquy they earned in others' eyes, and refuse to be shamed by them. Only when he has been brought to respect and love someone, as he does with Dunya, must he sense his own unworthiness before her. Then he must choose whether to see his actions as they are and seek grace, following her example, or to kill himself and deny his knowledge. Dostoevsky created Dunya as a Beatrice refused by an unfaithful Dante, one who is comfortable in Hell but is ashamed to rise higher, convinced that it is she he seeks rather than the God he sees reflected in her. Svidrigailov's disorientation before his suicide beautifully enacts Gregory of Nyssa's words about what a soul sees when it looks beyond the material world:

> Imagine a sheer steep crag with a projecting edge at the top. Now imagine what a person would probably feel if he put his foot on the edge of this precipice and, looking down into the chasm below, saw no solid footing nor anything to hold onto. This is what I think the soul experiences when it goes beyond its footing in material things, in its quest for that which has no dimension and which exists from all eternity. (page number not provided)

Svidrigailov's dreams before his death are some of the most horrific emblems of the modern world found in literature because they show the nature of his refusal to go beyond his will to control the material world. Those dreams stem from his waking feelings of love and pity for Dunya and the position in which he had placed her. His first dream is of a potentially Edenic world: a Whit Sunday full of warmth, cool breezes and abundant flowers. In an English-style cottage he finds that 'The floor was strewn with fragrant freshly cut hay, the windows were open, a cool, fresh, gentle breeze blew into the room, birds were chirping under the windows, and in the middle of the room, on tables shrouded in white satin, stood a coffin' (487). In the coffin lies the young servant girl who drowned herself after being seduced by Svidrigailov. Perhaps for the first time he sees that she is 'savagely wounded by the outrage that had amazed and horrified her young childish conscience, overwhelmed her soul, pure as an angel's, with unmerited shame, and torn from her a last cry of despair' (487). This dream is replaced by a vision of the waters rising to flood St Petersburg, a flood into which Svidrigailov intends to walk until he finds a shivering five-year-old girl, soaked to the skin. When he attempts to help her, in pure charity and pity undressing her from her drenched clothes and putting her to bed, she turns into a seductive, suggestive child-prostitute. Svidrigailov is touched with real horror at such corruption in the face of a child and calls her, 'Accursed creature!' before he awakes (490).

What the cynical man above the law sets loose on the world by his destruction of the innocence of the young servant girl comes back, like a flood over the social body, to haunt its creator. The amusing game of violating the peace and beauty of Eden comes to haunt him as the world is darkened into hovels where children know as much vice as he has ever practised. Yet he will not give up the world he has helped bring to birth. As he cuttingly remarks to Raskolnikov: 'If you are so sure that one can't listen at doors, but any old woman you like can be knocked on the head, then you'd better be off at once to America somewhere' (466). In the end it is he who repeats to the old guard, 'Achilles', the words 'I said I was off to America' as he puts a bullet in his brain (490). Svidrigailov, like Raskolnikov, finally finds himself weak, incapable of living in a world that his evil has darkened. For seven years he bears the images of dead servants and mistresses. Yet even he cannot bear the loss of his Rachel nor the image of the rising generation of children that he and his fellow corrupters have helped to fashion. He has been brought to see the weakness behind his assumed strength and can only submit to justice and grace or kill himself in a last denial.

Sonya, who lives out the humiliation of prostitution, is the only character who understands more fully than Svidrigailov that her human will is worth next to nothing unless turned towards God in a true humility. One by necessity and one by choice has lived out the destruction of all that society thinks noble. That Sonya's self-renunciation originates in her saintliness is a critical commonplace, but it is important to remember that her selling herself to support her family has left her feeling so dead in soul that she is a fit companion for Raskolnikov after he commits his murders. When she reads the story of the raising of Lazarus from the dead, Sonya is shaken by the same sort of feverish trembling and sense of guilt as Raskolnikov is when he thinks of the dead pawnbroker. Sonya requires the resurrecting power the Lord extended to Lazarus, just as does Raskolnikov.

For his part, if Svidrigailov is typologically linked to a false Jacob, then Raskolnikov is more firmly linked to Esau. Like many in Dostoevsky's modern world he gives up his inheritance in scorn. First he abandons his place in a Christian civil world by murder for a mess of roubles; then in a more noble-seeming but morally-suspect act he gives over his very family to Razumikhin. It is easy to mistake Svidrigailov as being truer to the type of Esau since he eagerly rejects the very idea of the good. Yet Svidrigailov is far more sinister since he lives out a secular religion based on defilement. Raskolnikov, like the thoughtless Esau, merely throws away by default all of the good which his culture offers him, thus leaving the role of Jacob to be filled by one whose type Yeats would come to call 'the worst < ... > full of passionate intensity'.

Raskolnikov's own rebirth occurs in at least two movements. The first part of that conversion is affected, of course, when he is brought to confession in Sonya's dwelling at the Kapernaumovs. As at the Biblical Capernaum, where Christ brought the demoniac back to right reason (Mk. 1:21–28), Sonya is able to bring Raskolnikov to an awareness that he is not the Napoleonic superman who can trample all law and custom. At this point Raskolnikov achieves what Orthodoxy calls nepsis, a state of sobriety and watchfulness, of coming back to oneself. No longer will he fall into fever and delirium as if out of his mind. Previously Raskolnikov's constant self-doubt and self-contempt, based on his apophatic critique of his willpower, led him near to an almost hysterical humiliation. That period is over; but he refuses to think past the argument that others in the world—indeed, millions of others—are as evil as he. He clings to the delusion that recognising his transgression for what it is makes him superior to lesser men. Of course he defines his real transgression as weakness and cowardice, not as murder. Having looked at his own weakness, he turns that gaze into an occasion for vanity. In this act he is developing some of the same cynicism, even in prison, that moulds a Svidrigailov. He threatens to become the sort of Cathar who places himself above the world of the flesh by asceticism, just as Svidrigailov tried to become the sort who proves the irrelevance of the body by immersing himself in filth.[13]

But Raskolnikov's image of self-sufficiency is shattered when Sonya falls ill and he realises his need for her. In an image remarkably resonant with Hawthorne's Ethan Brand, Raskolnikov stops work as a lime burner to look out upon the freedom of the steppes and the tents of nomads who seem the children of Abraham. Then Sonya appears. This time he does not repel her but holds her hand and 'suddenly he seemed to be seized and cast at her feet' (526). This time he is hurled to his knees by the Spirit, not looking for justice but for the grace of love itself. Emptied out of himself he has rejoined the community as a fellow sufferer who is a wanderer in the hands of God. In his linkage with the tents of Abraham he approaches identification with the kind of people who, Sergy Bulgakov writes, 'are so characteristic of Orthodoxy, above all Russian Orthodoxy: those who are not of this world and who have here "no abiding city"; pilgrims, the homeless "fools for Christ" who have renounced human reason, accepted the appearance of folly, voluntarily to experience outrages and humiliations for the love of Christ.'[14] Of course his motives are not yet fully understood or directed towards the God behind Sonya but, as Dostoevsky says, that is the beginning of another story.

Thus Raskolnikov is finally able to escape from his false self-image and from the deadly and deadened example of Svidrigailov who had offered himself as a false messiah, telling the young murderer, 'you shall see how easy-going I am. You shall see that it is possible to live with me' (419). These phrases, with their echo of Christ's pronouncement, 'My yoke is easy and my burden is light' (Mat. 11:30), once tempted Raskolnikov, but he follows the much more arduous path of Sofya/Sophia, Sonya's real name, which translates, of course, as Plato's Wisdom. The arrogant murderer who would not endure to be laughed at by the brilliant Porfiry Petrovich had allowed himself, at Sonya's urging, to confess to a man he found so insignificant as to call him 'The Squib'. At that moment Raskolnikov believed he was drinking fully of the cup from which Christ also drank. But Vladimir Lossky notes that in the deepest traditions of Orthodox thought 'If it is true that penitence is the beginning of this way, "the gateway of grace," this is not to say that it is a passing moment, a stage to be left behind. It is in fact not a stage but a condition which must continue permanently, the constant attitude of those who truly aspire to union with God.'[15] Raskolnikov's confession was only one step on the road to penitence, and it is a recognition of the intellect, not of the heart. So he is hated by his fellow prisoners in Siberia who sense his denial of the need for forgiveness even as he suffers the effects of justice. Only when he has submitted to Sonya's spiritual leadership, cast down at her feet by a power beyond him, can he begin to open himself to grace. The Squib to whom Raskolnikov had confessed, for his part, was not so lowly that he could not scorn women, whom he thinks below him, as he shows in his foolish yet meaning-laden joke about women as midwives 'Who push themselves into the Academy and study anatomy; well, tell me, if I fall ill am I going to call in a girl to cure me? He, he!' (509). Of course Dostoevsky is both criticising the 'New' woman and also recalling that Socrates described himself as a midwife in Plato's *Symposium*. As the wise woman from Mantinea, Diotima, helped Socrates bring forth his soul in beauty and reach Sophia or wisdom, so Sonya serves as a midwife for the soul of Raskolnikov, even as a spiritual physician who helps cure him of his madness, pace the Squib.

If Svidrigailov insists on using women as objects in a game of power disguised as liberation, the intellectual Raskolnikov must submit to the humiliation of being healed by an uneducated woman who has herself known the depths of shame. What must be done in the eyes of Dostoevsky is so radically unacceptable to the modern world that we are glad Raskolnikov is so grotesque a sinner. Otherwise the words of St Mark the Monk might be applicable to us: 'Unless a man gives himself entirely to the Cross, in a spirit of humility and self-abasement; unless he casts himself down to be trampled underfoot by all and despised, accepting injustice, contempt and mockery ... he cannot become a true Christian'.[16]

NOTES

1. Kallistos Ware, *The Orthodox Way* (London, 1981), 12–32.

2. V. Lossky, *The Mystical Theology of the Eastern Church* (New York, 1976), 37.

3. Gregory of Nyssa, *Select Writings and Letters*, trans. William Moore and Henry Wilson, *The Nicene and Post-Nicene Fathers of the Christian Church*, 5, 2nd series 1892 (Grand Rapids, MI, 1979), 264

4. *Ibid.*, 265.

5. *Ibid.*, 265.

6. Ware (1981), 17.

7. Lossky (1976), 65.

8. Ware (1981), 57.

9. R. P. Blackmur, *'Murder in Your Own Room'. Eleven Essays in the European Novel* (New York, 1964), 151.

10. F. M. Dostoevsky, *The Brothers Karamazov*, ed. Ralph Matlaw, trans. Constance Garnett (New York, 1976), 299.

11. F. M. Dostoevsky, *Crime and Punishment*, trans. Jessie Coulson, ed. George Gibian (New York, 1975), 179.

12. *Ibid.*, 477.

13. The Cathars were a Gnostic heresy of great power from the tenth to the fifteenth century that had adherents all over Europe, but who are best known from sects like the Bogomils and Albigensians. Calling themselves 'the pure' or 'Cathari', they saw all flesh as

Satan's domain. They were reported to show their contempt for all but pure spirit by living lives either of extreme asceticism or vicious sensualism. They also advocated suicide, especially by starvation, as an act of purity.

14. S. Bulgakov, *The Orthodox Church*, trans. T Hopko (New York, 1988), 151.

15. Lossky (1976), 204.

16. Reference not provided.

ANTONY JOHAE

Towards an iconography of
'Crime and Punishment'

I take as my starting point the first of several dreams depicted by
Dostoevsky in his novel *Crime and Punishment* (1866).[1] It is made to occur
shortly before the protagonist, Raskolnikov, carries out his crime and, like
the dreams which occur after the murder, is charged with violence. In his
dream, Raskolnikov recalls the scene of his provincial childhood. He is on his
way with his father to visit the grave of his grandmother and of his baby
brother. But in the dream the progress of father and son is arrested by a
violent incident which occurs outside the tavern on the road to the church.
A crowd of drunken peasants has been invited to get on a huge cart to which
a mare has been harnessed; but it is incapable of pulling such a load.
Infuriated by this, the intoxicated owner, goaded on by the other peasants,
proceeds to beat the horse to death. The boy tries to stop the onslaught
himself, but his father pulls him away from the crowd saying: 'It's not our
business. Come along!' The boy appeals to his father, but the father merely
responds with: 'Come along, son, come along! < ... > let's go home < ... >
They're drunk' (75). The dream narrative ends: 'He put his arms round his
father < ... > He tried to draw a breath, to cry out and—woke up' (78).

It has been suggested by W. D. Snodgrass in a well-known essay
entitled 'Crime for punishment: The tenor of part one'[2] that Raskolnikov's
history is mirrored in his dream: a return to the Christian faith (symbolised

---

From *Dostoevsky and the Christian Tradition*. © 2001 by the Cambridge University Press.

by his walk to the church and cemetery with his father) is interrupted by the murder of the pawnbroker and her half-sister (represented in the dream by the killing of the mare outside the tavern). In this interpretation the dream is not treated as though it were irrelevant to the final outcome, but rather is given the status of prediction or prophecy, so that the final outcome—Raskolnikov's salvation—appears to have been validated by the patterning of the dream. Images are not seen as picked-up residues of the day disguising repressed wishes (Freud), but as archetypal figures which, when illuminated, verify the world as an ordered and meaningful whole (Jung).

To offer further support for this proposition, it is necessary first to piece the images together to form a system, a symbology, a theology even. Let us begin this process by examining part of the dream narrative or, to be precise, the descriptive passage which provides the context for the action outside the tavern.

> Not far from the tavern was a road, a rough country road [which] stretched windingly away in the distance, and about three hundred yards farther on it turned to the right, skirting the town cemetery. In the middle of the cemetery was a stone church with a green cupola to which he used to go twice a year to morning Mass with his father and mother, when a service was held in memory of his grandmother < ... > For the service they always used to take with them a special funeral dish on a white plate and wrapped in a white napkin, and the Funeral dish was of sweetened rice and raisins stuck into it in the shape of a cross. He loved that church with its ancient icons < ... > and the old priest with the shaking head < ... > [E]very time he visited the cemetery he used to cross himself over the grave religiously and reverently, and bow down and kiss it. (73)

If we are fully to appreciate the significance of this description, it will need to be visualised in more detail than has been directly represented here. We are told that the funeral dish of sweetened rice has been marked out by raisins in the form of a cross and that on each occasion the boy, Raskolnikov, visits the graveside of his baby brother, he makes the sign of the cross bowing down to kiss the grave. This duplication of cross imagery ought to draw our attention to the fact that the description is potentially replete with such images. The cemetery would be filled with crosses marking the numerous graves; the 'stone church with a green cupola' would certainly be crowned with a cross; and 'the old priest', intermittently crossing himself, would also be likely to be looked down upon by an icon representing the Crucifixion.

Apart from the shared communal value of such imagery, which would be transparently clear to many readers, it is also highly significant in terms of the protagonist's individual history, because the cross imagery may have been embedded in the text as a symbolic prefiguration of Raskolnikov's ultimate return to the faith of his childhood. But in order for the cross to carry such symbolic weight at a personal level (as distinct from the communal) we might first look for a further duplication of the primary image in one guise or another, treating each manifestation of it as signalling the way to Raskolnikov's ultimate redemption. To do this we need to pass over the threshold of dream (and of childhood) and to follow the trajectory of Raskolnikov's conscious (and adult) life. In doing so we are immediately struck by the fact that, having killed the old pawnbroker, Raskolnikov discovers two crucifixes—'one of cypress wood and another of copper, and in addition, a little enamelled icon' (97)—which are attached to a ribbon around the murdered woman's neck. There is also a purse bulging with money which he keeps for himself, but the crucifixes he throws on the body of the dead woman. Seconds later, the old woman's half-sister, Lizaveta, enters the flat and Raskolnikov is panicked into committing a second murder.

The action of throwing away the crosses would perhaps not have signified much beyond Raskolnikov's rejection of a Christian standard and his confirmed criminality—he commits a second murder and steals the purseful of money—had it not been revealed later that Lizaveta and the prostitute, Sonya, had exchanged similar crosses. 'She gave me her [copper] cross and I gave her my little icon', Sonya explains after Raskolnikov has made his confession to her (435). She then offers him the cross made of cypress wood, but Raskolnikov refuses the cross because Sonya has made it clear to him what its acceptance signifies: 'We'll suffer together', she tells him, 'so let us bear our cross together' (435). He must, in other words, confess his crime publicly and submit to the humiliation of punishment. Acknowledging that he is not yet ready to take the first step, Sonya says: 'When you go to accept your suffering, you will put [the cross] on. You will come to me and I'll put it on. We shall pray and go together' 436). Thus, when Raskolnikov eventually returns to Sonya and says to her: 'I've come for the crosses, Sonya' (533), the meaning is clear: he will make his public confession and accept the consequences.

It can be seen here how the cross as symbol works at both a private and public level. At first it is worn as a personal token of mutual relation (Lizaveta and Sonya support each other in their suffering) and of sacrifice (Sonya devotes her life to Raskolnikov). These, moreover, are affective exchanges and are quite different from the pecuniary exchanges negotiated between Raskolnikov and the pawnbroker or, even, between Raskolnikov and his mother.

A crucifix, furthermore, is usually worn hanging from the neck and is often hidden against the heart, thus betokening the private, affective nature of the gesture. But at the same time the cross symbol has the potential to make public: especially when displayed by the priest during the Divine Liturgy. Correspondingly, Raskolnikov's crime cannot remain a secret between him and Sonya: he must, as Sonya has told him, 'Go to the cross-roads, bow down to the people, kiss the earth < ... > and proclaim in a loud voice to the whole world: I am a murderer!' (536).

One can observe here the way in which a macrocosmic dimension has been given to the cross symbol ('cross-roads < ... > the whole world') as opposed to the small scale of the crucifixes and the 'little icon'. The effect of this enlargement of the symbol is to reinforce its function in the public domain. A similar correspondence may also be remarked between the behaviour of the child, Raskolnikov, as recorded in the dream—'[E]very time he visited the cemetery he used to cross himself over the grave religiously and reverently, and bow down and kiss it' (73)—and its virtual recurrence at the crossroads before he goes to make his deposition to the police—'He knelt down in the middle of the square, bowed down to the earth, and kissed the filthy earth with joy and rapture' (537). The circumscribed childhood experience, already breached by his witnessing the violent incident outside the tavern (and for readers in English translation the publicness of the place would be denoted in the name 'public house') has been enlarged into the adult experience of actually committing a crime and coming to the point of public confession at the cross-roads.

Although psychological regression (i.e. a return to childhood in dream) seems here to form a paradigm of Raskolnikov's reversion to an amoral and primal violence (his murder of the two sisters), a prophetic projection into the future is made potentially possible by the symbols of the dream and, in particular, the recurring image of the cross, the shared communal value of which signals the way to Raskolnikov's return to Christian fellowship.

It can be understood more clearly here what Erich Auerbach meant when he asserted in his *Mimesis* that Dostoevsky had written his novels in the 'old-Christian' manner as opposed to modern occidental realism.[3] Although one could not deny a clearly delineated horizontal temporal continuum in Dostoevsky's fiction conforming to occidental realism, the vertical figural dimension cannot be overlooked either. Auerbach's thesis may be more readily accepted if it is recognised that an iconographic mode of representation coming from Orthodox Church art was still endemic to Russian culture in the nineteenth century (as it had been in the European Middle Ages) and that the aesthetic principles upon which it was founded would likely have influenced the practice of a Russian novelist such as

Dostoevsky for whom the tenets of an unqualified secular realism would have been alien. Thus, by implanting discrete metaphysical symbols into the literal representation, the author has effectively transcended the limitations of nineteenth-century secular realism (as indeed Mikhail Bakhtin has shown Dostoevsky to have overcome the limitations of nineteenth-century monologic narrative in the creation of his polyphonic discourse).[4]

It is perhaps not accidental that this combination of horizontal movement in time and space and the vertical and atemporal stasis of iconographic representation, when delineated, form the shape of a cross, a kind of watermark on the pages of the novel.[5] This would seem to support my contention that a resolution in *Crime and Punishment* is well founded and not simply a popular response to a surface reading of the text ('they lived happily ever after', or words to that effect).

The vertical dimension, furthermore, is not solely represented by religious symbol; the dream narratives are themselves synchronic breaks in the temporal progression of the plot and have as much potential for symbolic representation as do icons in a church. Dreams may signify in a condensed symbolic form the essential, or existential, core of the dreamer's being: a coalescence of his past life, his present dilemmas and his wishes for the future.

The symbolic thrust of Dostoevsky's fiction cannot, of course, be demonstrated on the strength of a single image; rather it has to be shown that a network of opaque signs resides in the text which, once acknowledged, calls for elucidation. Duplication may contribute to such an awareness as in the example of the recurring cross image; or hidden meanings may be stored in nomenclature (though less opaque to a reader of Dostoevsky in the original Russian than in translation). The name Raskolnikov, for example, is derived from *raskol'nik* meaning, in Russian, schismatic or heretic, thus giving a clue to the deeper functional level at which the naming process operates. Recognition of this kind of structure, furthermore, ought to alert us to the possibility of an internal network of nomenclatural symbols representing not merely the externality of the characters (the names they go by), but the hidden well-springs of their being. To illustrate: Porfiry, the name given to the examining magistrate in charge of the murder investigation, is also recognisably the name of a hard and highly-valued purple marble. Richard Peace has also observed that 'Porphyra' was the name given to 'the purple cloak which was the attribute of the Byzantine emperors',[6] all of which seems a far cry from the Porfiry who suffers from haemorrhoids (352) and who can say of himself. 'The good Lord has given me a figure that arouses nothing but comic ideas in people. A buffoon' (356). But Porfiry is here referring to his external appearance (as others see him) and not to his inner self from whence come his resourcefulness and integrity, qualities which in turn allow him to gain an insight into (or to 'see through') the split (*raskol*) psyche of the criminal who with a hatchet, has 'split open' the heads of his two victims.

One could at this point set up a symbolic contrast between the blood spilt by the criminal and the purple inherent in the examining magistrate's name, a proposition which would seem quite feasible if it is remembered how essential colour symbols are to the art of iconography. The purple in the name Porfiry ought to illuminate the text as it is hoped my exegesis of the cross symbol has done. Indeed, there is a direct relationship in ecclesiastical symbology between the image of the cross and the colour purple, for purple is the colour of the Passion when the sufferings leading up to the crucifixion of Christ are commemorated. During this period in the Church year the vestments worn are purple.

I am not intimating here that Porfiry's haemorrhoids represent the sum total of his suffering. These are only external signs of his discomfort, as his name is an external sign of his identity. On the other hand, the purple part of Porfiry establishes an ontological status for him: if he at first appears to be a mundane lawyer endeavouring to trick the criminal into revealing himself, he covertly, and figuratively, performs a sacred role as sage, or priest, whose function it is to hear the sinner's confession of guilt, to share his spiritual suffering, and to guide him towards the expiation of his crime through punishment. Thus, 'the purple cloak ... of the Byzantine emperors' (who, incidentally, held semi-divine status) falls into place: Porfiry offers Raskolnikov protection (a reduction of his sentence) if he will 'go to the police and make a full confession' (469) (rather as the Imperial Tsar of Russia commuted Dostoevsky's sentence to hard labour as he was about to face the firing squad).

It is noteworthy in connection with the protective cloak of suffering which the examining magistrate, Porfiry, as it were, holds out to the criminal, that Sonya, about to accompany Raskolnikov to the police station to make his deposition, picks up a shawl and puts it over her head. We are told: 'It was a green drap-de-dames shawl ... "The family shawl"' (534–35). And, at the penal settlement in Siberia, she is wearing the same shawl at the moment when Raskolnikov is finally reconciled to their union (557). The recurring image of the green shawl reinforces at an iconographic level what is already made explicit in the narrative: Sonya's protective influence over Raskolnikov. But we may go further than this by drawing on Richard Peace's additional observation that 'The full name of Sonya is Sofya (Sophia) which evokes the great Orthodox cathedral of Constantinople—Hagia Sophia (The Holy Wisdom of Orthodoxy).'[7] Nomenclature here, as elsewhere, harbours in it the potential for a radical transformation of surface representation (Sonya, the prostitute, but who is called 'little mother' by the convicts) into a profoundly metaphysical meaning (Sonya: Mother Church). This proposition can be supported by referring once again to our original paradigm: Raskolnikov's dream of childhood which, as has already been noted, appears to anticipate his eventual return to the Church: 'In the middle of the cemetery was a stone church with a green cupola, to which he used to go twice a year to morning Mass with his father and mother' (73). It will not have gone unremarked that the colour of the church cupola (that is, its protective vault) is green, and that green is also the colour of Sonya's shawl. This effectively illustrates how leitmotifs, whether colours, names or objects, converge on one another to give the imagery an illuminated status as symbol.

It could be argued, however, that what we are seeing here is no more than a coincidence of colour (green) with object (church and shawl) without any causal connection between them. This might be so if no repetition could be observed. But let us join Raskolnikov on the Nikolayevsky Bridge overlooking the River Neva the day after he has committed the murder. He has narrowly escaped being run over by a carriage, the driver of which has whipped him across the back (itself both a reflection of Raskolnikov's dream and presaging the way in which Sonya's father, Marmeladov, is to die). The people nearby mock him because they think that he is drunk (like Marmeladov, and like Raskolnikov himself when he goes to the cross-roads). He then becomes aware that a coin has been placed in his hand: 'He looked up and saw an elderly, well-to-do woman of the merchant class, in a bonnet and goatskin shoes, accompanied by a young girl wearing a hat and carrying a green parasol, probably her daughter. "Take it, my dear, in Christ's name"' (132).

The green parasol (a kind of vault giving protection from the sun) might still be thought of as mere coincidence were it not for the descriptive passage which follows: 'The cupola of the cathedral, which nowhere appears to better advantage than when seen from < ... > the bridge < ... > glittered in the sunshine, and in the clear air every ornament on it could be plainly distinguished' (132). That the girl on the bridge holding the green parasol is not Sonya matters no more than that the rouged prostitute on the boulevard with a 'little shawl < ... > thrown over her bare back' (64) is not Sonya (or that the red-lipped roué who pursues her is not Svidrigailov). The protective and life-giving principle remains constant: the mother with the daughter holding a green parasol gives money out of compassion. 'Take it, my dear, in Christ's name.' When Raskolnikov then turns his face in the direction of the Cathedral he realises what he has lost. 'His past seemed to be lying at the bottom of some fathomless cavern, deep, deep down, where he could only just discern it dimly, his old thoughts, problems, subjects, impressions, and that magnificent view [of the cathedral cupola], and himself, and everything, everything' (133).

The clear implication is that religion had been a part of his past (as is made explicit in the dream), but that now he is rejecting the protective wisdom of Mother Church as he now spurns the money given to him by mother and daughter: 'He opened his hand, stared at the silver coin, and, raising his arm, he flung it with a violent movement into the water < ... > He felt as though he had cut himself off from everyone and everything at that moment' (133). It is problematic, too, whether or not the murderer will soon throw himself off the bridge into the shapeless water (in contradistinction to the clear forms of the cathedral cupola and the green parasol).[8]

One could perhaps imagine an iconographic representation of the scene, with the murderer standing on the bridge (an image itself charged with symbolic potential) looking at the cathedral and about to throw the coin into the river. There might be included a triad of buildings: the cathedral at the top with its glittering cupola; on the left, the classical façade of the university which Raskolnikov has also forsaken. 'On his way to his lectures at the university < ... > he usually stopped here < ... > on this very spot, and gazed intently at this truly magnificent panorama, and every time he could not help wondering at the vague and mysterious emotion it aroused in him' (132); and at the bottom of the picture the Palais de Crystal, the tavern in the prostitute quarter of St Petersburg to which Raskolnikov resorts in order to read in a newspaper of the crime he has committed.

The name of the tavern is not fortuitous, for it can be seen as an emblematic travesty of English Utilitarianism, a philosophy which proposed the greatest happiness for the greatest number but which, according to Raskolnikov, means that in practical terms a percentage of young women (Sonya, for example, and even his sister, Dunya) must fall into prostitution 'so that the others [the majority of women] should be kept fresh and healthy and not be interfered with' (69). The locale for such activity was, of course, the tavern—*pivnaia*—meaning in Russian literally 'the place of beer'. No doubt Dostoevsky, in naming his tavern, had in mind the Crystal Palace, the building constructed in London for the Exhibition of the Industry of All Nations in 1851, a monument, as it were, to industrialism and the Utilitarian system of thought which supported it. For the purposes of our iconographic representation, it is worth noting that the original Crystal Palace was largely constructed of glass—an extremely fragile material (as Dostoevsky regarded the entire Utilitarian system of thought)—whereas the cathedral was made of stone, a durable substance born out by the fact that the cathedral is still standing, whilst the Crystal Palace was destroyed by fire in 1936.[9]

Now it has already been noted that the name Porfiry contains within it the 'purple marble' and that the colour purple carries an iconographic value. Is it possible, also, that the 'hard and valuable stone' in the name conveys a similar religious import? Is Porfiry 'as solid as a rock' as the Church is in its ancient traditions (in contradistinction to the ephemeral modernity of the Crystal Palace)? It could be argued that I am overstating the liaison between concrete images and symbolic meanings. The cathedral is not, after all, described as made of stone (though clearly it is). On the other hand, if one looks again at the dream paradigm, it will be recalled that 'in the middle of the cemetery was a *stone* church with a green cupola' (73, my emphasis, A. J.). This does not, of course, confirm a definitive liaison between the examining magistrate and the Russian Orthodox Church as religious institution; we need to look further at the texture of the text and to continue to identify the connecting threads which are often not seen individually when reading through impressionistically. It may have gone unnoticed that Porfiry's patronym is Petrovich (Peter's son) and that since Porfiry connotes 'stone', there may be reason to suppose that 'Petrovich' signifies something more than simply who his father is. Pyotr derives from the Latin *Petrus* ('stone'), so there is a direct semantic association of the two names. It should also not be forgotten that the very locale of Porfiry's criminal investigation is St Petersburg, a city which although built of stone was sited by the Tsar, Peter the Great, against all architectural logic on marshland. But this hardly seems a promising route to establishing Porfiry as someone whose integrity is solidly based, for the modern city of St Petersburg—topographically situated on marshland and philosophically modelled on a Western concept—would appear to be as ill founded as the ultra-modernity of the Crystal Palace in London.

St Petersburg is, of course, a German name (thus bearing out its Western character) meaning literally 'St Peter's castle'. This reminds us that within the city is the St Peter and St Paul Fortress, the prison where Raskolnikov would most certainly have been taken before being transported to Siberia (as Dostoevsky, after mock-execution, was himself imprisoned and from where he was transported). Since the St Peter and St Paul Fortress is going to play such a conspicuous role in Raskolnikov's destiny (after he has confessed, it will be the place of imprisonment, the prelude to penal servitude), a fourth building might be added to our imaginary icon—the St Peter and St Paul Fortress—placed on the right, or to the east (the direction of Siberia), as the university (the Academy of Sciences) with its classical portico has been placed on the left, or in the west.

The position of the Crystal Palace might be explained first of all because it is morally the polar opposite of the cathedral and, also, because on the religious plane the cupola of the cathedral, at the top, extends into the vault of Heaven whilst the Crystal Palace is engulfed in the formless waters of the River Neva (as analogously Raskolnikov throws the coin given him 'in Christ's name' into the water, or as the drunken woman throws herself off the bridge in an attempted suicide; or, again, as Raskolnikov himself contemplates such an act; and as Marmeladov dissolves in drink in the city underworld; hence, the Palais de Crystal tavern).

It can be seen that as an iconographic representation of Raskolnikov's spiritual journey at which stopping on the bridge is a moment of crux, the cathedral and the Crystal Palace have been placed in opposition to each other, the one leading 'upwards' (iconographically speaking) to salvation, the other 'downwards' to damnation. This does not necessarily imply that a choice has to be made by the criminal to repent or to remain obdurate. It is perhaps predestined (divinely planned, designed, drawn, painted or written) that he should lose his faith (the Church), dream up grandiose scientific ideas (at the university), commit murder to ensure the greatest happiness of the greatest number (the Crystal Palace), and that he should eventually submit to punishment (the St Peter and St Paul Fortress) before his ultimate return to the faith of his childhood (the Church). Here, there is no schismatic, or gnostic, pictorial denotation of, let us say, Good versus Evil or Heaven versus Hell, but an occult cyclical and symbolic unity which is concealed in the deep structure of the novel. The circle of experience has, as it were, been drawn around the four points of the cross of life's suffering, as there are four points of departure for Raskolnikov: the Church, the University, the Palais de Crystal, and the St Peter and St Paul Fortress.

It is possible to discern in this cyclical representation of the murderer's life at least a partial correspondence with the content of Raskolnikov's dream of childhood: his walk to the *church* where he used to go with his mother and father, is interrupted by the killing of the old mare outside the *tavern*; and in so far as there is a paradigmatic similarity between them, the dream does appear to anticipate, in a condensed form, the sequence of events that are recorded in Raskolnikov's history.

It may have been remarked that in the process of tracing the network of connecting threads in the novel, I have moved away from a consideration of the symbology of the patronym, Petrovich; and it is perhaps fitting, since we have returned to the childhood scene where the stone church with a green cupola stands, that our investigation should be resumed in that area. Attention has been drawn to the somewhat dubious status of St Petersburg in the iconography of the fiction: a city built of stone (unlike most Russian provincial towns where houses, up until the twentieth century, were built of wood) constructed on marshland. One is reminded here of Christ's parabolic injunction to build one's spiritual house on rock (Mt. 7: 24–25) and, furthermore, of his designation of the Apostle Peter as the 'rock' upon whom the Christian Church would be founded (Mt. 16: 15–20). It is not, then, by mere chance that the Christian name, Porfiry (purple stone), is juxtaposed with the patronym, Petrovich (son of a 'rock'). Rather, what we are seeing here is a vivid example of Dostoevsky's iconographic method at work.

It has already been asserted that the colour purple in Porfiry's name signals a sacred role for him on the vertical axis. We might go further and suggest that, since the names have been juxtaposed, there ought to be a symbolic liaison between the stone in Porfiry's name and the potential 'rock' in Petrovich. This seems likely bearing in mind the canonical value of purple: if Porfiry symbolically wears the vestments of the Passion by taking on collective responsibility for Raskolnikov's crime and, hence, his suffering (an endemic part of Russian Orthodox-Church thinking), it would also be possible to see him symbolically as a son, or priest, of the Church; that is, 'St Peter's son'. Once this is accepted, Porfiry takes on the role of protector, or 'little father' as priests are called in the Orthodox tradition, thus providing a complement to Sonya's 'little mother' as she is known by the convicts in the penal colony. Seen iconographically, what we have here is a diptych, with Porfiry inscribed on one side and Sonya on the other.

However, if the name of the examining magistrate, Porfiry Petrovich, bears such an affirmative iconographic signification, how is one to interpret what Richard Peace has described as the embodiment of 'a new type of pettifogging legal expert' in, precisely, *Pyotr Petrovich* Luzhin?[10] If it is the case that Luzhin's Christian name, Pyotr, and patronymic, Petrovich, appear to function complementarily (as they do in Porfiry Petrovich), it is certainly not so when they are juxtaposed as a pair with his family name; for the name, Luzhin, comes close to the Russian word *luzha*—'a puddle'—and, therefore, if inherent meaning is taken into account, must work antithetically to the stonelike properties of Pyotr and Petrovich. Since I have already posited the symbolic propensity of water as purporting formlessness, or loss of form, and 'stone/rock' as signifying substantive form, or the saving of human form, it will have become clear that the name, Pyotr Petrovich Luzhin, is invested with an irreconcilable duality similar to the disparate nomenclature given by Dostoevsky to the main protagonist of his novel, *The Idiot*: Prince Leo ('lion') Myshkin ('mousekin').[11]

The phonetic similarity of the name Luzhin with *luzha* ('puddle') also has relevance on a philosophical plane if it is remarked that Luzhin has been the 'student' of his former ward, Lebezyatnikov, whose adherence to the rationalistic values of Utilitarianism, symbolised by the Crystal Palace (and placed in the waters of the River Neva in our imaginary icon), is as unequivocal as was Raskolnikov's at the time of the murder. But Luzhin's avowal of the Utilitarian way of thinking learned from Lebezyatnikov is not born out of conviction, but because the notion of enlightened self interest suits his ruthless egoism; it is, in other words, a watered down philosophy— a mere puddle of an idea. Luzhin's actions have the effect of negating any altruistic moral value that his pseudo-Utilitarianism may purport to have: he merely seeks to profit by sowing discord, as when he falsely accuses Sonya of theft, or in his attempt to break up the Raskolnikov family by tempting Dunya to marry him so that she may be kept.

Clearly, the duality implicit in his names—Pyotr Petrovich, on the one hand, and Luzhin, on the other—is lived out in the divisiveness of his actions. Whereas Raskolnikov for all his schizoid behaviour did desire to put the world to rights—to bring it together again—Luzhin works at nothing but disuniting in the most petty and mean-spirited way; and it would not be too far-fetched, on a metaphysical plane, to call him 'diabolical' once we note that the word derives from the Greek *dia-bolos*, meaning literally 'to throw across', or 'to slander', a practice at which Luzhin is adept.[12] Contained within the word is the notion of division; Luzhin is diabolical precisely because he attempts to divide one person from another—Sonya from Raskolnikov, Dunya from her family—to break their integrity and to destroy their human solidarity with one another. Thus we can better understand the iconographic juxtaposition of the disparate nomenclature: Pyotr Petrovich (stone, son of stone) with Luzhin (*luzha*, 'puddle') which works counter to the fundamental integrity implicit in the name Porfiry Petrovich and, on a larger scale, the unifying symbol of the Christian cross. Again, seen iconographically, what we have here is a diptych with Pyotr Petrovich Luzhin placed on the left and Porfiry Petrovich on the right, but, unlike the spiritually complementary figures of Sonya the saint and Porfiry the sage, Luzhin and Porfiry are situated in opposition to each other on the moral scale.

If this once more seems to be in danger of overstating the case, let us counterbalance figurative stones in the name Porfiry Petrovich with the image of a literal stone:

> [Raskolnikov] suddenly noticed < ... > a huge unhewn stone, weighing about fifty pounds, and lying close against the outer stone wall < ... > He bent down over the stone, caught hold of the top of it firmly with both his hands, and, applying all his strength, turned it over. There was a small cavity under the stone, and he at once started throwing everything [he had stolen from the murdered money lender] out of his pockets into it. (127)

It is noteworthy here that Raskolnikov had intended throwing the stolen things into a canal, or the river, thus destroying the evidence against him (symbolically rendering them formless), but that he suddenly decides to hide them in a safe place under the stone (thus preserving their form). This turns out to be fortunate because, later at the trial, the examining magistrates and judges are clearly impressed that the accused man 'should have hidden the purse and various articles from the flat under a stone without attempting to make any use of them' (543), a fact which partly contributes to a lessening of the severity of his sentence. The stone, then, has preserved the evidence which will save the condemned man from a life sentence (or total loss of human identity) just as, correspondingly, Porfiry Petrovich has offered Raskolnikov a degree of protection if he will reveal all, which in practical terms again means that the life sentence will be commuted to a few years penal servitude.

We have discovered here in what a complex way Dostoevsky's symbology works. On the one hand, the image of a stone is represented literally and does not appear, in its isolated form, to carry any symbolic weight; the image fits inconspicuously into the framework of secular realism. On the other hand, once the latent symbolism of the names Porfiry Petrovich and Pyotr Petrovich Luzhin becomes fully realised, the language of the text is itself illuminated in such a way that literal images are found to have a capacity for extra-literal meaning. This agrees entirely with religious iconography, the purpose of which is to express on a spiritual plane what it is not possible to attain through literal representation only. There has to be an in-built figural dimension, the foundation, as it were, of the discursive narrative. At a surface level, the polyphony which Mikhail Bakhtin has postulated for Dostoevsky's poetics—a technical innovation which has the effect of destabilising the text ('the world')[13]—is brought under control by, or is even arrested by, the vertical figural dimension which cuts through the diachronic, horizontal plane of the discourse.[14] Time is brought to a standstill to make way for an instant (or an eternity) of teleological certitude. Symbology functions rather as the narrator might do in a monologic narrative, except that whereas the narrator may consciously know all, the symbols are hidden in the deep structure of the text, the realm of the text's unconscious. This difference can easily be accounted for by the fact that even if the voices are many, the visual perspective is limited: the world seen and experienced, for the most part, by one man: Rodion Romanovich Raskolnikov (*Crime and Punishment* was originally drafted as a first person narrative). It is natural, therefore, that with such a limitation imposed on him (as it is imposed on all of us) that the world should appear to the murderer chaotic, meaningless and absurd.

Conversely, once a network of symbols has been established and a hidden signification brought to light, it will be seen that symbols permeate the discourse with an attribute of what amounts to immanency, thus opening it up to inherent meaning. Moreover, this special status of symbol as the bearer of hidden meaning is metaphysical in thrust because it has the capacity to transcend the limitations of mundane discourse and to impose on it the stability which on the surface it seems to lack. As Mikhail Bakhtin has said: 'Dostoevsky destroys the flatness of the earlier artistic depiction of the world. Depiction becomes for the first time multidimensional.'[15]

NOTES

1. All quotations are from: F. M. Dostoevsky, *Crime and Punishment*, trans. D. Magarshack (Harmondsworth, 1970). Page references are given in brackets.

2. W. D. Snodgrass, 'Crime for punishment: The tenor of part one', *Hudson Review* 13, no. 2 (1960), 248.

3. E. Auerbach, *Mimesis: The Representation of Reality in Western Literature*, trans. W. R. Trask (Princeton, NJ, 1974), 521.

4. M. Bakhtin, *Problems of Dostoevsky's Poetics*, ed. and trans. C. Emerson (Minneapolis, MN, 1984).

5. See A. Johae, 'Idealism and the dialectic in *The Brothers Karamazov*', ed. L. Burnett, *F. M. Dostoevsky 1821–1881: A Centenary Volume* (Colchester, 1981), 111.

6. Richard Peace, *Dostoevsky: An Examination of the Major Novels* (Cambridge, 1975), 44.

7. *Ibid.*, 44–45.

8. See J. Catteau, *Dostoevsky and the Process of Literary Creation*, trans. A. Littlewood (Cambridge, 1989), 426.

9. For the significance of the Crystal Palace for Russians in the mid-nineteenth century, see M. Berman, *All That Is Solid Melts Into Air: The Experience of Modernity* (London, 1983), 235–48. I have traced the Crystal Palace motif in Chernyshevsky, Dostoevsky and Zamyatin in 'The Russian sources of George Orwell's *Nineteen Eighty-Four,*' *New Comparison*, 17 (1994)

10. See Peace, *Dostoevsky*, 23.

11. For an account of the ambiguities of name and character in Prince Leo Myshkin, see A. Johae, 'Retractive imagery: Dostoevsky and German Romanticism', *Germano-Slavica*, 8, no. 2 (1994), 10–12.

12. I am indebted to Hugh Drake for drawing my attention to the etymology of 'diabolical'.

13. Bakhtin, *Dostoevsky's Poetics*, 45–46.

14. Robert Louis Jackson in 'Bakhtin's Poetics of Dostoevsky' in *Dialogues with Dostoevsky: The Overwhelming Questions* (Stanford, CA, 1993), 283, has observed that Bakhtin 'projects < ... > a horizontal plane to the Dostoevsky novel on which exist multiple "consciousnesses" < ... > At the same time he [Bakhtin] suggests what we may term a vertical dimension in Dostoevsky's novelistic universe, a hierarchy of voices, orientations, or truths arising out of this sea of autonomous jostling truths.' On other religious readings of Dostoevsky's novels, see in the same volume, 'Chateaubriand and Dostoevsky: Elective affinities', 'Vision in his soul: Vyacheslav I. Ivanov's Dostoevsky' and 'Last stop: Virtue and immortality in *The Brothers Karamazov*'. None of these essays, however, give attention to the aesthetic sources of Dostoevsky's iconographic art in religious symbology.

15. M. Bakhtin, 'Towards a reworking of the Dostoevsky book', partly reproduced in Fyodor Dostoevsky, *'Crime and Punishment': The Coulson Translation: Backgrounds and Sources: Essays in Criticism*, ed. George Gibian, 3rd edn (New York, 1989), 655.

LINDA IVANITS

The Other Lazarus in Crime and Punishment

$\mathbf{A}$t the edges of Dostoevsky's novelistic world or, perhaps more accurately, of the hero's awareness, one frequently encounters the bustle of the Russian people (*narod*). This is especially true of *Crime and Punishment* (*Prestuplenie i nakazanie*, 1866), where a multitude of tradespeople, artisans, prostitutes, and beggars enter and exit at the periphery of the murder story. One reason that we often read past them—aside from the obvious fact that our interest is riveted on Raskolnikov—is that they lack the self-consciousness that we tend to postulate as the defining attribute of significant characters.[1] The hero may (or, as is more often the case, may not) absorb them into his inner deliberations, yet we are seldom privy to *their* thoughts and queries. Of course, the presence of the lower classes authenticates Dostoevsky's depiction of a squalid section of St. Petersburg and indicates that the humanitarian theme, which Belinsky had lauded twenty years earlier in *Poor Folk* (*Bednye liudi*, 1846), remains strong in *Crime and Punishment*.[2] But the common people of *Crime and Punishment* do more than round out the picture of social reality: they have an important voice of their own. Unobtrusive allusions to folklore and popular belief, which are embedded in the speech and thoughts of major personages and in mini-stories that we can patch together from street scenes, convey the ethical values of the *narod*.[3] The voice of the people runs counter to the rationalistic theories that Raskolnikov

From *The Russian Review* 61, no. 3 (July 2002). © 2002 by *The Russian Review*.

uses to justify the murder, and it is the voice that he must heed in order to be reintegrated into the human community.

The *Notebooks* attest both that Dostoevsky's use of folklore in *Crime and Punishment* was deliberate and that he softened its effect by removing excessive references from the published text.[4] On the whole, the writer chose to handle the popular tradition obliquely or to conceal it in symbol and metaphor. It is thus far less evident than the articulations of the environmentalist position, which justified eliminating harmful or useless members from society, or of the Napoleonic theory, which conjectured that a few extraordinary people had the right to bypass conventional morality to benefit humankind. As George Gibian suggests, Dostoevsky may have felt that an outright statement of the case for "acceptance of suffering, closeness to the life-sustaining Earth, and love" would sound "insipid and platitudinous."[5] While logical argumentation and direct statement suffice to explain the rationales for murder, the spiritual wisdom of the *narod* must be experienced in life itself through compassion and acts of kindness.

Several existing studies probe the working of the popular ethic in *Crime and Punishment*. V. P. Vladimirtsev shows how more than four hundred references to laments and tears create a background din in which we can discern the people's sympathetic bemoaning of the fate of Raskolnikov.[6] The "terrible, desperate howls" from the street that awaken Raskolnikov after the murder, the suppressed tears and prayers of Katerina Ivanovna as she and her children kneel during the last rites for Marmeladov, the whining voice of the beggar woman to whom Raskolnikov gives five kopeks on his way to surrender, and numerous other instances enter this collective lament for the young murderer.[7] Vladimirtsev suspects that Dostoevsky considered adding a Haymarket prostitute's lament about her terrible fate to this background noise, but opted instead for Razumikhin's casual mention of the Russian song, "I shall weep burning tears" (*Zal'ius' slez'mi goriuchimi*).[8] In another study, L. M. Lotman demonstrates that Marmeladov's pathetic tavern speech proclaiming forgiveness in the afterlife for even the greatest sinners is modeled largely on a widespread satirical legend about a drunkard arguing his way into heaven.[9] Here Dostoevsky conveys lofty notions about the all-inclusive mercy of God in a "debased and grotesque form" by placing them in the mouth of a drunkard who has mistreated and abandoned his family.[10]

The present article discusses a folklore subtext that has yet to be adequately studied: the spiritual song (*dukhovnyi stikh*) that retells the Gospel parable of the beggar Lazarus and the unmerciful rich man (Luke 16:19–31). Dostoevsky situates the one clear reference to this song in his hero's thoughts; as he is about to meet Porfiry Petrovich for the first time, Raskolnikov reflects, "I suppose I'll have to sing Lazarus to this one too"

(6:189). "To sing Lazarus" (*pet' Lazaria*) is a turn of speech for "to tell a tale of woes," "to solicit something ingratiatingly," "to put on a false front."[11] The Lazarus song, from which the idiom was derived, summed up Russian popular notions about justice; it expressed the belief of the *narod* that the relations between rich and poor should be governed by concrete charity as manifested in almsgiving (*milostynia*). In *Crime and Punishment*, allusions to the song thread their way through the text binding seemingly unrelated scenes and personages. Since the reference is buried in an idiom, Russian readers tend to overlook it. Not surprisingly, it usually fails to survive translation into English.[12]

The few studies that comment on Raskolnikov's thought of "singing Lazarus" focus on the idiom rather than the song. R. G. Nazirov suspects that this expression comes into Raskolnikov's mind because he has falsely assumed the role of a beggar.[13] M. S. Altman suggests that his thought of the song may mean that he is pretending when he tells Porfiry Petrovich that he believes in the resurrection of Lazarus.[14] True, on the day following the murder, when summoned to the police station because of his failure to pay his rent, Raskolnikov exaggerates his position as a "poor and sick student depressed ... by poverty" (6:80); and he intends to maintain this stance in front of Porfiry Petrovich, who may suspect him of murder. The song concealed beneath the idiom, however, directs us not so much to the hero's playacting as to his inner fragmentation (his name comes from the word "to split"—*raskolot'*). Something deep within Raskolnikov draws him to the lowly and the outcast (Sonia, his sickly fiancée, Lizaveta), and he gives alms to the destitute. Something else causes him to rebuke himself for his generosity and to reject help from others. Raskolnikov clings to the belief that he may be superior to the street rabble to whom he gives a few kopeks. As he phrases it in his confession to Sonia, he feels compelled to ascertain "whether he is a louse (*vosh'*), like everybody else, or a human being" (*chelovek*, 6:322). When he thinks about "singing Lazarus," he seems to express a subconscious awareness that he must choose between the way of giving *and receiving* alms (*milostynia*) and the way of power and reason, by which he can justify murder on the grounds that the old pawnbroker is a "louse" and not a "human being." Raskolnikov cannot have it both ways. Joseph Frank captures the starkness of his dilemma when he states, "On the one side there is the ethic of Christian *agape*, the total, immediate, and unconditional sacrifice of self ...; on the other, Raskolnikov's rational Utilitarian ethic, which justifies the sacrifice of *others* for the sake of a greater social good."[15]

Although critics seldom mention the beggar Lazarus, they almost universally perceive the novel's central religious meaning in the Gospel narrative of the resurrection of Lazarus (John 11: 1–45), which Sonia reads to Raskolnikov. John's narrative, they argue, contains the pledge that Raskolnikov, like the dead Lazarus, can awaken to new life.[16] In the novel, Dostoevsky highlights the Lazarus whom Jesus brings back from the tomb while downplaying Lazarus the beggar. While John's Lazarus captures the novel's metaphysical center, the Lazarus song directs us to the world of the impoverished inhabitants of Petersburg's back alleys and squares.[17] In *Crime and Punishment* the two Lazarus stories complement each other by fusing the themes of charity and resurrection into a single overarching religious vision. The novel links the action of giving and receiving alms to the theme of resurrected life, for the presence of God on earth becomes palpable in simple acts of charity, though the rich and the powerful may not see it.

In pre-Petrine Russia, Luke's parable about the rich man and Lazarus was a favorite subject for sermons and religious tracts.[18] The song, which took shape on the basis of written sources, was known virtually everywhere in the countryside by the nineteenth century. A narrative on the beggar Lazarus in some form or another would surely have been included among stories Dostoevsky heard as a child and again in Siberia. In his *Diary of a Writer* for July/August 1877, he wrote about the Russian people's love for such edifying tales:

> Yes, on the whole the Russian people love stories about holy things very much. Peasants, their children, the urban lower-middle class (*meshchane*), and merchants even listen to these stories with tenderness and sighs. There is, for example, the question of who has read the great *Menologion* (*Chet'i-Minei*)? ... And now would you believe that knowledge of the *Menologion* is extremely widespread throughout the entire Russian land, oh, not of course of the entire book, but at least its spirit is widespread? And why is this so? Because there are an exceedingly large number of men and women narrators of the saints' lives. ... I myself heard such stories in childhood even before I learned to read. Later I even heard these stories in the stockade among bandits, and the bandits listened and sighed. These stories are not transmitted by books, but are learned by heart. These stories, and stories about holy places, contain something that is, so to speak, penitential and purifying for the Russian people.[19]

In the early 1860s, the writer's activity as copublisher of *Time* (*Vremia*) and later *Epoch* (*Epokha*) brought him into the direct proximity of a number of publications containing the Lazarus song. In 1861, *Time* reviewed P. V.

Bessonov's *Wandering Pilgrims* (*Kaleki perekhozhie*), P. V. Kireevsky's *Songs* (*Pesni, sobrannye P. V. Kireevskim*), and N. Varentsov's *Collection of Russian Spiritual Songs* (*Sbornik russkikh dukhovnykh stikhov*).[20] The section of Bessonov's classic multivolume work that was under review (vol. 1, pt. 1) contains nine variants of the Lazarus song listed under the beading "Whom do Wandering Pilgrims Take as an Example" (*Kogo berut premerom kaleki perekhozhie*), thereby underscoring its special role in the beggars' understanding of their place in the world. Kireevsky's and Varentsov's anthologies both contain several variants of the Lazarus song.

Like the New Testament account, the spiritual song contrasts the earthly life of the rich man and the beggar with their reversal of fortunes after death: the rich man who failed to help the poor one goes to hell, while the beggar Lazarus goes to heaven. Both accounts imply that the beggar's condition inherently makes him a recipient of divine sympathy, whereas the rich man must earn this favor through acts of mercy. Russian folklore in general reinforces the ethic of the Lazarus song and shrouds the act of almsgiving with an aura of sacredness. In legends it is often Christ himself who, disguised as the beggar, seeks charity.[21] Even the formulaic request for an offering, "I beg/accept alms in the name of Christ" (*Proshu/primi milostyniu Khrista radi*), is sanctioned by a spiritual song in which Christ wishes to leave his beggar-brothers "mountains of gold and rivers of honey" at the time of his Ascension. John the Evangelist (sometimes John the Baptist or John Chrysostom) cautions him against leaving them riches, saying:

> Ah, you true Christ and Heavenly Tsar,
> Don't give them [beggars] mountains of gold.
> Don't give them rivers of precious metals.
> The powerful, the rich will take them away;
> And here there will be much murder,
> And there will be much blood-spilling here.
> Do give them your sacred name;
> They will remember you;
> They will give praise to you.
> They will be fed; they will be given something to drink,
> They will be clothed and given footwear.[22]

The Lazarus song pushes the contrast between good and evil further than Luke's parable by elaborating on the earthly life of the two men, the circumstances of their death, and, often, their conversation in the afterlife. It usually makes the rich man and the poor man brothers and underscores this relationship by naming both "Lazarus" (hence the common designation of this song as "The Two Lazaruses"). While the Gospel narrative is scanty in its details of the interaction between the rich man and the poor one, the song includes a scene in which the beggar asks his wealthy brother for alms in the name of Christ, is refused, and is thrown out of the house. Typically the rich man denies his kinship with the beggar and sets his "fierce" dogs on him. But the dogs, kinder than their owner, bring the poor brother crumbs from their master's table and, as in the Gospel account, lick his sores. Luke does not relate how the two men die, but the song shows the poor Lazarus beseeching God to take his soul. Though anticipating that his life in the next world will correspond to his earthly existence, he finds God's hell preferable to his brother's unkindness:

> The poor man went out into the open field,
> He looked up; he gazed at the heavens,
> The poor man shouted out in a loud voice:
> "Oh, Lord! Lord! Merciful Savior!
> Hear, Oh Lord, my prayer,
> My unrighteous prayer:
> Send me, Lord, terrible angels.
> Terrible, and restless, and unmerciful!
> Let them thrust a lance through my ribs to my soul,
> Let them place my soul on a harrow;
> Carry my soul into the burning tar."[23]

The rich brother, on the other hand, expects to enter heaven, for he imagines the afterlife as a continuation of the pleasure he knows on earth. Some variants of the song indicate that he believes his wealth will secure his way into paradise:

> And thus my soul reigned
> Living here in the expansiveness of the world,
> My soul drank, ate, and amused itself!
> For me, a rich man, there is the means to enter heaven,
> For me, a rich man, there is the means to save my soul
> A rich man has great possessions:
> Bread and salt, gold and silver.[24]

The ending of the Lazarus song differs sharply from that of Luke's parable. The Gospel story introduces the theme of resurrection: the rich man asks to be sent back to his father's house to warn his brothers, but Abraham responds, "If they do not listen to Moses and the prophets they will pay no heed even if someone should rise from the dead" (Luke 16:31). The song, on the other hand, keeps the emphasis on the wealthy brother's torments in hell. The rich man cries out for help to his poor brother, whose kinship he now acknowledges; the poor man responds that he cannot go against God's will ("Brother, my brother, ... it is not my will but the will of God").[25] Sometimes the ending includes a list of acts of charity akin to that noted in Matthew 25 that the rich brother failed to perform on earth:

[The rich man cried out:]
"Oh my brother, poor Lazarus!
Since you knew and were aware of eternal life,
Of the evil, eternal torment,
Why, my dear one, did you not tell me then?
Ah, I would not have been so concerned
        about my possessions and life,
Bread and salt, and gold and silver!
I would have given alms in the name of Christ,
I would have called you my own dear brother,
I would have summoned poor beggars into my house,
I would, my brother, have attended to widows and orphans,
I would have protected them with nightly lodgings,
I would have clothed the naked and the barefoot,
I would have given alms to those sitting along the road,
I would have brought light into the darkness of the dungeons,
I would have accompanied the dead in their coffins."[26]

For the Russian folk, the Lazarus narrative was a succinct presentation of the injustice reigning in the world and, at the same time, a powerful summons to live the Gospel commandment of love of neighbor.[27] Yet, in spite of the sharply negative portrayal of the rich Lazarus, it is not possible to claim that the song advocates a social upheaval that would equalize the distribution of wealth. It is clear, however, that wealth *ipso facto* bears with it the obligation of charity. The rich brother goes to hell not because he is wealthy, but because he failed to help the poor.

Within the educated milieu of Dostoevsky's time, the understanding of beggars and almsgiving differed sharply from that of the people. The radical intelligentsia in particular was prone to explain the existence of beggary, like that of crime, as an aberration of the social structure that would disappear once the system was set right. Several years prior to the writing of *Crime and Punishment* this position slipped into *Time* in a review of I. G. Pryzhov's book, *Beggars in Holy Russia* (*Nishchie na sviatoi Rusi: Materialy dlia istorii obshchestvennogo i narodnogo byta v Rossii*). The reviewer, M. Rodevich, rejected Pryzhov's historical schema that appeared to link the mid-nineteenth-century beggars crowding the streets of the Russian capitals to the pilgrims who were once the bearers of the spiritual songs and whom princes and monasteries sustained.[28] He viewed beggary as a phenomenon that "could not help but be connected with the very structure of social life in general" and beggars as a social blight that almsgiving aggravated: "Poverty is a social sin, a civic vice of the people; as it relates to the individual person it is a misfortune. Beggary is social charlatanism and religious virtue maintained by false notions about society."[29] The solution Rodevich advocated was to educate the people so that they would overcome their irrationality and the "mystical-religious urgings" that caused them to give alms: "teach them, open their eyes, let them understand that their almsgiving leads to nothing but bad."[30]

Dostoevsky disagreed with Rodevich, and in a passage that he omitted from the final text of *Crime and Punishment* he placed his objections in the mouth of Razumikhin:

> Certain good, big-hearted, and truly intelligent people will tell you that it is sad and difficult to help in an isolated fashion and that one must tear out the root of evil and implant good. Others, also fine and good people, but already too steeped in theory, will bring you entire volumes of proof—truly accurate (from one point of view)—that isolated instances of good do not help society. They forget that, among other things, they do help that particular individual, and they make you yourself better and uphold love in society. And so fools and rogues will immediately conclude that it is not necessary to help at all, and that this is progress.[31]

In the finished text, Dostoevsky carried on this polemic more indirectly. He placed the crucial statements in the mouth of the drunk Marmeladov, who introduces the theme of beggary in the tavern scene (bk. 1, chap. 2) with a parody of Rodevich: "Kind Sir ... poverty isn't a vice, that's the truth. ... But beggary (*nishcheta*), Kind Sir, beggary is a vice" (6:13). This deformation of the radical position continues in Marmeladov's explanation of why Lebeziatnikov, the novel's prime caricature of the men of the sixties, refuses to lend him money: "After all, he knows beforehand that I won't return it. From compassion? But following the latest ideas Mr. Lebeziatnikov explained the other day that in our time compassion is already forbidden by science" (6:14).

In the tavern scene the very relationship between the drunken civil servant and ex-student is suggestive of that between supplicant and almsgiver, and it may be precisely Marmeladov's beggarly mien that attracts Raskolnikov. Marmeladov is dirty and in rags; he has sold his clothing for drink and has spent five nights on a hay barge. Though Raskolnikov is hardly better dressed, the title by which Marmeladov repeatedly addresses him, "Kind Sir" (*Milostivyi gosudar'*), is revealing, It is, of course, a standard form of respectful address and here points to Marmeladov's clerical status; but it also contains the key word (*milostivyi*) of the spiritual songs and folk legends for a person who shows kindness (*milost'*) or gives alms (*milostynia*).[32] In the Lazarus song *milostivyi* describes Christ and the angels he sends to the beggar; its opposite, *nemilostivyi*, is used for the rich man and the angels Christ sends to him. The disjointed story Marmeladov tells Raskolnikov contains a number of mini-stories on the pattern of destitute seeker/(potential) benefactor. Katerina Ivanovna is reduced to a state of hopeless beggary and Marmeladov, unable to look on such suffering, offers her his hand; Sonia becomes a prostitute in order to feed small children who have not "seen a crust for three days"; Marmeladov appears before his superior, Ivan Afanasevich, dressed in rags, and the latter takes him back in the service; Marmeladov asks Sonia for money for drink and she gives him her last thirty kopeks (6:16, 17, 18, 20).

The terms "beggar" (*nishchii*) and "beggary" (*nishcheta*) are sprinkled throughout the text of *Crime and Punishment* and pertain not only to the riffraff of Petersburg's back streets, but to most of the main characters as well. The Marmeladovs are a destitute family in a tenement of beggars. A woman mistakes Raskolnikov for a beggar. Though the term is not specifically used of Razumikhin, we learn that he dresses in rags and that his poverty is so great that he sometimes does not light the stove in the winter (6:44). Luzhin fancies that his marriage to Dunia will lift her from beggary. At his trial Raskolnikov explains his murder partly as a result of his destitution (*nishcheta*), and his sentence is more merciful (*milostivee*) than could have been expected (6:411). Mention of beggars occurs even in contexts remote from the main action; thus, on the final night before his suicide Svidrigailov looks through a chink in the wall of his dank hotel room and, for some reason, espies one man reproaching another for being a beggar whom he "pulled out of the mud" (6:389).

The motif of almsgiving (*milostynia*) similarly occurs at almost every juncture of *Crime and Punishment*. Raskolnikov gives alms to the Marmeladovs, to an organ grinder, to a prostitute, and to a young girl who has just been seduced; even on his way to the police station to confess to the murder of the pawnbroker and her sister Lizaveta, he gives something to a woman with a child. The detail that he had used his meager resources to support an impoverished, consumptive student and his destitute father surfaces at his trial. We know very little about his former fiancée except that she was sick, dreamed of a convent, and loved to give alms to beggars. When Raskolnikov's landlady refuses to continue his board because he has not paid his bill, her servant Nastasia, seeing how sick and penniless he is, brings him food and drink in her own dishes. Sonia reproaches herself for refusing to give Katerina Ivanovna collars and cuffs. The corresponding passage in the *Notebooks* makes it clear that she considers herself a great sinner precisely because of this "sin against love" and not because of prostitution.[33] In Siberia, Sonia brings pies and sweet breads (*kalachi*) to the entire stockade at Christmas. Luzhin emerges as especially despicable by the standard of almsgiving. He imagines that his marriage to Dunia will free her from destitution, but he does not lift a finger to help her. Later, after Dunia has broken the engagement, he reproaches himself for not using expensive gifts to bind her to him. His treatment of Sonia subverts the meaning of almsgiving as an act of compassion. He gives her ten rubles for Katerina Ivanovna, whom he terms a "beggarly fool" and a "beggarly widow"; and then he slips another hundred in her pocket so that he can accuse her of stealing "from beggary."[34] Though he is an amoral debauchee whose portrayal contains demonic overtones, Svidrigailov takes the time before his suicide to make financial provisions for his young fiancée, Katerina Ivanovna's orphaned children, Sonia, and Raskolnikov.[35]

The relationship of the two Lazarus brothers is recapitulated in that between Alena Ivanovna and Lizaveta: the pawnbroker forces her half-sister to work for her like a slave, yet, like the rich Lazarus, she believes she can buy her way into heaven. She plans to leave all her wealth to a monastery where prayers will be said for her soul. As a merciless usurer, the pawnbroker constitutes precisely the sort of victim Raskolnikov needs to convince himself that he can improve the lot of the downtrodden by eliminating her ilk.[36] Immediately after his first visit to her, he overheard a discussion that coincided with his own thoughts: it would be possible to kill Alena Ivanovna without any pangs of conscience because she sucked the vital juices from "young creative forces" and on her money one could save dozens of families "from beggary (*nishcheta*), dissolution, destruction, debauchery, hospitals for venereal diseases.... One death and a hundred lives in exchange—after all, it's a matter of simple arithmetic" (6:54). In selecting Alena Ivanovna as the brunt of his attack, Raskolnikov appears to differentiate between predators and victims along the lines of the Lazarus song. But in yielding to the idea that it is his mission to bring about a "just" solution by destroying the oppressor, he usurps a right that the song leaves to divine providence.

Raskolnikov's apparently chance killing of Lizaveta along with her half-sister destroys the "simple arithmetic" of the calculation according to which she and other "poor Lazaruses" would benefit from the pawnbroker's death.

The theme of beggary moves to the center of narrative attention when Katerina Ivanovna takes to the streets with her children. The tie between this scene and the tavern scene becomes explicit when Katerina Ivanovna's six-year-old daughter sings "The Little Farm" ("Khutorok"), the same song that a seven-year-old was singing while Marmeladov was talking with Raskolnikov. Lazarus's plea to God in the song finds its counterpart in the desperate cry with which Katerina Ivanovna prefaces her move: "On the day of my husband's funeral, after my hospitality, I'm chased from my lodgings onto the street with my orphans! And where am I to go! ... Lord! ... is it possible that there is no justice (*spravedlivost'*)! Who is there for you to defend if not us, orphans that we are!" (6:311). Now Katerina Ivanovna adopts the role of a beggar asking for alms: "Let everybody see, all of Petersburg, how the children of a noble father beg for alms"; and, "We are a poor, noble family of orphans reduced to beggary" (6:329). Both Luke's account and the song illustrate the rich man's abundance by referring to his sumptuous meals; Katerina Ivanovna summons her husband's superior from his dinner at the house of a general "who feasts on grouse." Just as Lazarus is driven from his wealthy brother's house when he seeks help, so she, too, is driven from the house of the general. Her threat to walk by his window and beg every day echoes Luke's detail that Lazarus lay at the rich man's gate (Luke 16:20). Like Lazarus, Katerina Ivanovna is unsuccessful in her search for justice on earth. As she lies dying her focus seems to be not so much on what will come next as on the thought that death will release her from her misery: "Enough! ... It's time! ... Farewell, wretched creature! ... They've driven the nag (*kliacha*) to death! ... I've overexerted myself!" (6:334). Her use of *kliacha* underscores that her life was full of hardship and cruelty, for it is the same word used for the mare that is brutally beaten to death in Raskolnikov's dream. In the Lazarus song the poor man begs for death without any expectation of paradise. Katerina Ivanovna's statements may echo this motif: she emphasizes that there is no need to waste money on a priest (6:333). One might note that some variants of the song list priests along with boyars and merchants as the money-loving companions of the rich brother.[37]

Crime and Punishment thus contains a large number of scenes and situations that evoke the Lazarus song. But, while the song, as is customary for folklore narratives, turns on the sharp juxtaposition of good and evil and seldom elaborates on the hero's motivation, the novel leaves no doubt about the complex psychology of the destitute person, who may be both victim and perpetrator of suffering. In the case of the Marmeladovs, as Edward Wasiolek notes, Dostoevsky transforms the common sentimental situation "in which circumstances bring an unfortunate individual to misery and destitution ... into one in which the individual looks for his misery and destitution and derives some strange satisfaction from displaying it and even exaggerating it."[38] Dostoevsky develops the theme of beggary in such a way as to negate any notion that the human person is rational or can be made happy by social reorganization, and the compound motivations of this slum family stand as a clear refutation of Lebeziatnikov's flimsy notion that "the environment counts for everything, and the person (*chelovek*) is nothing."[39] Almsgiving, however, offers more than a kinder alternative to impersonal social reform for feeding the hungry. It represents a mutual exchange in charity in which the destitute person receives material sustenance and offers in return a prayer for the well-being of the benefactor.[40] The rite of giving alms places human interaction beyond the realm of logical argumentation for it assumes divine participation both in giving and in receiving. We can see this illustrated by the woman to whom Raskolnikov gives five kopeks on his way to surrender; she responds, "May God preserve you" (*Sokhrani tebia Bog*, 6:405), thereby blessing him for the ordeal that lies ahead.

Katerina Ivanovna accepts alms from Marmeladov, but fails to respond to his kindness with a blessing of pity for him. The *Notebooks* contain a passage in which she acknowledges her harsh treatment of her husband on her deathbed: "The poor thing would look at me, and I couldn't say a kind word to him" (7:192). Marmeladov remained sober for the first year of their marriage, but this was not sufficient to gain her acceptance. She could not forget that she attended a school for aristocratic girls and was his social superior. His decision to drink represents a perverse attempt to punish her and to harm himself, thereby gaining her attention. He seemed to be on the verge of lifting his family from beggary once he had been taken back into the service; but he chose instead to steal the money that had been saved and plunge them back into destitution. When Raskolnikov meets him, he is truly a beggar and is buying drinks with Sonia's last thirty kopeks. Marmeladov knows he is guilty before his loved ones and terms himself a "swine" and a "beast." But he places a good deal of the blame for his situation on Katerina Ivanovna, whom he describes as proud and, in her unpitying attitude toward him, unjust (*nespravedliva*). His account, which pictures her both as the wicked stepmother of the fairy tale who destroys her stepdaughter by forcing her into prostitution and as a penniless, consumptive mother with three hungry children, points to her psychological impasse. Katerina Ivanovna remains haughty in her destitution; even when she deliberately assumes the role of beggar and forces her children to dance and sing for alms, she cannot quite identify with others in her situation. She wants the children to sing French and German songs instead of "The Little Farm" as evidence that they are well-bred children and not common street urchins.

In Raskolnikov's case, the Lazarus song directs us to the area of his psyche where his rationales for murder vie with his sympathy for the downtrodden. As he gropes toward an understanding of why he killed Alena Ivanovna, he alternates between spontaneous compassion for the street people and the self-castigating fear that he may be a "louse" rather than a superior individual with the right to breach conventional morality.[41] This struggle is evident in his conflicting attitudes toward almsgiving. While impulsively generous, he himself refuses to accept alms. Raskolnikov objects to being typed as a beggar, but, as noted earlier, resolves to play the role of a penniless ex-student when he visits Porfiry Petrovich. Destitution, however, is more than a front that he adopts before the clever police inspector to elude suspicion of murder. Raskolnikov is truly poor and lives almost entirely on handouts. Nastasia feeds and nurses him throughout the novel, though he is loath to acknowledge his dependence on her. When he receives money— from pawning his father's watch, from his mother—he gives it away in what seems to be a burst of sympathy for the downtrodden (Katerina Ivanovna and her children, a girl who has been seduced). Afterward, when he has subjected his actions to analysis, he reproaches himself for wasting money (6:25, 42–43).

The rashness with which Raskolnikov gets rid of his money is one of several clues that he chooses his destitution. He gives up tutoring and avoids Razumikhin, who could supply him with work. Every bit as poor as his friend, Razumikhin also lives in a fifth-floor "closet" (*kamorka*—the same term used for Raskolnikov's room, 6:5), dresses in rags, and sleeps on a tattered couch (6:87). But Razumikhin (whose name signifies "reason" or "good sense"—*razum*)[42] manages to survive on lessons and translations and serves as an affirmation that Raskolnikov could scrape together a meager income if he wished. One might construe Raskolnikov's willful impoverishment as a test of his strength, a probe to determine just how much he can endure in preparation for the feat of freeing the oppressed from the likes of the vicious pawnbroker, whom he visits only after ceasing to work (6:52). But there is an additional possibility. While at the conscious level Raskolnikov rejects the image of himself as beggar, his option for destitution, like his attraction to social outcasts, may signal a subconscious identification with the suffering of those who seek alms and a vague recognition of the presence of God among them.

After the murder Raskolnikov intuitively finds his way to Razumikhin's where, as his muddled attempt to explain his visit indicates, he both seeks and refuses help: "Well, listen. I came to you because, besides you, I don't know anyone who could help ... to begin ... because you are better than anyone else, that is smarter, and you can reason it out.... But now I see that I don't need anything, you hear, absolutely nothing" (6:88). Raskolnikov leaves, having accepted a translation project and three rubles; but then he suddenly returns, places them on a table, and walks off without saying a word. A little later the pattern of accepting and rejecting alms is repeated on the Nikolaevsky Bridge. After sustaining the lash of a driver's whip for straying into the path of a carriage, Raskolnikov is dimly aware that a merchant lady and girl have thrust a coin into his hand saying, "Accept this, sir, for Christ's sake." He glances across the Neva and espies the cupola of the cathedral shining in the sun. Vague thoughts and memories run through his head, and he senses a breach with his past, which exists somewhere in the depths beneath him. Suddenly he becomes aware of the twenty-kopek piece in his fist, tosses it into the Neva, and has the sensation that "at that minute he had taken scissors and cut himself off from everything and everybody" (6:89–90). Nazirov believes that Raskolnikov's throwing away the coin signifies his rejection of Christian compassion.[43] This understanding is partially right, but it ignores the cry for help behind Raskolnikov's deeds. His spurning of Razumikhin's translation and the woman's alms no doubt represents a self-punitive refusal of pity, and he derives bitter satisfaction from taunting himself with the thought that he is severed from his past and any help is futile. At the same time, the very fact that he turns to Razumikhin for aid implies that he is seeking a way out of his predicament. The mention of the gleaming cupola as Raskolnikov clutches the twenty-kopek coin may be intended as a muted reminder that the protocol of almsgiving requires him to bless his benefactor. However, not yet ready to acknowledge that he is a "poor Lazarus" and to embrace his common brotherhood with the destitute, Raskolnikov cannot accept alms.

A slightly later instance of almsgiving reinforces the suspicion that Raskolnikov yearns for pity. After Marmeladov has been run down by a carriage (a motif that connects this incident with the one involving Raskolnikov on the Nikolaevsky Bridge), Raskolnikov helps carry him home, summons a doctor and, when he dies, gives Katerina Ivanovna all the money that his mother sent him. As he is leaving, Katerina Ivanovna's elder daughter Polechka overtakes him. Before the thin, frail child, Raskolnikov drops his defensive stance:

"And do you know how to pray?"
"Oh, of course, we know! For a long time now. Since I'm already big, I pray all by myself. But Kolia and Lidochka pray out

loud with Mama ..."

"Polechka, my name is Rodion; pray for me too sometimes. Just say 'and your servant Rodion'—no more."

"I'll pray for you throughout all my future life," the girl pronounced heatedly and suddenly started laughing again, threw herself at him, and again embraced him strongly. (6:147)

Raskolnikov's refusal to accept help from Razumikhin and the woman on the bridge truncates the almsgiving rite. In the above scene, however, it is complete. Of course, Raskolnikov has shifted to the more comfortable role of benefactor, but in asking Polechka to pray for him, he acknowledges his own need and thereby insures the full implementation of the ritual.

The encounter with Polechka has a powerful effect on Raskolnikov and, unable to cope with his emotion, he reinterprets it as a surge of power for the struggle ahead: "Enough! ... There is life! After all, didn't I just live? My life has not died along with the old woman! Let the kingdom of heaven be hers and—enough, my good lady, it's time for peace! Now for the kingdom of reason and light and ... and will and force ... and then we'll see! We'll measure ourselves now!" (6:147). Mocking himself for his religious fervor, Raskolnikov sets off for Razumikhin's housewarming party where he knows he will find Porfiry Petrovich; but by the time he arrives, his strength has dissipated and he feels too weak to enter. Razumikhin accompanies him home, and on the way Raskolnikov makes another incoherent attempt to explain himself: "Listen, Razumikhin, ... I was just with a dying man, a certain official died.... I gave away all my money there ... and besides just now a certain being kissed me, who, even if I had killed someone, would also ... in a word, I saw there a certain other being, with a fiery plume ... but I'm getting all mixed up" (6:149–50). In his presence at Marmeladov's deathbed, his kindness to Katerina Ivanovna, his first glimpse of Sonia, and, especially, his conversation with Polechka, Raskolnikov participated in the give and take of the almsgiving rite and, however much he attempted to suppress or twist its impact, experienced the touch of divine mercy.

The next day, when Raskolnikov visits Porfiry Petrovich and thinks about "singing Lazarus," he carries within him the residue of his experience with Polechka as well as his resolve to measure his strength against the police inspector. On the surface the encounter takes on elements of a mock almsgiving rite in which Raskolnikov adopts the role of a supplicant lacking the funds to redeem his father's watch vis-à-vis an important person who can grant or refuse his request. It is possible that the name "Porfiry," which comes from the word for "purple" (*porfira*), is intended to associate Porfiry Petrovich with the rich man whose role he unwittingly parodies and who in Luke's account dresses in purple (Luke 16:19; the Russian text uses *v porfiru*).[44] Toward the end of their encounter, Porfiry shifts the playacting implied in "singing Lazarus" to a serious level. After listening to Raskolnikov's theory of extraordinary men, he abruptly asks him if he believes in the New Jerusalem, God, and the resurrection of Lazarus. The insightful inspector clearly glimpses behind the young murderer's pose a struggle between his wish to be "extraordinary" and his search for a solution to his agony. Porfiry's curious question exposes the repressed side of Raskolnikov's psyche and creates a potential association between John's Lazarus and the beggar.

It is to Sonia that Raskolnikov takes Porfiry's query. That evening he visits her in her beggarly room (*v nishchenkoi komnate*, 6:251) and impels her to read to him the story of the resurrection of Lazarus. The *Notebooks* indicate that at one point Dostoevsky considered using Mark's Gospel for his resurrection account (7:91). His choice of John may have been predicated in part by his desire to connect the two Lazaruses.[45] The scene in which Sonia reads the Gospel story contains several references to almsgiving (*milostynia*) and justice (*spravedlivost'*). Sonia says that Katerina Ivanovna "believes that there should be justice in all things" and, as if contradicting her dead father, she affirms that Katerina Ivanovna is just (6:243); she asserts that Lizaveta was just and will "behold God" (*Ona boga uzrit*, 6:249). She reminds Raskolnikov that he gave his last kopek to Katerina Ivanovna and censures herself for cruelty in withholding collars and cuffs from her when, for her part, Katerina Ivanovna would give away everything she had (6:244–45). Raskolnikov taunts Sonia with the likelihood that Katerina Ivanovna and the children will end up on the streets and that Polechka will be sent to beg for alms or will become a prostitute; he emphasizes how quickly children begging for alms become perverted (6:245, 246, 252). His initial request that Sonia read him the story of the resurrection of Lazarus is so ambiguous that it may embed a second reference to Lazarus the beggar:

> "Where is the part about Lazarus?" he suddenly asked.
> Sonia stubbornly looked down at the floor and didn't answer.
> "Where is the part about the resurrection of Lazarus? Find it for me, Sonia."
> She glanced at him from the side.
> "Don't look there.... In the fourth Gospel." (6:249)

It appears that Sonia is not sure which Lazarus Raskolnikov is speaking about on his first request, and her answer leaves open the possibility that he may be looking in Luke's Gospel instead of John's.

Dostoevsky incorporates John's narrative in a manner that highlights the Gospel text's threefold movement—the affirmation of general resurrection; the relocating of resurrection in the person of Christ; and the miracle of resurrection within earthly life. Martha confesses her belief that her dead brother will rise on the last day; Jesus responds that He is "the resurrection and the life" (John 11:19–29); Jesus feels sorry for Martha and Mary, weeps, goes to the tomb, summons Lazarus, and the dead man emerges from the grave (John 11:32–45). The spaces between the quotations from the Gospel are filled with descriptions of Sonia's reading, which, hesitant at first, becomes triumphant as she nears the miracle.[46] Watching her tremble yet grow more confident as she reads, Raskolnikov understands that he has laid bare Sonia's most cherished secret, the reason she endures and does not throw herself into the canal and the reason why, though humiliated and impoverished, she can say that God does everything for her (6:248). In the *Notebooks* Sonia proclaims, "I myself was a Lazarus who had died and Christ resurrected me" (7:192).

John's story of resurrection is the capstone to the novel's debate about God and the afterlife. The Lazarus song offers an image of eternity that is fairly standard in Russian folklore: a just God welcomes the beggar to paradise and consigns the unmerciful rich man to the flames of hell. In *Crime and Punishment* Dostoevsky incorporates a different set of alternatives from that of the spiritual song: Marmeladov's vision of total forgiveness and Svidrigailov's image of a dank, sooty bathhouse with spiders in the corner.[47] While the Lazarus song promises a breakthrough to a better world after death for the destitute, Marmeladov's eternity does not exclude the unmerciful rich and, one can imagine, may even accommodate Svidrigailov, who anticipates instead a continuum with the dreariness of his life on earth. But for the living, only John's Lazarus holds genuine promise. The concept of the "afterlife" in John is fundamentally different from that of the Lazarus song or even Marmeladov's speech, both of which draw sharp boundaries between this world and the next. John's Lazarus is a pledge not just for the next world, but also for renewed life in the here and now. Raskolnikov had a foretaste of resurrected life in giving alms and receiving Polechka's blessing, and now he is moved by Sonia. But, still not ready to adopt her view of life, he attempts to pull her into his sphere: "What should you do? Break what must be broken once and for all, that's what: and take the suffering on yourself. ... Freedom and power, and most important, power! Over all trembling creatures, over the whole ant heap! ... That's the goal! Remember it!" (6:253).

In *Crime and Punishment* the Lazarus song forms an undercurrent in which we can discern the voice of Sonia and other street people. Their ethic of absolute charity enters into the novel's ideological debate, offering, in a nuanced rather than a rhetorical manner, a counterpoint to the two main theories that serve as pretexts for Raskolnikov's crime—the environmentalist (or utilitarian) theory and the Napoleonic one. The song encompasses the range of Raskolnikov's feelings about almsgiving and beggars. On the surface, his thought of the song implies that he intends to adopt the pose of a penniless ex-student in front of Porfiry Petrovich; at a deeper level it signals that in some mysterious way he is seeking divine mercy. But Raskolnikov, generous in giving alms, refuses the help of others, and thereby asserts his superiority and rejects his common brotherhood with the *narod*. The understanding of beggary nurtured among the people subverts his division into strong and weak (or extraordinary and ordinary), for the destitute person is sacred and must be viewed as Lazarus, or as Christ himself. Raskolnikov becomes open to new life only when he is able to view himself as poor enough to receive as well as give. By the end of *Crime and Punishment* the popular ethic seems to have prevailed, for Raskolnikov has recognized the falseness of his dream of being extraordinary and is able to love Sonia. As the novel closes, he picks up the copy of the Gospels from which Sonia read him the story of the resurrection of Lazarus and thinks, "Is it possible that her convictions will also be my convictions now?" (6:422).

NOTES

1. The understanding of self-consciousness as the *sine qua non* of a Dostoevskian hero is, of course, one of the major legacies of Bakhtin. See Mikhail Bakhtin, *Problems of Dostoevsky's Poetics*, ed. and trans. Caryl Emerson (Minneapolis, 1984), 49–50. An earlier version of this study was read at the Annual Meeting of the American Association for the Advancement of Slavic Studies, November 1994. Research for the article was supported in part by a grant from the International Researches and Exchanges Board (IREX) with funds provided by the National Endowment for the Humanities and the United States Information Agency and by a National Endowment for the Humanities Fellowship for University Teachers. I wish also to thank Irene Masing-Delic and *Russian Review*'s anonymous readers for their helpful and encouraging advice.

2. Donald Fanger, *Dostoevsky and Romantic Realism* (Chicago, 1967), 184–213 and elsewhere, discusses the social dimension of *Crime and Punishment*.

3. Most studies of Dostoevsky's use of folklore in *Crime and Punishment* agree that the writer used the popular tradition to present the moral perspective of the people. See, for example, V. A. Mikhniukevich, *Russkii fol'klor v khudozhestvennoi sisteme F. M. Dostoevskogo* (Cheliabinsk, 1994), 99; and T. B. Lebedeva, "Obraz Raskol'nikova v svete zhitiinykh assotsiatsii," in *Problemy realizma* (Vologda, 1976), 80–81.

4. Mikhniukevich, *Russkii fol'klor*, 100.

5. George Gibian, "Traditional Symbolism in *Crime and Punishment*," in Feodor Dostoevsky, *Crime and Punishment*, trans. Jessie Coulson, ed. George Gibian (New York, 1989), 526–27.

6. V. P. Vladimirtsev, "Narodnye plachi v tvorchestve F. M. Dostoevskogo," *Russkaia literatura*, 1987, no. 3:189.

7. F. M. Dostoevskii, *Prestuplenie i nakazanie*, in *Polnoe sobranie sochinenii v tridtsati tomakh*, ed. G. M. Fridlender (Leningrad, 1972–88), 6:70–71, 143, 405. All further references to Dostoevsky will be to this edition and will be indicated in the text, where appropriate, or in the notes as *PSS*, with volume and page references. Translations are mine.

8. *PSS* 6:160; Vladimirtsev, "Narodnye plachi," 189. See also Vladimirtsev's "Zal'ius' slez'mi goriuchimi," *Russkaia rech'*, 1988, no. 1: 119–23.

9. L. M. Lotman, "Romany Dostoevskogo i russkaia legenda," in her *Realizm russkoi literatury 60kh godov XIX veka* (Leningrad, 1974), 286–90. We can be almost certain that the writer was familiar with a variant of this legend in which the drunk reminds Peter that he denied Christ three times, David that he had Uriah murdered so that he could take his wife, and John the Evangelist that Christ's commandment to love one another came through him. John commands Peter to open the gates. See A. N. Afanas'ev, "Povest'o brazhnike," *Narodnye russkie skazki i legendy* (Berlin, 1922), 2:540–41.

10. Gibian, "Traditional Symbolism," 527. Diane Oenning Thompson, "Problems of the Biblical Word in Dostoevsky's Poetics," in *Dostoevsky and the Christian Tradition*, ed. George Pattison and Diane Oenning Thompson (Cambridge, England, 2001), 72, notes that Marmeladov enjoys a "carnival freedom from decorum" in his speech and claims that we must assume the presence of Christ in the tavern scene since "the whole meaning of His mission would collapse were He not present here, in the Petersburg misery."

11. V. I. Dal', *Tolkovyi slovar' zhivogo velikorusskogo iazyka* (St. Petersburg-Moscow, 1881), 2:234, gives the following: "'… To sing the Lazarus,' a song that beggars sing; to ingratiatingly solicit something." See also A. S. Al'tman, *Dostoevskii po vekham imen* (Saratov, 1975), 44–46.

12. Sidney Monas captures it well; he uses, "I'll have to play the part of Lazarus for him, too" (New York and London: Signet, 1968, 244). David Magarshack renders it, "I shall have to gush over him, too" (New York and London: Penguin, 1951, 263); Constance Garnett uses, "I shall have to pull a long face with him too" (New York: Random House, 1950, 242); David McDuff, "I'll have to complain about my lot to this fellow, too" (New York and London: Penguin, 1991, 298); and Jessie Coulson, "I shall have to make the most of my illness" (New York and London, Norton Critical Edition ed. by George Gibian, 1989, 208. This edition adds footnote explaining the literal meaning of the expression).

13. R. G. Nazirov, "Zhesty miloserdiia v romanakh Dostoevskogo," *Studia Russica* (Budapest), 1983, no. 6:249.

14. Al'tman, *Dostoevskii po vekham imen*, 44–45. See also Harriet Murav, *Holy Foolishness: Dostoevsky's Novels and the Poetics of Cultural Critique* (Stanford, 1992), 70.

15. Joseph Frank, *Dostoevsky: The Miraculous Years, 1865–1871* (Princeton, 1995), 132.

16. For example, Edward Wasiolek, *Dostoevsky: The Major Fiction* (Cambridge, MA, 1964), 81; Richard Peace, *Dostoyevsky: An Examination of the Major Novels* (Cambridge, England, 1971), 46; Michael Holquist, *Dostoevsky and the Novel* (Princeton, 1977), 102; and Frank, *Miraculous Years*, 131.

17. Fanger remarks both that Dostoevsky "grounds his metaphysical concerns with consummate care in the three-dimensional world" and that a social novel "was unthinkable for him except as it touched on moral resurrection" (*Dostoevsky and Romantic Realism*, 130, 190).

18. See A. N. Robinson, "K probleme 'bogatstva' i 'bednosti' v russkoi literature XVII veka: Tolkovaniia pritchi o Lazare i bogatom," in *Drevnerusskaia literatura i ee sviazi s novym vremenem*, ed. O. A. Derzhavina (Moscow, 1967), 124–55.

19. *PSS* 25:214–15. Dostoevsky probably knew the biblical version of the beggar Lazarus from very early childhood. In his family the children learned to read from a collection of 104 bible stories, and the deacon employed to teach them catechism told

bible stories with great feeling. See Andrei Dostoevskii, *Vospominaniia* (Moscow, 1999), 64–65. The writer's personal library at the time of his death contained E. Bers'e, *Beseda o bogatom i Lazare*, trans. A. Zabelin (St. Petersburg, 1880). See L. P. Desiatkina and G. M. Fridlender, "Biblioteka Dostoevskogo (Novye materialy)," in *Dostoevskii: Materialy i issledovaniia*, ed. G. M. Fridlender (Leningrad, 1980), 4:257.

20. *Vremia: Zhurnal literaturnyi i politicheskii*, 1861, no. 2:2:163–81.

21. For several legends of Christ as beggar see A. N. Afanas'ev, *Narodnye russkie skazki* 2:459–71.

22. P. Bessonov, *Kaleki perekhozhie: Sbornik stikhov* (Moscow, 1861), 1:1–2. Bessonov changes the more usual *kaliki* to *kaleki* in the title of his famous anthology. According to V. I. Dal', *kaleka* designates someone who is maimed or crippled (*Tolkovyi slovar'* 2:79–80). Dal' implies that *kaliki perekhozhie* is the more appropriate name for the wandering pilgrims who sought alms (*podaianiia*), but suspects that the terms *kaliki* and *kaleki* were confused because of their similarity.

23. Bessonov, *Kaleki*, 56–57.

24. Ibid., 58.

25. See, for example, V. Varentsov, *Sbornik russkikh dukhovnykh stikhov* (St. Petersburg, 1860), 76–77. Varentsov notes that in Arkhangelsk Province the term *kaliki* was used for bearers of spiritual songs (p. 5).

26. Bessonov, *Kaleki*, 59–60.

27. Fedotov, *Stikhi dukhovnye (Russkaia narodnaia vera po dukhovnym stikham)* (Paris, 1935), 86, 94.

28. *Vremia: Zhurnal literaturnyi i politicheskii*, 1862, no. 12:2:88–102.

29. Ibid., 100, 88.

30. Ibid., 102.

31. *PSS* 7:211. See also V. S. Nechaeva, *Zhurnal M. M. i F. M. Dostoevskikh*, "*Vremia*," 1861–1863 (Moscow, 1972), 199–200. Dostoevsky personally was very generous to beggars. Reports of those who knew him in the 1840s attributed his chronic lack of money in part to his excessive willingness to give away all that he had to anyone less fortunate. His second wife also testifies to the writer's lavish generosity toward all who asked for a handout. See A. E. Rizenkampf, "Nachalo literaturnogo poprishcha," and S. D. Ianovskii, "Vospominaniia o Dostoevskom," both in *F. M. Dostoevskii v vospominaniiakh sovremennikov* (Moscow, 1964), 1:116–17, 160; and Anna Dostoevsky, *Dostoevsky: Reminiscences*, trans. Beatrice Stillman (New York, 1975), 275–78.

32. Dal', *Tolkovyi slovar'* 2:426.

33. *PSS* 7:135. Frank notes the incident of the collars and cuffs, which causes Sonia to consider herself a great sinner, as an illustration of how Dostoevsky develops the conflict of Christian love versus restructuring society in the novel (*Miraculous Years*, 132).

34. *PSS* 6:281, 288, 305. Nazirov suspects that in this scene Dostoevskii is playing with a tendency prevalent among the bourgeoisie to regard poor people as thieves ("Zhesty," 250).

35. On the connections between Svidrigailov and evil spirits see Linda Ivanits, "Suicide and Folk Beliefs in Dostoevsky's *Crime and Punishment*," in *The Golden Age of Russian Literature and Thought*, ed. Derek Offord (London and New York, 1992), 138–48; and V. P. Vladimirtsev, "Russkie bylichki i pover'ia u F. M. Dostoevskogo," in *Zhanr i kompozitsiia literaturnogo proizvedeniia* (Petrozavodsk, 1989), 99–100.

36. Wasiolek, *Dostoevsky: The Major Fiction*, 61.

37. See Varentsov, *Sbornik*, 70.

38. Wasiolek, *Dostoevsky: The Major Fiction*, 63. On contradictions and ambiguity in the Marmeladov family see also Victor Terras, *Reading Dostoevsky* (Madison, 1998), 58–60, 70–71.

39. *PSS* 6:283. For a discussion of environmentalism in the novel see Derek Offord, "The Causes of Crime and the Meaning of Law: *Crime and Punishment* and Contemporary Radical Thought," in *New Essays on Dostoyevsky*, ed. Malcolm Jones and Garth Terry (Cambridge, England, 1983), 42–43.

40. According to S. V. Maksimov, *Brodiachaia Rus' Khrista-Radi, Sobranie sochinenii* (St. Petersburg, 1908–13), 5:149–52, Russian peasants tended to regard the prayers of beggars in response to almsgiving as very powerful. Maksimov notes a particularly interesting ritual of secret almsgiving practiced among some of the Old Believers of Vladimir Province (pp. 150–51). The recipient of such charity was obliged to pray for the anonymous benefactor, and such a prayer was thought to quickly deliver the giver from various misfortunes.

41. As Frank points out, Raskolnikov does not understand why he committed murder; "he becomes aware that the moral purpose supposedly inspiring him cannot explain his behavior" (*Miraculous Years*, 102). On Raskolnikov's inner dialectic see especially Robert L. Jackson, "Philosophical Pro and contra in Part One of *Crime and Punishment*," *The Art of Dostoevsky* (Princeton, 1981), 189–207. See also Philip Rahv, "Dostoevsky in *Crime and Punishment*," in *Dostoevsky: A Collection of Critical Essays*, ed. René Wellek (Englewood Cliffs, NJ, 1962), 19–22.

42. Here Dostoevsky's understanding of *razum* as a spiritual force enabling good judgment is close to that given by Dal' (*Tolkovyi slovar'* 4:53), and contrasts sharply with *rassudok*, which implies calculation and carries negative tonalities. Unable to obtain the axe he was counting on for the murder, Raskolnikov suddenly espies another and thinks, "Ne rassudok, tak bes" (*PSS* 6:60).

43. Nazirov, "Zhesty," 249. Nazirov also suggests that in handling the theme of beggary Dostoevsky accents something unnoticed before him—that the defectiveness of civilization consisted "not so much in the egoism of the well-fed as in the incapacity of the suffering to accept alms. Since in a bourgeois society alms serve to elevate the giver and debase the receiver, the acceptance of a handout is incompatible with the dignity of the personality" ("Zhesty," 249–50).

44. Peace suggests that Porfiry's name points to the purple cloak of the Byzantine emperors (*porphyra*) and that the police inspector is a sort of "secular priest" (*Dostoevsky*, 44).

45. Nazirov suggests that while the Gospels distinguish clearly between Luke's and John's Lazarus, the folk tradition tends to mix them up ("Zhesty," 249). In *Crime and Punishment*, he claims, Dostoevsky adheres to the popular tradition. I believe that Dostoevsky does not so much mix them up as make them complementary. For an interesting survey of apocryphal and legendary traditions about John's Lazarus see E. B. Rogachevskaia, "Voskresenie i zhizn': Obraz Lazaria v srednevekovoi Rusi, Evrope, i Vizantii," *Vestnik russkogo khristianskogo dvizheniia* (Paris) 5–6 (1998), no. 179:28–36.

46. On Dostoevsky's censorship problems with the chapter that includes this Gospel narrative see Frank, *Miraculous Years*, 93–95.

47. Svidrigailov draws on the folklore of the Russian bathhouse as a gathering place of devils and harmful spirits for this image. See my *Russian Folk Belief* (Armonk, NY, 1989), 59–60.

Chronology

1821	Fyodor Mikailovich Dostoevsky born October 30 in a Moscow hospital for the poor, where his father was a resident surgeon.
1837	Death of Dostoevsky's mother.
1838	Dostoevsky enters military engineering school in St. Petersburg.
1839	In the wake of increasingly harsh and abusive treatment, Dostoevsky believed, the serfs on Dostoevsky's father's estate castrate and murder their master. Recent evidence, however, casts doubt on the circumstances of his father's death.
1843	Dostoevsky finishes engineering course; joins engineering department of the War Ministry.
1844	Resigns from his post. Publishes his translation of *Eugenie Grandet*.
1845	Finishes his first novel. *Poor Folk*, which wins the acclaim of radical critic Belinsky.
1846	*Poor Folk* published in *St. Petersburg Miscellany*. *The Double* published in *Notes from the Fatherland* two weeks later.
1847	"A Novel in Nine Letters" published in *The Contemporary*. Dostoevsky frequents meetings of the Petrashevsky circle, a clandestine society of progressive thinkers. Publishes pamphlets in the *St. Petersburg Chronicle* and the *St. Petersburg News*.

1848	Publication of *A Strange Wife*, *A Faint Heart*, "The Stories of a Veteran," *The Christmas Tree and the Wedding*, *White Nights*, *The Jealous Husband*, and *The Landlady*, all in *Notes from the Fatherland*. The latter work draws harsh criticism from Belinsky.
1849	Dostoevsky arrested for his role in the Petrashevsky circle, and imprisoned in St. Petersburg's Peter and Paul Fortress. Sentenced to death, but at the last minute the sentence is commuted to four years of forced labor in Siberia. Sent to Omsk, where he remains until 1854.
1854	Dostoevsky enlists in the army as a private and is sent to Semipalatinsk, near the Mongolian border.
1856	Promoted to lieutenant.
1857	Marries Maria Dmitrievna Isaeva, a widow. *A Little Hero* published anonymously in *Notes from the Fatherland*.
1858	Released from army; leaves Semipalatinsk for Tver.
1859	Is permitted to return to St. Petersburg. "Uncle's Dream" published in *The Russian Word*; *A Friend of the Family* published in *Notes from the Fatherland*.
1860	Introduction and first chapter to *Notes from the House of the Dead* are published. Work meets opposition from the censor at *The Russian Word*.
1861	*Notes from the House of the Dead* in its entirety and *The Insulted and the Injured* are published in *Time*, a journal recently started by Dostoevsky's brother Mikhail.
1862	First trip abroad. "An Unpleasant Predicament" published in *Time*.
1863	*Winter Notes on Summer Impressions* published in *Time*. *Time* is suppressed. Second trip abroad.
1864	Publishes magazine, *Epoch*, with brother Mikhail. *Notes from Underground* published in *Epoch*. Death of Dostoevsky's wife, and, within a few months, his brother.
1865	*Epoch* ceases publication. Third trip abroad.
1866	*Crime and Punishment* serialized in *The Russian Herald*. Anna Grigorievna Snitkina comes to work for Dostoevsky's as a stenographer. *The Gambler* published.
1867	Marries Snitkina. The couple goes abroad to live for the next four years.

1868	*The Idiot* serialized in *The Russian Herald*. A daughter, Sofia, is born, but dies two months later.
1869	Daughter Lyubov' born in Dresden.
1870	"The Eternal Husband" published in *Dawn*.
1871–72	Returns to St. Petersburg. Son Fyodor born. *The Possessed* serialized in *The Russian Herald*.
1873–74	Editor of *The Citizen*. *Diary of a Writer* begins publication.
1875	Son Alexey (Alyosha) born. "A Raw Youth" serialized in *Notes from the Fatherland*.
1876	"A Gentle Spirit" published in *Diary of a Writer*.
1877	"Dream of a Ridiculous Man" published in *Diary of a Writer*.
1878	Death of son Alyosha. Dostoevsky visits Optina monastery with Vladimir Solov'yov; they meet Starets Amvrozy.
1879–80	*The Brothers Karamazov* serialized in *The Russian Herald*.
1881	Dostoevsky dies on January 28.

Contributors

HAROLD BLOOM is Sterling Professor of the Humanities at Yale University and Henry W. and Albert A. Berg Professor of English at the New York University Graduate School. He is the author of over 20 books, including *Shelley's Mythmaking* (1959), *The Visionary Company* (1961), *Blake's Apocalypse* (1963), *Yeats* (1970), *A Map of Misreading* (1975), *Kabbalah and Criticism* (1975), *Agon: Toward a Theory of Revisionism* (1982), *The American Religion* (1992), *The Western Canon* (1994), and *Omens of Millennium: The Gnosis of Angels, Dreams, and Resurrection* (1996). *The Anxiety of Influence* (1973) sets forth Professor Bloom's provocative theory of the literary relationships between the great writers and their predecessors. His most recent books include *Shakespeare: The Invention of the Human* (1998), a 1998 National Book Award finalist, *How to Read and Why* (2000), and *Genius: A Mosaic of One Hundred Exemplary Creative Minds* (2002). In 1999, Professor Bloom received the prestigious American Academy of Arts and Letters Gold Medal for Criticism, and in 2002 he received the Catalonia International Prize.

A.D. NUTTALL has been a Professor of English at the University of Sussex. He is the author of *Why Does Tragedy Give Pleasure?* as well as of numerous other books, some of which cover Shakespeare, Pope, Milton, and Blake.

MIKHAIL BAKHTIN (1895–1975) was a leading Soviet critic and literary theorist who, for political reasons, withdrew from an active literary life. He wrote numerous essays and books, such as *Art & Answerability: Early Philosophical Essays* and *The Dialogic Imagination: Four Essays*.

HARRIET MURAV teaches Russian at the University of California, Davis. She is the author of *Russia's Legal Fictions (Law, Meaning and Violence)*.

DAVID MATUAL has taught at Wright State University. He is the author of *Tolstoy's Translation of the Gospels: A Critical Study*.

LIZA KNAPP teaches Slavic languages and literature at the University of California at Berkeley. She is the editor of *Dostoevsky's* The Idiot: *A Critical Companion*.

NAOMI ROOD teaches classics at Colgate University. She has also written on *The Odyssey* and and ancient Greek poetry.

OLGA MEERSON teaches Slavic languages and literature at Georgetown University. She has a range of expertise, including Russian Orthodox liturgical poetics and musicology and contemporary Russian women poets.

VICTOR TERRAS is the author or editor of several books, including *Reading Dostoevsky* and *A History of Russian Literature*. He has also translated some of Dostoevsky's works.

JANET TUCKER teaches at the University of Arkansas. Her article in this volume is part of a book she plans to publish on *Crime and Punishment*. She is the editor of *Against the Grain: Parody, Satire, and Intertextuality in Russian Literature*.

HENRY M.W. RUSSELL teaches at Ave Maria College, Ypsilanti, Michigan.

ANTONY JOHAE teaches in the English department at Kuwait University. He has also taught in Britain, Germany, Ghana, and Tunisia. Aside from his essay in this volume, he has published others on Dostoevsky. Also, he has written on Zamyatin, Trotsky, Swift, Coleridge, and Dickens, to name a few.

LINDA IVANITS teaches in the Department of Germanic and Slavic Languages and Literatures at Penn State University. She is the author of *Russian Folk Belief*.

Bibliography

Anderson, Roger. "The Optics of Narration: Visual Composition in *Crime and Punishment*." Anderson, Roger, and Debreczeny, Paul, eds. *Russian Narrative and Visual Art: Varieties of Seeing*. Gainesville: University Press of Florida, 1994.

Anwar, Sarosh. "Rethinking Moral Absolutes: Dostoevsky's *Crime and Punishment*," *Gombak Review* 1, no. 2 (December 1996).

Bethea, David M. "Structure versus Symmetry in *Crime and Punishment*." Crook, Eugene J., ed. *Fearful Symmetry: Doubles and Doubling in Literature and Film*. Tallahassee: University Press of Florida, 1982.

Brody, Ervin C. "Meaning and Symbolism in the Names of Dostoevsky's *Crime and Punishment* and *The Idiot*," *Names: A Journal of the American Name Society* 27 (1979).

Burnett, Leon, ed. *F. M. Dostoevsky (1821–1881): A Centenary Collection*. Colchester: University of Essex, 1981.

Cassedy, Steven. "The Formal Problem of the Epilogue in *Crime and Punishment*: The Logic of Tragic and Christian Structures," *Dostoevsky Studies* 3 (1982).

Curtis, Laura A. "Raskolnikov's Sexuality," *Literature and Psychology* 37, nos. 1–2, 1991.

Dalipagic-Csizmazia, Catherine. "Razumov and Raskolnikov: The Path of Torments," *L'Epoque Conradienne* 19 (1993).

Danow, David K. "Dialogic Structures in *Crime and Punishment*," *Russian, Croatian and Serbian, Czech and Slovak, Polish Literature* 19, no. 3 (April 1, 1986).

Davydov, Sergei. "Dostoevsky and Nabokov: The Morality of Structure in *Crime and Punishment* and *Despair*," *Dostoevsky Studies* 3 (1982).

Dilman, Ilham. "Dostoevsky: Psychology and the Novelist." Griffths, A. Phillips, ed. *Philosophy and Literature*. Cambridge: Cambridge University Press, 1984.

Dodd, W. J. "Varieties of Influence: On Kafka's Indebtedness to Dostoevskii," *Journal of European Studies* 14, no. 4 (56) (December 1984).

Fiene, Donald M. "Raskolnikov and Abraham: A Further Contribution to a Defense of the Epilogue of *Crime and Punishment*," *International Dostoevsky Society Bulletin* 9 (1979).

Follinus, Gabor. "Thus Speaks the Devil: *Crime and Punishment*," *Studia Slavica Academiae Scientiarum Hungaricae* 37, nos. 1–4 (1991–1929).

Frank, Joseph. "The Genesis of *Crime and Punishment*." Belknap, Robert L., ed. *Russianness: Studies on a Nation's Identity*. Ann Arbor: Ardis, 1990.

_____. "The Making of *Crime and Punishment*." Polhemus, Robert M., and Henkle, Roger, B., eds. *Critical Reconstructions: The Relationship of Fiction and Life*. Stanford: Stanford University Press, 1994.

Gill, Richard. "The Bridges of St. Petersburg: A Motif in *Crime and Punishment*." *Dostoevsky Studies* 3 (1982).

_____. "'The Rime of the Ancient Mariner' and *Crime and Punishment*: Existential Parables," *Philosophy and Literature* 5, no. 2 (Fall 1981).

Hallissy, Margaret M. "Barthelme's 'Views of My Father, Weeping' and Dostoevsky's *Crime and Punishment*," *Studies in Short Fiction* 18, no. 1 (Winter 1981).

Holk, André van. "Moral Themes in Dostoevsky's *Crime and Punishment*," *Essays in Poetics: The Journal of the British Neo-Formalist School* 14, no. 1 (April 1989).

Ivanits, Linda. "Suicide and Folk Belief in Dostoevsky's *Crime and Punishment*." Offord, Derek, ed. *The Golden Age of Russian Literature and Thought*. New York: St. Martin's, 1992.

Jernakoff, Nadja. "*Crime and Punishment*: Svidrigailov—A Character in His Own Right," *Transactions of the Association of Russian-Americans* 14 (1981).

Johae, Antony. "Expressive Symbols in Dostoevsky's *Crime and Punishment*," *Scottish Slavonic Review* 20 (Spring 1993).

_____. "Hallucination in *Oliver Twist* and *Crime and Punishment*," *New Comparison: A Journal of Comparative and General Literary Studies* 9 (Spring 1990).

Johnson, Tamara, ed. *Readings on Fyodor Dostoevsky*. San Diego, CA: Greenhaven, 1998.

Jones, Malcolm V., and Terry, Garth M., eds. *New Essays on Dostoevsky*. Cambridge: Cambridge University Press, 1983.

Kanzer, Mark. "Dostoevsky's Matricidal Impulses." Coltrera, Joseph T., ed. *Lives, Events, and Other Players: Directions in Psychobiology*. New York: Aronson, 1981.

Koprince, Ralph G. "The Question of Raskol'nikov's Suicide," *Canadian-American Slavic Studies* 16, no. 1 (1982).

Lynch, Michael F. "Dostoevsky and Richard Wright: Choices of Individual Freedom and Dignity," *Chiba Review* 12 (1990).

Mann, Robert. "Elijah the Prophet in *Crime and Punishment*," *Canadian Slavonic Papers* 23, no. 3 (September 1981).

Martinsen, Deborah A. "Shame and Punishment," *Dostoevsky Studies* 5 (2001).

McMillan, Norman. "Dostoevskian Vision in Flannery O'Connor's 'Revelation,'" *The Flannery O'Connor Bulletin* 16 (1987).

Mitchell, Giles. "Pathological Narcissism and Violence in Dostoevskii's Svidrigailov," *Canadian-American Slavic Studies* 24, no. 1 (1990).

Morson, Gary Saul. "How to Read *Crime and Punishment*," *Commentary* 93, no. 6 (June 1992).

Murav, Harriet. "The Discourse of Ivrodstvo and the Discourse of Psychology in *Crime and Punishment*." Clayton, J. Douglas, ed. *Issues in Russian Literature Before 1917*. Columbus, OH: Slavica, 1989.

Ozick, Cynthia. "Dostoevsky's Unabomber," *New Yorker* (February 24, 1997–March 3, 1997).

Palumbo, Donald. "Coincidence, Irony, and the Theme of the Fortunate Fall in *Crime and Punishment*," *University of Dayton Review* 18, no. 3 (Summer 1987).

——————. "Coincidence in *Crime and Punishment* and *Light in August*: Evidence of Supernatural Agents at Work in the Novels of Dostoevsky and Faulkner," *Lamar Journal of the Humanities* 7, no. 1 (Spring 1981).

Rice, James L. "Raskol'nikov and Tsar Gorox," *Slavic and East European Journal* 25, no. 3 (Fall 1981).

Richardson, R. E. "Svidrigalov and the 'Performing Self,'" *Slavic Review* 46, nos. 3–4 (Fall-Winter 1987).

Rising, Catharine. "Raskolnikov and Razumov: From Passive to Active Subjectivity in *Under Western Eyes*," *Conradiana* 33, no. 1 (Spring 2001).

Sagarin, Edward. *Raskolnikov and Others: Literary Images of Crime, Punishment, Redemption, and Atonement.* New York: St. Martin's, 1981.

Straus, Nina Pelikan. "'Why Did I Say Women!'?': Raskolnikov Reimagined," *Diacritics* 23, no. 1 (Spring 1993).

Tamling, Jeremy. "Criminals from a Sense of Guilt: Dickens and Dostoevsky," *Cahiers Victoriens et Edouardiens* 55 (April 2002).

Ugrinsky, Alexej, and Ozolins, Valijak, eds. *Dostoevski and the Human Condition after a Century.* New York: Greenwood, 1986.

Wasiolek, Edward. "Conrad and Dostoevsky, and Natalia and Sonia," *International Fiction Review* 17, no. 2 (Summer 1990).

Weiner, Jack. "Spanish Elements in Dostoevsky's *Crime and Punishment* (1865) and *The Idiot* (1869)," *Discurso: Revista de Estudios Iberoamericanos* 7, no. 2 (1990).

Acknowledgments

"The Intellectual Problem II" by A.D. Nuttall. From Crime and Punishment: *Murder as Philosophic Experiment*: 53–85. © 1978 by A. D. Nuttall. Reprinted by permission.

"Characteristics of Genre and Plot Composition in Dostoevsky's Works" by Mikhail Bakhtin. From *Problems of Dostoevsky's Poetics*: 166–70. © 1984 by the University of Minnesota. Reprinted by permission.

"*Crime and Punishment*: Psychology on Trial" by Harriet Murav. From *Holy Foolishness: Dostoevsky's Novels & the Poetics of Cultural Critique*: 51–70. © 1992 by the Board of Trustees of the Leland Stanford Junior University. Used with the permission of Stanford University press, www.sup.org.

"In Defense of the Epilogue of *Crime and Punishment*" by David Matual. From *Studies in the Novel* 24, no. 1 (Spring 1992): 26–34. © 1992 by the University of North Texas. Reprinted by permission of the publisher.

"The Resurrection from Inertia in *Crime and Punishment*" by Liza Knapp. From *The Annihilation of Inertia: Dostoevsky and Metaphysics*: 44–65. © 1996 by Northwestern University Press. Reprinted by permission.

"Mediating the Distance: Prophecy and Alterity in Greek Tragedy and Dostoevsky's *Crime and Punishment*" by Naomi Rood. From *Russian Literature and the Classics*: 35–58. © 1996 by Overseas Publishers Association. Reprinted by permission.

"How Dostoevsky Inscribes 'Thou Shalt Not Kill' in a Killer's Heart. The Decalogue Taboo Internalized: The *It* of 'It'" by Olga Meerson. From *Dostoevsky's Taboos*: 53–80. © 1998 by Olga Meerson. Reprinted by permission.

"The Art of *Crime and Punishment*" by Victor Terras. From *Reading Dostoevsky*: 51–72. © 1998 by the Board of Regents of the University of Wisconsin System. Reprinted by permission of the University of Wisconsin Press.

"The Religious Symbolism of Clothing in Dostoevsky's *Crime and Punishment* " by Janet Tucker. From *Slavic and East European Journal* 44, no. 2 (Summer 2000): 253–265. © 2000 by the American Association of Teachers of Slavic and East European Languages of the U.S., Inc. Reprinted by permission.

"Beyond the Will: Humiliation as Christian Necessity in *Crime and Punishment*" by Henry M. W. Russell. From *Dostoevsky and the Christian Tradition*: 226–36. © 2001 by the Cambridge University Press. Reprinted by permission of Cambridge University Press.

"Towards an Iconography of *Crime and Punishment*" by Antony Johae. From *Dostoevsky and the Christian Tradition*: 173–88. © 2001 by the Cambridge University Press. Reprinted by permission of Cambridge University Press.

"The Other Lazarus in *Crime and Punishment*" by Linda Ivanits. From *The Russian Review* 61, no. 3 (July 2002): 341–57. © 2002 by *The Russian Review*. Reprinted by permission.

Index